Theories of Distributive Justice

Theories of Distributive Justice

JOHN E. ROEMER

Harvard University Press

Cambridge, Massachusetts

London, England

1996

Library of Congress Cataloging-in-Publication Data

Roemer, John E.
  Theories of distributive justice / John E. Roemer
    p.   cm.
  Includes bibliographical references and index.
  ISBN 0-674-87919-8 (alk. paper)
  1. Income distribution—Mathematical models.   2. Distributive
justice—Mathematical models.   3. Welfare economics—Mathematical
models.   I. Title
  HB523.R63   1996
  339.2—dc20

95-23768

To Natasha

Acknowledgments

I am deeply indebted to Richard Arneson, G. A. Cohen, David Donaldson, and John Weymark, who each read the manuscript and provided me with detailed comments, chapter by chapter and at times line by line. To be taken so seriously by such fine scholars is indeed a great compliment. In addition, Frédéric Gaspart and Ignacio Ortuño-Ortin gave me useful comments on several chapters. I thank Avinash Dixit for permission to use his unpublished lecture notes on Arrow's theorem, on which §1.3 is largely based. Figures 2.2 and 2.8 are redrawn with permission of Cambridge University Press from William Thomson and Terje Lensberg, *Axiomatic Theory of Bargaining with a Variable Number of Agents,* copyright © 1989 by Cambridge University Press. Finally, I am grateful to the graduate students on whom I tried out several chapters in a course taught at Harvard University during the fall of 1994. Their enthusiasm for the subject reinforced my belief that the topic of distributive justice deserves much more prominence in the economics curriculum than it currently has.

June 1995

Contents

Introduction

The theory of distributive justice—how a society or group should allocate its scarce resources or product among individuals with competing needs or claims—goes back at least two millennia. Aristotle and Plato wrote on the question, and the Talmud recommends solutions to the distribution of an estate among the deceased's creditors. Here I do not attempt an exhaustive review of this voluminous literature, to which a good fraction of the world's great minds have contributed, but rather attempt to examine the major theories of distributive justice that have been expounded since 1950. During the last fifty years new economic tools have been used either to propound new theories of justice or to examine old ones. There has been, as well, a renaissance, since the publication of John Rawls's magisterial *Theory of Justice* (1971), of philosophical interest in the question. My task is to evaluate the contributions of contemporary political philosophy, using these new economic tools, to the theory of distributive justice, and to evaluate the work of economists who have used these tools to study the topic.

Many economists who work in the areas of social choice theory and welfare economics are quite unfamiliar with contemporary philosophical thinking on distributive justice. I believe this seriously limits the value of their work, for the philosophers are writing about issues of fundamental importance for the normative evaluation of a society's method for allocating resources. Most economists are familiar with utilitarianism and the Rawlsian difference principle, of course, yet these two distributive principles, though important, occupy less than two chapters of this book. My central purpose is to increase the philosophical tool kit available to economists, with the aim of enriching their conception of what justice consists in—or at least of what those who have thought most deeply about the subject now think it consists in—and thereby rendering their policy evaluation, more generally their understanding of the fairness of resource allocation mechanisms, more sophisticated.

Let me first summarize some methodological differences between the economist's and the philosopher's ways of thinking. Many economists, when trying to read political philosophy, soon give up, because they find it too informal or too lacking in rigor to be tractable. The modern economist has been trained to take an interesting question and squeeze it as quickly as possible into a formal model. Axioms summarize certain primitive relationships among the terms which define the model, and knowledge comes from inferring conclusions from these axioms that do not obviously follow from them. The economist's main interest is in the inference procedure, her aesthetic sense most satisfied by a brilliant proof or a demonstration that a certain strong conclusion surprisingly follows from a set of apparently weak axioms. While the political philosopher will also appreciate such demonstrations, his real interest lies in the intellectual process that precedes formulation of the model. As one political philosopher put it to me, when a question becomes completely clear, it is of no more philosophical interest. The philosopher's job, then, is to take vague questions and to figure out how to render them less vague: What is the correct way of posing the question? What kinds of information are needed to answer the question? Thus a philosopher faced with an economist's model will usually challenge the terms and axioms of the model. He will offer counterexamples intended to show that the model has ignored, in its very specification, certain important cases of the question under study. He will find examples to show that the axioms have already implicitly answered certain questions that should remain open at the onset, or that the axioms have by fiat excluded certain important cases. The economist typically, and impatiently, views the philosopher's challenges as picayune and diversionary; the philosopher views the economist as thoughtlessly forcing subtle questions into her Procrustean bed.

My approach in this book is to play the role of the philosopher, so far as I am able to, when evaluating the work of economists on distributive justice (in Chapters 1–4, for the most part), and to think like an economist when evaluating the work of philosophers (in Chapters 5–8, for the most part). In the first four chapters, I outline the principal contributions of economists since 1950 to the study of distributive justice and criticize them for either incorrectly representing a philosophical problem (as, for example, in Harsanyi's claims about what utilitarianism consists in, see §§4.3 and 4.4) or for discarding too much of what's relevant for distributive justice in formulating the model (as, for example, in the application of Nash bargaining theory to distributive justice, see §§2.5, 2.6, 3.5, and 3.6). In the last four chapters, I apply economists' tools to study some of the "vague" formulations of philosophers: I read contemporary philosophical theories of distributive justice, that is to say, in a way that I think will help economists to understand them. The result is, often, that a philosopher's claims are inconsistent. More constructively, I also offer economic models to capture certain philosophical ideas in a way that will be, I hope, acceptable to both economists and philosophers: examples are found in §§5.7, 6.3, 6.4, 8.3, and 8.4.

I have said that my primary purpose is to present political philosophy in a digestible form to economists in order to increase the sophistication of their work on normative issues. What contribution do I believe economic analysis can make to the philosopher of distributive justice? I must say that, much as I might prefer to believe otherwise, I think economics is the handmaiden in this relationship. The economist's way of thinking can check the consistency of a philosophical theory or provide a concrete formulation (a model) to make precise some of its still vague assertions. It can often translate a philosophical view about distributive justice into a concrete social policy, such as a tax policy, or delineate the set of feasible social policies which are consistent with that view. These services are surely valuable, perhaps even indispensable. I do not, however, believe that the economist's way of thinking has produced, or will ever produce, important new insights into what distributive justice is. The key new concepts in the last thirty years in the theory of distributive justice—primary goods, functionings and capability, responsibility in its various forms, procedural versus outcome justice, midfare—have all come from the philosophical way of thinking. And it will not do to say that, after economic analysis, many of these concepts have been shown to be ill conceived, for as I hope to show in the last four chapters, these philosophical ideas have led to immense progress in our understanding of what justice consists in. To say that all the theories are somewhat lacking is just to recognize the exquisite subtlety of the problem.

The book presents the major developments in modified chronological order. "Modified," because after a major idea is introduced, I follow it through to its latest significant incarnation before turning to the next idea. Chapter 1 discusses Kenneth Arrow's approach to social choice, in particular his impossibility theorem, which was published in 1951. This theorem was at first viewed, pessimistically, as foreclosing the possibility of aggregating individual preferences into a social preference over various alternatives. For our purposes, the application might be that there is no ordering of possible allocations of resources among individuals in a society, according to their degree of justness, where justness must take account of individual preferences in certain apparently desirable ways (as summarized by the axioms of the theorem). During the 1970s, however, it was convincingly established that the impossibility result could be nullified by assuming that certain kinds of information are available about preferences that Arrow's framework forbade. Thus one could interpret the impossibility result as flowing not from some deep inconsistency in the idea of democracy, but from the paucity of information which Arrow admitted about individual preferences. More specifically, if interpersonal comparisons of utility are possible, then there do exist ways of aggregating individual preferences into a social preference. Chapter 1 develops this theory. In §1.4, I argue that it is not clear that the classical social choice framework is the right one for studying distributive justice, in that it ignores much information that is relevant for justice, and §1.5 presents a way of dealing with this criticism.

In 1950 John Nash proposed an axiomatic treatment of the two-person bargaining problem which was, in spirit, similar to Arrow's axiomatic approach. He characterized what has come to be known as the "Nash solution" with a set of apparently compelling axioms. Other axiomatic solutions to the bargaining problem were proposed by later writers, such as Ehud Kalai and Meir Smorodinsky (1975) and William Thomson and Terje Lensberg (1989). "Nash bargaining theory" has been applied in two ways in the study of distributive justice: first, some philosophers, such as David Gauthier (1986), have viewed justice as the outcome of a suitably defined bargaining problem, and second, some economists, notably Thomson, have chosen to use Nash's axiomatic *method* to characterize directly what justice requires, even though they do not believe that justice is characterized as the outcome of some bargaining problem. This work is presented in Chapter 2 and is criticized, in §2.5, for unacceptably simplifying the problem of distributive justice.

Chapter 3, the most technically demanding in the book, attempts to resolve the challenge posed for Nash bargaining theory in Chapter 2. Nash bargaining theory, illicitly from the viewpoint of distributive justice, ignores information on available resources and preference orders (utility functions) of individuals, reducing the problem of resource allocation immediately to one of "utility allocation." By so doing, it rules inadmissible by fiat many resource allocation mechanisms that might possibly implement distributive justice. This chapter attempts to put resources and preferences back into the problem: Can one reconstruct the essential insights of the Nash, axiomatic approach, where the objects of study are possible worlds replete with "economic" information, not just "utility" information? I show that this can be done. But a philosopher might still object that even more information is required than "economic information" for deliberations of justice, namely, information about what *kind* of "utility" is being measured by utility functions and what the *names* of goods are. Section 3.5 argues that this objection can be accommodated, but at a cost that might be philosophically unacceptable.

Utilitarianism is a venerable theory of distributive justice, which maintains that the just resource allocation (in a world with a fixed population) is that which maximizes the sum total of utility over persons. In Chapter 1 utilitarianism is shown to be the unique social choice rule consistent with certain informational assumptions on utility functions, and the other Arrovian axioms. Those informational assumptions are, however, somewhat too loose: in other words, the *uniqueness* of utilitarianism as the social recommendation is not compelling because we often believe we have much more information on utility than was admitted in the Chapter 1 characterization. Eric Maskin (1978), however, proved that, under stricter informational assumptions and other apparently attractive axioms, utilitarianism is still the unique social recommendation (§4.2). The chronological order of this chapter derives from the contributions of John Harsanyi (1953, 1955), who introduced the idea of the veil of ignorance as a Gedankenexperiment for the study of distributive justice. Moreover, Harsanyi purported to show that utilitarianism would emerge from the contemplation of souls behind a veil of ignorance. He also put forth a distinct argument that utilitarianism is the unique social choice rule when individual and social preferences satisfy the von Neumann–Morgenstern axioms (that is, when individuals and society behave "rationally" in the face of uncertainty). Harsanyi's theorems are evaluated in §§4.3 and 4.4. Finally, this chapter considers the question of optimal population size. The original Benthamite statement of utilitarianism was the view that society should allocate resources so as to achieve "the greatest good for the greatest number." This objective is not, as stated, coherent (one cannot maximize two things simultaneously), but it invites the question, What is the optimal population size for a world with a given finite resource base? Section 4.6 presents recent work on this subject.

Chapter 5 introduces contemporary views that justice consists in some kind of egalitarianism. Rawls (1971) inaugurated this inquiry with a theory of distributive justice that differed from utilitarianism principally in two ways: he argued that justice should focus not on welfare as such, but on the provision of certain kinds of goods he labeled "primary" for all persons, and that, rather than seeking to maximize the sum of some index of these goods across persons (analogous to utilitarianism), it should seek to maximize the smallest bundles of them (the difference principle). Rawls opened up the issue, which since then has been viewed as key in egalitarian theories of distributive justice, of *what* it is the just society should equalize (the equalisandum) across persons. Sections 5.2–5.4 evaluate Rawls's arguments for the difference principle, including his concern with primary goods. Serge-Christophe Kolm (1972) also advocated "maximin" or the difference principle, although his justification for it lay elsewhere: while Rawls invoked a veil-of-ignorance argument, Kolm appealed to the notion that, fundamentally, all persons are really identical (§5.5). The next step was taken by Amartya Sen (1980), who also argued for an egalitarian view of justice, but proposed that Rawls had got the equalisandum wrong: what justice requires is the equalization neither of welfare nor of primary goods but, rather, of something he called "capability," which lies between goods and welfare. A person uses goods to function in various ways—to be mobile, to understand the world around her, to have a social life, and so on. While functionings are *produced* by the consumption of various goods, they are *inputs* into welfare. Sen later argued that the just society equalizes the sets of available vectors of functionings (their *capabilities*) among its citizens (§5.6). Section 5.7 presents a model of Rawlsian or Senian justice somewhat different from conventional models, in that it is not assumed that the conditions of different persons (where that condition can be measured by the level of an index of primary goods or an index of functionings) are interpersonally comparable.

In 1974 Robert Nozick published *Anarchy, State, and Utopia,* probably the most important antiegalitarian contribution to contemporary political philosophy. Nozick argued that justice should concern itself not with patterns of outcome, but with the procedures by which agents interact economically. He apparently grounded his particular proposal for what just procedures consist in, in John Locke's view that, if a person mixes her labor with an unowned part of the natural world, then she is entitled to appropriate the product as her own, as long as she thereby leaves "enough and as good for others" of that natural resource. Section 6.2 summarizes some of the philosophical controversy surrounding Nozick's ideas. Locke's proviso may be inadmissibly strong, for in a world of scarcity, a time must come when no one can further appropriate objects which embody natural resources without meaningfully decreasing the amounts of those resources available for others. The question becomes, How might a neo-Lockean alter Locke's acquisition proviso when natural resources are scarce? Section 6.4 argues that Nozick's solution is only one of a set of possible solutions, and other solutions are presented that engender outcomes far more egalitarian than Nozick's. Thus far in this chapter, Nozick's premise that individuals are self-owners, in the sense that they are entitled to use their labor as they see fit and to appropriate the products of it, subject to some constraints, has not been challenged. Section 6.6 outlines recent arguments by G. A. Cohen that self-ownership is not an ethically attractive premise. If his arguments are appealing, there is an even more basic challenge to Nozick's theory of justice than those provided earlier.

In 1981 Ronald Dworkin published a pair of articles in which he took up the issue initially posed by Rawls and then elaborated by Sen: What is the right equalisandum for an egalitarian theory of justice? Dworkin argued that it is not welfare, for, among other reasons for rejecting welfare, a society committed to equalizing the welfare of all individuals would have to give more resources to those with expensive tastes, and this is ethically unacceptable. A society should not have to supply the champagne lover with more resources than the beer lover, for assuming the former is glad he has champagne tastes, he should take personal responsibility for acquiring the extra money required to satisfy them. Dworkin went on to argue that the right alternative to equalizing welfare is to equalize the bundles of resources available to persons. The subtlety, however, came in his view that the vector of resources must be considered to include certain nontransferable (inalienable) resources, such as native talents. Thus a physical equalization of resource bundles across persons could not be carried out. The question became: What allocation of transferable resources would appropriately compensate individuals for their fixed unequal bundles of nontransferable resources? Dworkin proposed an ingenious solution to the problem, that the distribution of resources should be deemed relevantly equal if it would have resulted from a prior situation in which individuals, from behind a veil of ignorance, could have taken out insurance against being born with paltry bundles of nontransferable resources. Thus, behind Dworkin's thin veil of ignorance, individuals know their preferences but not the bundles of inalienable resources they will receive in the "birth lottery," and they are each provided with the same amount of money with which such insurance can be purchased. The actual distribution of transferable resources (say, money) in the world is an "equal" one if it would have resulted from such an insurance scheme. Sections 7.3 and 7.4 criticize a number of Dworkin's formulations and, in particular, argue that the insurance mechanism does not implement an attractive kind of equality, one that a "resource egalitarian" would be happy with. Section 7.5 presents an axiomatic approach to the problem of finding a resource allocation mechanism which satisfies several apparent demands of a resource egalitarian view.

Dworkin brought to the fore in egalitarian thought the issue of responsibility. A concern with individual responsibility was present in Rawls and Sen, for both primary goods and functionings, the equalisanda of their theories, are only the inputs into a successful life; Rawls and Sen, at least implicitly, hold individuals responsible for transforming those inputs into a successful life. To put it another way: justice does not require, in their theories, equal welfares or equal degrees of success in the realization of life plans, but only equalization of what's needed to produce welfare and success. Nevertheless, responsibility is not a focal point in the writings of Rawls and Sen, while it emerges center stage in Dworkin's work. At the end of the 1980s, Richard Arneson (1989) and G. A. Cohen (1989) took Dworkin's ideas a step further. The key idea of Dworkin's work, they held, is that justice requires the equalization of some kind of advantage insofar as that advantage is the consequence of circumstances and traits for which persons should not be held responsible, but allows differentiation of advantage insofar as it results from circumstances and traits regarding which the person should be held responsible. What Arneson and Cohen quarreled with was Dworkin's placement of "preferences" on the side of what persons should be held responsible for. Arneson argued that all the arguments that Dworkin and Rawls had marshaled against equality of welfare were ineffective against a view that he called "equality of opportunity for welfare"; Cohen argued that the right conception of distributive justice is the very similar "equality of access to advantage." These proposals are both intellectual descendants of Dworkin's; they both feature the issue of personal responsibility, but differ from Dworkin on what kinds of things a person should be held responsible for. I analyze these proposals in §§8.1 and 8.2.

We can view the theories of Rawls, Dworkin, Arneson, and Cohen as theories advocating equality of opportunity, in the sense that they all believe in equalizing some kind of wherewithal that all people need to create mean-ingful and successful lives for themselves. But the "opportunities" they ad-vocate equalizing are much more encompassing than those equalized in the traditional, "thin" conception of equality of opportunity. In §§8.3–8.5, I propose a way of implementing, through tax policy, a kind of equality of opportunity that I associate with the proposals of Arneson and Cohen. More precisely, I propose a way that a society can design a tax policy that implements equality of opportunity for certain kinds of advantage (say, health, income, or welfare), consonant with its conception of what individ-uals should and should not be held responsible for. Section 8.6 presents other recent work by economists, in the axiomatic tradition, on how to equalize income or welfare when it is the consequence of causes only some of which persons should be deemed responsible for.

There are (at least) three topics which some might find inexcusably miss-ing from this book: the theories of exploitation, envy-freeness, and com-munitarianism. I do not deal with the theory of exploitation because, as I explain in Roemer (1994, pp. 65–96), after studying it for some time, I came to believe that it is not in itself a fundamental theory of (in)justice. I do not mean that workers are justly treated under capitalism, but rather that the view that what's unjust about their treatment is exploitation needs further articulation. For, according to Marx, or at least to my interpretation of his view (see Roemer 1994, Part I), the exploitation of the worker is en-tailed by his receiving wage goods which embody less labor than the labor he expended for that pay. Now the unequal exchange of "embodied labor" in goods for "direct labor" in production is by no means obviously unjust. Indeed, if the capitalist is the rightful owner of the factory, then why cannot we view the "surplus labor" (the difference between the embodied labor in the wage goods and the labor the worker expends in the factory) as a rent the worker pays for access to that factory, for access, that is, to what he needs to render his labor fruitful? Thus the existence of surplus value, or unequal labor exchange in the above sense, is not sufficient to ground the claim that the worker is unjustly treated. I think that some egalitarian the-ory, of the Rawls-Sen-Dworkin-Arneson-Cohen variety, is needed to justify the Marxian accusation that workers are unjustly treated under capitalism. It may be unjust, for example, for any small group to own a factory, if, in a market economy, that makes the equalization of opportunities impossi-ble. Or the method by which the capitalist came to acquire the factory may have been unjust. In either case, we need a deeper theory.

I do not give the theory of "envy-freeness," or what economists also call "fairness," a full chapter, because I do not find it to be at all compelling as a theory of justice. The idea does not appear (to my knowledge) in the writings of political philosophers with the exception of Dworkin (1981b) and Van Parijs (1995). In the Appendix I argue that "fairness" has become popular among economists because it enables one significantly to narrow down the set of Pareto optimal allocations without assuming any interpersonal comparability of utility. But justifying an interest in the concept for that reason is like only looking for the lost diamond under the streetlight because it's too dark to see elsewhere. I argue, moreover, that, when economists move beyond simple exchange economies to production economies, they modify the definition of "fairness" in a way that implicitly incorporates an element of interpersonal comparability. If we admit that this element of comparability is compelling in production economies, it must, I argue, also be compelling in exchange economies. Thus "fairness" loses the essential characteristic for which it is prized, its independence of any notion of interpersonal comparability.

I do not discuss communitarianism because it does not seem to me that economic analysis would be useful for critiquing or elucidating its main claims. There are the interesting books of Jon Elster (1992) and H. P. Young (1994), which argue that different "spheres" of social life seem to have different norms of distributive justice, an idea which resonates, to some extent, with some of the claims of communitarians (see, specifically, Walzer 1983). Elster lists twenty-odd allocation rules that are used to allocate scarce goods and necessary burdens in different spheres, and maintains that there is no (sufficiently simple) general theory which explains what rules are used in what cases. If he is right, then the scope for economic analysis of this important aspect of communitarianism is limited.

When I began to write this book, I conceived of it as a text for graduate students in economics who have taken a first-year course in microeconomic theory. Indeed, it should be fully accessible to a student with that amount of preparation. I intend the presentation of the philosophical ideas to be sufficiently self-contained that a reasonably sophisticated person, who has not read them in the original, will understand the issues. Still, if this book is used as a text, I strongly recommend that it be supplemented with the relevant philosophical readings. Those economists who wish to work in this area must, after all, learn to read political philosophy and not take it all second-hand from a small number of translators.

I also hope that political philosophers and, more generally, social scientists interested in distributive justice can learn from this book. There is a good deal of verbal discussion of the formal theorems, and even if their proofs cannot be understood by the economically untrained reader, I believe their statements usually can be. And certainly the nonformal material of the final four chapters can serve as an introduction to contemporary theories of distributive justice for the nonphilosophical reader.

In writing this kind of survey, the author must select judiciously what literature to comment upon, if not to prevent overwhelming the reader with too many trees, then at least to keep the book's price within reason. There is much work in economics which I have ignored that is at least marginally related, perhaps importantly applicable, to the topic of distributive justice. Fortunately, there are a number of recently published and forthcoming books presenting this material: I include Moulin (1988), Broome (1991), Gaetner and Klemisch-Ahlert (1992), Peters (1992), Young (1994), Thomson (1991, 1994), Moulin (1995), Hausman and McPherson (1995), and Kolm (1995). My main criterion has been to discuss work that I believe is philosophically important, or that flows directly from such work. I am mildly confident that my choices have not been too idiosyncratic.

1

The Measurement of Utility and Arrow's Theorem

1.1   The Measurability and Comparability of Utility

Utility as a term meaning the capacity of a good to satisfy a want of whatever kind can be traced back to Pufendorf's *De officio hominis et civis iuxta legem naturalem* (1724; see Black 1987) and to Ferdinando Galiani's *Della moneta* (1751; see Georgescu-Roegen 1987)—"the aptitude of a thing to procure us felicity." Jeremy Bentham, to whom is due the credit for introducing the term as a technical one in English political economy, wavered between viewing utility as a correlate of happiness and, later, finding no "sufficiently manifest connection between the idea of *happiness* and *pleasure,* on the one hand, and the idea of *utility,* on the other."[1] In his *Cours* (1896), Pareto introduced the term "ophelimity" to denote "the attribute of a thing capable of satisfying a need or a desire, legitimate or not," and later used that term to denote the satisfaction of individual desires, and utility to denote the attribute of things beneficial to society. In his early work, Pareto viewed ophelimity as a physicalist attribute, one subject to the laws of quantity. By 1900, however, he understood that the device needed to analyze individual choice was the individual's family of indifference curves, and that no particular numbers need be associated with these curves, that any ordinal indexing of them would do. He thus wrote that he had freed economic theory from all "metaphysical" ingredients.[2]

---

1. The quotation is taken from Georgescu-Roegen (1987).
2. The source for the information in this paragraph is Georgescu-Roegen (1987).

When Bentham wrote that the social goal should be to achieve "the greatest happiness for the greatest number," his principle of utility, he clearly conceived of utility as something the summation of which it was meaningful to perform across individuals.[3] Pareto's concept of optimality, however, was remarkable for not requiring such interpersonal comparability: it is what we now call a purely ordinal concept. (The cost of not assuming such comparability was, of course, the indeterminacy of Pareto optimality as a social prescription.)

General equilibrium theory, which came to full fruition with the work of Arrow and Debreu (1954), made perfectly clear that the economics of the market could be fully described using only the concept of indifference maps of individuals, that is, the notion of preference orders over commodity bundles. No notion of utility as a measurable quantity was needed, nor was it necessary to make any comparisons of "utility" between individuals. (This is, at least, true of a theory where no individual has any power to bargain or to "influence prices." For once interpersonal bargaining occurs, then notions of fairness may be required to describe its outcome, as a bargainer may refuse to accept an offer because he views it as unfair, a conclusion he may reach, inter alia, by making some comparison of his gain compared with his adversary's.) This success of general equilibrium theory—of describing completely the economic outcome in a market economy using only ordinal information on individual preferences—has doubtless encouraged the view, now held by many economists, that no other information regarding preference is *meaningful*, that it is incoherent to speak either of intensity of individual preference (in the sense of fixing a cardinal scale to index a person's indifference curves, where the difference of utility between states has meaning) or of interpersonal comparability of welfare. This inference is, of course, faulty. To understand why one object heats up faster than another, for example, one might need not know their colors, but that does not imply that the objects do not possess color. Whether it is meaningful to speak of intensity of individual preference or of one person being "better off" than another is not a question that can be solved by knowing what kind of information on preference a particular theory requires. Moreover, the parsimony of general equilibrium theory in regard to information on preferences does not imply that more information might not be needed for purposes other than a

---

3. Bentham's principle of utility leaves moot what it might mean to maximize two objectives at once, a topic I will address briefly in Chapter 3.

positive description of economic outcomes in market economies (or, as I have indicated, even in market economies where some agents have market power).

The modern viewpoint, that the preference orderings of persons over alternative states are the primitives of economic theory and that utility functions are merely convenient representations of those orderings, was first grasped by Pareto, as already noted.[4] Despite Pareto's insight, it was not until the 1970s that full clarity was reached on the meaning of utility functions, a clarity finally achieved as a result of the efforts of economists to understand fully the meaning of Arrow's "general possibility theorem," or, as some might say, of their efforts to escape its pessimistic proclamation. Although Arrow's theorem (1951, 1963) showed that society could not coherently choose from among alternative states if it adhered to some plausible, appealing axioms, Bergson (1938) had introduced the idea of a social welfare function some years earlier, a concept that continues to be used to this day. How could Arrow's theorem and common Bergsonian practice be reconciled? The answer lay in a full understanding of the connection between utility functions and preference orderings.

Let X be a set of social states, let H be a set of at least two individuals, and let R^h be a preference order of individual h over X. We write xR^hy to mean "h weakly prefers state x to state y." Formally, we can view R^h as a subset of $X \times X$, where a pair (x, y) is contained in the subset iff xR^hy. A subset of $X \times X$ is called a *binary relation* on X. Let P^h and I^h be the strict preference relation and indifference relation contained in R^h: that is, xI^hy iff xR^hy and yR^hx and xP^hy iff xR^hy and not yR^hx. (We say "contained in" since we can view R^h as a subset of $X \times X$.) We assume that R^h is complete, reflexive, and transitive: completeness means that for any $x, y \in X$, either xR^hy or yR^hx; reflexive means for all x, xR^hx; transitive means if xR^hy and yR^hz then xR^hz. A complete, reflexive, transitive binary relation on X is called an *order* on X. A binary relation that is reflexive and transitive is a *quasi-order*. The *choice set* $C(X, R)$, where R is a quasi-order, is $\{x \in X \mid (\forall y \in X)xRy\}$.

A utility function is a mapping $u: X \rightarrow \mathbf{R}$, where $\mathbf{R}$ is the set of real numbers, and a utility function *represents a preference order R on X* iff $u(x) \geq u(y)$

---

4. It is perhaps more accurate to say that "choice" is the primitive from the modern viewpoint. A preference order simply records how a person chooses, or would choose. Thus a utility function, which represents preferences as revealed choices, need not coincide with what makes a person happy, or with his interests, if the person does not always choose in line with his interests.

whenever xRy [which implies $u(x) > u(y)$ whenever xPy and $u(x) = u(y)$ whenever xIy]. There are an infinite number of utility functions that represent any given preference order R, if R can be represented by a utility function, but there are orders that have no such representation. If u represents R and $f : \mathbf{R} \to \mathbf{R}$ is any increasing function, then $f \circ u$, defined by $f \circ u(x) \equiv f(u(x))$, is also a utility function representing R.

Let $\rho = (R^1, R^2, \ldots, R^H)$ be a *profile* of preference orders for individuals in H (whom we conveniently number as $1, 2, \ldots, H$) over X. We can represent the profile R by a profile $u = (u^1, u^2, \ldots, u^H)$, if u^h is a utility function which represents the preference order R^h. Suppose, for the sake of argument, that we view each citizen's preferences as respecting the degree of happiness she enjoys in social states (that is, xR^hy iff h is at least as happy in x as in y), that happiness is measured in units called "haps," and that happiness is a perfectly commensurable quantity across individuals— the state of enjoying 100 haps, for any person, is associated with exactly the same set of neural reactions in the brain, giving rise to exactly the same chemical bath and electric stimuli of the relevant pleasure or satisfaction centers. Then there would be exactly one choice of u^h we would find acceptable for each citizen h, namely, the one that gives the number of haps she enjoys in the various states. The uniquely acceptable profile u would then contain much more information than is contained in the preference profile ρ.

Now suppose, in contrast, that we take the view that the only information about preferences that we know, or is relevant to our objective, is the information contained in ρ. Then *any* profile u, in which u^h represents citizen h's preference order, would be acceptable, and u^h would of necessity be some increasing transform of the "true" utility function described above.

There is a convenient way of specifying the information about preferences that we wish a profile of utility functions, u, to convey. We begin with one acceptable profile, u. We then ask: What transformations of the profile u engender another acceptable profile, u'? Let $f^h : \mathbf{R} \to \mathbf{R}$. If f^h is a strictly increasing function and u^h represents R^h, then $f^h \circ u^h$ represents R^h as well. Let $f = (f^1, f^2, \ldots, f^H)$ be an H-tuple of strictly increasing functions from $\mathbf{R}$ to $\mathbf{R}$, and write $f \circ u = (f^1 \circ u^1, f^2 \circ u^2, \ldots, f^H \circ u^H)$. What transformations f would be acceptable in the first case described above, when we insist that $u^h(x)$ measure the happiness of a person in state x in haps? Only one: the identity transformation, that is, $I^* = (I, I, \ldots, I)$, where I is the identity mapping from $\mathbf{R}$ to $\mathbf{R}$, for only this transformation leaves the profile u unchanged. In the second case above, where the profile u need only represent the information in ρ, there are a multitude of acceptable transformations, namely, all those transformations f where the f^h are each strictly increasing!

We can, quite generally, specify the kind of information that we require the profile u to convey by specifying the *group of transformations G* that can be acceptably applied to an acceptable profile u. In the first case above, that group consists of just one element; in the second, it consists of an infinity of elements. These sets of transformations are, indeed, algebraic groups with respect to the operation $*$ defined by $f * g = (f^1 \circ g^1, \dots, f^H \circ g^H)$, where $f \circ g$ is the ordinary composition of functions. That is, G always contains the identity transformation I^*; if it contains a transformation $f = (f^1, f^2, \dots, f^H)$, it also contains its "inverse," $f^{-1} := (f^{1^{-1}}, f^{2^{-1}}, \dots, f^{H^{-1}})$, where $f^{h^{-1}}$ is the inverse function of f^h; and if it contains two transformations f and g, it contains their composition, $f * g$. Let us define G^{AFC} to be the singleton group, consisting just of the identity transformation I^*. We say that utility is *absolutely measurable and fully comparable* iff we allow an acceptable profile u of utility functions to be transformed only by elements in G^{AFC}. Let G^{ONC} be the group consisting of all transformations f, where f^h is any strictly increasing function. We say that utility is *ordinally measurable and noncomparable* if we allow an acceptable profile to be transformed by any element of the group G^{ONC}.

We can define many other groups of transformations, which characterize the kind of information the utility functions are meant to convey. Suppose utility information is meant to convey cardinal meaning: for instance, we wish to consider the family of von Neumann–Morgenstern utility functions for a person in a situation with uncertainty, but there is no interpersonal comparability of utility intended. Or we wish differences in utility between states to be meaningful for each individual. The appropriate restriction for this kind of utility is then *cardinally measurable and noncomparable,* and it is characterized by allowing transformations in the group G^{CNC}, consisting of all increasing affine transformations of the form $f = (\alpha^1 I + \beta^1, \dots, \alpha^H I + \beta^H)$, where the β^h are any real numbers and the α^h are any positive real numbers. Given one acceptable profile of utility functions u, then application of any f in G^{CNC} produces another profile of utility functions that is acceptable for each individual. [For instance, if we wish utility differences to be meaningful, note that if $u(x) - u(y) > u(w) - u(z)$, then for any $\alpha^1 > 0$ and any β^1, if $v \equiv \alpha^1 u + \beta^1$, then $v(x) - v(y) > v(w) - v(z)$.]

Suppose we view utility as only carrying ordinal information for individuals, but interpersonal comparisons are meaningful. This is sometimes called co-ordinal utility. We say that a utility profile contains *ordinal full comparable* information (or utility is ordinally measurable and fully comparable) iff an acceptable profile u can be transformed by a transformation of the form $f = (f^1, f^1, \ldots, f^1)$, where f^1 is any strictly increasing transformation. Thus we can transform person h's utility function by any increasing transformation—so only ordinal information is contained in her u^h—but then we must transform everyone's utility function by the same transformation. Call the group of such transformations G^{OFC}. This means that interpersonal orderings of states are preserved: that is, if for one acceptable profile, $u^1(x) > u^2(y)$, then this order is maintained for all acceptable profiles, which is to say, it is meaningful to assert that citizen 1 is better off in state x than citizen 2 is in state y. It is noteworthy that utility profiles can contain meaningful information of interpersonal comparability without containing cardinal information individually—at least from the mathematical viewpoint, if possibly not from the philosophical.

Suppose that we wish to model the view that individual utility contains cardinal information (for example, von Neumann–Morgenstern, or the meaningfulness of utility differences between states for a person), that differences in utility between states are comparable for all citizens, but that absolute levels of utility for individuals can never be ascertained. We can model these requisites by allowing transformations of an acceptable profile u only by the group G^{CUC}, standing for *cardinally measurable and unit comparable,* where a typical element of the group is $f = (\alpha I + \beta^1, \alpha I + \beta^2, \ldots, \alpha I + \beta^H)$. Thus, if $(u^1, \ldots, u^H)$ is acceptable, so is $(\alpha u^1 + \beta^1, \ldots, \alpha u^H + \beta^H)$. This says that the levels of utility are meaningless, since we can alter the order of levels by adding appropriate and different constants β^h, but that statements of the form "$u^1(x) - u^1(y) > u^2(x) - u^2(y)$" are meaningful. Finally, G^{CUC} insists that cardinal information is meaningful, as only increasing affine transformations are allowed ($\alpha > 0$).

There are other kinds of information we might want utility profiles to describe, some of which will be defined in later chapters. The general observation is that the larger the group of allowable transformations, the less information is conveyed by the profiles. Thus when utility profiles are ordinally noncomparable, which is the only information required for general equilibrium theory, the group G^{ONC} is as large as possible: it contains all the other groups defined above. When the group is as small as possible, G^{AFC}, the utility profile contains as much information as it possibly can. The other groups listed lie between these two. Since G^{CUC} is a subgroup of G^{CNC}, utility profiles contain more information if they are cardinal unit comparable than if they are cardinal noncomparable. In some cases, neither of a pair of groups contains the other (for example, G^{CUC} and G^{OFC}). In these cases, we cannot say that one utility profile contains more information than the other.

It is sometimes convenient to be able to say that a utility profile contains *at least* CUC information (say). Thus we say a profile u satisfies CUC+ if and only if we allow transformations of u by a group $G \subseteq G^{CUC}$.

Consider a "Bergson-Samuelson social welfare function," W, for a society H. W associates to any vector of utility *numbers* $(\bar{u}^1, \ldots, \bar{u}^H) \in \mathbf{R}^H$ a real number, which is taken to be an ordinal measure of the welfare of a society in which individual h experiences utility level $\bar{u}^h$. Thus let u be an acceptable profile of utility functions for H, let x be a social state, and define $\tilde{W}^u(x) \equiv W(u^1(x), \ldots, u^H(x))$. Let us, I hope without any disturbing ambiguity, call $\tilde{W}^u$ a social welfare function as well. Suppose we have only limited information about utility profiles for the society—say we have cardinal-unit-comparable information (that is, we allow transformations of an acceptable profile by elements of G^{CUC}). How can we model the requirement that our social welfare function $\tilde{W}^u$ respect our informational knowledge?

We shall adopt the view here (although one might defend a different view) that we require of our social welfare function only that it give us an ordering of social states—that is, that $\tilde{W}^u$ give a social preference order R. Thus the social preference order induced by $\tilde{W}^u$ is the binary relation R^u defined by $\tilde{W}^u(x) \geq \tilde{W}^u(y)$ iff $x R^u y$, with indifference precisely when $\tilde{W}^u(x) = \tilde{W}^u(y)$. Continuing with the above example, we wish to express the requirement that the Bergson-Samuelson social welfare function W be meaningful when utility information is cardinal unit comparable: then we simply require that $\tilde{W}^u$ and $\tilde{W}^{u'}$ induce the same social preference order (that is, $R^u = R^{u'}$) whenever u and u' are both acceptable, that is, when $u = f \circ u'$ for some $f \in G^{CUC}$. More generally

Definition 1.1. A Bergson-Samuelson social welfare function W *respects information on utility profiles of type Y* iff, for any acceptable profile of utility functions u and any transformation $f \in G^Y$, $\tilde{W}^u$ and $\tilde{W}^{u'}$ induce the same ordering of social states, where $u' = f \circ u$.

Let us define the *utilitarian* social welfare function as $W(\bar{u}^1, \ldots, \bar{u}^H) = \sum \bar{u}^h$. We show that W respects cardinal-unit-comparable information on utility profiles. For, by definition, $\tilde{W}^u(x) = \sum u^h(x)$. Suppose $\tilde{W}^u(x) \geq \tilde{W}^u(y)$, that is, $\sum u^h(x) \geq \sum u^h(y)$. Let $f = (\alpha I + \beta^1, \ldots, \alpha I + \beta^H)$ be any transformation in G^{CUC}, and let $u' = f \circ u$. Then $\tilde{W}^{u'}(x) = \sum (\alpha u^h(x) + \beta^h) = \alpha \sum u^h(x) + \sum \beta^h \geq \alpha \sum u^h(y) + \sum \beta^h = \sum (\alpha u^h(y) + \beta^h) = \tilde{W}^{u'}(y)$. Therefore, $\tilde{W}^u$ and $\tilde{W}^{u'}$ indeed induce the same preference order over social states. We thus say that utilitarianism respects cardinal-unit-comparable information, or that utilitarianism is a coherent concept of social welfare even if utility information is only cardinally measurable and unit comparable.

Similar reasoning shows that utilitarianism does not respect ordinal noncomparable information, that is, that utilitarianism is incoherent given only ONC information on utility profiles. To see this, suppose there are two states, x and y, and two individuals, 1 and 2, and we have an acceptable utility profile that gives them utility levels $u^1(x) = 5$, $u^1(y) = 1$, $u^2(x) = 1$, $u^2(y) = 4$. Then utilitarianism chooses state x over state y, since $6 > 5$. Now subject the profile (u^1, u^2) to the transformation $f(z) = (z, z^3)$—that is, we leave u^1 unchanged but we cube the second person's utility function. This is a transformation in G^{ONC}. After the transformation, we have $u'^1(x) = 5$, $u'^1(y) = 1$, $u'^2(x) = 1$, $u'^2(y) = 64$. Now utilitarianism chooses y over x, since $65 > 6$. Thus utilitarianism changes its verdict when we transform the utility profile by an element of G^{ONC}. It is thus not a well-defined concept given only ONC information on utility.

Consider another well-known social welfare function, $W(\bar{u}^1, \ldots, \bar{u}^H) = \min_h \bar{u}^h$: social welfare is equal to the welfare of the least well-off person in society. This leads to the social decision problem

$$\max_{x \in X} \min_{h \in H} u^h(x),$$

hence the familiar "maximin utility." Does this W respect cardinal unit comparability? No. (This is left as an exercise for the reader.) W respects OFC information, however. Let $\tilde{W}^u(x) > \tilde{W}^u(y)$, for some acceptable utility profile u. This means that $\min_h u^h(x) = u^{h^1}(x) > \min_h u^h(y) = u^{h^2}(y)$, that is, the worst-off person in state x is h^1 and the worst-off person in state y is h^2. Now subject u to a transformation $f \in G^{OFC}$, $f = (f^1, \ldots, f^1)$. Note that h^1 remains the worst-off person in state x after f is applied, and h^2 remains the worst-off person in state y, and by monotonicity of f^1, we have $f^1(u^{h^1}(x)) > f^1(u^{h^2}(y))$, which says precisely that W continues to prefer state x to state y after the transformation by f.

The reader may also convince herself that utilitarianism does not respect OFC information. Thus utilitarianism and maximin are each social welfare functions that are coherent with certain kinds of information on utility profiles, but not others. There are informational situations in which, for a social planner, utilitarianism would be a coherent social welfare function but maximin would not be, and conversely.

If we have as much information on utility profiles as it is possible to have—that is, absolute measurability and full comparability—then all social welfare functions are coherent. With such measurability, there is only one admissible utility profile, so a social welfare function W gives rise to only one $\tilde{W}^u$. So, trivially, all acceptable $\tilde{W}^u$ give rise to the same preference order R of states. When an economist writes down a particular social welfare function and does not remark on the kind of utility information with respect to which it is coherent, one might charitably assume that he is assuming that utility is absolutely measurable and fully comparable, for in this case there are no restrictions on the social welfare function.

The key observation from this discussion is that the less information there is on utility profiles (that is, the larger the admissible group of transformations), the fewer coherent social welfare functions there are in the given framework. If the admissible group of transformations is G, then each $f \in G$ imposes a restriction on W—namely, that for any acceptable u, $\tilde{W}^u$ and $\tilde{W}^{f \circ u}$ induce the same preference order R. So less information on utility implies a larger group G, which implies more restrictions on W.

We might well ask: What social welfare functions are coherent if we assume the least possible amount of information on utility functions, namely, transformability by the group G^{ONC}? Arrow's "general possibility theorem," now more frequently called Arrow's impossibility theorem and recast as a statement about Bergson-Samuelson social welfare functions, asserts that none exists. It is thus not a statement that it is never possible for society to have a coherent social welfare function, but rather that, if only particularly poor information on utility profiles is usable, namely, ONC information, then there exists no coherent social welfare function.

For pedagogical reasons, I have adopted an anachronistic presentation of the topic. Although Arrow's theorem was proved in 1951, the conceptualization of the different kinds of information that might be conveyed by utility functions was not developed until the 1970s. Arrow did not work with utility functions at all, or with social welfare functions, but only with preference profiles, as I describe next.

1.2   The Arrow Impossibility Theorem

Let X be a finite set of alternative social states, and let $\mathcal{R}$ be the set of all orderings over X. A *social choice rule*[5] is a mapping ψ from a subset $\mathcal{D} \subseteq \mathcal{R}^H$ into $\mathcal{R}$. ($\mathcal{R}^H$ denotes the Cartesian product of $\mathcal{R}$ with itself H times.) That is, ψ associates to any profile of orderings an ordering. The interpretation is that ψ "aggregates" the preference orders of individuals in society into one social preference. What reasonable restrictions might one impose on the map ψ for it to respect the preferences of individuals? Arrow proposed the following, although not in just this form.

If $\rho = (R^1, \ldots, R^H)$ is a profile of preference orders, $x \rho y$ shall mean that, for all h, $x R^h y$. I shall also use the notation $R = \psi(\rho)$.

Condition WP (Weak Pareto Optimality).   If $x, y \in X$ and $x P^h y$ for all h then $x P y$.

This means that if all citizens rank x better than y, then society must rank x better than y.

Condition I (Binary Independence of Irrelevant Alternatives).   Let $\rho = (R^1, \ldots, R^H)$ and $\rho' = (R'^1, \ldots, R'^H)$ be two profiles, let x and y be any two states, and suppose that for all h, $x R^h y$ precisely when $x R'^h y$. Then $x R y$ iff $x R' y$.

In words, if no individual changes her ranking of x and y when her preferences change from R^h to R'^h, then society shall not change its ranking of x and y in the move from ρ to ρ'. The name of the axiom derives from the fact that the social ranking of the two states x and y does not depend on how the ranking of other states changes as the profile changes from ρ to ρ'.

Condition ND (Nondictatorship).   There is no individual k such that, for all profiles $\rho \in \mathcal{D}$ and for all $x, y \in X$, $x P^k y$ implies $x P y$.

If the negation of this held, then the society would always prefer one state x to another state y whenever individual k prefers x to y.

Condition U (Unrestricted Domain).   The domain $\mathcal{D}$ of ψ is $\mathcal{R}^H$.

---

5. Arrow calls this a "social welfare function," but I have already used that terminology to mean something else.

This says that the social choice rule must make a social prescription for any conceivable preference profile society may have.

The "impossibility" theorem states that there is no social choice rule satisfying WP, I, ND, and U. Define a social choice rule ψ to be a *dictatorship* if, for some k, and all profiles $\rho \in \mathcal{D}$, and for all $x, y \in X$, $x P^k y$ implies $x P y$: that is, the social preference between two states is always the preference ordering of citizen k, when k strictly prefers one state to the other. An alternative statement to the one just provided is:

Theorem 1.1. *Suppose* $|X| \geq 3$. *The only social choice rules satisfying WP, I, and U are the dictatorships.*

The impossibility theorem can be seen, from the viewpoint of the history of social choice theory, as a refinement of Condorcet's paradox. A natural social choice rule is the one defined by "majority vote." To keep things simple, suppose there is an odd number of individuals and we admit only preference orderings with no indifference (of two states, one is always strictly preferred to the other). Suppose, given a profile ρ, we define x socially preferred to y iff a majority of citizens prefer x to y. A quick check shows that this rule respects WP, I, ND, and U (at least, unrestricted domain of strict preference orderings). Why, then, is "majority rule" not a counterexample to Theorem 1.1? Because it does not define a preference *ordering* of states. Consider the following society with individuals 1, 2, and 3 and states x, y, and z, and suppose the preference order of individual h, for $h = 1, 2, 3$, is given by column h of the following table:

1	2	3
x	y	z
y	z	x
z	x	y

Write "P" for the majority rule relation. We have $x P y$, since both 1 and 3 prefer x to y; we have $y P z$ since both 1 and 2 prefer y to z. By transitivity— a property of an order—we must therefore have $x P z$. But note both 2 and 3 prefer z to x, and so $z P x$. Since P is a strict ordering (no indifference), this is a contradiction. That is, P is not, in fact, a strict ordering of X. Arrow's theorem states that this failure is not an aberration. (Strictly speaking, we can now see that I was being imprecise when I stated that "majority rule" obeys the four conditions, since it fails to be ordering, and those conditions referred to social orderings. This, however, is a small point, for majority rule does define a binary relation on X—that is, a subset of $X \times X$—and as a relation, it does enjoy the relevantly restated conditions WP, I, ND, and U.)

As an abstract mathematical statement, Theorem 1.1 is subject to any number of applications or interpretations. I have implicitly assumed, thus far, that the theorem says something about the impossibility of democratic rule—by thinking of the "individuals" as citizens in a society with preference orders over various social states among which society must choose. The restrictions WP, I, and ND are clear enough in their intent: WP and I are both ways of requiring the social preference ordering to respect the views of individuals, and ND is motivated by the same principle that makes "one man one vote" an attractive democratic principle. U, however, is harder to justify—why should society have to supply an aggregation procedure that will work for *any* profile of preferences? One justification of U is the view that ψ is a constitution, a procedure that a society describes intended to be workable for many years in the future and for many different kinds of social choice problems. Thus the relevant preference profiles cannot be predicted, and prudence suggests writing a constitution that will work regardless of what they may be.

There are other applications of the impossibility theorem, as an abstract mathematical statement. I shall describe two. The first is taken from MacKay (1980). Suppose we wish to design a scoring system to choose a winner of a quadrathalon, an athletic contest with four events. To be specific, suppose there are three athletes—Aziza, Bogdan, and Charles—and the events are the Run, the Jump, the Hurdle, and the Weights. The athletes' performances are given, in a particular instance, by:

	Run	Jump	Hurdle	Weights
Aziza	10.1″	6.0′	40″	150 lb
Bogdan	9.2″	5.9′	42″	140 lb
Charles	10.0″	6.1′	39″	145 lb

Let us think of each athletic event as an "individual" and each athlete as a "social state." (Granted, this seems strange, but watch what happens.) A "preference order" of individuals over states is a ranking of how the athletes do in the event. Thus individual "Run" ranks the states A, B, and C as follows in the instance of the table: A is preferred to C is preferred to B; "Jump" ranks the state C preferred to A preferred to B, and so on. Thus a scoring system for the quadrathalon should take as data the "profile" consisting of the preference orders of the four individuals (events) over the states (athletes). Should it obey condition WP? Yes, for this says that if A(ziza) does better than C(harles) in all events, she should receive a higher aggregate score than Charles. Should it obey condition I? This says the following: Suppose there are two quadrathalons, and in each event, B(ogdan) and A(ziza) have the same relative standing in both (for example, Bogdan beats Aziza in the Run in both, Aziza beats Bogdan in the Hurdle in both, and so on). Then, if Aziza is considered to defeat Bogdan in the first quad, she should also beat him in the second. Nondictatorship says that the scoring system cannot ignore all but one event and simply rank athletes according to how they do on the Run (say). Unrestricted domain says that the system must be able to score the contestants regardless of what the outcomes are in the four events. This condition is a reasonable one to impose if the events are testing skills that are "orthogonal" in the sense that knowing the outcome of one event does not help predict what the outcome will be in another. The conditions WP, I, ND, and U are therefore reasonable restrictions on a scoring system. Theorem 1.1 asserts that there is no scoring system with these attributes.

The second application is due to May (1954). Let us delve behind the problem a person Adam faces in forming preferences over commodity bundles. We may assume that Adam has preferences over certain fundamental characteristics that commodities have, or certain states of physical and mental well-being that they provide. These may be nutrition, shelter from the elements, opportunities to do interesting work, freedom from disease, gastronomic pleasure, and doing good for others. Let us suppose that Adam can rank all the relevant commodity bundles, or, more generally, life plans, according to each of these six criteria (a tall order already). We may view each criterion as an "individual" and the ranking of life plans (social states) as a preference order of that individual. Adam's problem is to construct a single ordering of life plans given the six preference orders. Should such an ordering satisfy the Weak Pareto condition? This simply says that if Adam prefers life plan x to life plan y according to all six criteria, then he should all around prefer x to y. Nondictatorship says that Adam's preference order should not simply discard the rankings according to five of the criteria and just follow the dictate of one. It is not hard to argue that, indeed, all four conditions of Theorem 1.1 are salient restrictions on the formation of an overall ordering; the implication is that no acceptable aggregate ordering exists for Adam. May (1954) goes on to provide a fascinating historical illustration of the cyclicity of preference that may be exhibited by a person who tries to make choices between alternatives by using "majority vote" among his characteristic preferences. (That is, if I prefer x to y according to four out of six of the above criteria, then I prefer x to y, *tout court.*) This is, of course, just an application of Condorcet's paradox to the situation at hand.

Thus the impossibility theorem gives us an unexpected bonus: it suggests why a "rational" individual might not have coherent preferences over states!

Theorem 1.1 uses as data only preference orderings: utility functions are not mentioned. It should be possible to restate the theorem in a framework where utility functions are employed, as those functions are representations of preference orderings. If this is done, then the theorem will have a premise stating that only ordinal noncomparable information about the utility functions is admissible—since only that information is captured in the preference orderings. We shall carry out this program in the next section. But it is apt to note, at this point, that one reason we may not be able to find an acceptable scoring system for the quadrathalon is that we admit no "interevent" orderings of athletes: that is, we do not allow statements of the form "Aziza did better on the Run than Bogdan did on the Hurdles." Similarly, in the problem of Adam, we do not use as data statements of the form "the nutrition Adam gets from commodity bundle x contributes more to his overall welfare than the amount of good Adam can do for others with commodity bundle y." Information of this kind is not available given only the profile of preference orderings. Were such "interindividual comparisons of utility" allowable, perhaps we could find a scoring system for the quadrathalon respecting WP, I, ND, and U, and, similarly, an overall preference aggregation rule for Adam.

1.3   Reformulation of the Impossibility Theorem with Utility Functions

To study this question, we must restate Theorem 1.1 using utility functions. Let $u = (u^1, \ldots, u^H)$ represent a generic profile of utility functions on X. Let $\mathcal{U}$ be the set of all such profiles. A *social welfare functional* F is defined as a mapping from a subset $\mathcal{D} \subseteq \mathcal{U}$ into $\mathcal{R}$; thus, it associates to any profile of utility functions in $\mathcal{D}$ an order on X. In the present formulation, F plays the same role as ψ did in the last section.[6]

---

6. In this section, I follow quite closely the unpublished lecture notes of Avinash Dixit (1978). Essentially the same methods are developed in Blackorby, Donaldson, and Weymark (1984).

We now translate the four conditions of the impossibility theorem into statements using the language of utility functions. Each condition is to be viewed as a restriction imposed on the behavior of F.

Condition WP* (Weak Pareto). Let $x, y \in X, u \in \mathcal{U}$. If for all h, $u^h(x) > u^h(y)$, then xPy, where $R = F(u)$ and P is the strict preference relation corresponding to R. (It is said that P is the *asymmetric factor* of R.)

Condition I* (Binary Independence of Irrelevant Alternatives). For all $x, y \in X$ and for all $u, u' \in \mathcal{U}$, if $u(x) = u'(x)$, and $u(y) = u'(y)$, then xRy iff $xR'y$, where $R = F(u)$ and $R' = F(u')$.

This condition restates Condition I in the new language.

Condition U* (Unrestricted Domain). $\mathcal{D} = \mathcal{U}$.

This is just the restatement of Condition U—the social choice functional must provide a social prescription for any possible profile of utility functions.

We next state for social choice functionals the analogous definition to Definition 1.1 for social welfare functionals.

Definition 1.2. *F respects information on utility of type Y iff for all profiles u and all transformations f in the group G^Y, $F(u)$ and $F(f \circ u)$ give the same ordering of X. [That is, if $R = F(u)$ and $R' = F(f \circ u)$, then xRy iff $xR'y$.]*

We can now state:

Theorem 1.2. *Let $|X| \geq 3$. Let U* hold. F satisfies WP*, I*, and respects ordinal noncomparable (ONC) information on utility if and only if F is a dictatorship.*

F is a dictatorship means: For some k and for all profiles u, and for all pairs $x, y \in X$, if $u^k(x) > u^k(y)$, then xPy where P is the asymmetric factor of $F(u)$.

I have taken the opportunity of stating Theorem 1.2 as an "if and only if" statement: that could also have been done with Theorem 1.1. We shall prove the impossibility theorem in the form of Theorem 1.2. I prefer the viewpoint of Theorem 1.2 as it naturally invites the question: What happens if we replace ONC information in its statement with some other kind of information, say, CUC? That invitation is not extended in the Arrovian formulation of Theorem 1.1, as utility functions do not appear there. Our program, then, shall be to prove a series of theorems, beginning with 1.2, in which we vary the kind of information we require the social choice functional to respect, and inquire into what, if any, social choice functionals are thus characterized.

Let me state another useful restriction on F:

Condition INW (Irrelevance of Non-Welfare Characteristics). Let x, y, $x', y' \in X$, let $u, u' \in \mathcal{U}$, and let $R = F(u)$ and $R' = F(u')$. Suppose that $u(x) = u'(x')$ and $u(y) = u'(y')$. Then xRy iff $x'R'y'$.

In words: Suppose, under two different profiles, the utilities experienced by members of society are exactly the same for states x and x' and for states y and y'. Then the social ordering of x and y given the first profile must be the same as the social ordering for x' and y' given the second profile. This condition states, as its name says, that the social choice functional F ranks states just using the utility information available about those states. If x and x' generate identical vectors of utility *numbers,* and y and y' do likewise, then, even though these numbers are associated with different profiles of utility functions, F's social prescription vis-à-vis x and y is invariant as the profile changes.

We proceed by establishing several lemmata, but first we define:

Condition PI* (Pareto Indifference). Let u be a profile, and suppose, for all h, $u^h(x) = u^h(y)$. Then $F(u)$ ranks x indifferent to y.

Lemma 1.1.   *If F satisfies U*, I*, and PI* then it satisfies INW.*

Proof: Let x, x', y, and y' be four distinct states and consider profiles u and u' satisfying the premise of INW. We summarize this information by the first two rows of the following table, where r and s are H-tuples of numbers:

	x	y	x'	y'
u	r	s		
u'			r	s
u''	r	s	r	s

(In the table, there are four elements not filled in.) By U*, we can construct a profile u'' with utility numbers r and s as indicated. Let $R = F(u)$,

$R' = F(u')$, and $R'' = F(u'')$. By I*, xRy iff $xR''y$. By PI*, $xR''y$ iff $x'R''y'$. By I*, $x'R''y'$ iff $x'R'y'$. Consequently, xRy iff $x'R'y'$, and INW is established for this case. Similar arguments can be made when x, y, x', and y' are not distinct. ∎

We next state:

Definition 1.3.   Let F be a social choice functional and W a Bergson-Samuelson social welfare function: W is a function mapping $\mathbf{R}^H$ into $\mathbf{R}$. W is said to *represent* F iff for all x, $y \in X$ and $u \in U$, and $R = F(u)$, $W(u(x)) \geq W(u(y))$ precisely when xRy.

The virtue of using a Bergson-Samuelson social welfare function W for analysis instead of a social choice functional F is that the former is defined on a concrete Euclidean space, while the latter is defined on a quite abstract space of utility profiles. For example, we can graph social welfare functions—at least if there are not too many individuals—while we cannot graph social choice functionals. If W represents F, we can learn everything relevant about F by studying W.

Not all social welfare functionals F can be represented by Bergson-Samuelson social welfare functions. But we have:

Lemma 1.2.   *If F satisfies INW and U* then there is an order R_F of $\mathbf{R}^H$ such that for all x, $y \in X$ and for all profiles u, $xF(u)y$ iff $u(x)R_Fu(y)$. If in addition R_F is continuous, then F can be represented by a continuous Bergson-Samuelson social welfare function.*[7]

Proof: Given F, we define the ordering, R_F, on pairs of $\mathbf{R}^H$ as follows. Let $\bar{u} = (\bar{u}^1, \ldots, \bar{u}^H)$ and $\bar{\bar{u}} = (\bar{\bar{u}}^1, \ldots, \bar{\bar{u}}^H)$ be two arbitrary H-tuples of real numbers. By U*, there is a profile u and states x and y such that $u(x) = \bar{u}$ and $u(y) = \bar{\bar{u}}$. Define $\bar{u}R_F\bar{\bar{u}}$ iff xRy, where $R = F(u)$. Now INW tells us that this order of $\bar{u}$ and $\bar{\bar{u}}$ is independent of the particular x, y, and u we chose. It is left to show that R_F, so defined, is an order of $\mathbf{R}^H$: the only issue is its transitivity. To this end, let a, b, and c be three vectors in $\mathbf{R}^H$, and suppose aR_Fb and bR_Fc. By U*, we can find states x, y, and z and a profile u such that $u(x) = a$, $u(y) = b$, and $u(z) = c$. By INW and aR_Fb we have

---

7. An order on the Euclidean space $\mathbf{R}^H$ is *continuous* if the upper and lower contour sets of any point in the space are closed.

xRy, where $R = F(u)$; similarly, yRz. It follows that xRz, and therefore, by INW again it follows that aR_Fc.

Now, by Debreu's (1964) representation theorem, there is a continuous, numerical representation, W, of the order R_F. W is the required Bergson-Samuelson social welfare function. ∎

Condition INW is often called *strong neutrality* in the literature, or, using a term coined by Amartya Sen, *welfarism*. Welfarism states that the social ranking of states depends only on the utilities that citizens receive in those states, which is the content of INW. Sen (1979) gives examples like the following to impugn the attractiveness of welfarism. Suppose there are social states x, y, and z, individuals 1 and 2, and a utility profile assigning utilities to the individuals in the states as follows:

	u^1	u^2
x	4	10
y	7	8
z	7	8

Now suppose that in state x, 1 is hungry and 2 is eating a lot. In state y, some food has been redistributed from 2 to 1. In state z, the food allotment is as in state x, but 1 is whipping 2, an act from which 1 evidently derives utility. If our social choice functional prescribes that state y is preferred to state x, then it must prescribe that z is also preferred to x—this is simply an application of Pareto indifference, a weaker condition than welfarism, together with transitivity of the social ordering. Welfarism, by definition, does not allow consideration of nonutility information—such as the nature of the utility's source—in rendering the social ordering.[8]

Lemma 1.3.   *Let W be a Bergson-Samuelson social welfare function that represents the social choice functional F. Then F respects information on utility of a given type iff W does.*

---

8. Not all philosophers and economists agree that examples like this one are telling against welfarism. For instance, David Donaldson writes (in personal correspondence with me): "[Examples like this one use] a moral intuition—that torturing people is wrong—which we believe for welfarist reasons; torture makes people worse off in a heavyweight way. The example works by linking this intuition to an implausible claim about fact—that whipping can be a substitute for decent nutrition. If we really could make poor people better off in this way, the world's problems would be a lot easier to solve."

Proof: This follows by immediate application of Definitions 1.1, 1.2, and 1.3. ∎

Let transformations of utility profiles from a group of transformations G be allowable, and let $f \in G$. Lemma 1.3 says, in particular, that *if $\bar{u}$ and $\bar{\bar{u}}$ are two vectors in $\mathbf{R}^H$ which lie on the same W-indifference curve, then $f(u)$ and $f(\bar{\bar{u}})$ must also lie on the same W-indifference curve.* It is this key fact that shall be used to establish the next theorem. We shall not in fact prove Theorem 1.2, but the following somewhat weaker theorem:

Theorem 1.2*. *Let $|X| \geq 3$. There is no social welfare functional F satisfying U*, I*, WP*, PI*, and ND*, which respects ONC information, and such that R_F is continuous.*

Proof: We prove the theorem for the case of a two-person society, $H = 2$. General proofs of the Arrow impossibility theorem are found in many sources: see, for instance, Sen (1986) for a proof and bibliography.

1. Let F satisfy the premises of the theorem. By the three lemmata above, F can be represented by a continuous social welfare function W which respects information of type ONC, and hence the key fact italicized in the paragraph above the statement of Theorem 1.2* holds.

2. Since W is continuous, it possesses indifference curves. Suppose $a = (a^1, a^2)$ and $a' = (a^1 + k^1, a^2 + k^2)$ lie on the same indifference curve, as in Figure 1.1. By WP*, we cannot have both k^1 and k^2 positive or both negative. Suppose that one is positive and the other negative—let k^1 be positive and k^2 negative as in the figure. Consider the linear transformation given by $\varphi(z^1, z^2) = (f^1(z^1), f^2(z^2)) = (2z^1 - a^1, \frac{1}{2}(z^2 + a^2))$. φ is in G^{ONC}— indeed, φ is in the smaller group G^{CNC}, since its component functions are both linear. It therefore follows that $W(a^1, a^2) = W(a^1 + 2k^1, a^2 + \frac{1}{2}k^2)$— this is just the statement that $W(\varphi(a)) = W(\varphi(a'))$, applied to the vectors a and a'. Hence $W(a^1 + k^1, a^2 + k^2) = W(a^1 + 2k^1, a^2 + \frac{1}{2}k^2)$. But this contradicts WP*, since $a^1 + 2k^1 > a^1 + k^1$ and $a^2 + \frac{1}{2}k^2 > a^2 + k^2$. Therefore the only possibility is that k^1 or k^2 is zero.

3. Suppose it is k^1 that is zero. Then a and a' lie on a vertical segment of a W-indifference curve. But it then follows that the entire indifference curve on which a lies is a vertical line in $\mathbf{R}^2$. For suppose there were some point a'' that was indifferent to a but did not lie on that vertical line. Then, by the argument of step 2, it must lie on a horizontal line through a. But

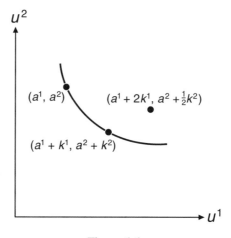

Figure 1.1

then we could apply the argument of step 2 to the points a' and a'', which lie on a straight line that is oblique to the axes, and deduce a contradiction.

4. This shows that each indifference curve of W is either a vertical or a horizontal line. But therefore, since one such curve is a vertical line, they all must be—for any horizontal indifference curve would intersect the vertical line that is the indifference curve on which a lies, and two indifference curves cannot intersect.

5. The indifference map consisting of vertical indifference curves is dictatorship by individual 1—only his utility matters for social preference. On the other hand, had k^2 been zero and k^1 positive in step 3, then the indifference map would have consisted of horizontal indifference curves, which is the dictatorship by individual 2. But these two social choice functionals are ruled out by ND*, and the theorem is proved. ∎

We have in fact proved a theorem stronger than 1.2*: we can replace "ordinal noncomparable" information in the statement with "cardinal noncomparable" information. (This follows since the transformation f used in the proof is in the group G^{CNC}.) Thus weakening the restriction on the social choice functional from ONC to CNC does not enable an escape from the impossibility result.

Let us define:

Condition AN* (Anonymity). Let the profile u' be a permutation of the profile u. Then $F(u) = F(u')$.

AN* says the names of individuals do not matter for the social order. AN* implies ND*.

Proceeding with the announced program, we shall now replace "ONC" in the statement of Theorem 1.2 with "OFC," and we have:

Theorem 1.3. *F satisfies PI*, WP*, I*, AN* and U*, respects ordinal full comparable (OFC) information on utility, and R_F is continuous, iff F is a positional dictatorship.*

A *positional dictatorship* occurs when the social preference order always coincides with the preference order of a particular *position*—such as the individual in the worst-off position or the best-off position. In a two-person society, these are the only two positions. Positional dictatorship of the worst-off yields the "maximin" social choice functional: the social order mimics the preferences of the individual with minimal utility. Positional dictatorship of the best-off is "maximax."

Proof of Theorem 1.3: Again, we prove this theorem for $H = 2$. For general finite H, see Gevers (1979, Theorem 4) and Roberts (1980a, Theorem 4).

1. Given F satisfying the premise of Theorem 1.3. Again, we proceed by studying the indifference curves of the Bergson-Samuelson social welfare function W that represents F, which exists and is continuous.

2. Consider any point $a' = (a, a)$ in the plane, and another point $a'' = (a + k^1, a + k^2)$ on the same W-indifference curve as a', and suppose $k^1 \geq 0$ and $k^2 \leq 0$. We shall apply the transformation $\varphi \in G^{OFC}$ defined by $\varphi(z^1, z^2) = (f(z^1), f(z^2))$, where

$$f(z) = \begin{cases} 2z - a & \text{for } z \geq a \\ \frac{1}{2}z + \frac{1}{2}a & \text{for } z < a. \end{cases}$$

Note that f is, indeed, strictly increasing. By our "key fact," it follows that $\varphi(a')$ and $\varphi(a'')$ must lie on the same W-indifference curve; but $\varphi(a') = a'$ and $\varphi(a'') = (a + 2k^1, a + \frac{1}{2}k^2)$. Thus it follows that $(a + 2k^1, a + \frac{1}{2}k^2)$ and a'' lie on the same indifference curve (since they both share the same indifference curve with a'). If $k^1 > 0$ and $k^2 < 0$, this would be impossible, by WP*. Therefore either $k^1 = 0$ or $k^2 = 0$.

3. Thus a'' lies either on a horizontal line segment to the right of a' or on a vertical line segment below a'. Suppose the former. Then all points of the form $a''' = (a + k^1, a + k^2)$ with $k^1 \geq 0$ and $k^2 \leq 0$ and which are

indifferent to a' must lie on a horizontal line segment to the right of a': for the alternative is that such a point a''' would lie on a vertical line segment below a', and then the positions of a''' and a'' would contradict WP*, as a'' would lie to the northeast of a'''.

4. We now take a point $a^* = (a + k^1, a + k^2)$ with $k^1 \leq 0$ and $k^2 \geq 0$, and repeat steps 2 and 3, which shows that a^* lies either on a vertical line segment above a' or a horizontal line segment to the left of a'. All points of the form a^* must then lie either on such a horizontal to the left of a' or a vertical above a'.

5. Combining these observations, we are left with four possibilities for what the indifference curves of W look like, illustrated in Figure 1.2. The cases of Figure 1.2c and 1.2d are the two positional dictatorships, dictatorship of the worst-off and best-off, respectively. The cases of Figure 1.2a and 1.2b are ruled out by AN*.

6. The converse part, that the positional dictatorships indeed satisfy the conditions WP*, I*, U*, AN*, respect information OFC, and generate continuous orders R_F, is left to the reader. ∎

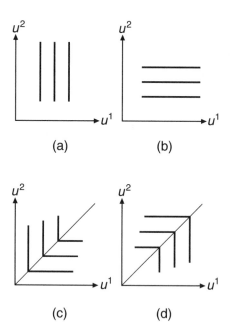

(a)   (b)

(c)   (d)

Figure 1.2

"Maximax" is not an attractive social choice rule—"give everything to him who hath." It can be eliminated by the insistence on some kind of minimal equity requirement. Hammond (1976) proposed an axiom similar to the following:

Axiom of Minimal Equity (ME). For some $u \in \mathcal{U}$, there exists $x, y \in X$ and $j \in H$ such that, for all $i \neq j$, $u^j(x) > u^j(y) > u^i(y) > u^i(x)$ implies yRx, where $R = F(u)$.

In the case of $H = 2$, ME states that there is at least one profile u where the social preference between two states follows the preference of the individual who is worse off, when the two individuals disagree on the ranking of the two states. ME eliminates the "maximax" rule. Thus we have:

Corollary 1.1. *F satisfies PI*, WP*, I*, U*, ME, AN*, respects ordinal level comparable information, and R_F is continuous iff F is the "maximin" social choice functional.*

Let us perturb the information requirement of Theorem 1.2* once more.

Theorem 1.4. *F satisfies PI*, WP*, I*, U*, AN* and respects cardinal unit comparability, and generates a continuous order R_F iff F is the utilitarian social choice functional.*

Recall that the utilitarian F can be represented by the Bergson-Samuelson social welfare function $W(a^1, \ldots, a^H) = \sum a^h$.

Proof: We prove the theorem for $H = 2$. For general finite H, see d'Aspremont and Gevers (1977, Theorem 3).

1. Let F satisfy the premises; we again study the W-indifference curves for its representing social choice function. Let $a = (a^1, a^2)$ and $a' = (a^1 + k^1, a^2 + k^2)$ lie on the same W-indifference curve. Consider the transformation $\varphi(z^1, z^2) = (rz^1 + (1-r)a^1, rz^2 + (1-r)a^2)$, where r is any positive number. Then $\varphi \in G^{CUC}$. Now $\varphi(a) = a$ and $\varphi(a') = (a^1 + rk^1, a^2 + rk^2)$. By the "key fact," a and $(a^1 + rk^1, a^2 + rk^2)$ are on the same indifference curve, which implies that a' and $(a^1 + rk^1, a^2 + rk^2)$ are on the same indifference curve. But this argument holds for *any positive r*. The points $(a^1 + rk^1, a^2 + rk^2)$, as r varies, trace out a straight line of slope k^2/k^1. Therefore the indifference curves of W are straight lines.

2. Because the indifference curves extend infinitely far in each direction (they are lines, not line segments), it follows that they must be parallel straight lines; otherwise they would intersect.

3. Anonymity requires that the indifference curves be symmetric with respect to the $45°$ line in the plane. Therefore we must have $k^2/k^1 = -1$. (We know k^2 and k^1 have opposite signs, or else WP* would be violated.) But this characterizes the Bergson-Samuelson utilitarian W.

4. As usual, the reader can convince herself that the converse statement holds: indeed, I have shown earlier that utilitarianism respects information of the cardinal-unit-comparable type. ■

None of the informational conditions we have imposed in the above theorems allows the Bergson-Samuelson social welfare function to be strictly quasi-concave—that is, to permit smooth trade-offs between the utilities of different individuals. As Blackorby, Donaldson, and Weymark (1984) point out, some such social welfare functions are compatible with utility that is "translation scale, fully measurable" [that is, $\varphi(z) = (z^1 + a, z^2 + a, \ldots, z^H + a)$]. As I mentioned earlier, all strictly increasing Bergson-Samuelson social welfare functions are compatible with absolutely measurable and fully comparable utility.

Theorems 1.2*, 1.3, and 1.4 thus allow a "resolution" of the Arrow impossibility theorem, if such "impossibilities" require resolution, for they show that the "impossibility of social choice" with the Arrovian postulates is due to the particularly impoverished information available to the social planner or the constitution framers. Indeed, the theorems suggest that the key to the existence of social choice rules is the admission of some kind of interpersonal comparisons of utility: for simply strengthening the measurability information available on individual utility from ordinal to cardinal does not provide an escape from impossibility. Both OFC and CUC permit types of interpersonal comparison—one of utility levels, the other of utility differences. This is the first of many times in this study that we shall see the important role played by the allowable amount of information in the interpretation of mathematical results pertaining to distributive justice.[9]

---

9. More characterization theorems, using various informational restrictions on utility, can be found in Gevers (1979), Deschamps and Gevers (1978), Hammond (1976, 1979), Sen (1976, 1986), and Strasnick (1976a, b).

1.4   The Connection between Arrovian Social Choice and Distributive Justice

The most obvious application of the Arrow framework to the question of distributive justice is to view the individuals as citizens of a society, the preferences or utility functions as being defined over commodity bundles, and the social states as alternative allocations of commodities among citizens. One might, then, be tempted to conclude from §1.3 that if there is only ordinal or cardinal noncomparable information on utility, there is no just allocation possible; if utility is ordinal fully comparable, then justice requires the "maximin" choice, and so on. But there are two criticisms of the validity of this inference. (I) The unrestricted domain assumption requires that we admit any preference ordering over commodity bundles, and that we admit any profile of such preferences for a society. Thus the conclusion cannot apply to a conventional economic environment, in which individuals care only about the commodities they receive, and their preferences are *monotone increasing* in goods. Clearly, allowing citizens to be concerned about what others get will not improve the situation significantly. Assumption U is just completely inappropriate in this context. (II) Why should distributive justice be so intimately linked to the preferences of individuals? Consider, again, the conventional economic environment in which all have self-regarding preferences (that is, no one derives any utility or disutility from the consumption of others). The Arrovian postulates may model the idea of democracy-respecting social choice; but, first, why should distributive justice be determined by a democratic procedure, where citizens vote in a self-interested way? Democratic social choice may, for example, permit majorities to exploit minorities in ways inconsonant with justice. And second, why should we treat preferences as representing the true *interests* of citizens, formed as they may be under conditions of unequal opportunity? Elster (1979), among others, has alerted us to the role of cognitive dissonance in the formation of preferences: the slave may adopt slavery-liking preferences in order to cope with his condition, but surely such preferences should not count in deciding whether slavery is just. Generally, if distributive justice is concerned with interests, and preferences do not correlate with interests because, for example, of restrictions on individuals' autonomy during the period of preference formation, then distributive justice should not depend too heavily on preferences.

Criticism I, indeed, requires reformulation of the interpretation of the social choice model I proposed in the opening sentence of this section.

Suppose, alternatively, we view X as a set of different possible rules by which a society may be governed—including but not limited to the kinds of property relations, for instance, that a society may allow. The unrestricted domain assumption then becomes more palatable, especially if X consists of not too many alternatives (laissez-faire capitalism, welfare capitalism, centrally planned socialism, market socialism, worker-managed industrial democracy, and so on). It is then not absurd to think that citizens may exist with any possible preference order over X, and that societies may exist with any possible profile of such preferences. The unrestricted domain assumption, that is, may be acceptable. This resolution of criticism I, however, weakens considerably the appeal of the theorems as dicta about distributive justice. Surely one would prefer that a theory of distributive justice tell us which *allocations of commodities* are just, but the unrestricted domain assumption renders Arrovian social choice theory irrelevant for that task. Social choice theory on a domain of commodities with economic preferences is the topic of the next section.

The simplest response to criticism II is to suppose that the "preference" profile $(R^1, \ldots, R^H)$ [or the utility profile $(u^1, \ldots, u^H)$] represents the interests of persons, not their choice behavior. Interests, for instance, may diverge from preferences (that is, choice-revealed preference) because of the "sour grapes" phenomenon or because of misinformation. Exactly how to formulate a person's interests is one of the deep problems of political philosophy: Rawls, Sen, Arneson, and Cohen provide different answers with their uses of primary goods, functionings, opportunity for welfare, and access to advantage, respectively, as will be discussed in Chapters 5–8. Although we may interpret the social choice problem as one of seeking a fair aggregation of individual interests, not one modeling democratic decision making, this does not get us very far in understanding what justice consists in without a theory of interests.

1.5   Social Choice on Economic Environments

There is an "economic" approach that modifies the Arrovian framework in direct response to criticism I. Can we reformulate the Arrovian axioms in a more concrete, economic context, where X does not stand for any abstract set of social states but, rather, consists in the possible allocations of commodities in an economy, and where the domain axiom is replaced by one which requires utility functions to be monotone increasing in commodities, continuous and concave or quasi-concave? Modulo criticism II, such a reformulation would restrict our attention precisely to the question of the justice of commodity distributions rather than the justice of an abstract social state. The answer is that this reformulation can be carried out, and, perhaps remarkably, the cognates of the Arrovian theorems stand in the economic context.

We shall now identify X^m as the set of allocations of m commodities to H persons; so $x \in X^m$ is a non-negative vector in $\mathbf{R}^{mH}$. Write $x = (x^1, \ldots, x^H)$, where x^h is the commodity vector in $\mathbf{R}^m$ that goes to individual h. We define $\mathcal{U}^{Ec}$ as the set of profiles $u = (u^1, \ldots, u^H)$ where each u^h is a continuous, self-regarding,[10] increasing, quasi-concave utility function on $\mathbf{R}^m$. Thus the domain $\mathcal{U}^{Ec}$ consists of "reasonable" economic preferences; it is a sharply restricted domain compared with $\mathcal{U}$. We can call the pair $(X^m, \mathcal{U}^{Ec})$ an *economic environment*.

Let $\mathcal{RC}^m$ consist of all continuous orders of X^m. The social choice functionals we shall consider are mappings F of profiles in $\mathcal{U}^{Ec}$ into $\mathcal{RC}^m$. If $F: \mathcal{U}^{Ec} \to \mathcal{RC}^m$, we say it is a *continuous-valued* social choice functional.

Condition C (Continuous-valued).   The ordering $F(u)$ is a continuous ordering of X^m for all u.

A social choice functional F is said to be *constant* if the ordering on allocation space generated by the function $F(u)$ is independent of u. [Pick any $R \in \mathcal{RC}^m$, and let $F(u) = R$ for all profiles u.] A social choice functional F is an *inverse dictatorship* of individual h iff $R = F(u)$ and $x R y$ precisely when $u^h(x^h) \le u^h(y^h)$. That is, the social preference is always the opposite of h's preference.

We have the following result:

Theorem 1.5.   *Let F satisfy C and respect ordinal noncomparable information on utility.[11] F satisfies I^* iff it is constant, dictatorial, or inverse dictatorial.*

Proof: See Theorem 13 in Campbell (1992), p. 136. (I have restated the theorem as it appears in Campbell using the utility-function approach.)

---

10. Self-regarding means that the individual utility depends only on the consumption of the individual. No "consumption externalities" are allowed. Hence the domain of u^h is R^m.

11. We must here define the group of acceptable transformations $\tilde{G}^{ONC}$ to consist of all strictly increasing continuous transformations of utility. Then transformations of profiles in $\mathcal{U}^{Ec}$ by elements of $\tilde{G}^{ONC}$ remain in $\mathcal{U}^{Ec}$.

Note there is no Pareto axiom in Theorem 1.5. However, we can easily deduce:

Corollary 1.2.   *Let F satisfy C and respect ordinal noncomparable information on utility. F satisfies I* and WP* iff F is a dictatorship.*

Proof: Of the three possibilities for what F can be, from Theorem 1.5, only the dictatorships satisfy WP*. The converse is immediate.   ∎

Corollary 1.2 is, of course, an analogue of Theorem 1.2. The requirement that F be continuous-valued is certainly a strong condition, and necessary for the result, but it is arguably a desirable condition. Theorem 1.5 is pessimistic, as it says that on a domain of economic environments, independence of irrelevant alternatives (I*) and anonymity rule out weak Paretianism—because anonymity rules out dictatorship and inverse dictatorship, and the constant social welfare functionals do not satisfy WP*, for $m > 1$. [To see the latter, let $x, y \in X^m$ be two allocations such that, for all h, neither x^h nor y^h vector-dominates the other—such allocations can be found since $m > 1$. Then there exists a profile in $\mathcal{U}^{Ec}$ such that $u(x) > u(y)$. It follows from WP* that $F(u)$ ranks x strictly preferred to y. But there exists another profile $u' \in \mathcal{U}^{Ec}$ such that $u'(y) > u'(x)$. Thus $F(u')$, by WP*, must rank y strictly preferred to x. It follows that F is not constant.]

Another approach to social choice on economic environments has been studied by Donaldson and Roemer (1987). First, we further restrict the domain of individual utility functions to be concave (as well as increasing, self-regarding, and continuous). In fact, we require a further technical condition, that any utility function u^h satisfy the following property: $\lim_{t \to \infty} t^{-1} u^h(tx^h) = 0$. Call the domain of utility profiles so defined, and when the commodity space is R^m, $\mathcal{U}_m^{Ec}$. The main innovation is to allow the dimension of the commodity space, m, to vary. Thus we define a social choice functional as consisting of a set of mappings $\{F^m, m = 1, \ldots, \infty\}$ where F^m is a social choice functional (in the earlier sense) mapping $\mathcal{U}_m^{Ec}$ into the set of orderings $\mathcal{R}C^m$. Our domain assumption is:

Condition D. F is a map that associates, for any m, any profile in $\mathcal{U}_m^{Ec}$ with a continuous order on X^m. We write $F = \{F^m\}$.

We replace the axiom I* by an axiom that, on its face, is of a very different kind, and arguably has some ethical appeal from a distributive justice viewpoint, namely:

Axiom of Consistency of (Social) Orderings across Dimension (COAD). Let $F = \{F^m\}$ be a social choice functional. Denote by (x, r) an allocation in $\mathbf{R}^{(m+n)H}$, where (x^h, r^h) is the commodity bundle assigned to individual h, and $x^h \in \mathbf{R}^m$ and $r^h \in \mathbf{R}^n$. Let $\bar{r} \in \mathbf{R}^{nH}$, and let $u \in \mathcal{U}^{Ec}_{m+n}$ and $\tilde{u} \in \mathcal{U}^{Ec}_m$ be two profiles such that, for all h and all vectors $x \in \mathbf{R}^m$:

(Pr) $\tilde{u}^h(x) = u^h(x, \bar{r}^h).$

Then, for any pair of allocations $(y, \bar{r})$ and $(z, \bar{r})$ in $\mathbf{R}^{(m+n)H}$, $F^{m+n}(u)$ ranks $(y, \bar{r})$ socially preferred to $(z, \bar{r})$ iff $F^m(\tilde{u})$ ranks y socially preferred to z.

In words, COAD imposes the following restriction on F. Suppose the planner faces an allocation problem in which the commodity space is $\mathbf{R}^{m+n}$, the profile is u, and the allocations of goods which must be ranked are (y, r) and (z, r). Call this the First Situation. In particular, the last n goods are distributed identically among individuals in the two allocations. The planner applies her social choice functional F^{m+n} and concludes, say, that (y, r) is preferred to (z, r). Now suppose the planner faces a different problem— one of comparing allocations y and z in $\mathbf{R}^m$. It so happens that the utility profile that characterizes the population is $\tilde{u}$, where condition (Pr)— standing for "projection"—is satisfied: call this the Second Situation. Condition (Pr) says that the Second Situation is one in which the individuals appear to be identical to the individuals in the First Situation, except every h is now consuming the commodity bundle r^h that he was consuming in the First Situation. COAD says that, in this case, F^m must also rank y preferred to z.

The following application of COAD may indicate its relevance to problems of distributive justice. Suppose that we must distribute m commodities among persons in a society H who have utility functions $\tilde{u}^h$ defined on $\mathbf{R}^m$. Suppose each person is characterized as having a natural endowment of some n internal goods—that is, suppose we can model the person's chemistry as the endowment of a certain bundle of goods in a commodity space $\mathbf{R}^n$. The internal endowment of person h is the bundle r^h (of endorphins, synaptic connections, and so on). We can view person h as in fact having a utility function, u^h, over all $m + n$ goods, such that, for any vector $x^h \in R^m$, $\tilde{u}^h(x^h) = u^h(x^h, r^h)$. Her utility is really defined over both transferable and internal goods, but it so happens that the endowment of internal goods is fixed (and undepletable). The planner, of course, does not have the opportunity to reallocate the "commodities" r^h among individuals—these bundles are nontransferable. Her problem is to decide between alternative allocations of transferable commodities $1, \ldots, m$—which is to be preferred, allocation y or z in $\mathbf{R}^{mH}$? But the planner may wish to take into account the unalterable distribution of the internal goods in her decision: to be precise, she may wish to choose between y and z in the same way that she *would* choose between (y, r) and (z, r), were the problem posed in that way. This is exactly the content of COAD. The distribution of transferable goods should be consistent with how she would distribute those goods were she instructed to view the individuals' consumptions as including their internal goods on the larger commodity space.

Definition 1.4. A social choice functional $F = \{F^m\}$ is *completely welfarist* iff there is an ordering R_F of $\mathbf{R}^H$ such that, for any pair of allocations $x, y \in \mathbf{R}^{mH}$ and profile $u \in \mathcal{U}_m^{Ec}$, $F^m(u)$ ranks x weakly socially at least as good as y exactly when $u(x) R_F u(y)$.

If in addition R_F is continuous, then it can be represented by a continuous Bergson-Samuelson social welfare function, as in §1.4.

Every social choice functional that is completely welfarist satisfies COAD. (This fact is not hard to see, and is left to the reader.) The surprising fact is that, with the addition of Pareto Indifference (PI), the converse is also true.

Definition 1.5. A social choice functional F satisfies *Pareto Indifference* (PI) iff for all m and for all profiles $u \in \mathcal{U}_m^{Ec}$, $u(x) = u(z)$ implies $F^m(u)$ ranks x indifferent to z.

Lemma 1.4. *Let the social choice functional F satisfy D. Then F satisfies COAD and PI iff it is completely welfarist.*

Proof: See Donaldson and Roemer (1987), Theorem 1.[12]

---

12. Part of the proof offered of this lemma, called "Lemma 1" in our 1987 paper, is incorrect, namely, the part at the beginning of the appendix of that paper and preceding the statement of Lemma 1. The existence of the profile U that we need is due to the concave extension theorem of Howe (1987): our short-cut attempt at proving Howe's result is wrong. I do not present the proof of Lemma 1.4 here, because the proof of Theorem 3.6, which is very similar in spirit to Lemma 1.4, is presented.

Thus, together, D, COAD, and PI play the role that U, I*, and PI* play in lemmata 1.1 and 1.2.

We are now ready to reintroduce the various notions of measurability and comparability of utility. Because we are working on a domain of concave utility functions, the definitions require a slight alteration of previous phrasing.

Definition 1.6. A social choice functional F respects *ordinal noncomparable* utility information iff for all m and for all profiles $u, u' \in \mathcal{U}_m^{Ec}$, if there is a transformation $f \in G^{ONC}$ such that $u = f \circ u'$, then $F^m(u)$ and $F^m(u')$ yield the same ordering of R^{mH}.

We must define the concept of F respecting ordinal level comparable in the analogous way. The other definitions, which use transformations by affine functions only, remain the same.

We can now state the analogues of the theorems of §1.2.

Theorem 1.6. *If F satisfies D, COAD, and WP* and respects CNC utility information, then F is a dictatorship: there is an individual h such that for all m and $y, z \in \mathbf{R}^{mH}$, $u^h(y^h) > u^h(z^h)$ implies $F^m(u)$ ranks y higher than z.*[13]

Proof: WP* and D imply that F satisfies PI. By Lemma 1.4, COAD and PI imply complete welfarism. By the domain axiom D, $F^m(u)$ is a continuous order on X^m. It follows that R_F (in the definition of complete welfarism) is a continuous order on $\mathbf{R}^H$. The rest of this proof is the same as that of Theorem 1.2*.

Theorem 1.7. *If F satisfies D, COAD, WP*, and AN and respects OFC utility information, then F is a positional dictatorship.*

Proof: Again, the proof of Theorem 1.3 applies.

Theorem 1.8. *If F satisfies D, COAD, WP*, and AN, and respects CUC utility information, then F is utilitarian.*

Proof: The proof of Theorem 1.4 applies.

---

13. In fact, the dictatorship must be strong [that is, $u^h(x) = u^h(y)$ implies that $F^m(u)$ ranks y and z indifferent], because of continuity.

I shall describe one more social choice theorem on economic environ-ments, as it employs two axioms which are both arguably attractive from an ethical viewpoint. Thus far, we have not introduced scarcity into economic environments: the description of an economic environment contains no datum of the amounts of goods available. Let ω be viewed as an aggregate social endowment of commodities in $\mathbf{R}^m$. Denote by $A(\omega)$ the set of all pos-sible allocations to members of H that are feasible with social endowment ω, assuming all goods are freely transferable among individuals:[14]

$$A(\omega) = \left\{ x \in R^{mH} \mid \sum x^h \leq \omega \right\}.$$

Let the "utility possibilities set" associated with the feasible allocations $A(\omega)$ and the profile u be denoted $S(\omega, u)$:

$$S(\omega, u) = \{ \bar{u} = (\bar{u}^1, \ldots, \bar{u}^H) \in \mathbf{R}^H \mid \exists \ x \in A(\omega) \quad \text{s.t.} \quad u(x) = \bar{u} \}.$$

Given a social choice functional $F = \{ F^m \}$ which is continuous-valued (that is, F^m is continuous-valued for all m), there is a set of "socially best" ele-ments in $A(\omega)$ according to $F^m(u)$, since $F^m(u)$ induces a continuous or-dering on a compact domain: call the set of best elements $B^F(\omega, u)$. We can now state:

Axiom of Symmetric Choice (SC).   For all m, for all $\omega \in \mathbf{R}^m$, if $u \in \mathcal{U}_m^{Ec}$ has all its components equal ($u^1 = \ldots = u^H$), and if $x \in B^F(\omega, u)$, then $u^1(x^1) = \ldots = u^H(x^h)$.

SC says that the best elements for an economy with scarcity, if all individuals have identical utility functions, give all individuals equal utility. This is a weaker axiom than anonymity.

Suppose we have two economies with the same individuals, but the ag-gregate endowment vector in one vector-dominates the endowment in the other: $\hat{\omega} \geq \omega$. The next axiom states that there is a socially best element in the economy with less scarcity that makes each individual at least as well off as she is under a socially best element in the other economy.

---

14. The following convention on vector orderings is followed throughout the book. If $x \in \mathbf{R}^n$ and $y \in \mathbf{R}^n$, then "$x \geq y$" means $x_i \geq y_i$ for all components i; "$x \geq y$" means $x \geq y$ and $x \neq y$; $x > y$ means $x_i > y_i$ for all i.

Axiom of Resource Monotonicity (RMON).   For all m, for all $u \in \mathcal{U}_m^{Ec}$, if $\hat{\omega}, \omega \in \mathbf{R}^m$ and $\hat{\omega} \geq \omega$, then there exist $\hat{x} \in B^F(u, \hat{\omega})$ and $x \in B^F(u, \omega)$ such that $u(\hat{x}) \geq u(x)$.

Theorem 1.9.   *Let F satisfy D, COAD, WP*, SC, and RMON. Then for each m, F^m is the "maximin" rule, that is, $F^m(u)$ ranks x at least as good as y iff $\min\{u^h(x)\} \geq \min\{u^h(y)\}$.*

Proof: (Donaldson and Roemer 1987, Theorem 8.)

1. As in the proof of Theorem 1.6, we may represent F by a continuous ordering, R_F, of $\mathbf{R}^H$. Let P_F stand for its asymmetric part.

2. Let 1_H be the vector $(1, 1, \dots, 1)$ in $\mathbf{R}^H$, and 0_H be the zero vector in $\mathbf{R}^H$. Let $\hat{u} = (\hat{u}^1, \dots, \hat{u}^H)$ be any vector in $\mathbf{R}^H$ not all of whose components are equal. Let $\gamma \in \mathbf{R}$ be any non-zero number such that $\min_h = \hat{u}^h < \gamma < \max_h \hat{u}^h$. Without loss of generality, let us say $\hat{u}^1 < \gamma < \hat{u}^2$. Our task is to show that $\gamma 1_H P_F \hat{u}$. The theorem will then follow easily.

3. Let $\varepsilon > 0$ and define $\tilde{u} \in \mathbf{R}^H$ by $\tilde{u}^h = \hat{u}^h + \varepsilon$, for all h, choosing ε small enough so that $\tilde{u}^1 < \gamma < \tilde{u}^2$. Choose a vector $(a^1, \dots, a^H) \in \mathbf{R}_+^H$ and a number $c \neq 0$ such that

(1.1a) $$\sum_h a^h \gamma = c$$

and

(1.1b) $$\sum_h a^h \tilde{u}^h = c.$$

[(1.1a) and (1.1b) are assured if $\sum a^h(\hat{u}^h + \varepsilon - \gamma) = 0$. By choice of ε and γ, there is a positive vector a as required.]

4. Choose $\beta < \min \tilde{u}^h$. Let e^h be the hth unit vector in $\mathbf{R}^H$. We next choose a profile of utility functions $U \in \mathcal{U}_{H+1}^{Ec}$ (that is, $H + 1$ goods) such that $U^h(0_{H+1}) = \beta$ and

$$U^h(e^h, x) = \begin{cases} \beta + \alpha^h x & \text{if } x \leq H \\ \beta + \alpha^h H & \text{if } x > H, \end{cases}$$

where

$$\alpha^h = \frac{c(\gamma - \beta)}{\gamma a^h H}.$$

(Note $\alpha^h > 0$.) Further assume that individual h cares only for goods h and $H + 1$: her utility from other goods is zero. Now consider the economy with an endowment $(1_H, H) \in \mathbf{R}_+^{H+1}$ and profile U. The reader may compute that

$$S((1_H, H), U) = \left\{ u \in \mathbf{R}^H \mid \beta 1_H \leqq u \text{ and } \sum a^h u^h \leqq c \right\}.$$

5. In addition, we may require that

$$U^h(0_H, x) = \begin{cases} \beta + \alpha^h x & \text{for } x \leq \frac{\gamma - \beta}{\alpha^h} \\ \\ \gamma & \text{for } x > \frac{\gamma - \beta}{\alpha^h}. \end{cases}$$

The reader may compute that the conditions imposed on U^h in this step and step 4 are consistent with monotonicity and concavity of U^h.

Consider, now, the economy with endowment $(0_H, H)$. We have:

$$S((0_H, H), U) = \{ u \in \mathbf{R}^H \mid \beta 1_H \leqq u \leqq \gamma 1_H \}.$$

6. We next consider an economy with two goods. The social endowment is $(0, H)$. The utility profile, $\bar{U} \in \mathcal{U}_2^{Ec}$, has all the utility functions identically equal to φ, where

$$\varphi(0, x) = \begin{cases} \beta + (\gamma - \beta)x & \text{for } x \leq 1 \\ \gamma & \text{for } x > 1. \end{cases}$$

Then $S((0, H), \bar{U}) = \{ u \in \mathbf{R}^H \mid \beta 1_H \leqq u \leqq \gamma 1_H \} = S((0_H, H), U)$. By SC and WP, $\bar{B}^F((0, H), \bar{U}) = \{\gamma 1_H\}$, and by full welfarism, it follows that $\bar{B}^F((0_H, H), U) = \{\gamma 1_H\}$, where the notation $\bar{B}^F(e)$ means the vectors of utility numbers in $\mathbf{R}^H$ associated with the best allocations, $B^F(e)$, of the economy e according to F.

7. By RMON, since $(1_H, H) \geq (0_H, H)$ it follows that there must be a utility vector in $\bar{B}^F((1_H, H), U)$ which gives each individual utility at least γ. But there is only one such vector in $S((1_H, H), U)$, the vector $\gamma 1_H$. There-

fore $\gamma 1_H \in \bar{B}^F((1_H, H), U)$. In particular, $\gamma 1_H R_F \tilde{u}$. Because $\tilde{u} P_F \hat{u}$, it follows that $\gamma 1_H P_F \hat{u}$, and the claim asserted in step 1 is proved.

8. Now let $\bar{u} \in \mathbf{R}^H$ be any vector not all of whose components are equal, and suppose $\min \bar{u}^h > \min \hat{u}^h$. We must show that $\bar{u} R_F \hat{u}$. Choose $\gamma \neq 0$ so that $\min \bar{u}^h > \gamma > \min \hat{u}^h$. WP implies $\bar{u} P_F \gamma 1_H$. If $\gamma > \max \hat{u}^h$, then WP implies $\gamma 1_H P_F \hat{u}$; if $\gamma < \max \hat{u}^h$, then we are in the case studied in steps 2–7, and again $\gamma 1_H P_F \hat{u}$. Thus, in any case, by transitivity, $\bar{u} P_F \hat{u}$.

9. We have essentially proved that R_F is the "maximin" ordering. The other cases to check, when $\bar{u}$ and/or $\hat{u}$ have all components equal, or have $\min \hat{u}^h = \min \hat{u}^h$, follow from the continuity of the relation R_F. ∎

Theorem 1.9 is remarkable, as it tells us that only "maximin" is acceptable, although a priori any Bergson-Samuelson welfare function is a candidate. (Note, for instance, that utilitarianism satisfies all the other axioms of Theorem 1.9's premise.) This suggests that the RMON axiom is very powerful: for with it, we get a characterization of a unique social choice functional without any "invariance" axiom.

A version of RMON was initially introduced in Roemer (1986a) and will appear again in Chapter 3. Although it has an apparent ethical appeal from an egalitarian standpoint (everyone should weakly gain when the economy in aggregate becomes "richer"), there are reasons to remain skeptical about its ethical standing—indeed, those reasons are the same reasons to be skeptical of "maximin" itself. Consider the case of two individuals, Andrea and Bob. There are two goods, a drug called endorphinate, and lobsters. Without endorphinate, Bob derives almost no utility from lobsters—only with endorphinate does he perk up and become capable of enjoying life's finer pleasures (like steamed lobster). Andrea, in contrast, has an excellent endocrine system, and endorphinate does nothing to enhance her pleasure from lobster consumption. Consider two aggregate endowments: under ω, there are L lobsters but no endorphinate, under $\hat{\omega}$ there are L lobsters and a plentiful supply of endorphinate. Under ω, one might be tempted to give almost all the lobsters to Andrea, as Bob derives hardly any pleasure from them. But under $\hat{\omega}$, one would allocate all the endorphinate to Bob, and give him a fair share of lobster also. This implies that Andrea becomes worse off as commodities become less scarce, violating RMON. If we insist that Bob derive no utility from lobster without endorphinate, then the argument becomes even more compelling.

The ethical skepticism about RMON that the Andrea-Bob story may engender is the same skepticism one may have about "maximin" itself. For in the world with endowment ω, maximin requires that we allocate the lobster between Andrea and Bob so as to equalize their utilities (assuming such an allocation exists), even though this may mean that Andrea gets only a *soupçon* of lobster.

For further literature on social choice theory applied to economic environments, the reader is advised to consult Border (1983), Donaldson and Weymark (1988), Bordes and Le Breton (1989, 1990), Campbell (1992), and Le Breton and Weymark (1994).

1.6 Conclusion

I have shown that Arrow's impossibility theorem is usefully viewed as one of a family of characterization theorems, in which utility functions are supposed to convey different kinds of information. I have interpreted the "impossibility" of social choice in Arrow's framework as a consequence of the lack of interpersonal comparability of utility. When various kinds of interpersonal comparability are admitted, we have shown that utilitarianism and maximin emerge as social choice rules that satisfy Arrow's (other) axioms.

This, however, is not a cause for rejoicing, for one might hope that many social choice rules would become acceptable with the insistence on cardinal-unit-comparable or ordinal-level-comparable utility, which is not the case.

The restriction to welfarist social choice rules, which is a consequence of various combinations of axioms in this chapter (for example, U, PI, and I, or D, COAD, and PI), is somewhat disturbing in the framework of the abstract environments of §1.2, for the reasons that Sen gives: one is thereby precluded from considering ethically relevant nonutility information that one may have about societies. For example, welfarist social choice allows no considerations of the morality of counting utility that arises from sadistic acts. (This is sometimes called the "offensive tastes objection.") There is a different problem with the welfarist restriction in the framework of economic environments: many distributional mechanisms exist that take into account information about resources/commodities that cannot be described with just utility information.

For example, a resource allocation mechanism that should be prominent in a study of distributive justice is "equal division Walrasian equilibrium." If a society has an aggregate endowment ω to allocate among individuals, divide the endowment equally among all of them and allow trade to a competitive (or, more precisely, Walrasian[15]) equilibrium. At least one such allocation exists for each utility profile in $\mathcal{U}^{Ec}$. An equal division Walrasian equilibrium (EDWE) allocation is a natural Pareto efficient allocation associated with an obvious notion of just initial conditions—that each begin with an equal share of society's aggregate endowment of goods. We might wish society to prefer allocations that are EDWE. To this end, define the set $C(\omega, u)$ as the set of EDWE allocations when $\omega \in \mathbf{R}_+^m$ is the aggregate endowment and u is the profile. $C(\omega, u)$ is always nonempty. We might capture the desirability of EDWE allocations by saying that the best allocations according to the social choice functional are the EDWE allocations:

Condition EDW (Equal Division Walrasian). F satisfies EDW iff for all $\omega \in \mathbf{R}_+^m$ and $u \in \mathcal{U}_m^{Ec}$, $B^F(\omega, u) = C(\omega, u)$. [See p. 44 for definition of $B^F(\omega, u)$.]

Condition EDW is undemanding from the point of view of utility information: to be precise, even insisting that F respect ONC information is unproblematic, since the set $C(\omega, u)$ is invariant over all utility profiles u that are ordinally equivalent. (This is just a way of saying that Walrasian equilibria depend only on [ordinal] preferences, not on utility representations.) But there is no social choice rule that satisfies both I* and EDW, or both COAD and EDW. To see the former statement, let $x, y \in A(\omega)$ be Walrasian equilibria for some profile u, and suppose F^m satisfies I* and EDW. Now choose another profile u' with respect to which x is EDWE but y is not, and $u'^h(x^h) \geq u'^h(y^h)$ iff $u^h(x^h) \geq u^h(y^h)$. (This can always be done.) Thus $F^m(u)$ ranks x and y as indifferent, and $F^m(u')$ ranks x strictly better than y. Now let $f \in \tilde{G}^{ONC}$ be a transformation such that for each h, $f^h(u'^h(x^h)) = u^h(x^h)$ and $f^h(u'^h(y^h)) = u^h(y^h)$, and call $f \circ u' = u''$. Since u' and u'' are ordinally equivalent, it follows that x is a member of $C(\omega, u'')$

---

15. The distinction between Walrasian and competitive equilibrium is as follows. A *Walrasian equilibrium* in an exchange economy is an allocation and a price vector such that, if all individuals treat prices as given (that is, parametrically), markets clear when all individuals supply and demand goods by maximizing utility subject to their budget constraints, where those budgets are derived from individual private endowments. A *competitive equilibrium* is a Walrasian equilibrium in which it is rational for all individuals to treat prices parametrically, that is, no individual has any market power. The distinction between the two concepts is important in the work of Ostroy (1980).

but y is not. Thus by EDW, $F^m(u'')$ ranks x superior to y. But by I*, $F^m(u'')$ and $F^m(u)$ must rank x and y in the same way, which is a contradiction. That no F satisfies COAD and EDW is also easily demonstrated. Thus welfarism rules out social choice functionals that pay attention to commodities or property rights in the sense that EDW requires.

When the environment is an economic one, it is natural to think that various notions of property rights in commodities or resources may be of the essence in considerations of distributive justice. Perhaps, at the end of the day, we may decide that property rights are after all unimportant for justice, but a theory which renders allocation rules inadmissible just because they depend on defining certain property rights, in the sense that EDW does, surely prejudges the question. This is what welfarism on economic environments does. The previous paragraph has, I hope, caused the reader to be skeptical of the independence axiom, at least when economic environments are at issue. Note that this criticism of welfarism is quite different from the offensive tastes objection.

While I initially concluded in §1.4 that the social choice framework was not appropriate for the problem of distributive justice—because the unrestricted domain axiom is far too strong when the set X consists of alternative distributions of commodities—the analysis of §1.5 responded to that criticism by showing that essentially the same sorts of characterization theorems can be reproduced on economic domains where preferences of individuals are restricted to be economically meaningful. Furthermore, theorems like 1.9 are examples of social-choice-functional characterizations that rely on axioms arguably motivated by ethical, not merely democratic, considerations. There is no obvious reason that democratic processes of preference aggregation would respect COAD or RMON, but there may well be ethical reasons for resource allocation rules to respect them. Hence, Theorem 1.9 responds to both criticisms I and II levied against Arrovian social choice theory in §1.4. But now another issue has surfaced, concerning the indefensibly narrow scope of any welfarist theory for addressing the issue of *distributive* justice.

2

Axiomatic Bargaining Theory

2.1 Justice as Rational Prudence

The view that "justice is simply rational prudence pursued in contexts where the cooperation of other people is a condition of our being able to get what we want" (Barry 1989, p. 6) goes back, according to Brian Barry, at least to Hobbes and Hume. With the development of game theory in the last fifty years, beginning with von Neumann and Morgenstern's (1944) treatise, it has become possible to state precisely what rational prudence in a situation requiring mutual cooperation consists in—or, I should say, may consist in, for there is no agreement as yet on what the appropriate solution concept for the n-person game is. The contemporary political philosopher most clearly associated with this view of justice is Gauthier (1986), although some interpretations of Rawls (see Chapter 5) make him a fellow traveler as well.

Barry calls the view of justice enunciated in the quotation of the opening sentence "justice as mutual advantage," and he contrasts it with a second view, "justice as impartiality," in which "a just state of affairs is one that people can accept not merely in the sense that they cannot reasonably *expect* to get more, but in the stronger sense that they cannot reasonably *claim* more" (Barry 1989, p. 8). To comprehend Barry's meaning, the two uses of "reasonably" must be distinguished: people cannot "reasonably expect" more in the bargaining sense, but they cannot "reasonably claim" more in the ethical sense—that to do so would violate the norm that justice is impartial, plays no favorites, among individuals. To articulate what the first "reasonably" means requires a theory of bargaining; to articulate what the second "reasonably" means requires a theory of fairness. Rawls's theory of justice is the prime example of the second view, and indeed, Rawls calls his view "justice as fairness."

The modern, mathematical formulation of the bargaining problem began with Nash's (1950) brief and elegant statement. Although neither Arrow nor Nash mentions the work of the other—and the publication dates suggest that these works were carried out essentially simultaneously—their similarity is remarkable. The great insight that Arrow and Nash both had was to change the focus of the social choice problem, or the bargaining problem, from the *single society* or *problem* to the *rule* or *solution* that would give an answer for *all societies* or *problems*. An interesting problem in the history of social science, I think, is to understand why the idea of so changing the focus was "in the air" at this time. Although this procedure now seems natural, one must recognize that its implications were fairly startling: it implies that one cannot say how a society should make a choice, or how a pair of traders should solve their bargaining problem, without simultaneously saying how any society should make its choice, or how any pair of traders should reach a bargain. The move from viewing the particular society as the main object to viewing it as simply one point in the domain of a function was both methodologically powerful and, I contend, philosophically contentious. Indeed, the failure to subject this move to sufficient philosophical scrutiny may have resulted in giving the theorems produced by it more influence than they should have had in political philosophy. This point, posed in interrogative form, is a subterranean one of this book.

Although Nash was concerned with the bargaining problem—and, as such, his work and its later elaborations are relevant to distributive justice insofar as one adheres to the "justice as mutual advantage" view—a subtle transformation has occurred in the use of Nash bargaining theory. Nash's axioms were intended to have only "positive" content, as ones describing the process by which traders would bargain. But in recent years, particularly in the work of Thomson (1991) and Thomson and Lensberg (1989), the axioms have taken on "normative" content or, more precisely, ethical content. (There is an ambiguity in the word "normative" as it is used by economists: it can mean either "should" in the sense of ethically mandated or "should" in the sense of what pure rationality requires. To say that a person should ignore sunk costs, for example, is a normative statement of the second kind. I shall use normative in the sense of "ethically should.") Thus modern axiomatic bargaining theory of the Thomson-Lensberg variety can be often interpreted as a study of justice as impartiality.

Hence, although this chapter begins by studying Nash's bargaining problem as one way of articulating justice as mutual advantage, it will eventually apply the same mathematical tools to articulate an approach to justice as impartiality.

2.2 The Nash Bargaining Solution

Nash illustrates the bargaining problem with an example in which two boys, Bill and Jack, wish to reach an agreement on how to divide a set of indivisible objects: a book, whip, ball, bat, box, pen, toy, knife, and hat. Initially, Bill owns some of these things, and Jack the others. Should they fail to reach an agreement, each keeps his initial endowment. There is uncertainty concerning whether an agreement will be reached, and hence Bill and Jack must have preferences over lotteries—specifically, over lotteries in which one outcome is the initial-endowment distribution. Nash assumes that the boys' preferences over lotteries obey the von Neumann–Morgenstern axioms and hence can be represented up to positive affine transformations by a pair of von Neumann–Morgenstern utility functions. He also proposes that all lotteries involving sets of objects be viewed as feasible. Fix a pair of utility functions for the two players. Note that there will be a utility possibilities set S consisting of all utility pairs $(\bar{u}^1, \bar{u}^2)$ that can be achieved for the players as expected utilities of possible lotteries among the objects. By linearity of the von Neumann–Morgenstern utility functions in the probabilities, S will be convex. It will also be compact, since there are only a finite number of sets of objects. Nash now takes a key step: he says we can ignore the objects and utility functions and restrict our attention to pairs of the form (S, d), where S is the utility possibilities set and d is the utility pair associated with the initial-endowment allocation, the utilities the players will receive should they fail to reach agreement. "d" is called the *threat* or *impasse point*.

From now on, Nash describes the general bargaining problem as an abstract pair (S, d), where S is any compact, convex set in $\mathbf{R}^2$ and $d \in S$. The economic environment giving rise to this abstract pair is forgotten. Further, he proposes to shift attention from the individual pair (S, d), to functions which map objects of the form (S, d) into points in S. Thus let F be a mapping from the set of all such objects (S, d) into $\mathbf{R}^2$, with the property that $F((S, d)) \in S$. F is called a *solution*; it is the analogue of Arrow's social choice rule.

Before proceeding further, one should note that the concept of "solution" differs in two ways from that of a social choice functional, apart from the fact that the two kinds of mapping are defined on different domains. First, on economic environments, a social choice functional induces a choice set of favored allocations. A Nash-type solution, however, always chooses just one allocation (or, more precisely, just one point in utility space). Second, on economic environments, social choice functionals induce an ordering of allocations; Nash-type solutions just choose which allocation is the best.

Nash proposes to characterize bargaining by stating axioms that the solution F must obey. These are:

Axiom of Pareto Efficiency (P).   For any $\mathcal{E} = (S, d)$, $F(\mathcal{E})$ is Pareto optimal in S.

This axiom is motivated by the view that the two players will never propose an allocation of the underlying goods (bats, balls, whips, and so on) which can be dominated in utility terms by another allocation.

Axiom of Scale Invariance (S.INV).   Let $a \in \mathbf{R}^2_{++}$ and $b \in \mathbf{R}^2$, let $S \subset \mathbf{R}^2$ and define S' as the set of points of the form $(a^1 s^1 + b^1, a^2 s^2 + b^2)$ for $s \in S, s = (s^1, s^2)$. Let $\mathcal{E} = (S, d)$ be a bargaining problem and let $\mathcal{E}' = (S', d')$, where S' is defined as above, and $d' = (a^1 d^1 + b^1, a^2 d^2 + b^2)$. Then $F(\mathcal{E}') = (a^1 F^1(\mathcal{E}) + b^1, a^2 F^2(\mathcal{E}) + b^2)$.

It will be convenient to denote the set S' by $aS + b$, and d' by $ad + b$.

S.INV is motivated by the implicit assumption that S and d are associated with a particular choice of von Neumann–Morgenstern utility functions, u^1 and u^2. For any $a \in \mathbf{R}^2_+$ and $b \in \mathbf{R}^2$, the utility functions $a^1 u^1 + b^1$ and $a^2 u^2 + b^2$ will do just as well; the bargaining solution should not change its underlying allocation of objects if the problem, in utility space, changes by virtue of a change in the choice of von Neumann–Morgenstern utility functions to represent the same preferences.

Axiom of Symmetry (S).   Suppose $d = (0, 0)$, and for any $(\bar{u}^1, \bar{u}^2) \in S$, $(\bar{u}^2, \bar{u}^1) \in S$ also. Then $F((S, d)) = (\bar{u}, \bar{u})$ for some number $\bar{u}$.

Nash motivates this axiom as one asserting that the players have equal bargaining skill. If the two players have identical preferences over lotteries, then the problem can be represented by choosing the same von Neumann–

Morgenstern utility function for them, giving rise to a symmetric set S with a threat point of $(0, 0)$. Equal bargaining skill means they should reach a bargain in which each receives the same utility.

Axiom of Contraction Consistency (CC).[1]   Let $\mathcal{E} = (S, d)$, $\mathcal{E}' = (T, d)$ and $S \subset T$. If $F(\mathcal{E}') \in S$ then $F(\mathcal{E}) = F(\mathcal{E}')$.

The axiom is motivated as follows. Suppose that the set of lotteries in the bargaining problem $\mathcal{E}$ is a strict subset of the set of lotteries available in the problem $\mathcal{E}'$, but the impasse allocations of objects are the same in the two problems. Suppose, further, that in the problem with the larger set of lotteries, the solution chooses a lottery which indeed is feasible in the smaller problem. CC states that this same lottery should be chosen by the solution in the problem with the restricted set of lotteries.
  Finally, Nash assumed an unrestricted domain axiom:

Axiom of Unrestricted Domain (U).   The domain of F consists of all pairs (S, d), where S is any convex, compact set in the plane containing a point $s > d$ and $d \in S$.

Define a point $s \in S$ as *individually rational* in the problem (S, d) iff $s^i \geq d^i$ for $i = 1, 2$. We next define a particular solution F^N:

Definition 2.1.   The *Nash bargaining solution* F^N maps a problem (S, d) into that point $(\bar{u}^1, \bar{u}^2)$ in S that maximizes the product $(u^1 - d^1)(u^2 - d^2)$ on the set of individually rational points in S.

Theorem 2.1.   *Given U, solution F obeys axioms P, S.INV, S, and CC iff it is the Nash bargaining solution.*[2]

  Proof:

  1. F^N is easily seen to obey the five axioms. We prove the other direction.

---

1. Nash called this axiom "independence of irrelevant alternatives." We shall use another term, to avoid confusion with Arrow's axiom.
  2. Nash did not restrict his solution to examining only individually rational points, but without this restriction, his theorem is false. I will demonstrate this after the proof of Theorem 2.1.

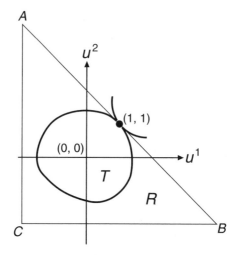

Figure 2.1

2. We begin with any problem $\mathcal{E} = (S, d)$. Denote by $\bar{s}$ the point $F^N((S, d))$ in S. We may choose a positive vector $a \in \mathbf{R}^2_{++}$ and a vector $b \in \mathbf{R}^2$ so that $ad + b = (0, 0)$ and $a\bar{s} + b = (1, 1)$. (This is left as an exercise for the reader.) We shall consider the transformed problem $\mathcal{E}' = (T, d')$, where $T = aS + b$ and $d' = ad + b = (0, 0)$.

3. In T, we know that the point $(1, 1)$ maximizes the Nash product $t^1 t^2$ on the set of individually rational points, since maximization of the Nash product is a property preserved under positive affine transformations. Thus, by convexity of T, there is a rectangular hyperbola, $t^1 t^2 =$ constant, tangent to T at the point $(1, 1)$: see Figure 2.1.

4. The line $t^1 + t^2 = 2$ separates that rectangular hyperbola from the set T at the point $(1, 1)$, as illustrated. Now construct a new bargaining problem (R, d'), where R is a "large" triangle, illustrated in the figure. By U, (R, d') is a feasible bargaining problem. Note that R is symmetric in the sense that the axiom S requires. Hence, by axioms P and S, $F((R, d')) = (1, 1)$. But the problems (R, d') and (T, d') are related to each other as the premise of axiom CC requires. Therefore $F((T, d')) = (1, 1)$. Now, by scale invariance, $F((S, d)) = \bar{s}$, which concludes the proof.[3] ∎

---

3. Nash's original proof used a large rectangle to enclose the set T. The idea of using a large triangle is due to Antonio Rangel. This may seem to be an unimportant amendment here, but in Theorem 2.10, having the triangle is decidedly more convenient.

Now to the comment promised in note 2. The product $(s^1 - d^1)(s^2 - d^2)$, without the restriction to individually rational points, might well be maximized at a point on the "southwest" boundary of S, where both utilities are numbers that are negative and large in absolute value. Hence the Nash solution is not that point that maximizes the unrestricted product $(s^1 - d^1)(s^2 - d^2)$.

Nash's theorem might appear to provide a compelling argument that bargainers should always choose that allocation that maximizes the Nash product. An alternative interpretation views the bargaining problem as one that is solved by an arbitrator. Surely the arbitrator would choose a Pareto optimal point (P), and would want his solution to be invariant with respect to different von Neumann–Morgenstern representations of the bargainers' preferences (S.INV). The arbitrator might impose CC on himself as a compelling consistency requirement. Why would he respect S? Perhaps out of some conception of fairness. I do not think we can rationalize the arbitrator's respect of Symmetry by invoking Nash's assumption that the bargainers are equally skilled, for in actual cases they may not be, but the arbitrator may still be guided by a notion of fairness that Symmetry represents.

There are three kinds of criticism of the Nash bargaining solution as a model of bargaining and, therefore, as a prescription for distributive justice between two persons under the "justice as mutual advantage" view. First, some say that the axioms are not really descriptive of bargaining. In particular, the CC axiom is most often challenged, and as we shall see in §2.4, other axioms have been offered to replace it. Second, the predominant current view among economists is that bargaining is best represented by a noncooperative game approach: it is methodologically incorrect to dream up axioms that should characterize the *end* of the bargaining process; rather, one must model the *process itself* explicitly as a noncooperative game which takes place in finite time. The outstanding example of the noncooperative approach is Rubinstein's (1982) model of alternating offers. Third, one can argue that the Nash approach gives no compelling reason that bargainers should ignore the underlying economic environment: why should the data of the problem be restricted to the abstract pair (S, d), and not include consideration of the actual *preferences* of bargainers and the *objects* that are to be distributed? Recall that in the social choice framework we began with *preferences* and *alternative states* and then deduced that, under certain axioms, we could restrict ourselves to only utility possibilities. But Nash simply states (perhaps cavalierly) that only utility possibilities matter. We shall pursue this criticism in §2.5.

Despite these criticisms, there is a stronger case to be made for the Nash bargaining solution (as a description of the outcome of the idealized bargaining process) than I have made thus far. What Rubinstein and others have called the "Nash program" consists in trying to construct noncooperative models of bargaining that give rise to the Nash solution—models, that is, that do not begin by specifying axioms that a solution F should obey, but rather examine one bargaining problem in isolation as a noncooperative game. I shall next outline four examples of the Nash program.

Nash's Demand Game

Nash (1953) proposed the following game that bargainers might play.[4] Suppose the players are unsure exactly what the set of utility possibilities is. Player 1 will announce a utility x and player 2 a utility y simultaneously. If $(x, y) \in S$, then that is the agreement reached; if $(x, y) \notin S$, then there is an impasse, and they receive the allocation associated with the threat point utilities. The players agree that there is a function $p(x, y)$ giving the probability that a point (x, y) lies in S. What will the players do?

Facing a proposal y by player 2, player 1 will choose x to maximize her expected utility, $p(x, y)x + (1 - p(x, y))d^1$. This gives rise to the first-order condition:

(2.1) $$\frac{\partial p}{\partial x}(x - d^1) = -p(x, y).$$

Similarly, given a proposal x by the first player, player 2's choice will satisfy the first-order condition:

(2.2) $$\frac{\partial p}{\partial y}(y - d^2) = -p(x, y).$$

Hence, the equilibrium announcement is characterized by the equation:

(2.3) $$\frac{y - d^2}{x - d^1} = \frac{\partial p/\partial x}{\partial p/\partial y}.$$

Now suppose that the actual Pareto frontier of the set S is described by the function $y = f(x)$, where f is a differentiable function. Then the Nash

---

4. For an alternative analysis of Nash's demand game, see Binmore and Dasgupta (1987, chap. 4).

product maximizes $(x - d^1)(f(x) - d^2)$. Hence the first derivative of that expression with respect to x must be zero at the Nash solution, or:

$$(2.4) \qquad f'(x) = -\frac{y - d^2}{x - d^1}.$$

Here's the key assumption. The bargainers, of course, do not know that $y = f(x)$ describes the boundary of S. But let us suppose that they assign the same probability, some constant k, to the event that $(x, f(x))$ lies in S for any x. [That is, they are not sure that $(x^1, f(x^1))$ lies in S, but they think that that event is equally likely to the event that $(x^2, f(x^2))$ lies in S for any x^2.] Then we can write $p(x, f(x)) = k$ as an identity in x, and differentiation of this equation gives us:

$$(2.5) \qquad f'(x) = \frac{-\partial p/\partial x}{\partial p/\partial y}.$$

But (2.3) and (2.5) imply (2.4): hence the Nash equilibrium of Nash's bargaining game is the Nash bargaining solution.[5]

The Zeuthen Bargaining Process

According to Harsanyi (1977a, pp. 149–153), Zeuthen (1930) proposed a bargaining process in which players make alternating offers. At each stage, the player whose move it is may repeat his last offer, accept his opponent's latest offer, or propose a new offer which gives him a utility intermediate between the two latest proposals. In the first case, we say he refuses to make a concession. If both players in succession refuse to make a concession, then an impasse is reached—each gets the utility of the impasse point. Zeuthen proposes a theory of who rationally should make the next concession, based on the latest proposals. Harsanyi shows that the equilibrium of Zeuthen's process is the Nash bargaining solution. The weakness of this justification of the Nash bargaining solution, from the modern viewpoint, is the ad hoc nature of Zeuthen's concession rule.

The Binmore-Rubinstein-Wolinsky (1986) Model

Binmore, Rubinstein, and Wolinsky (1986) display two noncooperative bargaining games, based on the alternating-offers model of Rubinstein

---

5. Readers must not confuse *Nash equilibrium*, the central equilibrium concept of noncooperative games, with the Nash bargaining solution.

(1982), and show that in the limit (to be described momentarily), the equilibrium in each game is the Nash bargaining solution. In the first game, there are two players bargaining over the division of a divisible pie. The players make alternating offers to each other until an agreement is reached. This process takes real time, and the players' utility depends not only on the outcome but on when the outcome is reached (thus each player has a time discount rate). There is a unique subgame-perfect equilibrium in this noncooperative game, and the authors show that as the time interval between offers approaches zero, the equilibrium approaches that allocation that maximizes the product of utility differences from the impasse point, which is defined as the utility players receive if they never reach an agreement. Note that risk does not enter in this formulation. The second problem is one in which players have no preferences over when the agreement is reached, but there is a probability that, after any move, nature will end the game. (For instance, the pie to be divided will disappear.) Here, preferences for risk are salient. The authors show that as the probability of breakdown goes to zero, the solution of the game approaches the Nash bargaining solution. It should be noted that, even if the players remain the same in the two problems described, their utility functions will change: for preferences over time are not represented by the same utility function as preferences over risk. The authors note that it is reasonable to assume that preferences over time can be represented by a utility function that is specified up to an increasing affine transformation, and so the scale invariance property holds.

The Rubinstein-Safra-Thomson (1992) Model

Rubinstein, Safra, and Thomson (1992) work on an economic environment of the form $(X, D, \geq^1, \geq^2)$ where X is a set of lotteries, D is the impasse lottery, and the preferences of player i over X are given by $\geq^i$. Let us choose von Neumann–Morgenstern utility functions to represent preferences such that $u^1(D) = u^2(D) = 0$. Rubinstein et al. propose that players make alternating offers, and at each stage, there is a probability $1 - p$ (which can be a function of the history of the game) that the result of the player's action at that stage will lead to an impasse. Thus if player 1 insists on an offer x, his expected utility is $pu^1(x) + (1 - p)u^1(D) = pu^1(x)$. The authors argue that a lottery $y^* \in X$ is a solution to the game if, no matter what offer x the moving player (say it is 1) makes, either:

(i) it is credible for the other player (2) to insist on y^*, when she takes into account the probability $1 - p$ of possible impasse [that is, $pu^2(y^*) \geq u^2(x)$], or

(ii) it is not credible for the other player to reject x, but the moving player does not have an incentive to propose x against y^* [that is, $pu^2(y^*) < u^2(x)$ implies that $u^1(y^*) > pu^1(x)$].

The mathematical statement in (ii) is equivalent to the statement:

for all p and x such that $\quad p < \dfrac{u^2(x)}{u^2(y^*)}$,

it follows that $\quad p < \dfrac{u^1(y^*)}{u^1(x)}$,

which means:

for all x, $\quad \dfrac{u^2(x)}{u^2(y^*)} \leq \dfrac{u^1(y^*)}{u^1(x)}$, $\quad$ or $u^1(y^*)u^2(y^*) \geq u^1(x)u^2(x)$.

But the last statement means that y^* is the Nash bargaining solution.

The approach here is similar to the Zeuthen approach, although the equilibrium condition encapsulated in (i) and (ii) is more convincing than Zeuthen's argument about who should make concessions.

Thus the Nash bargaining solution appears to be an equilibrium of various noncooperative games which bargainers might play. This makes it more compelling as a prediction of the outcome of self-interested, rational bargainers than it may have appeared from Nash's original axiomatic characterization.

2.3   Other Axiomatizations of the Nash Solution

A number of alternative axiomatic characterizations of the Nash solution have been given in the literature. Two are presented in this section. The first, by Roberts, illustrates how the Nash solution can emerge in a social choice framework.

We return, then, to the social-choice-functional approach of §1.3. Roberts introduces the following axiom:

Axiom of Partial Independence of Irrelevant Alternatives (PIIA).   There is a state $\bar{x} \in X$ such that for any profiles $u, u' \in \mathcal{U}$, and any $A \subseteq X$, $u(x) =$

$u'(x)$ for all $x \in A \cup \{\bar{x}\}$ implies that $F(u)$ and $F(u')$ give the same ordering of states in A.

This axiom is weaker than Binary Independence of Irrelevant Alternatives (I*). For example, consider the social choice functional that, for some fixed state $\bar{x}$, ranks states x according to the magnitude of $\min_i(u^i(x) - u^i(\bar{x}))$. The rule could be called "maximize the minimal gain from the status quo $\bar{x}$." This social choice functional satisfies PIIA, but not I*.

We have:

Theorem 2.2 (Roberts 1980b, Theorem 7). *If a social choice functional F satisfies U*, WP*, A, PIIA, and respects cardinal noncomparable utility, then it is the Nash social choice functional; that is, F ranks x socially preferred to y whenever*

$$\prod_{i=1}^{H}(u^i(x) - u^i(\bar{x})) > \prod_{i=1}^{H}(u^i(y) - u^i(\bar{x})).$$

Theorem 2.2 is in a sense a more complete result than Nash's bargaining theorem, because welfarism is *deduced* in the social choice framework from primitive postulates, as we have shown, whereas Nash simply assumes welfarism—that is, he discards the economic information that motivates the problem without any axiomatic justification.

A second, notable alternative axiomatization of the Nash solution is due to Thomson and Lensberg—this time, in the bargaining-theory framework of Nash, where F is a solution acting on the domain of problems of the form (S, d). The domain of Thomson and Lensberg, however, is expanded in the following way. Let $\mathcal{P}$ be a countably infinite set of individuals. Let P be a finite subset of $\mathcal{P}$ of size $p = |P|$. The set Σ^P is the set of convex, comprehensive,[6] compact sets of $\mathbf{R}_+^P$ with at least one point whose coordinates are all positive; thus a set $S \in \Sigma^P$ can be viewed as a utility possibilities set for the set of agents P, with threat point at the origin. Thomson and Lensberg define a bargaining solution as a set of mappings $F = \{F^P\}$, one for every "coalition" P, where the domain of F^P is Σ^P and its range is $\mathbf{R}_+^P$. In fact, for $S \in \Sigma^P$, $F^P(S) \in S$. To be slightly more precise, a *bargaining problem for the coalition P* is a pair (S, P), where $S \in \Sigma^P$ (S is viewed as the utility

---

6. A set S in a real space is comprehensive if $x \leq y$ and $y \in S$ implies $x \in S$. If S is viewed as a utility possibilities set, comprehensiveness can be interpreted as the free disposability of utility. To say that a set S is comprehensive in $\mathbf{R}_+^n$ means that the above condition must hold whenever $x, y \in \mathbf{R}_+^n$.

possibilities set for P, and the threat point is normalized to be the origin). A solution F associates to each pair (S, P) the point $F^P(S)$.

It is clear what it means for the set of mappings F to satisfy Pareto optimality and scale invariance—it simply requires those axioms to hold for every F^P. Thomson and Lensberg introduce a new axiom, which they call Multilateral Stability (M.STAB). The idea is as follows. We begin with two coalitions of individuals, P and Q with $P \subset Q$. Suppose $T \in \Sigma^q$ and $F^Q(T) = x$. The vector x is in $\mathbf{R}^q$, and its components are interpreted as the utility received by the various members of Q. In particular, some "subvector" of x corresponds to the utilities of members of P—call it x^P—which is the projection of x onto the appropriate p-dimensional subspace associated with the utilities of members of P. Indeed, if we hold fixed the components of x associated with members of Q not in P—call that the subvector $x^{Q\backslash P}$—there will be a subset S of T in R^p sliced out: we write $S = t_P^x(T)$. Formally, $t_P^x(T)$ is defined as the set $\{x' \in R^p \mid (x', x^{Q\backslash P}) \in T\}$, where the notation $(x', x^{Q\backslash P})$ is meant to denote the vector whose components x' are associated with the coalition P and whose components $x^{Q\backslash P}$ are associated with the members $Q\backslash P$. See Figure 2.2, which illustrates the set $t_P^x(T)$ when Q consists of three individuals and P of two. We can now state the condition:

Multilateral Stability (M.STAB). Given $P, Q \in \mathcal{P}$, with $P \subset Q$, and given $S \in \Sigma^p$ and $T \in \Sigma^q$ such that $S = t_P^x(T)$ where $F^Q(T) = x$, then $F^P(S) = x^P$.

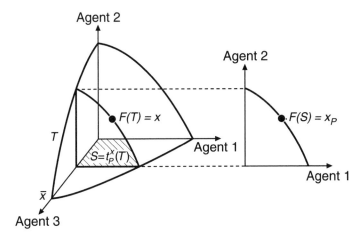

Figure 2.2

In words, suppose that the solution F assigns the utility point x in a bargaining problem T with bargainers consisting of the set of bargainers Q. Now fix the utilities of the individuals in $Q \backslash P$ at the levels assigned at x. This leaves a certain "utility pie" left over which the individuals in P can bargain over [defined by the set $t_P^x(T)$]. M.STAB says that in the smaller-dimensional bargaining problem that now takes place among the members of P, the solution will assign them precisely the utilities that they received at x in the original problem.

The axiom can be viewed as one of "stability with respect to partial implementation of the solution outcome." Thomson and Lensberg give the following example. Suppose a bricklayer, a carpenter, and a painter bid a certain amount to build a house and agree on how to divide the payment among them. After the contract is signed, the bricklayer sets the foundation and collects his share of the payment. M.STAB says that there can now be no meaningful renegotiation between the painter and the carpenter for the remainder—the solution of the bargaining problem between them would award them just what they originally agreed to when all three decided upon the shares.

In the next theorem, "AN" is the anonymity axiom:

Axiom of Anonymity (AN). For any sets of individuals P and P' of the same cardinality, if γ is a one-to-one mapping of P onto P' (that is, a permutation), if (S, P) and (S', P') are bargaining problems such that S is mapped onto S' by the permutation γ, then $F^{P'}(S')$ is the image of $F^P(S)$ under the permutation γ.

In particular, AN implies S, but not conversely.

Theorem 2.3 (Thomson and Lensberg 1989, Theorem 7.1). *A solution* $F = \{F^P\}$ *satisfies P, S.INV,*[7] *AN, and M.STAB iff it is the Nash solution; that is, for all P, $F^P(S)$ is that point that maximizes the product of the utilities in S.*

Theorem 2.3 thus replaces CC by M.STAB, and strengthens S to AN. Note, as well, that it postulates a much larger domain of bargaining problems:

---

7. Since the domain of bargaining problems described above normalizes the threat point to be always at the origin, the scale invariance axiom must permit transformation of utility sets by positive transformations of their coordinates only (with no additive constants).

indeed, it requires the admission of bargaining problems with arbitrarily large numbers of individuals (more than there will ever be on Earth). One might well ask whether a theorem which requires a domain axiom covering situations that will, for sure, never occur, is one that tells us something important about our own world. Exactly this question, of course, can be posed about the theorems in Chapter 1 that used the axiom COAD, for that axiom requires the admission of economic environments with arbitrarily large numbers of goods.

Thomson and Lensberg give an ethical justification for the axiom of multilateral stability. Imagine, now, that F is a solution to all possible problems of distributive justice, that is, we interpret the bargaining problem (S, P) as a utility representation of the problem of dividing a fixed set of resources among a set of individuals P, where S is the set of utility possibilities that are generated by all possible distributions, and the origin of S is identified as the utility vector that people get at an allocation that we deem to be in some sense fair. Multilateral stability says that, if a certain distribution of the resources, call it x, among a set of agents Q is just, and if we look at the *aggregate* resources that the subgroup P of Q gets at x, then the just allocation of that aggregate among the individuals in P is exactly the distribution assigned by x. Or, more informally, if a distribution of all resources available on Earth is just, then the distribution of resources assigned to each country (province, family) must also be just within that country (province, family).

We can also interpret AN as a principle of just distribution (justice should be blind to the names of persons); Pareto optimality is also a desirable property of a just distribution. Indeed, we can give Pareto optimality a completely normative interpretation, as follows: any person should be permitted to replace a proposed distribution by another one, as long as his substitution makes no one worse off than in the original proposal. (I do not here specify a rule for the order in which citizens are recognized in the town meeting in which these proposals and substitutions are made.) The only proposals which will stand unaltered under this process are the Pareto optimal ones. Scale invariance is justified, as in Nash, as modeling the view that utilities are generated by preferences over lotteries that obey the von Neumann–Morgenstern axioms. This axiom, however, is only attractive in the context of viewing the bargaining problem as one of distributive justice if there is some uncertainty involved in the selection of an allocation.

Given this interpretation of the axioms, we are on the way to viewing

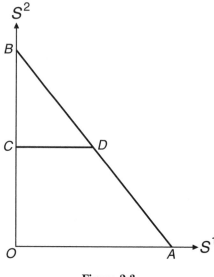

Figure 2.3

Theorem 2.3 as one that proposes a solution to the problem of "justice as impartiality": we no longer are interpreting the axioms as ones that describe bargaining among rational players. But to make this interpretation precise will require considerably more work, for reasons whose discussion I will postpone until §2.5.

2.4   The Kalai-Smorodinsky and Egalitarian Solutions

2.4.1   *The Kalai-Smorodinsky Solution*

Nash's CC axiom has been criticized for being inaccurate as a characterization of bargaining. In Figure 2.3, there are two utility possibilities sets, the triangle OAB, and the trapezoid OADC. Suppose the threat point, for both problems, is the origin O. Suppose the solution in the triangle problem OAB is at point D: then by CC, the solution in the trapezoid problem OADC must also be at point D. But this seems unreasonable: for at D, the second player gets his maximum possible utility. In particular, one might think that player 2 has a weaker bargaining position in the trapezoid problem than in the triangle problem, which would suggest she should get less utility in the former than in the latter. CC does not permit this.

To model this idea, Kalai and Smorodinsky (1975) replaced Nash's CC axiom with an axiom of "individual monotonicity." For a bargaining problem (S, d), represent any point in S as $s = (s^1, \ldots, s^H)$, where H is the dimension of the real space in which S sits. Define $a^h(S, d) = \max\{s^h \mid s \in S, s \geq d\}$: $a^h(S, d)$ is the most that individual h can possibly get at points in S that dominate the threat point. $a(S, d)$ is the point in R^H whose h^{th} coordinate is $a^h(S, d)$. It is sometimes called the *ideal point* of the problem (S, d).

Axiom of Individual Monotonicity (I.MON). Let (S, d) and (T, d) be two bargaining problems in $\mathbf{R}^2$ with $T \supset S$. If $a^1(S, d) = a^1(T, d)$, then $F^2((T, d)) \geq F^2((S, d))$. Similarly, if $a^2(S, d) = a^2(T, d)$ then $F^1((T, d)) \geq F^1((S, d))$.

In particular, the premise of the axiom applies to the two problems in Figure 2.3, where $S = $ trapOADC and $T = \triangle$OAB. I.MON asserts that the second player should receive at least as much utility in the triangle problem as in the trapezoid problem. Of course, since the inequality is weak, it does not violate the axiom for D to be the solution in both problems.

Definition 2.2. The *Kalai-Smorodinsky solution* F^{KS} is the mapping that associates to each bargaining problem in the plane, (S, d), the point on the Pareto frontier of S that lies at its intersection with the line joining d and $a(S, d)$. See Figure 2.4.

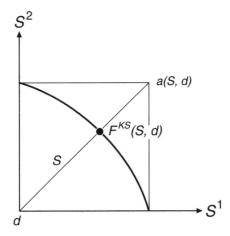

Figure 2.4

We have:

Theorem 2.4 (Kalai and Smorodinsky 1975).   *Let F satisfy U, P, S, S.INV, and IMON. Then $F = F^{KS}$.*

Proof:

1. We are given an arbitrary problem in the plane (S, d). There is an increasing affine transformation that maps the plane into itself and sends the point $a(S, d)$ into $(1, 1)$ and d into $(0, 0)$. [This uses the fact that $a(S, d) > d$, which is true by the domain axiom U.] Call the new bargaining problem so attained (T, O). By S.INV, the solution under F on (S, d) maps into the solution on (T, O) under this transformation.

2. The solution F^{KS} on (T, O) is a point with equal coordinates—call it (a, a). This follows because the line connecting the threat point to the point $a(T, O)$ has slope one. See Figure 2.5.

3. Construct a quadrilateral T' inside T as illustrated in Figure 2.5, by connecting the point (a, a) to the points $(1, 0)$ and $(0, 1)$. The quadrilateral T' so formed (whose other two sides are the segments along the axes) generates an acceptable bargaining problem (T', O), by axiom U. The problem (T', O) is symmetric, and so by axioms S and P, $F((T', O)) = (a, a)$.

4. Now (T', O) and (T, O) are related to each other in the way required by the premise of I.MON. Since $a^i(T', O) = a^i(T, O)$ for $i = 1$ and 2, it fol-

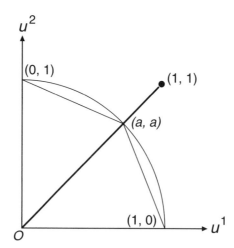

Figure 2.5

lows, by I.MON, that $F^i(T, O) \geq F^i(T', O)$ for $i = 2$ and 1. Thus $F(T, O) \geq (a, a)$ and so $F(T, O) = (a, a)$. But (a, a) is the Kalai-Smorodinsky solution on (T, O), so $F(T, O) = F^{KS}(T, O)$. By S.INV, it follows that $F(S, d) = F^{KS}(S, d)$. ∎

The motivation given above for I.MON was not an ethical one; it had to do with the relative strength of the players' bargaining positions. But again Thomson and Lensberg have provided an alternative characterization of the Kalai-Smorodinsky solution, in which I.MON is replaced with a normatively appealing axiom.

As before, Thomson and Lensberg work on the domain consisting of problems Σ^p, for any dimension p. Again the new axiom they introduce involves comparing the action of the solution in two worlds where the number of individuals varies. The idea behind the new axiom, which they call "population monotonicity," is that if two problems have the same bundle of resources to distribute, but there are more people in problem 1 than problem 2, then no one should end up better off under the solution in problem 1 than he does in problem 2. This can be viewed, as the authors say, as an axiom of solidarity: that when new people come into the community bringing *no* resources with them, the earlier citizens of the community should all chip in to support them.

The axiom, however, is stated entirely in terms of utilities—not in terms of resources—as, in the classical bargaining theory context, there are no resources provided in the data of the problem (S, d). Given two sets of individuals P, Q with $P \subset Q$, where the group of citizens Q faces a bargaining problem $T \in \Sigma^q$, let $S = T_P$ be the projection onto $\mathbf{R}^P_+$ of the set T. We can view the set S as the utility possibilities available to the coalition P in the original problem if all individuals in $Q \backslash P$ are held to the utilities they receive at the threat point (the origin, in the Thomson-Lensberg domain). Or, to put the point in a way consistent with the Thomson-Lensberg interpretation, we can view S as the utility possibilities set for the group P, and T as the utility possibilities set for Q when the new citizens $Q \backslash P$ bring with them no resources and the threat point (the origin in utility space) is associated with the utilities citizens receive when they consume no resources. We can now state:

Axiom of Population Monotonicity (P.MON).   A solution $F = \{F^P\}$ satisfies *population monotonicity* if, for any sets P, Q with $P \subset Q$, if $T \in \Sigma^q$ and $S = T_P$, then $F^P(S) \geq F^Q_P(T)$, where $F^Q_P(T)$ denotes the coordinates of the utility vector $F^Q(T)$ associated with the individuals in P.

To state the next theorem requires defining the conditions of weak
Pareto optimality and continuity:

Weak Pareto (WP). A solution $F = \{F^P\}$ is *weakly Pareto optimal* if for any
$S \in \Sigma^p$, there is no $s \in S$ such that $F^P(S) < s$.

Continuity (CONT). A solution $F = \{F^P\}$ is *continuous* if for all P and for
all sequences $\{S^k\} \subset \Sigma^p$ which converge to some set $S \in \Sigma^p$ in the Hausdorff topology,[8] $F^P(S^k)$ converges to $F^P(S)$.

This axiom says that if two utility possibilities sets are "close," then the
solutions in the two problems must be close.
    We have:

Theorem 2.5 (Thomson and Lensberg 1989, Theorem 3.1). *A solution*
$F = \{F^P\}$ *satisfies WP, AN, S.INV, CONT, and PMON iff it is the Kalai-
Smorodinsky solution.*[9]

    Just as Theorem 2.3 opened up the possibility of interpreting the Nash
solution as a prescription for justice as impartiality, so Theorem 2.5 opens
up the possibility of interpreting the Kalai-Smorodinsky solution as such
a prescription. It should again be emphasized that there is a fundamental shift from Theorem 2.4 to Theorem 2.5, as Theorem 2.4 is relevant
for justice only insofar as we interpret justice as "mutual advantage"—
assuming, that is, that I.MON is a correct attribute of bargaining between
self-interested players.

---

8. The Hausdorff topology is induced by the following metric on the set of compact
sets in $\mathbf{R}^n$: for two such compact sets S and S', define $\mathrm{dist}(S, S') = \max\{\max\{\delta(x, S) \mid x \in
S'\}, \max\{\delta(x, S') \mid x \in S\}\}$, where $\delta(x, S)$ is the distance of the point x to the set S (that
is, the minimal distance of x to points in S).
    9. The axiom WP can be replaced by P, and CONT can be dropped from the state-
ment of the theorem, if we restrict the domain of bargaining problems to consist only
of "strictly comprehensive" utility possibilities sets. A strictly comprehensive set is one
whose weak Pareto frontier is identical to its Pareto frontier. Alternatively put, the weak
Pareto boundary of such a set in $\mathbf{R}^2$ contains no segment parallel to either coordinate
axis. In $\mathbf{R}^n$, the weak Pareto boundary contains no segment parallel to a coordinate subspace. Thus WP and CONT can be viewed as essentially technical conditions which are
needed to prove the theorem on the full domain which includes nonstrictly comprehensive sets.

Gauthier (1986) subscribes to the Kalai-Smorodinsky solution as the realization of distributive justice, but from the viewpoint of justice as mutual
advantage: he views F^{KS} as the correct characterization of the outcome
of self-interested players in a bargaining game. He holds this view not
because he is convinced that the axioms of Theorem 2.4 characterize
rational bargaining, but because there is a characterization of the Kalai-
Smorodinsky solution as the outcome of a noncooperative bargaining
process, somewhat akin to the Zeuthen-Harsanyi justification of the Nash
solution referred to in §2.2. To explain Gauthier's reasoning, it is convenient to refer to allocations of commodities as well as to points in utility
space. Let H be the set of bargainers and D the allocation associated with
the "initial bargaining position"—presumably, specifying the pretrade endowment position of each player. Let d^h be the utility that player h gets
if he consumes his initial endowment. The bargaining problem is one of
the form (S, d), in utility space. Let u^h be a von Neumann–Morgenstern
utility function for player h. Let $\bar{u}^h = a^h(S, d)$ be the maximum utility
that player h could get if all other players are held to their threat *utilities*. (This does not mean that they consume their initial endowments,
for in this case, player h would be held to his threat utility as well.) Thus
$(\bar{u}^1, \bar{u}^2, \ldots, \bar{u}^H)$ is the ideal point, $a(S, d)$. Gauthier says that, as an initial
claim, it is rational for each bargainer h to propose the allocation where
she receives the utility $\bar{u}^h$. It is not feasible for every player simultaneously to receive $\bar{u}^h$, of course, so from these initial claims, players must
start to make concessions. Suppose a player h proposes, as a solution to
the bargaining problem, an allocation C of commodities. Gauthier defines
the *absolute concession* that the player makes at this offer as $\bar{u}^h - u^h(C)$—
as the utility loss he suffers at that allocation from his initial claim. Gauthier
defines the *relative magnitude of the concession of a player h at an allocation*
C as the ratio $\left(\bar{u}^h - u^h(C)\right)/(\bar{u}^h - d^h)$, the ratio of his absolute concession at C to the utility gain he would enjoy were he to receive his initial
claim. Now each rational player must seek to minimize the relative magnitude of the concession for himself. The crux of Gauthier's argument
is that, when a proposal for an allocation C is on the table, then the
next concession must (rationally) be made by the player who enjoys the
smallest relative magnitude of the concession at C, assuming there is a
player who enjoys a smaller relative magnitude than other players. (We
will return to this claim momentarily.) It follows that an allocation C is
an equilibrium of the game if and only if no one must make a further
concession, which is to say that the relative magnitudes of all players' con-

cessions are equal at C. But this defines precisely the Kalai-Smorodinsky solution.

Why, then, must a rational bargainer make a concession if, at a proposal C, he enjoys a smaller relative concession than the other player? (Let us suppose we have a two-person problem, for simplicity.) Gauthier says this principle " . . . expresses the equal rationality of the bargainers. Since each person, as a utility-maximizer, seeks to minimize his concession, then no one can expect any other rational person to be willing to make a concession if he would not be willing to make a similar concession" (1986, pp. 143–144). He believes this means that each person proposes a concession from his initial claim in which he suffers a relative magnitude of concession no greater than that of any other player.

I do not see why "magnitude of relative concession" is the equalisandum required by rationality. As a characterization of rational claims among self-interested bargainers, the Rubinstein-Safra-Thomson interpretation of the Nash solution is far more convincing. First of all, in regard to Gauthier's claim, it is unclear what a *ratio* of two utility differences means. It is true that this ratio is an invariant of the representation of a person's preferences over lotteries by von Neumann–Morgenstern utility functions; but if one person suffers a greater relative magnitude of concession than another at an allocation, why does it follow that others must make further concessions to him? Gauthier gives no explanation for his view grounded in the pursuit of rational self-interest in a bargaining environment.[10]

2.4.2 The Egalitarian Solution

The final solution I shall discuss does not involve the axiom of scale invariance, nor is it cogently viewed as a bargaining solution. Mathematically, however, we can characterize it in a Nash-type environment. Let us define the domain $\tilde{\Sigma}^p$ as the set of strictly comprehensive, convex, compact sets in $\mathbf{R}_+^p$, and let us specify a problem as a pair (S, P) where P is a set of individuals and $S \in \tilde{\Sigma}^p$ is conceived of as their utility possibilities set. Let us call the domain of all such problems $\tilde{D}$. We shall, for the present, be vague about the interpretation of the origin in S. A solution shall be viewed as a set of mappings $F = \{F^P\}$, as before.

We introduce the condition:

---

10. See also Binmore (1993) for a critique of Gauthier's conception of rationality, and Gauthier (1993) for a partial admission that he erred.

Monotonicity (MON).   Let (S, P) and (T, P) be two problems, and $S \subset T$. Then $F^P(T) \geqq F^P(S)$.

The axiom has an ethical justification. We may view the set T as the utility possibilities in a world where there are strictly more resources or commodities than in S. MON states that, when resources increase, the solution F should make no individual worse off than he was in the world with fewer resources. MON can be viewed as a solidarity axiom: for it also says that, when the resource bundle decreases, everyone should (weakly) tighten his belt.

We next define a useful class of solutions. First, an *unbounded monotone path from the origin in* $\mathbf{R}^n_+$ is a mapping $\varphi : \mathbf{R}_+ \to \mathbf{R}^n_+$ such that $t^1 > t^2$ implies $\varphi(t^1) \geq \varphi(t^2)$, $\varphi(0) = 0$, and the Euclidean length of the vector $\varphi(t)$ is unbounded in t.

Definition 2.3.   A solution $F = \{F^P\}$ is a *monotone utility path* (MUP) *solution* if for each positive integer p there is an unbounded monotone path from the origin in $\mathbf{R}^p_+$, call it φ^p, such that, for any $S \in \tilde{\Sigma}^p$, and any set of individuals P of cardinality p, $F^P((S, P))$ is the intersection of the Pareto frontier of S with the path φ^p.

An MUP solution is illustrated in Figure 2.6.

We define the *egalitarian solution* on $\tilde{\Sigma}^p$ as the mapping E^p that maps any $S \in \tilde{\Sigma}^p$ into the Pareto optimal point in S whose coordinates are all equal. Since S is strictly comprehensive, there is such a point.

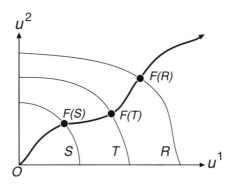

Figure 2.6

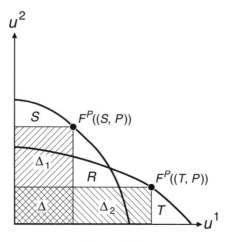

Figure 2.7

We have:

Theorem 2.6. *Let F be a solution on $\tilde{D}$ satisfying P, Sy,*[11] *and MON. Then, for all p, F^P is the egalitarian solution on $\tilde{\Sigma}^p$.*

(Theorem 2.6 is closely related to a theorem of Kalai [1977].)

Proof:

1. We shall first prove that the domain assumption, P, and MON imply that F^P must be a monotone utility path solution for all P. Suppose, to the contrary, that F^P is not such a solution: then there are two problems (S, P) and (T, P) with $S, T \in \tilde{\Sigma}^p$ such that neither of the points $F^P((S, P))$ and $F^P((T, P))$ dominates the other componentwise. See Figure 2.7 for an illustration in $\mathbf{R}^2$. Consider the set $R = S \cap T$; R is strictly comprehensive, and is therefore in $\tilde{\Sigma}^p$. Therefore F^P prescribes a solution for the problem (R, P). Since $R \subset S$, it follows by MON that $F^P((R, P))$ lies in the rectangle Δ^1 constructed to the southwest of the point $F^P(S)$—see again Figure 2.7. Since $R \subset T$, it follows that $F^P((R, P))$ lies in the rectangle Δ^2 to the southwest of the point $F^P((T, P))$. Therefore $F^P((R, P))$ lies in the intersection of these two rectangles $\Delta = \Delta^1 \cap \Delta^2$. Now every point in Δ^1 except $F^P((S, P))$ lies in the interior of S, since S is strictly comprehensive,

---

11. The axiom Sy is the symmetry axiom S, but stated on the domain $\tilde{D}$.

and similarly, every point in Δ^2 except $F^P((T, P))$ lies in the interior of T. Therefore Δ lies in the interior of R. Therefore no point in Δ is Pareto optimal in R. But since we have shown that $F^P((R, P))$ must lie in Δ, we have a contradiction to the Pareto condition. This proves that F^P is a monotone utility path solution.

2. For any p, construct an infinite sequence of symmetric sets $\{S^k\}$, $S^k \in \tilde{\Sigma}^p$, which is unbounded (that is, the sets S^k get arbitrarily large). By symmetry and Pareto, the solution under F^P on (S^k, P) must be the equal utility point with the largest coordinates that lies in S^k. But these points trace out an unbounded monotone path in $\mathbf{R}_+^p$. By step 1, this path completely determines the solution F^P. The monotone utility path solution associated with this monotone path is E^p, and the theorem is proved. ∎

Theorem 2.6 offers an apparently compelling solution to the problem of distributive justice: if we agree that Pareto, symmetry, and monotonicity are ethically attractive properties of a solution, then the solution must, in any problem, equalize the utilities of the individuals—welfare egalitarianism— where the problem is normalized so that $u^h(0) = 0$ for all h. Thus far, we have not thought about the measurability properties of the underlying utility functions. In fact, if scale invariance were imposed as an additional premise in Theorem 2.6, there would be an impossibility result: since the egalitarian solution is not scale invariant, there are no solutions that satisfy P, S, MON, and S.INV on $\tilde{D}$. We can substitute scale invariance for symmetry, and then we get a possibility result, but an unpleasant one.

Definition 2.4. A solution $F = \{F^P\}$ is *dictatorial* if for each coalition P there is an integer $j \leq p$ such that $F^P((S, P)) = a^j(S)$, where $a^j(S)$ is defined as the Pareto optimal point in S at which all players except the jth one receive zero utility.

Theorem 2.7.   *Let F be a solution on $\tilde{D}$ satisfying P, S.INV, and MON. Then F is dictatorial.*

Proof:

1. The argument of Theorem 2.6, step 1, applies: for any P, F^P must be a monotone utility path solution. But the only monotone paths that are invariant to the positive transformations permitted under the scale

invariance axiom are the paths defined by the coordinate axes themselves. This means that F^P is dictatorial. ∎

How, then, can we interpret Theorem 2.6? The easiest way, I think, is to view the underlying utility functions as concave functions which are cardinally measurable with full comparability.[12] Concavity of the functions guarantees that, in an economy with a convex set of feasible allocations, the utility possibility sets are convex, and the assumption of cardinal measurability and full comparability does not destroy concavity. The egalitarian solution respects utility information which is cardinally measurable and fully comparable. Thus it appears that we can interpret Theorem 2.6 as a distributive prescription in an economic environment, where an aggregate endowment of goods must be distributed among citizens with concave utility functions, all of whom receive the same utility when consuming no goods, which can be normalized to zero.

Thomson and Lensberg also have a characterization of the egalitarian solution using the axiom of population monotonicity.

Theorem 2.8 (Thomson and Lensberg 1989, Theorem 4.2).   *A solution defined on $\tilde{D}$ satisfies P, Sy, CC, and PMON iff it is the egalitarian solution.*

(Here CC is the statement of the "contraction consistency" axiom on the relevant domains $\tilde{\Sigma}^P$.)

Proof:

1. I shall outline the proof for a special case; Thomson and Lensberg's argument shows this case is not restrictive. Let $S \in \tilde{\Sigma}^2$, and consider the problem (S, P), where $P = \{1, 2\}$. Further, suppose that $a^1(S) + a^2(S) < 3$ and that the Pareto optimal equal utility point in S is $(1, 1)$. Write $e_P = (1, 1)$. Consider a third individual, and the group $Q = \{1, 2, 3\}$, and let $T = \{(t^1, t^2, t^3) \mid t^i \geq 0 \text{ and } \Sigma t^i \leq 3\}$. Note that $T \in \tilde{\Sigma}^3$. In particular, the Pareto optimal equal utility point in T is the point $e_Q = (1, 1, 1)$. Note that $S \subset T$. See Figure 2.8.

2. By Pareto optimality and symmetry, $F^3((T, Q)) = e_Q$. Consider now the convex, comprehensive hull of the point e_Q and the set S—that is, the

---

12. Full comparability is defined by specifying the utility profile up to the same affine transformation $\varphi(z) = az + b$ for all players, where $a \in \mathbf{R}_+$ and $b \in \mathbf{R}$.

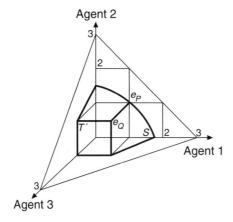

Figure 2.8

smallest comprehensive, convex set in $\mathbf{R}_+^3$ containing e_Q and S. Call this set T'—see Figure 2.8. Note that $T' \in \tilde{\Sigma}^3$. By contraction consistency, since T' is contained in T and $e_Q \in T'$, we have $F^3((T', Q)) = e_Q$.

3. By construction, the set S is the projection of the set T' onto the 1–2 plane. It follows from PMON that individuals 1 and 2 cannot get more utility in the problem (S, P) than they do in the problem (T', Q)—that is, $e_P \leqq F^2((P, S))$. But since e_P is Pareto optimal in S, it follows that $e_P = F^2((P, S))$. Thus on the problem (S, P), F is egalitarian. ■

I have noted an argument against Nash's CC axiom from the viewpoint of bargaining theory, but it may still be an attractive axiom of "collective rationality" for a rule of distributive justice. I have argued that the axioms P, Sy, and PMON have ethical justifications: thus Theorem 2.8 appears to offer another attractive ethical justification of welfare egalitarianism.[13]

While I have discussed the various solutions for two-person environments, the Nash and egalitarian solutions extend to n-person environments, as do their characterizations. The natural extension of the Kalai-Smorodinsky solution to n-person environments fails in general to satisfy Pareto optimality; Thomson (1991) defines the "lexicographic Kalai-

13. There are several other bargaining solutions discussed in the literature that I will not review here. The interested reader is urged to consult Roth (1979), Kalai (1985), Peters (1992), and Thomson (1991).

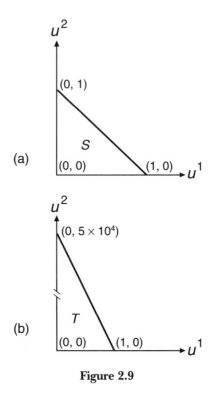

Figure 2.9

Smorodinsky solution," which does. For a discussion of the extension of these solutions in the *n*-person context, see Thomson (1991, chap. 2).

2.5   A Criticism from the Economic Point of View

Consider the problem of two bargainers who must decide who gets an indivisible object worth $1 to each of them. Their preferences over lotteries are identical and can be represented by the von Neumann–Morgenstern utility $u(x) = x$, where $x \in \mathbf{R}$. If they fail to reach an agreement on the lottery, neither gets the object. The utility possibilities set for this problem is illustrated in Figure 2.9a. According to the Nash, the Kalai-Smorodinsky, and the egalitarian solutions, the players should agree on the lottery giving each of them probability $\frac{1}{2}$ of receiving the object: that is, they should flip a fair coin. (Indeed, this is required by the symmetry and Pareto axioms alone.)

Now consider another bargaining problem, where there are two objects, a silver dollar (object A) and a Rolls Royce (object B). The same two players are involved as in the first problem. The set of lotteries consists of all lotteries of the following form: with probability p, the first player gets object A and the second player gets nothing, and with probability $(1 - p)$ the second player gets object B and the first player gets nothing. The utility possibilities set is illustrated in Figure 2.9b. This utility possibilities set is a scale-invariant transformation of the one in Figure 2.9a, where the first coordinate remains unchanged and the second one is multiplied by 5×10^4. S.INV states that the lottery chosen by the players should be the same one that was chosen in the problem of Figure 2.9a: that is, the players should flip a fair coin, and if it lands heads, the first player gets the dollar, while if it lands tails the second player gets the Rolls Royce. Thus both the Nash and Kalai-Smorodinsky solution will propose the coin flip in the problem of Figure 2.9b.

But this seems crazy—certainly from an ethical viewpoint, but also from a bargaining viewpoint. Most people would think that in the bargaining problem of Figure 2.9b, player 1 will be able to insist on a probability much closer to one. Certainly from an ethical viewpoint, it appears that the fair agreement will consist in a probability p close to 1. What's wrong?

The problem is that one cannot distinguish between two very different changes in the underlying economic environment that could have engendered the change of S into T: in one possible change, we simply replace the second person's von Neumann–Morgenstern utility function u^2 by the equally good utility function $a^2 u^2$, where a^2 is a large positive number; in the second possible change, the prizes available to the participants have changed, but the utility functions have not, as in the story told above. Nash-type bargaining theory cannot distinguish between these two kinds of change, for they look exactly the same in utility space. This is the content of the implicit welfarist axiom supposed by Nash, an (unstated) axiom specifying that bargainers treat as relevant only the information contained in the abstract pair (S, d).

Unfortunately this problem afflicts all of the axioms discussed thus far, with the exception of Pareto optimality. Consider the symmetry axiom S. Nash's intention was that this axiom apply to a problem in which the two players have the same von Neumann–Morgenstern preferences over a set of lotteries that is symmetric in the obvious sense: the problem that generated Figure 2.9a is an instance. Now consider another problem of two players who must divide a bundle of two goods between them, the aggregate endowment of which is $(1, 1)$. The first has a Cobb-Douglas utility function $u^1(x_1, x_2) = x_1^{.5}x_2^{.5}$, and the second has linear preferences $u^2(x_1, x_2) = .5(x_1 + x_2)$. The Pareto optimal allocations, which equalize their marginal rates of substitutions, require that each person receive the same amount of both goods. If individual one gets x of both goods, her utility is x; then individual 2 gets $(1 - x)$ of both goods, and his utility is $1 - x$. Thus the Pareto frontier is the set of points $(x, 1 - x)$, for all x between 0 and 1. But this generates exactly the set S of Figure 2.9a. By symmetry, the players must agree to divide the goods so that each receives the utility allocation $(.5, .5)$. Now this may indeed happen, but the reasoning cannot be justified by Nash's justification of the symmetry axiom, because the players do not have identical preferences over all divisions of the endowment. Welfarism renders the axiom much stronger than Nash originally intended, in the sense that it enforces an equal division of utility even in cases when the players are not identical.

Consider next the monotonicity axiom (MON). The ethical justification of MON was a story in which the amount of resources increases between two problems, while the individuals remain the same. But MON enforces monotonicity of outcomes on a much larger set of problems—namely, for any two economic environments in which the utility possibilities set of one contains the other. Clearly this can happen on account of preferences changing as well as on account of resources changing. We have no obvious intuition that "monotonicity" should apply if one economic environment is related to another by a change in preferences (that is, of individuals), but MON enforces monotonically related outcomes in that case as well.

The same reasoning applies to the axioms M.STAB and P.MON: they enforce consistency and solidarity (respectively) even when the change in utility sets that they postulate comes about for reasons entirely different from the stories that were told to motivate the axioms.

It is useful to state the implicit welfarist axiom of Nash bargaining theory formally. To this end, I shall define a domain of appropriate economic environments. (This can be done in many different ways.) Let B be a finite set of r objects. There will be two players. Let $\mathcal{B}$ be the set of ordered partitions of B into three elements, some of which may be empty. A *lottery* is a probability distribution on $\mathcal{B}$. The interpretation is that the objects in the first (second) element of a partition are allocated to the first (second) player, and the objects in the third element go to neither player. For example, if $B = \{a, b\}$, then $\mathcal{B}$ consists of the nine partitions $(a, b, \emptyset)$, $(b, a, \emptyset)$,

$(ab, \emptyset, \emptyset)$, $(\emptyset, ab, \emptyset)$, $(a, \emptyset, b)$, $(\emptyset, a, b)$, $(b, \emptyset, a)$, $(\emptyset, b, a)$, and $(\emptyset, \emptyset, ab)$. A probability distribution over $\mathcal{B}$ is a vector $(p_1, \ldots, p_9)$ with non-negative components that sum to one. For example, taking the partitions as ordered above, the lottery $(\frac{1}{2}, 0, 0, \frac{1}{2}, 0, 0, 0, 0, 0)$ is the lottery "with probability one-half, the first player receives a and the second player receives b, and with probability one-half, both objects go to the second player."

We define an economic environment as a tuple $e = \langle B, \Omega, u^1, u^2, \omega^* \rangle$ where B is the set of objects, Ω is a set of lotteries over $\mathcal{B}$, u^1 and u^2 are von Neumann–Morgenstern utilities for the two players over lotteries of the objects in B, and $\omega^* \in \Omega$ is a fixed lottery. A utility function is defined by specifying the utility received from every possible subset of B. By the expected utility property, the utilities on lotteries are just the appropriate probability-weighted sums of these numbers. We may write the utility for player i when he faces the lottery p as $u^i(p)$. I shall also write $u^i(C)$, for C a subset of B, to mean the utility that player i has when she consumes the bundle C: I hope this notational duplicity will not be a source of confusion. Define $\mathcal{A}(e)$ as the utility possibilities set generated by the environment e—that is, $\mathcal{A}(e) = \{(a, b) \mid \exists\, p \in \Omega \text{ such that } u^1(p) = a, u^2(p) = b\}$. For purposes of exposition, it will not harm to fix the set of objects B once and for all, and to write an economic environment from now on as $e = \langle \Omega, u^1, u^2, \omega^* \rangle$.

Let $\mathcal{D}$ be a class of such economic environments. A *mechanism* φ on $\mathcal{D}$ maps any $e \in \mathcal{D}$ into a lottery which is a member of its Ω,[14] denoted $\varphi(e)$. We can state:

Axiom of Welfarism (W). Let F be a mechanism on $\mathcal{D}$. If $e = \langle \Omega, u^1, u^2, \omega^* \rangle$ and $e' = \langle \Omega, v^1, v^2, \omega \rangle$ are two environments in $\mathcal{D}$ such that $\mathcal{A}(e) = \mathcal{A}(e')$, then $u^1(\varphi(e)) = v^1(\varphi(e'))$ and $u^2(\varphi(e)) = v^2(\varphi(e'))$.

The axiom states that, if two economic environments give rise to the same utility possibilities set, then the mechanism must assign solutions for the two problems which are indistinguishable in terms of utility. Nash bargaining theory can be viewed as a theory that begins on economic environments but imposes the welfarism axiom right away; hence, all further

---

14. To be absolutely precise, it is sometimes appropriate to view φ as a correspondence that maps a given environment into a lottery and all other lotteries that are Pareto-indifferent to it. Thus φ is a correspondence that induces a function in utility space, the mapping $u \circ \varphi = (u^1(\varphi(\cdot)), u^2(\varphi(\cdot)))$.

axioms can be stated in the language of the form (S, d), where S is the utility possibilities set of the underlying economic environment, and d is the utility vector the players receive at the specified lottery ω^*.

How powerful is the axiom of welfarism? One way to study this question is to restate Nash's axioms directly on a domain of economic environments $\mathcal{D}$, and then to compute the class of mechanisms that satisfy these axioms on $\mathcal{D}$—but without postulating welfarism. If only the Nash bargaining solution satisfies the axioms, then the welfarism axiom could have been dispensed with by Nash. But if there are many mechanisms that satisfy the "Nash" axioms when reformulated directly on economic environments, then the welfarism axiom is powerful—it was eliminating many mechanisms.

We proceed with this program. Fixing B, let $\mathcal{D}$ be the class of economic environments of the form $e = \langle \Omega, u^1, u^2, \omega^* \rangle$, where Ω is any compact, convex set of lotteries (as defined above), u^i are any von Neumann–Morgenstern utilities for two players defined on Ω, and ω^* is any point in Ω that is not on the weak Pareto frontier [that is, there exists a lottery $p \in \Omega$ such that $u^1(p) > u^1(\omega^*)$ and $u^2(p) > u^2(\omega^*)$]. The "Nash" axioms are as follows.

Axiom of Domain (U*).   The mechanism φ is defined on $\mathcal{D}$.

Axiom of Scale Invariance (S.INV*).   Let $e = \langle \Omega, u^1, u^2, \omega^* \rangle$ and $e' = \langle \Omega, v^1, v^2, \omega^* \rangle$ where u^i is a positive affine transformation of v^i, for $i = 1, 2$. Then $\varphi(e) = \varphi(e')$.

This is exactly what Nash intended with his axioms S.INV—that if two problems differ only by the utility representations of the same preferences, then the solution should be the same in both.

Next, we need to define a symmetric set of lotteries. Note that any partition in $\mathcal{B}$ has its "inverse partition"; if (X, Y, Z) is a partition, then its inverse is (Y, X, Z) (just switch the bundles going to the two players). The only partition which is its own inverse is $(\emptyset, \emptyset, B)$—when neither player receives any object. In the example above, when $B = \{a, b\}$, I have listed the partitions so that each partition is followed by its inverse. If p is a lottery, denote by p^* the lottery with the property that, if k and l are indices of a partition and its inverse in the ordered set $\mathcal{B}$, then $p_k = p_l^*$. A *set* of lotteries Ω is said to be *symmetric* if $(p \in \Omega \Rightarrow p^* \in \Omega)$. A *lottery* p is said to be symmetric if, whenever k and l are the indices of a partition and its inverse, $p_k = p_l$.

Axiom of Symmetry (S*).   Given a problem $e = \langle \Omega, u, u, \omega^* \rangle$ where Ω is symmetric and ω^* is symmetric, then $\varphi(e)$ is a symmetric lottery.[15]

The axiom S* is the obvious resource-based version of the Nash symmetry axiom. Note, in particular, that if the individuals have identical utility functions, and Ω is a symmetric set of lotteries, and ω^* is a symmetric lottery, then the utility possibilities set is a symmetric set in $\mathbf{R}^2$.

Axiom of Contraction Consistency (CC*).   Let $e = \langle \Omega, u^1, u^2, \omega^* \rangle$ and $e' = \langle \Omega', u^1, u^2, \omega^* \rangle$, with $\Omega' \subset \Omega$, and suppose $\varphi(e) \in \Omega'$. Then $\varphi(e') = \varphi(e)$.

This is exactly the motivation that Nash gave for his "independence of irrelevant alternatives" axiom: that if two problems differ only in that the set of lotteries for one is contained in the set of lotteries for the other, and if the solution on the problem with the bigger set lies in the smaller set, then that should also be the solution on the problem with the smaller set.

Pareto (P*).   If $e = \langle \Omega, u^1, u^2, \omega^* \rangle$, there does not exist a lottery $p \in \Omega$ such that $(u^1(p), u^2(p)) \geq (u^1(\varphi(e)), u^2(\varphi(e)))$.

We define:

Definition 2.5.   A finite collection of problems $\{e^1, e^2, \ldots, e^M\}$, where $e^i \in \mathcal{D}$ for all i is called a *regular* collection iff no two problems have individuals with the same pair of von Neumann–Morgenstern preferences, and no problem has the same von Neumann–Morgenstern preferences for both individuals.

We can now state:

Theorem 2.9.[16]   *Let $\{e^1, e^2, \ldots, e^M\}$ be a regular collection, and choose, for each e^i, an arbitrary Pareto optimal lottery $\sigma^i \in \Omega^i$. [$e^i = \langle \Omega^i, u^{1i}, u^{2i}, \omega^{*i} \rangle$.]*

---

15. There is a notational pitfall here. I have indicated that the two players have the same preferences (over objects in B) by assigning them each the utility function "u." But $u(p)$ means something different for each player: $u(p)$ will be the same number when p is a symmetric lottery. Thus, in particular, the threat point in e has equal utility coordinates, because ω^* is symmetric.

16. This theorem was originally presented in Roemer (1990), but the set-up and proof given there are incorrect. The errors are, I hope, eliminated in the version presented here.

Then there is a mechanism φ satisfying U*, S*, S.INV*, CC*, and P* such that $\varphi(e^i) = \sigma^i$ for all $i = 1, \ldots, M$. Furthermore, φ is continuous, in an appropriate topology, on the domain $\mathcal{D}$.

The theorem tells us that the Nash axioms, appropriately restated on a domain of economic environments, hardly restrict the mechanism at all, in precisely this sense: we can choose any regular collection of problems in the domain and choose arbitrary Pareto optimal lotteries in these problems, and there is a mechanism that obeys the axioms and chooses the specified lotteries as the solutions of the given problems. Furthermore, this can be done in a continuous way, so the mechanism does not jump around on $\mathcal{D}$.

If in addition to the axioms stated in Theorem 2.9 we impose the welfarism axiom, then there is only one mechanism that is admissible: the *Nash mechanism*, which assigns for each problem that lottery p^* that maximizes the product $(u^1(p) - u^1(\omega^*))(u^2(p) - u^2(\omega^*))$:

Theorem 2.10. *Let the set B contain at least one object. Let φ be a mechanism on $\mathcal{D}$ that satisfies U*, S*, S.INV*, CC*, P*, and W. Then φ is the Nash mechanism.*

Proof: The proof builds on the proof of Theorem 2.1. Note that the utility possibilities sets associated with problems in $\mathcal{D}$ are convex, compact sets, since the sets of lotteries Ω are compact and convex.

1. We begin with an arbitrary problem $e = \langle \Omega, u^1, u^2, \omega^* \rangle$ in $\mathcal{D}$ and a mechanism F satisfying the axioms. Let $\bar{p} \in \Omega$ be the "Nash lottery" in Ω, that is, the lottery that solves the problem

$$\max_{p \in \Omega} (u^1(p) - u^1(\omega^*))(u^2(p) - u^2(\omega^*)).$$

As in the proof of Theorem 2.1, construct the problem $e' = \langle \Omega, v^1, v^2, \omega^* \rangle$, where $v^1 = \alpha^1 u^1 + \beta^1$, $v^2 = \alpha^2 u^2 + \beta^2$, $v^1(\bar{p}) = 1 = v^2(\bar{p})$, and $v^1(\omega^*) = 0 = v^2(\omega^*)$: there are positive numbers α^1 and α^2 and numbers β^1 and β^2 such that this is true. Denote $\mathcal{A}(e') = T$: see Figure 2.1. [$\bar{p}$ remains the Nash lottery of the problem e'.]

2. The next step is to construct a problem in $\mathcal{D}$ whose utility possibilities set is the triangle R in Figure 2.1, as follows. Let $a \in B$, and choose utility functions $\hat{u}^1$ and $\hat{u}^2$ so that the coordinates of point A in Figure 2.1 are $(\hat{u}^1(\emptyset), \hat{u}^2(\{a\}))$, the coordinates of point B in Figure 2.1 are

$(\hat{u}^1(\{a\}), \hat{u}^2(\emptyset))$, and the coordinates of point C are $(\hat{u}^1(\emptyset), \hat{u}^2(\emptyset))$. Note that $\hat{u}^1$ and $\hat{u}^2$ have the same values on $\{a\}$ and $\emptyset$, and we may extend them to be identical on all subsets of B. Let Γ be the set of all lotteries which assign zero probability to all partitions in $\mathcal{B}$ except the partitions $(a, \emptyset, B \backslash a)$, $(\emptyset, a, B \backslash a)$, and $(\emptyset, \emptyset, B)$. Then the utility possibilities set associated with $\langle \Gamma, \hat{u}^1, \hat{u}^2 \rangle$ is precisely the triangle R of Figure 2.1; $\hat{\omega}$, the threat lottery, is chosen to give the same point in utility space as the threat point of the bargaining game associated with the set T in Figure 2.1. Define $\hat{e} = \langle \Gamma, \hat{u}^1, \hat{u}^2, \hat{\omega} \rangle$.

3. In fact, by construction, $\hat{e}$ is a symmetric bargaining problem, and axiom S* applies. By S* and P*, $F(\hat{e})$ is the lottery generating the utility point $(1, 1)$ in R. Write $F(\hat{e}) = \hat{p} \in \Gamma$.

4. Of course, $R \supset T$. Let $\Gamma' = \{p \in \Gamma \mid (\hat{u}^1(p), \hat{u}^2(p)) \in T\}$. Since T is compact and convex, so is Γ'. It follows that $\hat{e}' = \langle \Gamma', \hat{u}^1, \hat{u}^2, \hat{\omega} \rangle$ is a problem in $\mathcal{D}$. Compare $\hat{e}'$ with $\hat{e}$: by CC*, it follows that $F(\hat{e}') = \hat{p}$. Now apply welfarism (W) to the problems $\hat{e}'$ and e': since $\mathcal{A}(\hat{e}') = \mathcal{A}(e')$, it follows that $F(e')$ is that lottery generating the utility point $((\hat{u}^1(\hat{p}), \hat{u}^2(\hat{p})) = (1, 1)$.

5. Finally, apply S.INV* to the problems e' and e: it follows that $F(e)$ is indeed the Nash lottery $\bar{p}$, as was to be shown. ∎

We proceed to prove Theorem 2.9. The first step is to demonstrate the following mathematical fact.

Lemma 2.1. *Let $(\alpha^1, \beta^1), \ldots, (\alpha^M, \beta^M)$ be M distinct vectors in $\mathbf{R}_+^r \times \mathbf{R}_+^r$, where $\alpha^i, \beta^i \in \mathbf{R}_+^r$, $\alpha^i \neq \beta^i$ for all $i = 1, \ldots, M$. Let $\gamma^1, \gamma^2, \ldots, \gamma^M$ be M vectors in $\mathbf{R}_+^2$. Then there exists a continuous function $\psi : \mathbf{R}_+^r \times \mathbf{R}_+^r \to \mathbf{R}_+^2$ such that:*

(i) $\psi(\alpha^i, \beta^i) = \gamma^i$ *for all $i = 1, \ldots, M$;*

(ii) $\psi(\alpha, \alpha) = (1, 1)$ *for all $\alpha \in \mathbf{R}^r$.*

Proof:

1. Given any $(\alpha, \beta) \in \mathbf{R}_+^r \times \mathbf{R}_+^r$, we define $\psi(\alpha, \beta)$ as follows. Let d^i be the distance from (α, β) to (α^i, β^i), for $i = 1, \ldots, M$, and let d^0 be the distance from (α, β) to the closed subset $D = \{(\alpha, \alpha) \in \mathbf{R}_+^r \times \mathbf{R}_+^r\}$. Define the numbers λ^i, for $i = 0, 1, \ldots, M$, as follows:

$$\lambda^i = \frac{1/d^i}{\sum_j (1/d^j)}, \quad \text{if } d^j \neq 0 \text{ for all } j = 0, 1, \ldots, M, \text{ and}$$

$$\lambda^i = 1, \lambda^j = 0, \qquad\qquad \text{for } j \neq i, \text{ if } d^i = 0, \text{ for some } i.$$

Note that at most one of the distances d^i can be zero, since all the points (α^i, β^i) are distinct and none lies in D. Now define:

$$\psi(\alpha, \beta) = \lambda^0(1, 1) + \sum_{j=1}^M \lambda^j \gamma^j,$$

and observe that ψ satisfies conditions (i) and (ii) and maps into $\mathbf{R}_+^2$.

To see that ψ is continuous, consider a sequence of points $\{(a^l, b^l), l = 1, 2, \ldots\}$ converging to a point (a^∞, b^∞), where $a^l, b^l \in \mathbf{R}_+^r$. If $(a^\infty, b^\infty) \notin D$ and, for all i, $(\alpha^i, \beta^i) \neq (a^\infty, b^\infty)$, then the observation that $\psi(a^l, b^l)$ converges to $\psi(a^\infty, b^\infty)$ is straightforward. Suppose, however, that $(a^\infty, b^\infty) = (\alpha^k, \beta^k)$ for some k. Then $\psi(a^\infty, b^\infty) = \gamma^k$. Letting $d^{il} := \text{dist}((a^l, b^l), (\alpha^i, \beta^i))$ and

$$\lambda^{il} := \frac{1/d^{il}}{\sum_j (1/d^{jl})},$$

we have $d^{kl} \to 0$ while, for all $j \neq k$, d^{jl} does not approach zero; it follows that $\lambda^{kl} \to 1$ and $\lambda^{jl} \to 0$ for all $j \neq k$. Hence $\psi(a^l, b^l) \to \gamma^k$, which shows that ψ is continuous. A similar argument obtains if, finally, $(a^\infty, b^\infty) \in D$. ∎

We can now prove Theorem 2.9.

Proof of Theorem 2.9:

1. We are given a regular collection, where $e^i = \langle \Omega^i, u^{1i}, u^{2i}, \omega^{*i} \rangle$. Choose the von Neumann–Morgenstern utilities $\hat{u}^{1i}$ and $\hat{u}^{2i}$ for the two players such that $\hat{u}^{ji}(\omega^{*i}) = 0$ and $\hat{u}^{ji}(B) = 1$, for $j = 1, 2$. This is possible, since by the hypothesis U^*, each player would strictly prefer to receive all the objects to the lottery ω^{*i}. Now define $\alpha^i = (\hat{u}^{1i}(C^1), \ldots, \hat{u}^{1i}(C^n))$ and $\beta^i = (\hat{u}^{2i}(C^1), \ldots, \hat{u}^{2i}(C^n))$, where $\{C^h\}$ are the subsets of B. Define $\gamma^i = (\hat{u}^{1i}(\sigma^i), \hat{u}^{2i}(\sigma^i))$. By Lemma 2.1, there is a continuous function ψ satisfying conditions (i) and (ii) of the lemma.

2. Now let $e = \langle \Omega, u^1, u^2, \omega^* \rangle$ be any problem in $\mathcal{D}$, and let $e' = \langle \Omega, \hat{u}^1,$ $\hat{u}^2, \omega^* \rangle$ be defined by choosing the utility functions $\hat{u}^1$ and $\hat{u}^2$ as described in step 1. Define the vectors α and β as $\alpha = (\hat{u}^1(C^1), \ldots, \hat{u}^1(C^n))$ and $\beta = (\hat{u}^2(C^1), \ldots, \hat{u}^2(C^n))$. We define the action of the mechanism φ on e as follows. Recall that $\mathcal{A}(e')$ is the utility possibilities set generated by e'. Consider the ray from the origin in $\mathbf{R}^2$ through the point $\psi(\alpha, \beta)$; this ray intersects the Pareto frontier of $\mathcal{A}(e')$ in a point, call it A. Define $\psi(e)$ as that lottery in Ω that generates the utility point A. This defines φ on the domain $\mathcal{D}$. See Figure 2.10 for an illustration.

3. By property (i) of ψ, φ maps the problem e^i into σ^i for $i = 1, \ldots, M$. By property (ii), for any symmetric problem e, φ chooses the Pareto optimal symmetric point. By the definition of φ, S.INV* is satisfied—since all problems which are equivalent up to scale invariance have their solution defined by the same reference problem (with normalized von Neumann–Morgenstern preferences). CC* is satisfied, since if two problems are related by the premise of the CC* axiom, the solutions of their normalized problems lie on the same ray in utility space. Finally, the map φ induces a function in utility space which is continuous in the data of the economic environment. ∎

In sum, when Nash bargaining theory is restated on the domain of economic environments that motivates the Nash axioms, those axioms are weak, in the sense that many mechanisms exist that satisfy them. Theo-

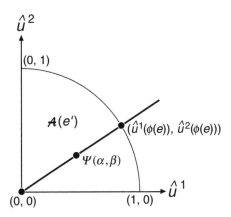

Figure 2.10

rems 2.9 and 2.10 together show the power of the axiom of welfarism. Thus, we must consider more carefully the justification of the axiom of welfarism, which does so much of the work in the theorems discussed earlier in this chapter.

Before turning to that consideration, I will mention a theorem of Binmore (1987) that gets a very different result from Theorem 2.9 when modeling Nash's axioms on a domain of economic environments. Binmore considers a two-person, two-commodity world, where initially person 1 owns an amount of fish $\bar{f}$ and person 2 owns an amount of wheat $\bar{w}$. Lotteries over trades in fish and wheat between them are considered, and the players have von Neumann–Morgenstern preferences over these lotteries, with some restrictions (quasi-concavity of preference). Let u be an admissible profile of preferences and $\mathcal{E}$ a set of possible trades between the players and lotteries on those trades ($\mathcal{E}$ need not consist of all physically feasible trades and lotteries). It is further specified that a pair $(u, \mathcal{E})$ is an admissible element in the domain only if the Walrasian equilibrium of that economy (with the given initial endowments) is unique and lies in $\mathcal{E}$. Let $\mathcal{G}$ be the domain of such problems (all with the specified initial endowment). A *solution* is a map F that associates each element $(u, \mathcal{E}) \in \mathcal{G}$ with a trade in $\mathcal{E}$. Note that F always chooses a trade, not a lottery of trades. Call Binmore's domain axiom U^B. The axioms of Pareto efficiency, scale invariance, and symmetry are basically the same as the ones in Theorem 2.9, translated so as to apply to the domain $\mathcal{G}$, and so I shall represent them as P*, S.INV*, and S*, respectively.

The contraction consistency axiom that Binmore uses, however, is much stronger than CC*. It really consists of two axioms. The first is the equivalent of CC*, and I shall denote it by CC* (always with the understanding that the axiom is stated on the domain $\mathcal{G}$). Let ω^* stand for the initial endowment point. The other part of the axiom I will call:

Axiom of Binmore Consistency (CC^B).   Let $(u, \mathcal{E})$ and $(u', \mathcal{E})$ be two elements of $\mathcal{G}$, with $s = F((u, \mathcal{E}))$ and $s' = F((u', \mathcal{E}))$, and let $u(s) = u'(s)$ and $u(\omega^*) = u'(\omega^*)$. Further, suppose that for all $t \in \mathcal{E}, u(t) \leqq u'(t)$. Then $s = s'$.

The axiom says that if preferences differ in the postulated way on two elements in the domain with the same set of possible lotteries, then the solution just chooses the same trade in those two problems. The utilities of both players in one problem must, for all lotteries, be less than or equal to the utilities of both players in the other, with equality at least at the initial endowment point and the solution. The reader will note that, if she draws a picture of the utility possibilities sets to represent the premise of CC^B, she will get the familiar picture of Nash's contraction consistency axiom. Thus CC^B and CC^* are both statements of contraction consistency on economic environments: they each describe a special case of pairs of economic environments that generate nested utility possibilities sets.

Theorem 2.11 (Binmore 1987, Theorem 1).   *Let F satisfy U^B, S.INV*, S*, P*, CC*, and CC^B. Then $F((u, \mathcal{E}))$ is the Walrasian equilibrium of the economy $(u, \mathcal{E})$.*

We see, then, that the axiom CC^B suffices, in addition to the other axioms of Theorem 2.9, completely to determine the solution F as the Walrasian equilibrium allocation. Despite the elegance of the result, it is not clear that it advances our understanding of the problem of distributive justice, conceived of either as mutual advantage or as impartiality. For Binmore offers no justification of the axiom CC^B, as descriptive of either bargaining or fairness, nor is any such justification apparent to me.

2.6   Conclusion

In this section I shall discuss two items of unfinished business: the plausibility of the axiom of welfarism, and the plausibility of the conception of justice as mutual advantage.

2.6.1   The Plausibility of the Axiom of Welfarism

There are two questions: is the axiom of welfarism a good assumption for a theory of bargaining, and is it a good assumption for a theory of distributive justice?

As I wrote earlier, the modern approach to bargaining theory begins with the specification of the economic bargaining problem and models the process of alternating concessions directly (for example, Rubinstein 1982), instead, à la Nash, of imposing axioms on the bargaining solution, viewed as a function on the space of all problems. In the noncooperative formulation it is assumed that players each try to maximize utility, but this is certainly not equivalent to welfarism, which is the different statement that the solution should depend only on the utility possibilities set and the threat point. In the Binmore-Rubinstein-Wolinsky model, for example, welfarism holds, but this is deduced, not postulated. Thus, given the state of the art in mathematical bargaining theory, one could conclude that Nash's assumption of welfarism has "microfoundations," that is, it can be deduced from more primitive assumptions about the behavior of rational bargainers. Against this view, however, one must mention the ideas of Schelling, in particular, the view that "salience" plays an important role in bargaining. An example of a salient solution is to split the prize equally (if it is divisible), or if there are several indivisible prizes, to split them into two bundles so that the market values of the two are roughly equal. Neither of these two solutions is welfarist: that is, from knowing the utility possibilities set and the threat point, one cannot implement either of these proposals. Alternatively put, it is possible to specify two economic environments which have the same utility possibilities sets and threat outcomes, but in which equal division of the prize or prizes will lead to different outcomes in utility space.

I must mention as well, at this point, one important view about the consequences of bargaining in a *large economy* with many players, each of whom enters the game with an endowment of goods. One of the classical proposals for the solution of an economic bargaining problem among many players is the core of the economy. An allocation is in the core of the economy if and only if no coalition of traders can, by "withdrawing" from the game with the private endowments of its members, arrange trades among themselves with the consequence that each member ends up better off than at the proposed allocation. Thus the core focuses on the possibility of coalition formation, a phenomenon that is ignored in the multiperson Nash bargaining problem. A basic result in general equilibrium theory is that, for economies with an infinite number of traders, the core consists of exactly the Walrasian equilibria of the economy, and as economies get large, the core "shrinks" to the set of Walrasian equilibria. (See, for discussion of this theorem, Hildenbrand and Kirman [1988].) But the mechanism that assigns to an economy its set of Walrasian equilibria is not welfarist: one cannot, that is, find the Walrasian equilibria—or the utility points associated with these equilibria—simply from information on the utility possibilities set and the initial endowment allocation of the economy. An alternative solution for the bargaining problem, which also takes serious account of coalition formation, is the "bargaining set," proposed by von Neumann and Morgenstern. Mas-Colell (1989) has shown that, for large economies, the bargaining set also shrinks to the set of Walrasian equilibria. Thus it is not at all obvious that welfarism is a property of the solution to the many-person bargaining problem.

It is even less arguable, I think, that welfarism is an attractive axiom for distributive justice. We have seen, in Chapter 1, Sen's argument against welfarism, but the point here is quite different. Sen's example (of the sadistic hungry individual) arises when individuals have preferences that are not self-regarding—they derive pleasure from interfering in the lives of others or from the sufferings of another. For purposes of studying distributive justice, let us assume that all citizens have self-regarding preferences—if we can at least solve *that* problem, we will have gotten a long way. Then one of Sen's criticisms of welfarism dissolves.[17] But the criticisms of §2.5 do not. The most obvious example is that, surely, the mechanism which assigns the Walrasian equilibrium from equal division of the social endowment should be a candidate for distributive justice. But this mechanism does not satisfy the axiom of welfarism. Put equivalently, in the Nash framework, this solution does not exist. The welfarist axiom rules out "most" mechanisms which can be defined on the domain of economic environments (Theorem 2.9). All this does not mean that, in the end, we will conclude that the mechanism that implements distributive justice is not welfarist; rather, it means that if that mechanism is welfarist, the fact should be deduced from more basic and primitive assumptions, not postulated *ab initio*.

2.6.2 *Justice as Mutual Advantage*

The question posed in §2.1, whether justice is properly conceived of as mutual advantage or impartiality, is purely philosophical and, as such, is beyond the scope of this study. Readers are referred to Gauthier (1986) for an argument *pro* justice as mutual advantage, and Barry (1989) for an argument *contra*. Nevertheless, some brief remarks are in order. As Ronald Dworkin points out, all contemporary theories of justice begin by proclaiming that all people (or at least all citizens of the community under discussion) are to be treated as equals. The differences between theories arise when the perquisites of this equality are delineated. Any theory of justice as mutual advantage, or as Gibbard (1991) calls it, "justice as ideal bargaining outcome," must therefore present the ideal bargaining problem, whose

---

17. But certainly not all his criticisms. Sen also criticizes welfarism, for example, because it gives too few resources to the "tamed housewife" who has learned to be happy with what others would call truncated opportunities, a trait she has adopted perhaps due to cognitive dissonance. Nosey preferences are not why welfarism is a poor guide to justice in the case of the tamed housewife.

outcome is to be the distributively just solution, sterilized of its real-world aspects that compromise initial equality of persons. For instance, the initial endowments of bargainers that define the threat point should themselves be just—not the consequences of plundering others (unless we would consider plundering a legitimate action flowing from one's morally legitimate use of one's strength to advance one's position). Should inequalities in "bargaining skill" be laundered out, or are those inequalities justified by virtue of being personal talents to which their holders are morally entitled? Should aspects of the players' preferences be laundered if they were developed under conditions of severe inequality of opportunity? Suppose, for example, one player has a very high rate of time discount, a trait that was imprinted by his cultural community, who themselves "rationally" adopted high rates of time preference because they lived in such miserable conditions of exploitation that life expectancy was very short. In the present bargaining problem, a high rate of time preference handicaps our subject, who is not willing to forestall consumption long enough to engage in a protracted sequence of alternating offers, and hence accepts a poor split offered by his opponent in the early stages of the game. My own view is that a great deal of laundering, of both resource endowments and preferences, would be necessary to render the players appropriately "equal" in a bargaining problem whose outcome could be described as just. This is the problem Rawls encountered in trying to propose the morally appropriate conditions under which the social contract should be negotiated: he ended up eradicating all differences between persons and posing the problem of justice as a *decision* problem of one soul behind a thick veil of ignorance (see Chapter 5).

Perhaps I display my prejudice that "justice as mutual advantage" is no justice. Although it may be possible to launder preferences and endowments so much that the just allocation can be captured as an outcome of the bargaining problem, I think the exercise would end up being a roundabout way of specifying justice as impartiality. From a mathematical viewpoint, this poses no problem: I mean the obvious point that, given an economic environment and any Pareto optimal allocation for it that we might consider just, there always exists a choice of threat point and of von Neumann–Morgenstern utilities for the players such that the prechosen point is the Nash bargaining solution for that environment. (In fact, there are an infinite number of specifications of preferences and threat points that will lead to the "right" solution.) It is not clear to me that the morally appropriate specification of the threat point and laundered preferences would not simply carry out this program. And with such steril-ized (or, rather, bleached) preferences and endowments, it does not seem appropriate to describe the "game" as one of "mutual advantage," as the characters in the contest would be quite different from real persons who pursue their own interests in an aggressive and ruthless (if rule-abiding) way. Laundering does not seem an inappropriate procedure, however, if one's aim is to model impartiality, for in that case it is natural to ask citi-zens to put themselves in the shoes of others, that is, to disregard aspects of their own situation (endowments, preferences).

I should, however, remark that "justice as ideal bargaining outcome" and "justice as social contract" are not equivalent, and the above considerations do not obviously apply against the latter. For a social contract may involve people making concessions to each other not because they rationally must (in the sense that not doing so would bring about an impasse in bargain-ing, resulting in the threat utilities), but because they (ethically) should by virtue of living in a community with others.

3

Axiomatic Mechanism Theory
on Economic Environments

3.1 Introduction

In this chapter I attempt to resolve the criticism against Nash-type bargaining theory lodged in §2.6.1. The motivations for the axioms in Nash theory come from resource-based intuitions, but the axioms, stated in utility space, restrict the action of the solution F far more than the intuitions warrant. Working in utility space eliminates many plausible mechanisms from consideration, mechanisms like "equal division Walrasian equilibrium (EDWE)"—it is impossible to define equal division of resources when no resources exist in the class of environments under consideration. We saw two concrete instances of the trouble one gets into from working in utility space: the Rolls Royce problem and Theorem 2.9. That theorem showed that, if we work on a domain of economic environments, then the economic counterparts of the Nash axioms hardly restrict the behavior of the allocation mechanism at all. Evidently when the Nash axioms are stated "correctly," that is, in a way which captures precisely the economic intuitions that motivate them, they are far too weak to characterize a unique allocation mechanism.

Here I show how we can recover the powerful characterization theorems of Chapter 2 on economic environments. The key is to use an axiom that enforces a certain kind of "dimensional consistency" on the allocation mechanism. (We have seen a version of this axiom already in the social choice context, COAD.) This axiom, called CONRAD, is a weak version of welfarism—sufficiently weak to be arguably a reasonable axiom in the context of distributive justice (as welfarism, I claimed, is not). The CONRAD axiom, along with other plausible axioms, turns out to imply welfarism. This chapter could be subtitled "Economic Foundations of Welfarism."

The domain of Nash bargaining theory, consisting of objects of the form (S, d), is informationally impoverished. We cannot refer to resources or utility functions in this domain, only to allocations of utility. The domain of economic environments is far richer, enabling us to refer to resources (and therefore to property rights) and to utility functions. But there is reason to believe, in the theory of distributive justice, that we might want even more information, namely, the *names* of goods. Some goods satisfy needs and some desires, and a theory of distributive justice arguably should distinguish between these kinds of satisfaction. In §3.5, I discuss axiomatic mechanism theory on environments with named goods, and in §3.6 I arrive at a perhaps sobering conclusion.

3.2   The Domain of Economic Environments

In §2.5 we worked on a domain of economic environments consisting of sets of lotteries and von Neumann–Morgenstern utility functions over lotteries. Here I shall work on a more conventional domain for distributive justice, where an environment consists of a problem in which a given bundle of resources must be divided among H persons with given utility functions. Let $\mathcal{U}^{(n)}$ be the set of all (real-valued) monotone, concave, continuous functions defined on $\mathbf{R}^n_+$, such that $u(0) = 0$. An *economic environment* is a vector

$$\mathcal{E} = \langle n; \bar{x}; u^1, \ldots, u^H \rangle,$$

where $n \geq 1$ is an integer, $\bar{x} \in \mathbf{R}^n_+$ and $u^h \in \mathcal{U}^{(n)}$. The interpretation is that $\bar{x}$ is the aggregate endowment vector to be allocated among H individuals with utility functions $\{u^h\}$. The theorems in this chapter are true for environments with any finite number of agents; I shall present them for two-person environments for simplicity's sake.[1]

What cannot be avoided is admitting economic environments of arbitrary finite dimension. Thus a key assumption of the analysis is that the domain consists of all environments $\mathcal{E}$, where n can be any positive inte-

---

1. In fact, whenever a classical theorem in bargaining theory is true for H players, its reformulation on economic environments is also true for H players.

ger, $\bar{x} \in \mathbf{R}^n_+$ is arbitrary, and u, $v \in \mathcal{U}^{(n)}$ are arbitrary. Let $\Sigma^{(n)}$ be the class of all admissible economic environments of dimension n. Let $\Sigma = \cup_n \Sigma^{(n)}$.

It is often convenient to work on the subclass of "strictly comprehensive" environments. Let $\mathcal{A}(\mathcal{E})$ be the *utility possibilities set* of $\mathcal{E}$,

$$\mathcal{A}(\mathcal{E}) = \{(\bar{u}, \bar{v}) \in \mathbf{R}^2_+ \mid \exists \bar{x}^1, \bar{x}^2 \in \mathbf{R}^n_+, \bar{x}^1 + \bar{x}^2 \leqq \bar{x}, u(\bar{x}^1)$$

$$= \bar{u}, v(\bar{x}^2) = \bar{v}\}.$$

$\mathcal{A}(\mathcal{E})$ is a closed, comprehensive, convex set in $\mathbf{R}^2_+$ containing the origin. It is convex since u and v are concave; it is comprehensive since the utility functions are continuous and goods can be freely disposed of. Call $\mathcal{E}$ a *strictly comprehensive* environment if the Pareto frontier of $\mathcal{A}(\mathcal{E})$ contains no level segments. Let $\Gamma^{(n)}$ be the class of all n-dimensional strictly comprehensive economic environments, and let $\Gamma = \cup_n \Gamma^{(n)}$.

The analysis here is limited to economic environments without production. This is, however, also an assumption made for simplicity's sake. Much (if not all) of the theory can be generalized to economic environments with convex production sets. One can substitute for the vector $\bar{x}$ in the definition of an economic environment an arbitrary convex set Ω lying in $\mathbf{R}^{2n}$, which can be interpreted as the production set for the economy.

An *allocation mechanism* F is a correspondence which associates to each economic environment $\mathcal{E} = \langle n, \bar{x}, u, v \rangle$ a set of feasible allocations. It will be assumed, however, that F induces a function in utility space; therefore F is said to be *essentially a function*. That is, if $(x^1, x^2) \in F(\mathcal{E})$ and $(\hat{x}^1, \hat{x}^2) \in F(\mathcal{E})$, then $u(x^1) = u(\hat{x}^1)$ and $v(x^2) = v(\hat{x}^2)$. Call the induced utility mapping μ_F:

$$\mu_F(\mathcal{E}) := (u(F^1(\mathcal{E})), v(F^2(\mathcal{E}))),$$

where $F^i(\mathcal{E})$ is the set of bundles which F may assign to agent i. The notation $u(F^1(\mathcal{E}))$ is unambiguous since F is essentially a function. Furthermore, it is assumed that F chooses *all* the allocations associated with a given point in utility space. That is,

$$(x^1, x^2) \in F(\mathcal{E}) \text{ and } u(x^1) = u(\hat{x}^1), v(x^2) = v(\hat{x}^2),$$

$$\text{then } (\hat{x}^1, \hat{x}^2) \in F(\mathcal{E}).$$

An allocation mechanism having this property will be called a *full correspondence*. Fullness is simply the assumption of Pareto indifference (PI): if two allocations deliver the same utility levels for the individuals, and one is acceptable, so is the other.

The theorems will all be proved on a slightly more restricted domain than Σ or Γ. Let $\hat{\mathcal{U}}^{(n)}$ be the class of all functions u in $\mathcal{U}^{(n)}$ such that

(3.1) $\forall x \in \mathbf{R}_+^n \lim_{t \to \infty} \frac{1}{t} u(tx) = 0.$

Let $\hat{\Sigma}^{(n)}$ be the class of all environments in $\Sigma^{(n)}$ whose utility functions are taken from $\hat{\mathcal{U}}^{(n)}$. Define $\hat{\Gamma}^{(n)}$ analogously and let $\hat{\Sigma} = \cup_n \hat{\Sigma}^{(n)}$ and $\hat{\Gamma} = \cup_n \hat{\Gamma}^{(n)}$. $\hat{\Gamma}$ and $\hat{\Sigma}$ are the domains for which the theorems are proved. It is a technical point to extend the theorems to the larger domains Σ and Γ. The domain assumptions are:

Axiom $D^{\hat{\Sigma}}$. The allocation mechanism F is a full correspondence which is essentially a function and is defined on the class of economic environments $\hat{\Sigma}$.

Axiom $D^{\hat{\Gamma}}$. The allocation mechanism F is a full correspondence which is essentially a function and is defined on the class of economic environments $\hat{\Gamma}$.

I shall comment on the relationship of these domain assumptions to the Nash domain assumption U below in §3.5. In a sense that will be then made clear, the present domain assumptions are stronger than assumption U.

3.3   Axioms and Theorems on Economic Environments

In this section, I state axioms which are weaker than their Nash-type counterparts, and which capture underlying resource-based intuitions that motivated the Nash-type axioms. To review, I state two of the Nash-type axioms:

Axiom of Welfarism (W).   Let $\mathcal{E}$, $\mathcal{E}' \in \hat{\Sigma}$ be economic environments with $\mathcal{A}(\mathcal{E}) = \mathcal{A}(\mathcal{E}')$. Then $\mu_F(\mathcal{E}) = \mu_F(\mathcal{E}')$.

Axiom W says that an allocation mechanism must treat identically (in terms of utility distribution) any two economic environments which have the same utility possibilities set. Note this axiom is stated to hold on $\hat{\Sigma}$; thus it is extremely strong, as it holds even if $\mathcal{E}$ and $\mathcal{E}'$ are of different dimension.

Axiom of Monotonicity (MON).   Let $\mathcal{E}$, $\mathcal{E}' \in \hat{\Sigma}$ be economic environments with $\mathcal{A}(\mathcal{E}) \subset \mathcal{A}(\mathcal{E}')$. Then $\mu_F \mathcal{E} \leqq \mu_F(\mathcal{E}')$.

MON says that as long as one utility possibilities set is contained in another, then neither utility should decrease under F's action in the "more abundant" environment. Note how inadmissibly strong MON is: for instance, it commits the mechanism to increases in both individuals' utilities even when the underlying economic environments have commodity spaces of different dimension. Thus MON cannot be justified by reference to an increase in the aggregate resource vector, since the resource vectors in $\mathcal{E}$ and $\mathcal{E}'$ are generally in different commodity spaces. It is therefore an axiom than can have only a welfarist motivation.

Now for the resource-based axioms. The first is an axiom that says that if the resource endowment increases, no one shall be worse off in the new, more abundant, environment.

Axiom of Resource Monotonicity (RMON). Let

$$\mathcal{E} = \langle n, \bar{x}, u, v \rangle$$
$$\mathcal{E}' = \langle n, \bar{x}', u, v \rangle$$

be two economic environments and $\bar{x}' \geq \bar{x}$. Then $\mu_F(\mathcal{E}') \geqq \mu_F(\mathcal{E})$.

RMON commits the mechanism to increasing (weakly) both utilities only when the two environments $\mathcal{E}$ and $\mathcal{E}'$ are the same except for an unambiguous increase in resources. RMON is a weakening of the Nash-type axiom MON. MON, stated on the domain of economic environments, commits the mechanism to (weakly) increasing both utilities even when $\mathcal{E}$ and $\mathcal{E}'$ differ in utility *functions* and in dimension of *commodity space*—as long as $\mathcal{A}(\mathcal{E}') \supset \mathcal{A}(\mathcal{E})$.

I shall adopt the shorthand of referring to the set of allocation mechanisms that satisfy an axiom by the name of that axiom. Thus, for instance, RMON means "the set of allocation mechanisms satisfying RMON." Formally, the strength of MON relative to RMON is stated as MON $\subset$ RMON. If a mechanism satisfies MON, then it surely satisfies RMON, but not conversely.

Definition 3.1. In an economic environment $\mathcal{E} = \langle n, \bar{x}, u, v \rangle$ an agent is said *not to like good* j iff he is indifferent to the amount of good j he consumes, for any levels of consumption of the other goods.

Axiom of Individual Resource Monotonicity (I.RMON). Let $\mathcal{E} = \langle n, \bar{x}, u, v \rangle$ and $\mathcal{E}' = \langle n, \bar{x}', u, v \rangle$, where $\bar{x}' \geq \bar{x}$ and $\bar{x}'_j > \bar{x}_j$ only for goods j not liked by the first (second) agent. Then $\mu_F^2(\mathcal{E}') \geq \mu_F^2(\mathcal{E})(\mu_F^1(\mathcal{E}') \geq \mu_F^1(\mathcal{E}))$.

Note that I.RMON is an economic axiom that might motivate the Kalai-Smorodinsky axiom IMON. In $\mathcal{E}'$, some goods are more abundant than in $\mathcal{E}$, but only goods that just one of the individuals likes. The axiom states that that individual's utility should not decrease in the more abundant environment. Formally, we have IMON $\subset$ I.RMON (draw the utility sets associated with $\mathcal{E}$ and $\mathcal{E}'$ and see what IMON implies).

Axiom of Economic Symmetry (Sy). If $\mathcal{E} = \langle n, \bar{x}, u, u \rangle$ then $(\bar{x}/2, \bar{x}/2) \in F(\mathcal{E})$.

Sy says that when the two individuals have the same utility function, the mechanism splits the resources equally between them. Note S $\subset$ Sy.

Axiom of Cardinal Noncomparability (CNC). If $\mathcal{E} = \langle n, \bar{x}, u, v \rangle$ and $\mathcal{E}' = \langle n, \bar{x}, \alpha u, \beta v \rangle$ for $\alpha, \beta \in \mathbf{R}_{++}$, then $F(\mathcal{E}) = F(\mathcal{E}')$.

Note S.INV $\subset$ CNC. As I said in Chapter 2, it is really the axiom CNC that Nash intended when he wrote the much more powerful axiom S.INV.

Axiom of Economic Continuity (ECONT). For any dimension n, μ_F is a continuous function in its arguments $\bar{x}$, u, and v, with the topology of pointwise convergence for the functional arguments.

Note CONT $\subset$ ECONT.

Finally, we state the key consistency axiom. Note that no axiom stated thus far ensures any coherence of the mechanism F as the dimension n of the economic environment changes. The next axiom imposes such coherence.

Axiom of Consistency of Resource Allocation across Dimension (CONRAD). Let $\mathcal{E} = \langle n + m; (\bar{x}, \bar{y}); u, v \rangle$ be an environment with $u, v \in \hat{\mathcal{U}}^{(n+m)}$ and let $((\hat{x}^1, \hat{y}^1), (\hat{x}^2, \hat{y}^2)) \in F(\mathcal{E})$, where each of the y-goods ($j = n + 1, \ldots, n + m$) is liked by at most one of the agents. Define u^*, v^* by

$$\forall x \in \mathbf{R}^n_+, \qquad u^*(x) = u(x, \hat{y}^1)$$
$$v^*(x) = v(x, \hat{y}^2).$$

If $u^*(0) = v^*(0) = 0$ then $u^*, v^* \in \hat{\mathcal{U}}^{(n)}$ and in this case consider the admissible environment $\mathcal{E}^* = \langle n, \bar{x}, u^*, v^* \rangle$. If $\mathcal{A}(\mathcal{E}^*) = \mathcal{A}(\mathcal{E})$ then $(\hat{x}^1, \hat{x}^2) \in F(\mathcal{E}^*)$.

Note, first, that W $\subset$ CONRAD. For CONRAD commits the mechanism to choosing resource allocations in $\mathcal{E}$ and $\mathcal{E}^*$ which generate the same point in utility space when these two environments are related to each other in a certain intimate way. CONRAD appears to be a much weakened version of W.

CONRAD enforces the same kind of dimensional consistency as does the COAD axiom (§1.5). I shall state the axiom verbally. Suppose the mechanism F is asked to choose an allocation in an $n + m$ dimensional environment, where the last m resources are "personalized"—each is liked by at most one individual. F chooses an allocation $((\hat{x}^1, \hat{y}^1), (\hat{x}^2, \hat{y}^2))$. Now fix the y goods at the allocation $(\hat{y}^1, \hat{y}^2)$, and consider the restriction of u and v to the lower dimensional space $\mathbf{R}^n$. Were the mechanism to be asked to distribute just the x goods ($\bar{x}$) between individuals with these restricted utility functions, it would again choose the allocation $\hat{x}$.

At this point, I ask the reader to accept CONRAD simply as an arguably attractive kind of dimensional consistency. In Chapter 7, we shall see that CONRAD in fact has an interpretation that is relevant for Dworkin's theory of resource egalitarianism.

Finally, a stronger version of CONRAD is sometimes needed:

Axiom of Strong Consistency of Resource Allocation across Dimension (SCONRAD). Let $\mathcal{E} = \langle n + m; (\bar{x}, \bar{y}); u, v \rangle$ be an environment with $u, v \in \hat{\mathcal{U}}^{(n+m)}$ and let $((\hat{x}^1, \hat{y}^1), (\hat{x}^2, \hat{y}^2)) \in F(\mathcal{E})$, where each of the y-goods ($j = n + 1, \ldots, n + m$) is liked by at most one of the agents. Define u^*, v^* by

$$\forall x \in \mathbf{R}^n_+, \qquad u^*(x) = u(x, \hat{y}^1)$$
$$v^*(x) = v(x, \hat{y}^2).$$

If $u^*(0) = v^*(0) = 0$ then $u^*, v^* \in \hat{\mathcal{U}}^{(n)}$ and in this case consider the admissible environment $\mathcal{E}^* = \langle n, \bar{x}, u^*, v^* \rangle$. Then $(\hat{x}^1, \hat{x}^2) \in F(\mathcal{E}^*)$.

The strength of SCONRAD lies in dropping the requirement, present in CONRAD, that the restricted economic environment $\mathcal{E}^*$ have the same utility possibilities set as the original environment $\mathcal{E}$.

By drawing a picture in utility space of what SCONRAD says, the reader will note that SCONRAD is a weak version of the Nash contraction consistency axiom CC: CC $\subset$ SCONRAD.

We may now state several theorems. F^N is the Nash mechanism (that selects the resource allocations at which the product of utilities is max-

imized), F^{KS} is the Kalai-Smorodinsky mechanism (that selects the resource allocations that generate the utility point at which the line connecting the ideal point and the origin intersects the Pareto frontier), and E
is the egalitarian mechanism (that chooses those resource allocations at
which utility is equalized at the highest possible level). A *dictatorship* is a
mechanism that assigns all of the goods to one individual.

Theorem 3.1. $D^{\hat{\Sigma}} \cap SCONRAD \cap PO \cap CNC \cap Sy = \{F^N\}.$

Theorem 3.2. $D^{\hat{\Gamma}} \cap CONRAD \cap RMON \cap PO \cap Sy = \{E\}.$

Theorem 3.3. $D^{\hat{\Gamma}} \cap CONRAD \cap CNC \cap Sy \cap PO \cap I.RMON = \{F^{KS}\}.$

Theorem 3.4. $D^{\hat{\Gamma}} \cap CONRAD \cap RMON \cap PO \cap CNC = \{the \ dictatorships\}.$

Theorem 3.5. $D^{\hat{\Sigma}} \cap CONRAD \cap RMON \cap WPO \cap Sy \cap ECONT = \{E\}.$

These theorems recover the characterization results of Theorems 2.1,
2.4, and 2.6, but with axioms that are faithful to the resource-based
intuitions that motivated the Nash-type axioms of Chapter 2. They thus
constitute a generalization of Nash-type bargaining theory to economic
environments. They are actually not stronger results than their Nash-type
counterparts, however, for although the "substantive" axioms here are
weaker than their Nash-type counterparts, the domain axiom is, as I remarked earlier, stronger.

What is the interpretation of the utility functions in these economic environments? In Theorems 3.1, 3.3, and 3.4, the utility functions are any
cardinal noncomparable utility functions; they are not conveniently interpreted as von Neumann–Morgenstern utilities, as the space on which they
operate is not a set of lotteries. In Theorems 3.2 and 3.5, we may assume
that the utility functions are absolutely measurable and comparable, since
no invariance axiom is needed for the results.

Indeed, as we shall see, Theorem 3.2 is true even when the utility functions are restricted to a smaller domain, which I call $\hat{U}^P$, consisting of
that subset of $\hat{U}$ in which the utility functions are bounded above by unity
[that is, $u(x) \leq 1$ for all x]. A function u in $\hat{U}^P$ can be given the following interpretation: $u(x)$ is the degree to which or probability that one's
life plan will be fulfilled when allotted a resource vector x. The condition
"$u(0) = 0$" states that, with no resources, the probability of fulfilling one's
life plan is zero. Thus we may interpret Theorem 3.2 as saying that if distributive justice obeys CONRAD and requires Pareto optimality, resource

monotonicity, and symmetry, then it must equalize the degrees to which or probabilities that individuals fulfill their life plans.

Finally, I remark on the relationship between CONRAD and welfarism. Although CONRAD may appear to be significantly weaker than welfarism, we have:

Theorem 3.6. *If F obeys $D^{\hat{\Gamma}}$ or $D^{\hat{\Sigma}}$ and CONRAD, then it satisfies W on those domains.*

Since these domain axioms include the fact that F is a full correspondence (that is, Pareto indifference), Theorem 3.6 is an analogue to Lemma 1.4. Theorem 3.6 provides an economic foundation for welfarism. It is a more compelling foundation for welfarism than Lemma 1.1, because the domain assumption U of Lemma 1.1 is both extremely powerful and unacceptable from the economic point of view, as I pointed out in §1.4—for U does not even require utility functions to be monotone increasing in resources, let alone concave. The appeal of the theorems in this chapter is that they hold on domains where the utility functions are economically reasonable— they are monotonic, concave, continuous functions. The relative difficulty of the proofs that follow is due to this economically meaningful domain restriction.

3.4   Proofs of Theorems

These theorems were originally proved in Roemer (1988). The proofs that follow are essentially equivalent to the proofs presented in that article, with one amendment. In the article, I relied on a result of Billera and Bixby (1973) (not the simple Lemma 3.2 below, which also is due to Billera and Bixby). That result states that any comprehensive, convex set in $\mathbf{R}^H$ can be represented as the utility possibilities set for an economic environment in which each of the H utility functions is concave, monotone, and continuous. In the following proofs, I avoid using that result. For this reason, the following proofs are more elementary than the ones in Roemer (1988).[2]

---

2. There is another reason to avoid using the Billera-Bixby representation result. The domain of utility functions that I employ, for which Condition (3.1) holds, is not exactly the same domain of functions that Billera-Bixby use. Thus rigor would require that I demonstrate the Billera-Bixby construction with Condition (3.1). I avoid this problem by proceeding as I do below.

We shall prove Theorem 3.6 first, and use it to deduce the other theorems. The proofs rely on two basic lemmata.

Lemma 3.1 (Howe 1987). *Let $u, v \in \hat{\mathcal{U}}^{(n)}$ and $u \geq v$ on $\mathbf{R}_+^n$. Then*

$$\exists w \in \hat{\mathcal{U}}^{(n+1)}, \quad \text{such that}$$

$$\forall x \in R_+^n, \qquad u(x) = w(x, 1)$$

$$v(x) = w(x, 0).$$

Remark. There is no simple representation for the function w in terms of u and v. For a proof of Lemma 3.1, readers should consult Howe (1987).

Corollary 3.1. *Let $u, v \in \hat{\mathcal{U}}^{P(n)}$ and $u \geq v$ on $\mathbf{R}_+^n$. Then*

$$\exists w \in \hat{\mathcal{U}}^{P(n+1)}, \quad \text{such that}$$

$$\forall x \in R_+^n, \qquad u(x) = w(x, 1)$$

$$v(x) = w(x, 0).$$

Proof of corollary: Since $\hat{\mathcal{U}}^{P(n)} \subset \hat{\mathcal{U}}^{(n)}$, it follows from Lemma 3.1 that there exists a function $w^* \in \hat{\mathcal{U}}^{(n+1)}$ such that $u(x) = w^*(x, 1)$ and $v(x) = w^*(x, 0)$. Define $w(x, r) = \min(w^*(x, r), u(x))$. The minimum of concave functions is concave, so w is concave. The reader can easily verify that w is monotonic in x and r, and is bounded by 1. Therefore $w \in \hat{\mathcal{U}}^{P(n+1)}$. w is the required function. ∎

Lemma 3.2 (Billera and Bixby 1973). *Let $\mathcal{E}_1, \mathcal{E}_2 \in \hat{\Sigma}$:*

$$\mathcal{E}_1 = \langle n, \bar{x}, u^1, v^1 \rangle$$
$$\mathcal{E}_2 = \langle m, \bar{y}, u^2, v^2 \rangle.$$

Define the environment $\mathcal{E}_1 \wedge \mathcal{E}_2 \in \hat{\Sigma}^{(n+m)}$ by

$$\mathcal{E}_1 \wedge \mathcal{E}_2 = \langle n + m, (\bar{x}, \bar{y}), u^*(x, y), v^*(x, y) \rangle,$$

where

$$u^*(x, y) := \min(u^1(x), u^2(y))$$
$$v^*(x, y) := \min(v^1(x), v^2(y)).$$

Then $\mathcal{A}(\mathcal{E}_1 \wedge \mathcal{E}_2) = \mathcal{A}(\mathcal{E}_1) \cap \mathcal{A}(\mathcal{E}_2)$.

Proof: Note, first, that $u^*, v^* \in \hat{\mathcal{U}}^{(n+m)}$. This follows since the minimum of concave functions is concave.

We prove that $\mathcal{A}(\mathcal{E}_1) \cap \mathcal{A}(\mathcal{E}_2) \subset \mathcal{A}(\mathcal{E}_1 \wedge \mathcal{E}_2)$. Let $(\bar{u}, \bar{v}) \in \mathcal{A}(\mathcal{E}_1) \cap \mathcal{A}(\mathcal{E}_2)$. Then there is an allocation $(\bar{x}^1, \bar{x}^2)$ of $\mathcal{E}_1$ such that $u^1(\bar{x}^1) = \bar{u}$ and $v^1(\bar{x}^2) = \bar{v}$ and an allocation $(\bar{y}^1, \bar{y}^2)$ of $\mathcal{E}_2$ such that $u^2(\bar{y}^1) = \bar{u}$ and $v^2(\bar{y}^2) = \bar{v}$. It follows that $u^*(\bar{x}^1, \bar{y}^1) = \bar{u}$ and $v^*(\bar{x}^2, \bar{y}^2) = \bar{v}$. Thus $(\bar{u}, \bar{v}) \in \mathcal{A}(\mathcal{E}_1 \wedge \mathcal{E}_2)$, as was to be shown.

The converse direction is left as an exercise for the reader. ∎

Let us call the environment $\mathcal{E}_1 \wedge \mathcal{E}_2$ the *convolution* of $\mathcal{E}_1$ and $\mathcal{E}_2$.

Lemma 3.1 (and Corollary 3.1) says that if one concave, monotone utility function dominates another on a common domain, then we can view these two functions as being projections of a *single* concave, monotone function w defined on a commodity space with one more good. In this larger commodity space, the individual with the dominating utility is viewed as consuming one unit of the new good, while the other individual consumes zero units of it. Thus the consumption of the new good can be viewed as "explaining" what appeared as a difference in utility functions at a lower dimension. The lemma thus implements a reduction of different utility functions to "fundamental preferences," discussed by Kolm (1972), a topic to which we return in §5.5. Lemma 3.2 shows how we can construct an economic environment whose utility possibilities set is the intersection of the utility possibilities sets of two given environments. The necessity of going to a higher dimension in this construction is what necessitates our assuming a domain of economic environments with commodity spaces of any finite dimension.

Proof of Theorem 3.6:

1. Let $F \in D^{\hat{\Gamma}} \cap$ CONRAD: let $\mathcal{E}_1, \mathcal{E}_2 \in \hat{\Gamma}$ and $\mathcal{E}_1 = \langle n, \bar{x}, u^1, v^1 \rangle$, $\mathcal{E}_2 = \langle m, \bar{y}, u^2, v^2 \rangle$, and let $\mathcal{A}(\mathcal{E}_1) = \mathcal{A}(\mathcal{E}_2)$. To show: $\mu_F(\mathcal{E}_1) = \mu_F(\mathcal{E}_2)$.

2. Construct the convolution $\mathcal{E}^* \equiv \mathcal{E}_1 \wedge \mathcal{E}_2$. $\mathcal{E}^* \in \hat{\Gamma}$ and by Lemma 3.2,

$\mathcal{A}(\mathcal{E}^*) = \mathcal{A}(\mathcal{E}_1) = \mathcal{A}(\mathcal{E}_2)$. I will prove that $\mu_F(\mathcal{E}_1) = \mu_F(\mathcal{E}^*)$. In like manner it will follow that $\mu_F(\mathcal{E}_2) = \mu_F(\mathcal{E}^*)$, and the theorem will follow. (The same argument works if we begin with $F \in D^{\hat{\Sigma}}$.)

3. Write $\mathcal{E}^* = \langle n + m, (\bar{x}, \bar{y}), u^*, v^* \rangle$. Construct the environment $\hat{\mathcal{E}}_1 = \langle n + m, (\bar{x}, \bar{y}), \hat{u}^1, \hat{v}^1 \rangle$, where $\hat{u}^1$ and $\hat{v}^1$ are the "flat extensions" of u^1 and v^1:

$$\forall(x, y) \in \mathbf{R}_+^{n+m}, \qquad \hat{u}^1(x, y) := u^1(x)$$
$$\hat{v}^1(x, y) := v^1(x).$$

4. From the definitions of $\mathcal{E}^*$ and $\hat{\mathcal{E}}_1$:

$$\forall(x, y) \in \mathbf{R}_+^{n+m}, \qquad \hat{u}^1(x, y) \geq u^*(x, y)$$
$$\hat{v}^1(x, y) \geq v^*(x, y).$$

By Lemma 3.1, it follows that $\exists U \in \hat{\mathcal{U}}^{(n+m+1)}$,

$$\forall(x, y) \in \mathbf{R}_+^{n+m}, \qquad U(x, y, 1) = \hat{u}^1(x, y)$$
$$U(x, y, 0) = u^*(x, y),$$

and $\exists V \in \hat{\mathcal{U}}^{(n+m+1)}$,

$$\forall(x, y) \in \mathbf{R}_+^{n+m}, \qquad V(x, y, 1) = \hat{v}^1(x, y)$$
$$V(x, y, 0) = v^*(x, y).$$

5. Now construct the flat extensions of U and V:

$$\left. \begin{array}{l} \hat{U}(x, y, r, s) := U(x, y, r) \\ \hat{V}(x, y, r, s) := V(x, y, s) \end{array} \right\} \quad \forall(x, y, r, s) \in \mathbf{R}_+^{n+m+2}.$$

6. Construct the extended environments

$$\tilde{\mathcal{E}}_1 = \langle n + m + 2, (\bar{x}, \bar{y}, 1, 1), \hat{U}, \hat{V} \rangle$$

and

$$\tilde{\mathcal{E}}^* = \langle n + m + 2, (\bar{x}, \bar{y}, 0, 0), \hat{U}, \hat{V} \rangle.$$

Note that $\mathcal{A}(\tilde{\hat{\mathcal{E}}}_1) = \mathcal{A}(\hat{\mathcal{E}}_1) = \mathcal{A}(\mathcal{E}_1)$, because only the first agent in $\tilde{\hat{\mathcal{E}}}_1$ likes the r-good and only the second agent likes the s-good, and

$$\hat{U}(x, y, 1, 0) = \hat{u}^1(x, y) = u^1(x)$$

and

$$\hat{V}(x, y, 0, 1) = \hat{v}^1(x, y) = v^1(x).$$

Thus no utility possibilities exist in $\tilde{\hat{\mathcal{E}}}_1$ which are not already available in $\mathcal{E}_1$. In like manner, it follows that $\mathcal{A}(\tilde{\mathcal{E}}^*) = \mathcal{A}(\mathcal{E}^*)$, since

$$\hat{U}(x, y, 0, 0) = u^*(x, y)$$

and

$$\hat{V}(x, y, 0, 0) = v^*(x, y).$$

7. Since $\mathcal{A}(\tilde{\hat{\mathcal{E}}}_1) = \mathcal{A}(\hat{\mathcal{E}}_1)$, it follows that $\mu_F(\tilde{\hat{\mathcal{E}}}_1) \in \mathcal{A}(\hat{\mathcal{E}}_1)$ and so there is an allocation $((\tilde{x}^1, \tilde{y}^1), (\tilde{x}^2, \tilde{y}^2))$ in $\hat{\mathcal{E}}_1$ such that $\mu_F(\tilde{\hat{\mathcal{E}}}_1) = (\hat{u}^1(\tilde{x}^1, \tilde{y}^1), \hat{v}^1(\tilde{x}^2, \tilde{y}^2))$. Therefore $\mu_F(\tilde{\hat{\mathcal{E}}}_1) = (\hat{U}(\tilde{x}^1, \tilde{y}^1, 1, 0), \hat{V}(\tilde{x}^2, \tilde{y}^2, 0, 1))$ by the definitions of U and V. By fullness of F, we conclude that the allocation $\hat{\eta}$ of $\hat{\tilde{\mathcal{E}}}$ defined by $\tilde{\eta} = ((\tilde{x}^1, \tilde{y}^1, 1, 0), (\tilde{x}^2, \tilde{y}^2, 0, 1))$ is in $F(\tilde{\hat{\mathcal{E}}}_1)$. Calculate the CONRAD-restriction of $\tilde{\hat{\mathcal{E}}}_1$ associated with $\tilde{\eta}$ by fixing the allocation of the r- and s-goods as they are assigned in $\tilde{\eta}$. By step 6, the restricted economy is precisely $\hat{\mathcal{E}}_1$, and since $\mathcal{A}(\tilde{\mathcal{E}}_1) = \mathcal{A}(\hat{\mathcal{E}}_1)$, CONRAD implies

$$\mu_F(\hat{\mathcal{E}}_1) = \mu_F(\tilde{\hat{\mathcal{E}}}_1).$$

Since neither agent likes the y-goods in $\hat{\mathcal{E}}_1$, CONRAD further implies

$$\mu_F(\mathcal{E}_1) = \mu_F(\hat{\mathcal{E}}_1),$$

as we can perform a permissible CONRAD restriction of $\hat{\mathcal{E}}_1$ with respect to the y-goods, and get $\mathcal{E}_1$. Hence

$$\mu_F(\mathcal{E}_1) = \mu_F(\tilde{\hat{\mathcal{E}}}_1).$$

8. Since $\mathcal{A}(\tilde{\mathcal{E}}^*) = \mathcal{A}(\tilde{\hat{\mathcal{E}}})$ (from steps 2 and 6), there must be a feasible allocation $\hat{\eta} = ((\hat{x}^1, \hat{y}^1, 0, 0), (\hat{x}^2, \hat{y}^2, 0, 0))$ in $\tilde{\mathcal{E}}^*$ inducing the same utility point as the allocation $\tilde{\eta} = ((\tilde{x}^1, \tilde{y}^1, 1, 0), (\tilde{x}^2, \tilde{y}^2, 0, 1))$ induces in $\tilde{\hat{\mathcal{E}}}$. But note that $\hat{\eta}$ is a feasible allocation in $\tilde{\hat{\mathcal{E}}}_1$, too. Since F is full, $\hat{\eta} \in F(\tilde{\hat{\mathcal{E}}}_1)$ because $\hat{\eta}$ and $\tilde{\eta}$ induce the same utility pair. Perform the CONRAD restriction of $\tilde{\hat{\mathcal{E}}}_1$ with respect to $\hat{\eta}$ by fixing the allocation of the last two goods at $(0, 0), (0, 0)$. This induces the environment $\mathcal{E}^*$ (see step 6), and since $\mathcal{A}(\mathcal{E}^*) = \mathcal{A}(\tilde{\hat{\mathcal{E}}})$ CONRAD applies, and

$$\mu_F(\mathcal{E}^*) = \mu_F(\tilde{\hat{\mathcal{E}}}_1).$$

9. From the conclusion of steps 7 and 8, it follows that

$$\mu_F(\mathcal{E}^*) = \mu_F(\mathcal{E}_1)$$

and the theorem is proved (see step 1). ∎

We next establish a series of lemmata using both Theorem 3.6 and its method of proof.

Lemma 3.3. $D^{\hat{\Gamma}} \cap RMON \cap W \subset MON.$

Proof:

1. Let $\mathcal{E}_1 = \langle n, \bar{x}, u^1, v^1 \rangle$, $\mathcal{E}_2 = \langle m, \bar{y}, u^2, v^2 \rangle$ for $\mathcal{E}_1, \mathcal{E}_2 \in \hat{\Gamma}$ and $\mathcal{A}(\mathcal{E}_1) \supset \mathcal{A}(\mathcal{E}_2)$. Let $F \in D^{\hat{\Gamma}} \cap RMON \cap W$. To show: $\mu_F(\mathcal{E}_1) \geq \mu_F(\mathcal{E}_2)$.

2. Construct $\mathcal{E}^* = \mathcal{E}_1 \wedge \mathcal{E}_2$, the convolution of $\mathcal{E}_1$ and $\mathcal{E}_2$; let $\mathcal{E}^* = \langle n + m, (\bar{x}, \bar{y}), u^*, v^* \rangle$. Let $\hat{\mathcal{E}}_1 = \langle n + m, (\bar{x}, \bar{y}), \hat{u}^1, \hat{v}^1 \rangle$, where $\hat{u}^1$ and $\hat{v}^1$ are the flat extensions of u^1 and v^1, as in step 3 of the proof of Theorem 3.6.

3. Note $\mathcal{A}(\mathcal{E}^*) = \mathcal{A}(\mathcal{E}_1) \cap \mathcal{A}(\mathcal{E}_2) = \mathcal{A}(\mathcal{E}_2)$ by Lemma 3.2.

4. Exactly as in steps 4 and 5 of the proof of Theorem 3.6, construct the Howe extension environments $\tilde{\hat{\mathcal{E}}}_1$ of $\mathcal{E}_1$ and $\tilde{\mathcal{E}}^*$ of $\mathcal{E}^*$. It follows that $\mathcal{A}(\tilde{\hat{\mathcal{E}}}) = \mathcal{A}(\mathcal{E}_1)$ and $\mathcal{A}(\tilde{\mathcal{E}}^*) = \mathcal{A}(\mathcal{E}^*)$.

5. Examine $\tilde{\hat{\mathcal{E}}}$ and $\tilde{\mathcal{E}}^*$. They are environments which are identical except that the aggregate endowment vector in $\tilde{\hat{\mathcal{E}}}$ dominates the aggregate endowment vector in $\tilde{\mathcal{E}}^*$. By RMON,

$$\mu_F(\tilde{\hat{\mathcal{E}}}) \geq \mu_F(\tilde{\mathcal{E}}^*).$$

6. Since $F \in W$,

$$\mu_F(\tilde{\hat{E}}) = \mu_F(E_1)$$

and

$$\mu_F(\tilde{E}^*) = \mu_F(E^*),$$

by step 4.

7. From steps 3, 4, and 5,

$$\mu_F(E_1) = \mu_F(\tilde{\hat{E}}_1) \geq \mu_F(\tilde{E}^*) = \mu_F(E^*) = \mu_F(E^2),$$

where the last equality follows from step 3 and the fact that $F \in W$. ∎

Lemma 3.4. $D^{\hat{\Sigma}} \cap SCONRAD \subset CC.$

Proof:

1. Let $F \in D^{\hat{\Sigma}} \cap$ SCONRAD. To show: $F \in CC$. Let E_2 and E_1 be any two environments with $\mathcal{A}(E_2) \subset \mathcal{A}(E_1)$, and $\mu_F(E_1) \in \mathcal{A}(E_2)$. To show: $\mu_F(E_2) = \mu_F(E_1)$. Note that $F \in W$ by Theorem 3.6, since SCONRAD $\subset$ CONRAD.

2. As in the proof of Theorem 3.6, steps 1 through 6, construct

$$\tilde{\hat{E}}_1 = \langle n + m + 2, (\bar{x}, \bar{y}, 1, 1), \hat{U}, \hat{V} \rangle$$
$$\tilde{E}^* = \langle n + m + 2, (\bar{x}, \bar{y}, 0, 0), \hat{U}, \hat{V} \rangle.$$

Only the first agent likes the r-good and only the second agent likes the s-good.

3. $F \in W$ implies $\mu_F(\tilde{\hat{E}}_1) = \mu_F(E_1)$ and $\mu_F(\tilde{E}^*) = \mu_F(E_2)$.

4. Since $\mu_F(E_1) \in \mathcal{A}(E_2) = \mathcal{A}(\tilde{E}^*)$, there is an allocation $\zeta = ((\bar{x}^1, \bar{y}^1, 0, 0), (\bar{x}^2, \bar{y}^2, 0, 0))$ in $\tilde{E}^*$ whose associated utility vector is $\mu_F(E_1)$. But ζ is also a feasible allocation in $\tilde{\hat{E}}_1$. Since F is a full correspondence, $\zeta \in F(\tilde{\hat{E}}_1)$ by step 3.

5. Let $\tilde{\hat{E}}^*_{\dagger}$ be the economic environment gotten by taking the SCON-RAD restriction of $\tilde{\hat{E}}_1$ with respect to the last two components of ζ. Then $\mathcal{A}(\tilde{\hat{E}}^*_{\dagger}) = \mathcal{A}(\tilde{E}^*) = \mathcal{A}(E_2).$

6. By SCONRAD, $\mu_F(\tilde{\hat{\mathcal{E}}}_1^*) = \mu_F(\mathcal{E}_1)$. By step 5, since $F \in W$, it follows that $\mu_F(\mathcal{E}_2) = \mu_F(\mathcal{E}_1)$. ∎

Lemma 3.5.[3] $D^{\hat{\Gamma}} \cap Sy \cap W \subset S$.

Proof:

1. Let T be a symmetric, strictly comprehensive utility possibilities set arising from some economic environment $\mathcal{E}'$. It suffices to show that $T = \mathcal{A}(\mathcal{E})$, where $\mathcal{E} = \langle n, \bar{x}, u, u \rangle$ is a symmetric economic environment. For if $F \in Sy$ then $\mu_F(\mathcal{E})$ must be an equal utility point in $\mathcal{E}$ and if $F \in W$ then $\mu_F(\mathcal{E}') = \mu_F(\mathcal{E})$ and it follows that $F \in S$.

2. Let the Pareto frontier of T be defined by the concave function $v = f(u)$. (This uses strict comprehensivity of T.) Consider the environment $\mathcal{E} = \langle 1, 1, u, u \rangle$ defined by

$$u(x) = \begin{cases} 2ax, & 0 \leq x \leq \frac{1}{2} \\ f(2a(1 - x)), & \frac{1}{2} \leq x \leq 1 \end{cases},$$

where (a, a) is the symmetric point on the Pareto frontier of T. $u(x)$ is concave, continuous, and monotone. The Pareto frontier $\mathcal{A}(\mathcal{E})$ is the set of points $\{(u(1 - x), u(x)) \mid 0 \leq x \leq 1\}$.

3. We check that $\mathcal{A}(\mathcal{E}) = T$ by verifying that $f(u(x)) = u(1 - x)$ for $x \in [0, 1]$. Let $x = \frac{1}{2} - \varepsilon$ for $\varepsilon \geq 0$. Then $f(u(x)) = f(2ax) = f(a - 2a\varepsilon) = f\left(2a\left(\frac{1}{2} - \varepsilon\right)\right) = u(1 - x)$. A similar calculation holds for $\varepsilon \leq 0$. Hence $\mathcal{E}$ is the required symmetric economic environment in $\hat{\Gamma}$ which generates the given symmetric strictly comprehensive set T. This proves the lemma, according to step 1. ∎

Lemma 3.6. $D^{\hat{\Sigma}} \cap I.RMON \cap W \subset IMON$.

Proof:

1. Let F satisfy the axioms and given $\mathcal{E}_1$ and $\mathcal{E}_2$ generating utility possibilities sets as in Figure 3.1. We need to show $\mu_F^1(\mathcal{E}_1) \geq \mu_F^1(\mathcal{E}_2)$.

---

3. I thank Karl Vind for the construction in step 2 of this lemma.

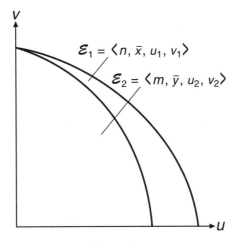

Figure 3.1

2. Construct the flat extension economy of $\mathcal{E}_1$:

$$\hat{\mathcal{E}}_1 = \langle n + m, (\bar{x}, \bar{y}), \hat{u}^1, \hat{v}^1 \rangle$$

with

$$\hat{u}^1(x, y) = u^1(x), \qquad \hat{v}^1(x, y) = v^1(x), \qquad \forall (x, y) \in \mathbf{R}^{n+m}.$$

Since $\mathcal{A}(\mathcal{E}_1) = \mathcal{A}(\hat{\mathcal{E}}_1)$, $\mu_F(\hat{\mathcal{E}}_1) = \mu_F(\mathcal{E}_1)$ because $F \in \mathrm{W}$.

3. Construct the convolution $\mathcal{E}^* = \mathcal{E}_1 \wedge \mathcal{E}_2 = \langle n + m, (\bar{x}, \bar{y}), u^*, v^* \rangle$. By Lemma 3.2, $\mathcal{A}(\mathcal{E}^*) = \mathcal{A}(\mathcal{E}_1) \cap \mathcal{A}(\mathcal{E}_2) = \mathcal{A}(\mathcal{E}_2)$ so $\mu_F(\mathcal{E}^*) = \mu_F(\mathcal{E}_2)$ because $F \in \mathrm{W}$.

4. Construct $\hat{\mathcal{E}}_{11} = \langle n + m, (\bar{x}, \bar{y}), \hat{u}^1, v^* \rangle$. Note $\mathcal{A}(\hat{\mathcal{E}}_1) \supset \mathcal{A}(\hat{\mathcal{E}}_{11})$ since the utility functions in $\hat{\mathcal{E}}_1$ dominate those in $\hat{\mathcal{E}}_{11}$ and the endowments of the two environments are identical.

5. To show $\mathcal{A}(\hat{\mathcal{E}}_1) \subset \mathcal{A}(\hat{\mathcal{E}}_{11})$: let $(\bar{x}^1, \bar{x}^2)$ be an allocation in $\mathcal{E}_1$. Consider in $\hat{\mathcal{E}}_{11}$ the allocation $\eta = ((\bar{x}_1, 0), (\bar{x}_1, \bar{y}))$. Note that

$$\hat{u}^1(\bar{x}^1, 0) = u^1(\bar{x}^1), \quad v^*(\bar{x}^2, \bar{y}) = \min(v^1(\bar{x}^2), v^2(\bar{y})) = v^1(\bar{x}^2),$$

and so η yields the same utility pair in $\mathcal{A}(\hat{\mathcal{E}}_{11})$ as it does in $\mathcal{A}(\mathcal{E}_1)$. [Note that this step uses the hypothesis that $v^1(\bar{x}) = v^2(\bar{y})$.] Hence $\mathcal{A}(\mathcal{E}_1) = \mathcal{A}(\hat{\mathcal{E}}_1) \subset \mathcal{A}(\hat{\mathcal{E}}_{11})$.

6. From steps 4 and 5, $\mathcal{A}(\hat{\mathcal{E}}_1) = \mathcal{A}(\hat{\mathcal{E}}_{11})$ so $\mu_F(\hat{\mathcal{E}}_{11}) = \mu_F(\hat{\mathcal{E}}_1)$, since $F \in W$.

7. Compare $\hat{\mathcal{E}}_{11}$ with $\mathcal{E}^*$. They differ only in the utility function of the first agent and $\hat{u}^1 \geq u^*$. By Lemma 3.1,

$$\exists U \in \mathcal{U}^{(n+m+1)}, \quad \text{such that} \quad U(x, y, 1) = \hat{u}^1(x, y)$$
$$U(x, y, 0) = u^*(x, y).$$

Define $V^*(x, y, r) \equiv v^*(x, y)$, for all (x, y, r). $V^* \in \mathcal{U}^{(n+m+1)}$.

8. Construct

$$\tilde{\hat{\mathcal{E}}}_{11} = \langle n + m + 1, (\bar{x}, \bar{y}, 1), U, V^* \rangle$$
$$\tilde{\mathcal{E}}^* = \langle n + m + 1, (\bar{x}, \bar{y}, 0), U, V^* \rangle.$$

Note $\mathcal{A}(\tilde{\hat{\mathcal{E}}}_{11}) = \mathcal{A}(\hat{\mathcal{E}}_{11})$ and $\mathcal{A}(\tilde{\mathcal{E}}^*) = \mathcal{A}(\mathcal{E}^*)$. By W, $\mu_F(\tilde{\hat{\mathcal{E}}}_{11}) = \mu_F(\hat{\mathcal{E}}_{11})$ and $\mu_F(\tilde{\mathcal{E}}^*) = \mu_F(\mathcal{E}^*) = \mu_F(\mathcal{E}_2)$.

9. $\tilde{\hat{\mathcal{E}}}_{11}$ and $\tilde{\mathcal{E}}^*$ differ only in the endowment of the r good, which only the first agent likes. Axiom I.RMON applies, and so $\mu_F^1(\tilde{\hat{\mathcal{E}}}_{11}) \geq \mu_F^1(\tilde{\mathcal{E}}^*)$. The various equivalences demonstrated show that

$$\mu_F^1(\mathcal{E}_1) = \mu_F^1(\tilde{\hat{\mathcal{E}}}_{11}) = \mu_F^1(\tilde{\hat{\mathcal{E}}}_{11}) \geq \mu_F^1(\tilde{\mathcal{E}}^*) = \mu_F^1(\mathcal{E}^*) = \mu_F^1(\mathcal{E}_2). \quad \blacksquare$$

Remark. Lemmata 3.2–3.6 remain true if we work on the domain of utility functions $\hat{\mathcal{U}}^p$, because whenever a proof uses Lemma 3.1, we can use Corollary 3.1 instead. The domain of functions $\hat{\mathcal{U}}^p$ is closed under all other constructions employed in the proofs.

We are now prepared to prove Theorems 3.1–3.5.

Proof of Theorem 3.1:

1. Given the preceding lemmata, we can now reconstruct the proof of Theorem 2.1 on the domain $\hat{\Sigma}$. Let $\mathcal{E} = \langle n, \bar{x}, u, v \rangle$ be an environment in $\hat{\Sigma}$. Let $(\hat{x}^1, \hat{x}^2)$ be an allocation for $\mathcal{E}$ which maximizes $u(x^1)v(x^2)$ on the feasible allocations of $\mathcal{E}$. Define positive numbers α and β by $\alpha u(\hat{x}^1) =$

$\beta v(\hat{x}^2) = 1$, and consider the environment $\mathcal{E}' = \langle n, \bar{x}, \alpha u, \beta v \rangle$. We know that $(\hat{x}^1, \hat{x}^2)$ maximizes the Nash product on $\mathcal{E}'$ as well.

2. Define the function $w : \mathbf{R}_+ \to \mathbf{R}_+$ by

$$w(x) = \begin{cases} x & \text{if } x \leq 2 \\ 2 & \text{if } x > 2 \end{cases}$$

Note $w \in \hat{\mathcal{U}}^{(1)}$. Consider the environment $\mathcal{E}^* = \langle 1, 2, w, w \rangle$. Note that the utility possibilities sets of $\mathcal{E}'$ and $\mathcal{E}^*$ are as illustrated in Figure 3.2. We know that the hyperplane $u^1 + u^2 = 2$ separates $\mathcal{A}(\mathcal{E}')$ from the rectangular hyperbola $u^1 u^2 = 1$, so the picture in Figure 3.2 is legitimate.

3. The axioms $D^{\hat{\Sigma}}$ and SCONRAD imply W (Theorem 3.6); W and SCONRAD imply CC. By Sy, $(1, 1) \in F(\mathcal{E}^*)$; by CC and fullness, $(\hat{x}^1, \hat{x}^2) \in F(\mathcal{E}')$; by CNC, $(\hat{x}^1, \hat{x}^2) \in F(\mathcal{E})$. ∎

Proof of Theorem 3.2:

1. We reconstruct the proof of Theorem 2.6. We first prove that F must be a monotone utility path mechanism (MUP). Suppose $F \notin$ MUP. Then there are two environments $\mathcal{E}^1 = \langle n, \bar{x}, u^1, v^1 \rangle$, $\mathcal{E}^2 = \langle m, \bar{y}, u^2, v^2 \rangle$ such that neither of the points $\mu_F(\mathcal{E}^1), \mu_F(\mathcal{E}^2)$ dominates the other componentwise. By Lemma 3.2, $\mathcal{A}(\mathcal{E}^1 \wedge \mathcal{E}^2) = \mathcal{A}(\mathcal{E}^1) \cap \mathcal{A}(\mathcal{E}^2)$. Refer again to Figure 2.7.

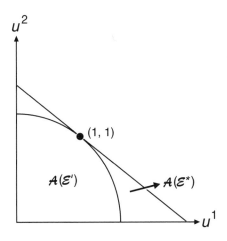

Figure 3.2

2. By $D^{\hat{\Gamma}}$ and CONRAD, $F \in W$ (Theorem 3.6); by RMON and W, $F \in$ MON (Lemma 3.3). Hence $\mu_F(\mathcal{E}^1) \geqq \mu_F(\mathcal{E}^1 \wedge \mathcal{E}^2)$ and $\mu_F(\mathcal{E}^2) \geqq \mu_F(\mathcal{E}^1 \wedge \mathcal{E}^2)$. It then follows that $F(\mathcal{E}^1 \wedge \mathcal{E}^2)$ is not Pareto optimal in $\mathcal{E}^1 \wedge \mathcal{E}^2$, a contradiction. Therefore $F \in$ MUP.

3. We can construct a sequence of symmetric environments to show that the monotone path is indeed the equal utility path, as in Theorem 2.6. ∎

Proof of Theorem 3.3:

1. We reconstruct the proof of Theorem 2.4 on economic environments. Let $\mathcal{E} = \langle n, \bar{x}, u, v \rangle$ be an arbitrary environment in $\hat{\Sigma}$; let $a(\mathcal{E})$ be the ideal point (see §2.4 for definition) of $\mathcal{A}(\mathcal{E})$. Choose $\alpha, \beta \in \mathbf{R}_+$ so that the ideal point of $\mathcal{E}' = \langle n, \bar{x}, \alpha u, \beta v \rangle$ is $(1, 1)$.

2. The mechanism F^{KS} chooses a resource allocation generating an equal-utility point on $\mathcal{E}'$: call that point (a, a). Consider the utility possibilities set, T, which is the convex hull of the four points $(0, 0)$, $(0, 1)$, $(1, 0)$, (a, a). See Figure 2.5.

3. We shall construct an economic environment whose utility possibilities set is T. Define

$$w^1(x) = \begin{cases} x & \text{if } x \leq 1 \\ 1 & \text{if } x > 1 \end{cases}$$

$$w^2(x) = \begin{cases} \frac{a}{1-a}x & \text{if } x \leq 1 \\ \frac{a}{1-a} & \text{if } x > 1 \end{cases},$$

and define $\mathcal{E}_1 = \langle 1, 1, w^1, w^2 \rangle$ and $\mathcal{E}_2 = \langle 1, 1, w^2, w^1 \rangle$. Note that w^1, w^2 satisfy condition (3.1), and so $\mathcal{E}_1, \mathcal{E}_2 \in \hat{\Gamma}$. In fact, $\mathcal{A}(\mathcal{E}_1)$ is the triangle with vertices $(0, 0)$, $(1, 0)$, $\left(0, a/(1 - a)\right)$, and $\mathcal{A}(\mathcal{E}_2)$ is the triangle with vertices $(0, 0)$, $\left(0, a/(1 - a)\right)$, $(0, 1)$. Thus, by Lemma 3.2, $\mathcal{A}(\mathcal{E}_1 \wedge \mathcal{E}_2) = T$, as required.

4. Let F satisfy the axioms of the theorem. By $D^{\hat{\Sigma}}$ and CONRAD, $F \in W$. By W and Sy, $F \in S$ (Lemma 3.5). Hence $\mu_F(\mathcal{E}_1 \wedge \mathcal{E}_2) = (a, a)$. By W and I.RMON, $F \in$ IMON (Lemma 3.6). Hence $\mu_F(\mathcal{E}') = (a, a)$. By CNC, it now follows that F chooses the Kalai-Smorodinsky point on $\mathcal{E}$; hence $F = F^{KS}$, as was to be shown. ∎

Proof of Theorem 3.4:   In the proof of Theorem 3.2, we showed that $F \in D^{\hat{\Gamma}} \cap$ CONRAD $\cap$ PO $\cap$ RMON implies that F is an MUP mechanism. Suppose there is an environment $\mathcal{E} \in \hat{\Gamma}$ such that $\mu_F(\mathcal{E}) = (\bar{u}, \bar{v}) > 0$. By

CNC, we can easily construct a new environment $\mathcal{E}'$ such that $\mu_F(\mathcal{E}') = \left(\frac{1}{2}\bar{u}, 2\bar{v}\right)$. But this violates MUP, since neither $\mu_F(\mathcal{E})$ or $\mu_F(\mathcal{E}')$ dominates the other. Therefore, for all $\mathcal{E}$, $\mu_F(\mathcal{E})$ has at least one component that is zero. This implies that the monotone utility path associated with F is one of the coordinate axes; thus F is a dictatorship. ∎

Proof of Theorem 3.5: This follows from Theorem 3.2. Take any $\mathcal{E} \in \hat{\Sigma}\backslash\hat{\Gamma}$. $\mathcal{E}$ can be approximated as the limit of a sequence of environments $\{\mathcal{E}_i\}$, $\mathcal{E}_i \in \hat{\Gamma}$. By Theorem 3.2, $F(\mathcal{E}_i) = E(\mathcal{E}_i)$ for all i. By ECONT, $F(\mathcal{E}) = \lim E(\mathcal{E}_i)$. ∎

Remark. Theorems 3.2, 3.4, 3.5, and 3.6 remain true if we work with the domain of functions $\hat{\mathcal{U}}^P$ instead of $\hat{\mathcal{U}}$. This is so by virtue of Corollary 3.1 and the Remark after the proof of Lemma 3.6. ∎

3.5 Naming Utility and Goods

Although economic environments contain more information than utility possibilities sets, one might believe that even more information is needed for purposes of distributive justice, in particular, information concerning what utility represents and what the resources in question are. Yaari and Bar-Hillel (1984) conducted experiments to illustrate this point.

In one experiment, 163 students were given the following problem. Jones and Smith must divide between them an aggregate endowment of 12 grapefruit and 12 avocados. Jones can metabolize 100 mg of vitamin F from a grapefruit and nothing from an avocado; Smith can metabolize 50 mg of vitamin F from an avocado or a grapefruit. Thus their "nutrition functions" can be written:

$$v_J(x, y) = 100x, \qquad v_S(x, y) = 50x + 50y,$$

where $x(y)$ is consumption of grapefruit (avocados). The "utility" possibilities set for this problem is illustrated in Figure 3.3. Students were asked which of the following five distributions of the fruit is most just:

J(6, 6)	S(6, 6)	equal split
J(6, 0)	S(6, 12)	Nash solution over strong Pareto set
J(8, 0)	S(4, 12)	Maximin
J(9, 0)	S(3, 12)	Nash solution from equal split
J(12, 0)	S(0, 12)	utilitarianism, Nash from (0, 0), and EDWE

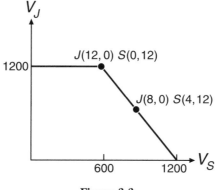

Figure 3.3

[The "Nash solution over the strong Pareto set" takes the threat point to be (600, 0) in utility space; "utilitarianism" maximizes the sum of the utilities; "EDWE" is Walrasian equilibrium where equal division of the fruit is the initial endowment position.]

Eighty-two percent of the students chose the maximin solution, which in this case equalizes the utilities of the two persons.

In the second problem, there is again a social endowment of (12, 12) of grapefruit and avocados. This time, the utility functions are "money metric utility." Jones likes grapefruit and is willing to pay $1 a piece for them; he detests avocado. Smith likes both fruits and is willing to pay $.50 for each. Thus their "utility" functions are exactly the same as in the first problem. Students were asked to choose among the five distributions. This time 28% chose maximin, 24% chose the Nash solution from equal split (which is also the Kalai-Smorodinsky solution from equal split), and 35% chose the Nash solution from a threat point of (0, 0).

Note that the economic information is identical in these two problems, that is, the resource endowment and the utility functions are the same. All that changes is the name of what utility is measuring—in one case, some kind of objective need, in the other, one presumes, a kind of gustatory satisfaction.

In a third problem, the social endowment of the two fruits remains (12, 12). Now we are told that each grapefruit contains 100 mg of vitamin F, and each avocado contains 100 mg of vitamin G. Jones needs vitamin F, but he requires .5 mg of G to metabolize 1 mg of F. Smith needs vitamin G, and can metabolize it directly. Thus their "utility" functions are:

$$v_J(x, y) = \min(100x, 200y)$$
$$v_S(x, y) = 100y.$$

It turns out that the utility possibilities set for this problem is the same as in the first two problems. This problem and the first one are identical in terms of what utility stands for (needs), but they have differing economic environments. This time, only 37% of the students voted for maximin (or equal utility), and 38% voted for the Nash solution from $(0, 0)$, which corresponds to the "corner" point on the utility possibilities set in Figure 3.3. [The distribution of fruit turns out to be $J(12, 6)$ $S(0, 6)$.]

The first and second experiments show that what utility measures appears to be important in the students' conceptions of justice, and the first and third experiments show that the economic environment is important (two problems with the same "names" yielding the same utility possibilities sets engender different choices for justice). One could argue that the students' responses are not well considered, which is to say they are not serious scholars of justice and are being misled by distinctions that should be irrelevant. For instance, one can rationalize the choice of allocation $J(12, 6)$ $S(0, 6)$ in the third problem as follows. It would be wasteful to give Jones fewer than 12 grapefruit, because Smith has no use for them. But if Jones gets 12 grapefruit, he needs 6 avocados to metabolize them (or else they go to waste). Thus, Jones gets $(12, 6)$, and the remainder $(0, 6)$ goes to Smith. There is no comparable possibility of waste in the first problem, and hence another criterion is used, namely, "equalize utility." Thus students appear to choose a "focal" criterion, and waste-avoidance is more prominent than equalization as a focus if waste is a possibility.

Perhaps, therefore, the Yaari–Bar-Hillel experiments are more predictive than normative, in the sense of indicating how societies may choose to divide resources, rather than how they *should* divide them. I think, nevertheless, it may well be the case that what goods do for people should matter in considerations of distributive justice, and so the difference between the students' responses in the first and second problems is on target: when it was a case of needs, the students were massively in favor of equality of needs' satisfaction, while in the case of gustatory satisfaction, no such clear focal point appeared. Indeed, Amartya Sen's theory of functionings and capability (see §§5.1, 5.6) takes precisely this viewpoint. Goods enable people to function in various ways, and some of those functionings may be more valuable than others (for example, being well nourished in contrast to having gustatory satisfaction). Thus for Sen, the names of goods matter, because specific goods are associated with specific functionings. In the remainder of this section, I study what happens if we introduce the names of goods into the environments of the theory.

Let us postulate the existence of an infinite set $\mathcal{N}$ of named goods. An *environment with named goods* is a tuple $\mathcal{E} = \langle N, n, \bar{x}, u, v \rangle$, where N is a (finite) subset of $\mathcal{N}$ of cardinality n, $\bar{x} \in \mathbf{R}_+^n$ is an aggregate endowment of those n goods, and u and v are utility functions of two individuals over those goods. Let us denote by $\Sigma^{(N)}$ the set of environments with named goods N whose utility functions are concave, continuous, monotone, with $u(0) = 0$ and satisfying condition (3.1), and by $\Gamma^{(N)}$ the subset of $\Sigma^{(N)}$ whose utility possibilities sets are strictly comprehensive. Let Σ be the union of $\Sigma^{(N)}$ over all finite $N \subset \mathcal{N}$ and Γ be the similar union of $\Gamma^{(N)}$.

If our allocation mechanism is defined on the domain Σ or Γ, then it may assign different allocations to two environments $\langle N, n, \bar{x}, u, v \rangle$ and $\langle M, n, \bar{x}, u, v \rangle$ which have the same economic information but involve different sets of goods. Thus our theory of distributive justice can take the functions of goods into account, as the students in the Yaari–Bar-Hillel experiments apparently do.

We must refine the previous axioms to conform to our intuitions, now that goods come with names. For example, the new resource monotonicity axiom is:

Axiom of Resource Monotonicity (RMON*).   Let

$$\mathcal{E} = \langle N, n, \bar{x}, u, v \rangle$$
$$\mathcal{E}' = \langle N, n, \bar{x}', u, v \rangle$$

be two economic environments and $\bar{x}' \geq \bar{x}$. Then $\mu_F(\mathcal{E}') \geqq \mu_F(\mathcal{E})$.

Thus our intuition only tells us that utility monotonicity should attain if the two environments in question involve exactly the same set of goods.

Axiom of Consistency of Resource Allocation across Dimension (CONRAD*).   Let $\mathcal{E} = \langle N \cup M, n + m, (\bar{x}, \bar{y}), u, v \rangle$ be an environment where $N \cap M = \emptyset$, with $u, v \in \hat{\mathcal{U}}^{(n+m)}$ and let $((\hat{x}^1, \hat{y}^1), (\hat{x}^2, \hat{y}^2)) \in F(\mathcal{E})$, where each of the y-goods $j = (n + 1, \ldots, n + m)$ is liked by at most one of the agents. Define u^*, v^* by

$$\forall x \in \mathbf{R}^n_+, \qquad u^*(x) = u(x, \hat{y}^1)$$
$$v^*(x) = v(x, \hat{y}^2).$$

If $u^*(0) = v^*(0) = 0$ then $u^*, v^* \in \hat{\mathcal{U}}^{(n)}$ and in this case consider the admissible environment $\mathcal{E}^* = \langle N, n, \bar{x}, u^*, v^* \rangle$. If $\mathcal{A}(\mathcal{E}^*) = \mathcal{A}(\mathcal{E})$ then $(\hat{x}^1, \hat{x}^2) \in F(\mathcal{E}^*)$.

The new CONRAD* axiom also must include the premise that the set of goods N is identical in the environments $\mathcal{E}$ and $\mathcal{E}^*$.

The Pareto and Symmetry axioms have obvious formulations on the new domain; let us call them PO* and Sy*. The domain axiom D^Σ means that the allocation mechanism F is a full correspondence that is essentially a function and is defined for every environment with named goods in Σ, and D^Γ has an analogous meaning. We can indeed, with a little work, recover the egalitarian Theorem 3.2 on the new domain:

Theorem 3.7. $D^\Gamma \cap CONRAD^* \cap PO^* \cap RMON^* \cap Sy^* = \{E\}$.

Proof:

1. Let $\mathcal{E}_1 = \langle N, n, \bar{x}, u^1, v^1 \rangle$ and $\mathcal{E}_2 = \langle M, m, \bar{y}, u^2, v^2 \rangle$. We first prove that if $N \cap M = \emptyset$ then either $\mu_F(\mathcal{E}_1) \geq \mu_F(\mathcal{E}_2)$ or $\mu_F(\mathcal{E}_2) \geq \mu_F(\mathcal{E}_1)$.

2. Suppose, to the contrary, that neither inequality in step 1 holds. Form the convolution $\mathcal{E}_1 \wedge \mathcal{E}_2 = \langle M \cup N, m + n, u^*, v^* \rangle$ where $u^*(x, y) = \min(u^1(x), u^2(y))$, $v^*(x, y) = \min(v^1(x), v^2(y))$. By Lemma 3.2, $\mathcal{A}(\mathcal{E}_1 \wedge \mathcal{E}_2) = \mathcal{A}(\mathcal{E}_1) \cap \mathcal{A}(\mathcal{E}_2)$. The same proof as in Theorem 3.2 establishes a contradiction, and the claim in step 1 is established.

3. Now let $\mathcal{E} \in D^\Gamma$, $\mathcal{E} = \langle N, n, \bar{x}, u, v \rangle$, be any environment for which $\mu_F(\mathcal{E})$ is not an equal utility point. Let $E(\mathcal{E}) = (a, a)$. Choose a symmetric environment $\mathcal{E}' = \langle M, m, \bar{y}, w, w \rangle$ such that $\mu_F(\mathcal{E}') = (a, a)$ (by Sy*) and $M \cap N = \emptyset$ (which is possible by D^Γ). By step 1's assertion, it follows that either $(a, a) \geq \mu_F(\mathcal{E})$ or $\mu_F(\mathcal{E}) \geq (a, a)$. If the first inequality is true, then $\mu_F(\mathcal{E}) = (a, a)$, since $(a, a) \in \mathcal{A}(\mathcal{E})$ and F is Pareto optimal. If the second inequality is true then $\mu_F(\mathcal{E}) = (a, a)$, again a contradiction, which establishes the theorem. ■

In a similar manner, we can establish the other theorems on a domain of economic environments with named goods.

Theorem 3.7 might appear to be a compelling argument for welfare egalitarianism when we allow consideration of the names of goods in making distributive judgments. But I shall argue that it is not. The rub is in the domain axiom D^Γ, which, I claim, is unacceptably strong. The domain axiom asserts that for *any* finite set of goods N and for *any* utility functions u and v (and for any resource vector $x \in \mathbf{R}^n_+$), there is a "possible world" in which two individuals have utility functions u and v over the goods N. But if this were true, our ethical intuition that the names of goods should count for distributive justice would be wrong. For if we think that the names of goods should count, it is because we believe that certain goods (bread, shelter) always take precedence over certain other goods (scotch whiskey, caviar) at sufficiently low consumption levels.[4] Names of goods count because some goods satisfy needs and others satisfy only desires, and if there are basic human needs, then it is false to say that *any* possible preference ordering over *any* set of goods is humanly feasible.

To be specific, consider an environment with four goods {food, shelter, yachts, fast cars}, and in which two persons have utility functions u and v reflecting the "normal" attitudes toward these goods: food and shelter become indispensable below certain levels, which means that the individuals would be willing to trade off any amount of yachts and fast cars for small amounts of the necessities, at sufficiently low consumption levels of those necessities. Now consider another environment with the same set of named goods, but in which the individuals treat fast cars and yachts as necessities, and shelter and food as luxuries: the utility functions u^* and v^* in this environment simply permute the goods, that is, there is a permutation σ of $\{1, 2, 3, 4\}$ such that $u^*(x) = u(\sigma(x))$ and $v^*(x) = v(\sigma(x))$. Both of these environments are in our domain, but the second one should not be. Human nature precludes the existence of the second environment.

We may state this in terms of Amartya Sen's notion of functionings, discussed in Chapter 5. Sen argues that certain kinds of human functioning are necessary preconditions for any possible conception of a life plan (being adequately nourished, sheltered, able to move around, and so on). There are certain resources, in turn, that are required to deliver these functionings. It is not conceivable that a person would, for instance, assign no utility to the consumption of these resources, if utility measures the rela-

---

4. This might be captured by requiring the marginal rates of substitution between luxury goods and "basic" goods always to be large at low levels of basic goods' consumption. For further elaboration of this idea, see §5.7.

tive success of achieving one's life plan or of overall well-being. That is to say, it is wrong to assume an unrestricted domain of preference orderings over certain sets of goods which include both these "primary" resources and certain luxury goods.

The domain assumption D^{Γ} thus sterilizes the model against what the naming of goods was supposed to capture. For it implies that we cannot distinguish, by looking at the set of possible worlds, that some goods are more basic than others to the fulfillment of human aspirations.

Let us compare our earlier domain assumption on economic environments, $D^{\hat{\Gamma}}$, to the domain assumption D^{Γ}. The former assumption says that there is an economic environment corresponding to any tuple of information $\langle n, \bar{x}, u, v \rangle$. This means that, for any tuple $\langle n, \bar{x}, u, v \rangle$, there exists *some* set of goods N of size n such that $\mathcal{E} = \langle N, n, \bar{x}, u, v \rangle$ is a possible world. This part may well be acceptable. What is unacceptable about the domain assumption $D^{\hat{\Gamma}}$ is that, if there happen to be two possible worlds associated with the economic information $\langle n, \bar{x}, u, v \rangle$—namely, there is another set of goods N^* such that $\mathcal{E}^* = \langle N^*, n, \bar{x}, u, v \rangle$ is also a possible world—the axiom forces the allocation mechanism to treat $\mathcal{E}$ and $\mathcal{E}^*$ isomorphically. Formally speaking, the domain axiom $D^{\hat{\Gamma}}$ includes a prescription to treat goods anonymously. It was to avoid this insensitivity of $D^{\hat{\Gamma}}$ to the names of goods that we moved to consider economic environments with named goods. But the domain axiom that is then used to prove Theorem 3.7 on a domain of environments with named goods turns out to be unacceptable for the very reason that motivated the move to consider environments with named goods!

One should note that exactly this kind of problem occurs in moving from the Nash domain axiom U to the domain axiom $D^{\hat{\Gamma}}$ on economic environments. U asserts that "any" pair (S, d) describes a possible world. Since actual worlds contain economic information, this means that, for any convex, comprehensive set S in $\mathbf{R}^2_+$, there is a possible world described by *some* tuple of economic information $\mathcal{E} = \langle n, \bar{x}, u, v \rangle$, with $\mathcal{A}(\mathcal{E}) = S$. When we moved from Nash axiomatic bargaining theory to economic environments, the domain axiom we needed to retain the characterization results asserts that *any* tuple of information $\mathcal{E}' = \langle m, \bar{y}, u', v' \rangle$ such that $\mathcal{A}(\mathcal{E}') = S$ must be admitted as a possible world. This is obviously a stronger axiom than U, but I have not argued that it is unacceptably strong.

If the domain assumption of Theorem 3.7 is unacceptably strong, can we reconstruct the argument with a more palatable domain axiom? Indeed, I believe we can. For the proof of Theorem 3.7 to go through, the domain

Δ upon which the mechanism F is defined must be "closed" under the following operations:

(i) If $\mathcal{E}_1$ and $\mathcal{E}_2$ are in Δ, then $\mathcal{E}_1 \wedge \mathcal{E}_2$ is in Δ;

(ii) If $\mathcal{E}_1 = \langle N, n, \bar{x}, u^1, v^1 \rangle$ and $\mathcal{E}_2 = \langle N, n, \bar{x}, u^2, v^2 \rangle$ are in Δ and $u^1 \geqq u^2$ and $v^1 \geqq v^2$, then there exists $\mathcal{E}_3$ in Δ with $\mathcal{E}_3 = \langle n, N \cup \{r, s\}, (\bar{x}, 1, 1), U, V \rangle$, where r and s is some pair of goods not in N and $U(x, 1, 0) = u^1(x)$, $U(x, 0, 0) = u^2(x)$, $V(x, 0, 1) = v^1(x)$, and $V(x, 0, 0) = v^2(x)$;

(iii) if $\mathcal{E} \in \Delta$, then there exists $\mathcal{E}^* \in \Delta$ where the utility functions of $\mathcal{E}^*$ are the "flat extensions" of the utility functions in $\mathcal{E}$;

(iv) for any positive number a, there is a symmetric environment in Δ such that (a, a) is a Pareto optimal point.

If (i)–(iv) hold, then all the constructions necessary to prove Theorem 3.7 can be carried out. Now let Δ be a domain consisting of environments of named goods, all of which are "acceptable": there are no environments in Δ, for instance, in which "milk" and "shelter" enter utility functions as luxuries and "scotch" and "caviar" enter as necessities. Denote by $\bar{\Delta}$ the "closure" of Δ, the smallest domain of named environments including Δ as a subset on which (i)–(iv) hold. The question is: If all the environments in Δ are acceptable, does the same hold true for $\bar{\Delta}$? If so, we may take the domain axiom of Theorem 3.7 to be $D^{\bar{\Delta}}$, and reestablish the theorem on an acceptable domain.

I think the answer to the last question is arguably "yes." I have no trouble with conditions (ii), (iii), and (iv): "closure" with respect to these conditions never requires us to admit environments which would sterilize the naming of goods of the meaning we intend names to have. Condition (i) is perhaps more delicate. Let $\mathcal{E}_1 = \langle N, n, \bar{x}, u^1, v^1 \rangle$ and $\mathcal{E}_2 = \langle M, m, \bar{y}, u^2, v^2 \rangle$, $M \cap N = \emptyset$, where both environments are in Δ; we must justify the view that $\mathcal{E} = \langle M \cup N, m + n, (\bar{x}, \bar{y}), u^*, v^* \rangle$ is an acceptable environment, where $u^*(x, y) = \min(u^1(x), u^2(y))$ and $v^*(x, y) = \min(v^1(x), v^2(y))$. I continue, here, to use the interpretation of "utility" that I find most relevant for the application to distributive justice, namely, that $u(x)$ is the (expected) degree to which or probability that one's life plan will be achieved with resource bundle x. In $\mathcal{E}_1$, the first individual, Alan, has a life-plan conception to which is associated a "utility" function u^1 defined on the goods N, and in $\mathcal{E}_2$ the first individual, Betsy, has a life-plan conception to which is associated a "utility" function u^2 defined on the goods M. The acceptability of condition (i) above hinges on the acceptability of supposing there is a possible world in which the first individual has a "utility" u^* defined on the set of goods $M \cup N$. Consider a hypothetical individual, Carmen, who lives in a world where the set of goods is $M \cup N$. Carmen has two goals in life, the first of which corresponds to Alan's goal and the second of which corresponds to Betsy's goal. Carmen evaluates the degree of success in achieving her life plan as the minimum degree of achievement of these two goals. (She sets a rather tough standard for herself.) Her utility function, in a world with goods $M \cup N$, is given by the utility function u^*. This story suggests that performing the convolution of two environments each of which is acceptable produces an environment which is itself acceptable. I conclude that we may replace the axiom D^Γ in Theorem 3.7 with the axiom $D^{\bar{\Delta}}$, giving us a theorem which makes an argument for equality of welfare (conceived, at least, as degree or probability of life-plan fulfillment), and in which our intuition that some goods are more important than others in the fulfillment of human aspirations is preserved.

I summarize the technical part of this discussion with:

Theorem 3.8. *Let Δ be any domain of environments with named goods, and let $\bar{\Delta}$ be the closure of Δ with respect to conditions (i)–(iv). Then*

$$D^{\bar{\Delta}} \cap CONRAD^* \cap PO^* \cap RMON^* \cap Sy^* = \{E\}.$$

3.6 Conclusion

In §2.5, I challenged the appropriateness of using Nash-type bargaining theory to study distributive justice. The challenge was that Nash theory accomplishes its apparently powerful characterizations of solutions with small numbers of compelling axioms only by implicitly imposing an unacceptably strong axiom, Welfarism. Welfarism states that, for purposes of distributive justice, only utility possibilities sets matter—the Ministry of Justice can discard the economic information (resources, utility functions of individuals) which generate those sets. There are two related ways of seeing the unacceptable strength of Welfarism: first, it rules out of court many allocation mechanisms that can only be defined with reference to economic information (such as equal division of all resources, or Walrasian equilibrium from equal division); second, the Nash-type axioms which appear reasonable are, in fact, much stronger than their underlying intuitions warrant.

In this chapter, I have attempted to respond to that challenge by reconstructing the Nash-type characterization results, but without discarding a priori economic information. No axiom of welfarism was assumed. Indeed, welfarism was deduced as a *theorem*, from "economic foundations." Such a deduction is only appealing if the premises appear to be sufficiently "distant" from the conclusion: I argued that the linchpin of this theorem, the CONRAD axiom, is reasonably distant from welfarism. (As I noted, another motivation for CONRAD will be given in Chapter 7, where it plays an important role.) The characterization results of this chapter used "substantive" axioms that are weaker than their counterparts in Chapter 2, but the domain axiom used here is stronger than in Chapter 2.

But then a second challenge was raised against the appropriateness of modeling possible worlds as economic environments: in reality, goods come with names, and different goods enter differently into the "individual production functions" of persons, who use them to satisfy needs and desires. The new challenge consisted in saying that the names of goods, as proxies for what goods do for people, may well matter for distributive justice, for those names convey information about how urgently the goods are needed by people. Indeed, Scanlon (1975) has discussed the relevance of the distinction between desire and need fulfillment for distributive justice in an article significantly entitled "Preference and Urgency." So we reconstructed one of the important characterization theorems without treating goods anonymously. The problem was that this characterization result (Theorem 3.7) depends on an even stronger domain axiom, one that, I argued, actually sterilizes our very attempt to take account of the fact that some goods fulfill more urgent needs for people than others.

I next asked whether it was possible to reestablish Theorem 3.7 working on a smaller domain, one which admits only environments with named goods in which goods never enter weirdly into the production of human aspirations. Arguing that it is, I finally arrived at Theorem 3.8, which constitutes the most ethically appealing argument for equality-of-welfare given thus far.

One should not, however, be complacent with respect to the axiomatic analysis as it stands. One can still quite plausibly argue that the domain assumption $D^{\bar{\Delta}}$ is too strong: for instance, it requires us to admit as acceptable possible worlds which contain more goods than there are atoms in the universe. The next step in our program might well be to try to reconstruct the characterization theorems on domains consisting of environments of named goods where there is a reasonable upper bound on the number of goods in an environment. My conjecture is that this cannot be done: it is probably the case that if we place a bound on the dimension of the commodity space, we can always construct a mechanism that satisfies the (nondomain) axioms of Theorem 3.8 but does not equalize utility. (Here is a perhaps challenging exercise for the reader.)

Where does this leave us? We have, in this chapter, progressively added information to the abstract representations of possible worlds upon which our theory is defined in order to construct a theory which is capable of capturing ethical intuitions that are arguably valid. In the process of doing so, the domain axioms we had to use to preserve the simple characterization results of Nash-type theory become decreasingly palatable. Even the environments we end up with in our most careful construction (Theorem 3.8) are highly abstract: they exclude all kinds of information about persons that might well be salient for distributive purposes. If we proceed further down the path of injecting more information into the environments on which we work, we will, I believe, only be able to preserve "nice" characterization results by employing domain axioms that effectively sterilize our models against representing the intuitions that motivate the injection of that information. We will lose the compelling and simple characterization results of the kind proved in this chapter and the previous one.

The mathematics is telling us something important: there will be no compelling argument deriving a simple rule for distributive justice, by which I mean an argument that deduces one solution or mechanism as the consequence of a small number of clear, appealing axioms. Philosophical integrity will require us to move beyond the "simple characterizations" of social choice and axiomatic bargaining theory.

4

Utilitarianism

4.1 Introduction

Utilitarianism, perhaps the oldest position taken in social choice theory, is the belief that, in the words of Bentham, society should seek to achieve the greatest good for the greatest number. Without further definition, this phrase is incoherent, as it requires the maximization of two objectives at once. If the population size is fixed, then utilitarianism recommends that we choose that social alternative that provides the greatest good. The justification for this proposal is the view that all individuals should be treated as equals, and such equality requires giving equal weight to each person's well-being in the social calculus, which suggests that the right social alternative is the one that maximizes the sum of individual utilities. We shall treat the choice of population size in §4.6.

But this egalitarian justification does not imply that the right or just social state is the one that maximizes the *sum* of utilities. Why should treating individuals equally require that we add up their "utilities"? Why not advocate that social alternative that equalizes their utilities? Or that provides the most equal opportunities? As Sen (1992) says, every modern theory of justice begins from the premise that citizens must be treated as equals in some respect.

In this study I define utilitarianism as the view that the just social alternative is that which maximizes the sum of individual "utilities" (at least, when the population size is fixed). It should be remarked that philosophers often denote by utilitarianism what I have called "welfarism," that the justness of a social state can be evaluated by knowing only the utilities that that state delivers to individuals. For instance, much of the philosophical discussion of utilitarianism concerns the problem of "nasty" preferences. In finding the alternative that maximizes social welfare, should one count the pleasures that some people receive from the pain of others (as in Sen's sadistic, hungry person of §1.3)? Note that this question is salient for any welfarist theory, not just utilitarianism (in our sense). We shall not be further concerned with sadistic preferences, for we limit our investigation to problems of distributive justice, in which we assume that all individuals have self-regarding preferences over distributions of commodities or resources. Another example of the double use of "utilitarianism" can be seen in the view philosophers take of Rawls. Rawls views his work as a manifesto against utilitarianism in two ways: first, that he advocates a maximandum of an index of primary goods, not utility; second, that he advocates looking only at the minimum of a set of individual "welfare" levels, not the sum. The first point contrasts Rawlsian justice with welfarism in general, the second with utilitarianism (in our sense) in particular. In the philosophical literature, and in Rawls himself, both of these objections are seen as ones against utilitarianism.

One philosophical objection to the welfarism of utilitarianism is predicated on the view that individual utility is a measure of pleasure; the objection then runs that something as well as individual pleasures counts in assessing the goodness of a state. If, however, we take the modern view that a utility function is just a representation of an individual's preferences, then this objection is not so clearly appropriate: for a person may prefer one bundle of resources to another not because it gives him more pleasure but because, for instance, it enhances his opportunity for leading a meaningful life. With this understanding, "welfarism" ceases to be a hedonistic theory of social value. Note that the objections to welfarism that arose in Chapter 2 are not, as I said, like Sen's objection to sadism; they involve the observation that postulating welfarism precludes the consideration of many allocation mechanisms, a preclusion with no obvious justification. Finally, the "utility" functions that are summed in the utilitarian objective need not even be measures of subjective well-being: they could measure some objective characteristic of individuals, such as life expectancy.

Given the modern view that a utility function is simply a numerical representation of a preference order, what is the meaning of utilitarianism, that is, of taking the sum $\sum u^i(x)$, where u^i is a utility function for individual i and x is a social alternative? The only case in which this summation has a meaningful interpretation in terms of social welfare is when the utility function measures something that is interpersonally comparable. For instance, suppose $u^i(x)$ is the life expectancy of individual i in state x. Then $\frac{1}{H}\sum u^i(x)$ is the average life expectancy of the society in question: one might well advocate that the "best" state is the one that maximizes average life expectancy. What kind of measurability and comparability properties do we insist upon for u^i to measure life expectancy? We can allow transformations of a profile $u = (u^1, \ldots, u^H)$ only by monotonic transformations of the form $\Phi = (\varphi, \varphi, \ldots, \varphi)$ where $\varphi(z) = az$, for some positive number a. (That is, it does not matter if we measure life expectancy in years or decades or hours.) These transformations preserve both utility differences and utility ratios: thus it is meaningful to say both that one person's life expectancy is six years more than another's, and that one person's life expectancy is two-thirds that of another's. Blackorby and Donaldson (1982) call this kind of measurability "ratio-scale full comparability"; the group of such transformations will be called G^{RFC}. Note this is a stronger informational assumption than cardinal full comparability, which permits transformations of the type Φ above where $\varphi(z) = az + b$—utility ratios are not preserved under these transformations. A fortiori, RFC is a stronger informational requirement than cardinal unit comparability, which permits arbitrary assignments of the zero points to each individual. We know, from Chapter 1, that utilitarianism is a coherent concept as long as utility is cardinally measurable and unit comparable. We shall see in the next section that, with any less information, utilitarianism ceases to be coherent.

Just because utilitarianism is a coherent concept with CUC information —by which we mean that utilitarianism gives a well-defined order of social states regardless which utility profile, from the set of informationally acceptable ones, is chosen—does not mean that $\sum u^i(x)$ is philosophically meaningful. To see this, take the above example. Suppose there are two persons, whose life expectancies are given by $u^1(x) = 10x - 3$ and $u^2(x) = 75 - x$, with x taking on any value in the interval $[1, 8]$ and life expectancy measured in years. (Thus average life expectancy is maximized when $x = 8$ at 72 years.) Suppose we consider the transformation $\tilde{u}^1 = 2u^1$ and $\tilde{u}^2 = 2u^2$. Life expectancy is maximized at $x = 8$ (of course), and average life expectancy is 144 half-years: in particular, both the ratios and differences of life expectancies among individuals are preserved. Suppose, however, we make the transformation $\bar{u}^1 = u^1 + 1000$, $\bar{u}^2 = u^2 - 600$. Of course, the solution is invariant (at $x = 8$), but now we have lost some of the information that was meaningful to us before: it no longer makes sense to say one person's life expectancy is a certain fraction of another's.

The upshot is that utilitarianism is a meaningful concept for justice only when we have a conception of utility that is interpersonally comparable in a meaningful way. Life expectancy is an example of such a conception. Somewhat more abstractly, we may take the view that the preference orderings of all individuals represent their views about the degree of opportunity given alternatives will afford them to realize their life plans and, further, that those degrees are interpersonally comparable—say, up to positive *linear* transformation (as with life expectancy), or even a positive *affine* transformation (what we call cardinal full comparability), or perhaps even up to cardinal unit comparability (allowing arbitrary assignments of the zero points to the various individuals). We must begin with some such conception of utility, a conception that permits us meaningfully to speak of the average utility in the society [that is, $\frac{1}{H}\sum_{i=1}^{H}u^i(x)$]. This may seem like an obvious point. But we shall see, in this chapter, that much of the discussion of utilitarianism in the economics literature turns out not to be about utilitarianism, so conceived, at all: for in the discussion in question, no such conception of utility is posited. Since I take the doctrine of utilitarianism to consist in the advocacy of that state which maximizes the total or the average utility of individuals, where utility represents an attribute of persons which it is meaningful to sum, the discussion I refer to is irrelevant in evaluating the doctrine of utilitarianism.

A second, and major, philosophical objection to utilitarianism is its insensitivity to inequality: a utility allocation of $(1, 99)$ is judged indifferent to one of $(50, 50)$. A principal conclusion of this chapter will be that ethical observers who are disturbed by what this kind of inequality connotes about the lives of people have no reason to revise their views based on the arguments for utilitarianism that have been put forth in the social choice literature. The theorems on utilitarianism, it turns out, do not challenge the usual kind of aversion to inequality. This statement, which may at this point appear paradoxical, will, I hope, become transparent by the chapter's end.

4.2   Maskin's Theorem

We have seen, thus far, two theorems on utilitarianism: Theorem 1.4 and its correlate on economic environments, Theorem 1.8. These theorems both require the social choice functional to respect cardinal unit comparability. For many purposes, this is not enough. Suppose, for instance, that X is a set of social alternatives and $u^i(x)$ is the life expectancy of individual i in state x. Suppose we require the social choice functional F to respect ratio-scale full comparability (see §4.1) and also the other axioms of Theorem 1.4 (WP*, I*, U*, and AN*). Is utilitarianism determined? Assuredly not. For instance, if utilities are restricted to be non-negative, the functional that ranks states according to the value of $\sum(u^i)^2$ satisfies these axioms and ratio-scale full comparability. So in the context of the life-expectancy problem Theorem 1.4 is not useful, for it requires too much of the social choice functional, namely, that its prescription be invariant even when utilities are transformed in ways that are not meaningful when life expectancy is what is being measured. To conclude that maximizing average life expectancy in a population should be society's goal requires a characterization theorem of the sort that Theorem 1.4 is, but with "cardinal unit comparability" replaced by "ratio-scale full comparability." The premise of invariance with respect to the group G^{RFC} is much weaker than the premise of invariance with respect to the group G^{CUC}—because the latter group is larger—and so, with no other strengthening of the axioms of Theorem 1.4, we lose the unique determination of a social welfare functional.

The group of transformations that we can allow depends on the measurability properties of whatever our conception of utility is. The next result shows that, in an unambiguous sense, cardinal unit comparability is the weakest informational requirement that renders utilitarianism coherent.

Proposition 4.1. *Let F^{ut} be the utilitarian social choice functional, defined on an unrestricted domain of utility profiles, and suppose the order $F^{ut}(u)$ is invariant with respect to transformations of utilities by the group G, where G consists of transformations whose component functions are monotonic, continuous, and differentiable except at a finite number of points. Then $G \subset G^{CUC}$.*

Proof:

1. Let $\Phi \in G$, $\Phi = (\varphi^1, \varphi^2, \ldots, \varphi^H)$. We must show that there are numbers $a, b^1, \ldots, b^H$, with $a > 0$, such that $\varphi^i(z) = az + b^i$, for $i = 1, \ldots, H$.

2. We begin by proving the result for $H = 2$. F^{ut} is represented by the Bergson-Samuelson social welfare function $W(x^1, x^2) = x^1 + x^2$ (where x^i are now thought of as utility numbers). By the supposition, the indifference curves of W are the same as indifference curves of $W \circ \Phi$: that is, for any number k' there is a number k such that the set $I(k') \equiv \{(x^1, x^2) \mid x^1 + x^2 = k'\}$ is identical to the set $I^\Phi(k) \equiv \{(x^1, x^2) \mid \varphi^1(x^1) + \varphi^2(x^2) = k\}$. Define $\psi^1(z) = \varphi^1(z) - \varphi^1(0)$ and $\psi^2(z) = \varphi^2(z) - \varphi^2(0)$, and note that $\psi^i(0) = 0$, for $i = 1, 2$.

3. Let x^1 be any number, and let $(x^1, \bar{x}^2) \in I(k')$: we may write $\bar{x}^2 = k' - x^1$. Since $(x^1, \bar{x}^2) \in I^{\Phi}(k)$, we may write $\varphi^1(x^1) + \varphi^2(k' - x^1) = k$, or

(4.1) $\psi^1(x^1) + \psi^2(k' - x^1) = k - \varphi^1(0) - \varphi^2(0).$

Equation (4.1) is an identity in x^1. By substituting the values 0 and k' for x^1 in (4.1), we conclude that

(4.2) $\psi^1(k') = \psi^2(k').$

But this is true for any number k'; hence ψ^1 and ψ^2 are indeed the same function, call it ψ.

     4. Thus we may write (4.1) as

(4.3) $\psi(x^1) + \psi(k' - x^1) = k''.$

Differentiating (4.3), which is a valid operation except at a finite number of points, gives

(4.4) $\psi'(x^1) = \psi'(k' - x^1).$

We are free to choose x^1 and k' arbitrarily, and hence (4.4) implies that ψ' is a constant, that is, there is a positive number a such that

(4.5) $\psi'(x^1) = a.$

Integrating (4.5), we have $\psi(x^1) = ax^1 + b$; but $\psi(0) = 0$, and so $b = 0$. Thus

(4.6) $\psi(x^1) = ax^1.$

Indeed, (4.6) is true for *all* x^1, by the continuity of ψ.

     5. By definition of ψ^i, it now follows that

$$\varphi^1(z) = az + \varphi^1(0)$$

$$\varphi^2(z) = az + \varphi^2(0),$$

and hence $\Phi \in G^{CUC}$.

6. To prove the proposition for $H > 2$, we proceed as follows. Let $I(k') = \{(x^1, x^2, \ldots, x^H) \mid \sum x^i = k'\}$. We know there is a number k such that $I^\Phi(k) = \{(x^1, \ldots, x^H) \mid \sum \varphi^i(x^i) = k\}$ is identical to $I(k')$. Now fix an integer j, $1 < j \leq H$, and fix x^i for $i \neq 1$, $i \neq j$, at arbitrary values $\bar{x}^i$. Then we know the sets $\{(x^1, x^j) \mid x^1 + x^j = k' - \sum_{i \neq 1, j} \bar{x}^i\}$ and $\{(x^1, x^j) \mid \varphi^1(x^1) + \varphi^j(x) = k - \sum_{i \neq 1, j} \varphi^i(\bar{x}^i)\}$ are identical. But these are sets of the form $\{(x^1, x^j) \mid x^1 + x^j = k''\}$ and $\{(x^1, x^j) \mid \varphi^1(x^1) + \varphi^j(x^j) = k'''\}$. The argument of steps 1–5 now shows that $\varphi^1(x) = ax + \varphi^1(0)$ and $\varphi^j(x) = ax + \varphi^j(0)$, from some $a > 0$. But j was arbitrary, and so, for all i we have $\varphi^i(x) = ax + \varphi^i(0)$, which establishes that $\Phi \in G^{CUC}$. ∎

The content of the proposition is that we cannot begin to consider utilitarianism as a candidate for justice unless utility as we conceive of it in the problem at hand is at least cardinal unit comparable: but, according to the problem, we may require much more than this, as the life-expectancy example shows. I find it difficult to think of a conception of utility that is invariant with respect to the group G^{CUC}, and hence Theorems 1.4 and 1.8 do not seem, to me, to be compelling arguments for utilitarianism.

I can, however, conceive of utility as being fully measurable and comparable (that is, utility profiles u can be transformed by $\Phi = (\varphi, \varphi, \ldots, \varphi)$, where $\varphi(z) = az + b$, and $a > 0$): for instance, utility is measured in units like "degrees"—we can measure the extent to which state x allows persons to fulfill their life plans in either "Celsius" or "Fahrenheit." Call the group of such transformations G^{FC}. This is, of course, a stronger informational requirement than cardinal unit comparability, and a weaker requirement than ratio-scale full comparability. There *is* a characterization of utilitarianism, due to Eric Maskin, in which the prior conception of utility is fully measurable and comparable. We work in the social choice framework of Chapter 1. Two new axioms must be stated.

Axiom of Continuity (CONT).   Suppose F is represented by a Bergson-Samuelson social welfare function $W : \mathbf{R}^n \to \mathbf{R}$. F is said to be *continuous* iff the ordering of $\mathbf{R}^n$ induced by W is continuous.[1]

Axiom of Elimination of the Influence of Indifferent Individuals (EL). Let $u^1, u^2 \in \mathcal{U}$ and $M \subseteq H$; suppose $u^{1i} = u^{2i}$ for all $i \in M$ and for all $j \in$

---

1. W need not be a continuous function, although if F is continuous, there is a continuous Bergson-Samuelson social welfare function which represents it.

$H\backslash M$, for all $x, y \in X$, $u^{1j}(x) = u^{1j}(y)$ and $u^{2j}(x) = u^{2j}(y)$. Then $F(u^1)$ and $F(u^2)$ are the same order on X.

EL says the following. Suppose we fix utility functions $u^1, \ldots, u^M$ for a subset of individuals $1, \ldots, M$. Now suppose all the other individuals (in $H\backslash M$) are indifferent among all possible states. Then the social ordering should depend only on the utility functions of the individuals $1, \ldots, M$. Thus the levels of utility of the indifferent individuals are irrelevant for the social ordering.

Strong Pareto (SP*).   Let u be a profile. If $u(x) \geq u(y)$, then x is preferred to y under the order $F(u)$.

We can now state:

Theorem 4.1 (Maskin 1978).[2]   *Let F satisfy U*, SP*, I*, AN, CONT, and EL and respect cardinal full comparability (that is, invariance with respect to the group G^{FC}). Then F is utilitarianism. [That is, $x F(u) y$ iff $\sum u^i(x) \geq \sum u^i(y)$.]*

Proof:

1. By U*, I* and SP*, F is represented by a Bergson-Samuelson social welfare function W; by CONT, we may take W to be continuous. By EL, the order on $\mathbf{R}^{n-m}$ induced by W when the components corresponding to $\mathbf{R}^m$ are fixed is independent of the level at which those m components are fixed. These facts suffice to prove, according to a theorem of Debreu (1954, Theorem 3) that $F(u)$ is represented by a function of the form $\sum g^i(u^i(x))$. The functions g^i are strictly monotonic by SP*. By AN, the functions g^i are all the same, write $g^i = g$. g is continuous by CONT; we must prove g is linear. By full comparability, we can then choose $g(z) = z$.

2. By full comparability, we may choose g so that $g(0) = 0$ and $g(1) = 1$. Let ε be that number in $(0, 1)$ such that $2g(\varepsilon) = g(1) + g(0)$. ε exists and is unique by continuity and monotonicity of g. We have $(\varepsilon, \varepsilon, 0, \ldots, 0) F(u)(1, 0, \ldots, 0)$ since $2g(\varepsilon) + (H - 2)g(0) = g(1) + (H - 1)g(0)$. Full comparability therefore implies that, for $a > b$,

$$((a - b)\varepsilon + b, (a - b)\varepsilon + b, b, \ldots, b) F(u)(a, b, \ldots, b).$$

---

2. The statement of the theorem is somewhat different from Maskin's to make it accord with the theorems in Chapter 1.

Therefore

(1) $2g((a - b)\varepsilon + b) = g(a) + g(b)$ for $a \geq b$.

3. Letting $a = 1, b = 0$, we obtain from (1):

(2) $g(\varepsilon) = \frac{1}{2}$.

Letting $a = 1, b = \varepsilon$ we obtain:

(3) $g((2 - \varepsilon)\varepsilon) = \frac{3}{4}$.

Letting $a = 2 - \varepsilon, b = 0$ we obtain:

(4) $g(2 - \varepsilon) = \frac{3}{2}$.

Letting $a = 2 - \varepsilon, b = 1$ we obtain:

(5) $g(\varepsilon - \varepsilon^2 + 1) = \frac{5}{4}$.

By monotonicity of g [from (3) and (5)]:

$$\varepsilon - \varepsilon^2 + 1 > (2 - \varepsilon)\varepsilon.$$

Taking $a = \varepsilon - \varepsilon^2 + 1$ and $b = (2 - \varepsilon)\varepsilon$ in (1) we obtain:

(6)
$$2g([(\varepsilon - \varepsilon^2 + 1) - (2 - a)\varepsilon]\varepsilon + (2 - \varepsilon)\varepsilon) = g((2 - \varepsilon)\varepsilon)$$
$$+ g(\varepsilon - \varepsilon^2 + 1),$$

which simplifies to

$$g(-2\varepsilon^2 + 3\varepsilon) = 1.$$

By monotonicity and $g(1) = 1$ we have

$$-2\varepsilon^2 + 3\varepsilon = 1,$$

which shows that $\varepsilon = \frac{1}{2}$.

Thus (1) implies

(7)   for $a \geq b$, $g\left(\tfrac{1}{2}(a+b)\right) = \tfrac{1}{2}(g(a) + g(b));$

it follows by symmetry that (7) holds for all $a, b \in \mathbf{R}$. From (2), $g\left(\tfrac{1}{2}\right) = \tfrac{1}{2}$. Taking $a = 1$ and $b = \tfrac{1}{2}$, (7) implies $g\left(\tfrac{3}{4}\right) = \tfrac{3}{4}$. Taking $a = 0, b = \tfrac{1}{2}$, (7) implies $g\left(\tfrac{1}{4}\right) = \tfrac{1}{4}$. In this manner, we can show that for any integers n, k, $g(k/2^n) = (k/2^n)$. Since the set of numbers $\{k/2^n\}$ is dense in $\mathbf{R}$, continuity of g implies $g(z) = z$ for all z, which concludes the proof. ∎

As I have said, Theorem 4.1 is a more compelling argument for utilitarianism than Theorem 1.4. The contentious axiom in 4.1 is continuity. For continuity eliminates one of the egalitarian contenders of utilitarianism, namely, the "leximin" mechanism, short for lexicographic minimum. I shall first define the leximin order, L, for a two-person society. We say that $(a^1, a^2)L(b^1, b^2)$ if and only if either $\min(a^1, a^2) > \min(b^1, b^2)$ or $\min(a^1, a^2) = \min(b^1, b^2)$ and $\max(a^1, a^2) \geq \max(b^1, b^2)$. This extends to $H > 2$ persons in a natural way. Given two utility vectors $a = (a^1, a^2, \ldots, a^H)$ and $b = (b^1, b^2, \ldots, b^H)$, first reorder the components so they read from smallest to largest: call the reordered vectors $\tilde{a} = (\tilde{a}^1, \ldots, \tilde{a}^H)$ and $\tilde{b} = (\tilde{b}^1, \ldots, \tilde{b}^H)$. Let j be the first superscript for which $\tilde{a}^j \neq \tilde{b}^j$. Then a is leximin-preferred to b if and only if $\tilde{a}^j > \tilde{b}^j$. (Otherwise b is preferred to a.) Thus two utility vectors are leximin-indifferent if and only if the vectors $\tilde{a}$ and $\tilde{b}$ are identical.

The leximin ordering of $\mathbf{R}^H$ is not continuous. Recall that an ordering is continuous (which is to say, there exists a continuous Bergson-Samuelson social welfare function representing it) if and only if all its upper and lower contour sets are closed: the upper contour set of an order R associated with a point $a \in \mathbf{R}^H$ is defined as $\mathrm{up}(a) = \{b \in \mathbf{R}^H \mid bRa\}$ and the lower contour set is $\mathrm{lo}(a) = \{b \in \mathbf{R}^H \mid aRb\}$. To see that the leximin order L is not continuous (in $\mathbf{R}^2$), consider the sequence of points $\left(\tfrac{1}{n}, \tfrac{1}{n}\right)$. Each of these points is strictly preferred to $(0, 1)$ (since $\min\left(\tfrac{1}{n}, \tfrac{1}{n}\right) > \min(0, 1)$). But they converge to the point $(0, 0)$ which is not in upper contour set of $(0, 1)$ [that is, $(0, 0)$ is inferior to $(0, 1)$].

The leximin order of utilities is a natural conception of egalitarianism, for it says, choose that social alternative which makes the worst off as well off as possible, then the next worse off as well off as possible, and so on. Thus the continuity axiom in Theorem 4.1 eliminates a kind of egalitarianism—an example of how a seemingly innocuous "technical" assumption is not innocuous at all. In fact, if we drop CONT from Theorem 4.1 and replace full measurability and comparability with ordinal full comparability (OFC) and include a minimal equity axiom (see Corollary 1.1), we get a characterization of leximin.[3] (See d'Aspremont and Gevers 1977, Theorem 7.)

Continuity of social choice works against egalitarianism, in the leximin sense. On the other hand, the discontinuous nature of leximin is also the main argument *against* it from the point of view of distributive justice. To see this, again consider a two-person society, and consider a sequence of utility vectors given by $((n-1)/n, n)$, for $n = 1, 2, \ldots$ According to leximin, all of these vectors are (socially) dispreferred to the utility vector $(1, 1)$. In other words, no amount of utility for the second person can compensate society for the fact that the first person's utility stays below 1, even by an arbitrarily small amount.

As an argument for utilitarianism, it would be still better to have an axiomatic characterization when utility is assumed to be ratio-scale comparable, as I have argued above. This problem is attacked by Blackorby and Donaldson (1982), who show that, if RFC comparability is substituted for FC comparability in Theorem 4.1, then a class of social choice functionals is characterized which they call global means of order r. If utility is restricted to be non-negative, this class includes functionals represented by Bergson-Samuelson social welfare functions of the form $W(a^1, \ldots, a^H) = (\sum r a^h)^{1/r}$, for r positive. Thus further axioms would be needed to characterize utilitarianism if only ratio-scale full comparability is admitted.

In sum, and in my judgment, Theorem 4.1 is the strongest argument we have for utilitarianism as a solution to the problem of distributive justice. Theorem 1.4 does not provide a compelling argument, since it is difficult to conceive of a notion of utility that is meaningful, from the viewpoint of distributive justice, and that is invariant with respect to all cardinal-unit-comparable transformations. An even more compelling argument (than Theorem 4.1) for utilitarianism would exist if there were a characterization theorem in which the prior conception of utility were only ratio-and-difference comparable. The strongest possible argument would be one in which absolute comparability and measurability were assumed, for then

---

3. Alternatively, the function $W(a^1, \ldots, a^H) = \min\{a^1, \ldots, a^H\}$ is egalitarian and continuous, but does not satisfy the strong Pareto property.

one could think of utility as measuring amounts of (interpersonally comparable) satisfaction, and the sum of utilities would correspond to a total amount of satisfaction in society—this is, of course, the classical utilitarian conception.

If we replace "fully measurable and comparable" with "absolutely measurable and comparable" in the premise of Theorem 4.1, then, as can be seen from step 1 of the proof, the class of social choice functionals consists precisely of those representable by a Bergson-Samuelson welfare function of the form $\sum g(u^i)$, where g is strictly increasing. These are the "generalized utilitarian" functionals; note that such a social choice functional may be rendered extremely inequality averse, as utilitarianism is not, by choosing g to be suitably concave. But this class also includes extremely equality averse functionals, gotten by choosing g to be suitably convex.

The theorems discussed in this section take an abstract set X as the set of social alternatives; as such, they are open to the criticism of not modeling the problem of the distribution of resources, as such. Nevertheless, we could produce an analogue of Theorem 1.4 on economic environments with the methods of §1.5, using the COAD axiom, and working on the domain of economic environments posited there.

4.3   The Representation Theorems of Harsanyi and Myerson

In a famous paper, Harsanyi (1955) makes a very different argument for utilitarianism. Harsanyi begins with a collection of H individuals who have von Neumann–Morgenstern preferences u^{*h} over a set of lotteries. Let the lotteries be over a set of m prizes, where $m \geq 2$; a lottery can be viewed as a probability vector $p = (p^1, \ldots, p^m)$, where p^i is the probability of receiving prize i. Call the set of such lotteries L (not to be confused with the leximin order, in another context). We may designate the utility from a lottery as $u^{*h}(p)$, where u^{*h} is h's utility function in a profile u^*. Harsanyi wishes to deduce a social preference order over L. He contends that, if it is reasonable to assume that individuals' preference orders of lotteries obey the von Neumann–Morgenstern axioms, then it is reasonable to assume that society's preference order over L also obeys those axioms. Further, he proposes a Pareto axiom—that if all individuals prefer lottery p to lottery q, then so should society. The remarkable result is that these two axioms imply that the social ordering must be of the form $\sum a^h u^{*h}$, for some real numbers $\{a^h\}$: that is, society must order social states (lotteries) by a weighted utilitarian rule!

Harsanyi's original proof of the theorem was not correct, but since then, many authors have provided correct proofs of a multitude of versions of Harsanyi's theorem: see Domotor (1979), Border (1981, 1985), Fishburn (1984), Coulhon and Mongin (1989), Hammond (1992), Weymark (1993), and Zhou (1994). The proofs rely on versions of the separating hyperplane theorem. The most thorough discussion of the meaning of the "Harsanyi aggregation theorem" is by Weymark (1991), who also presents a catalogue of variations on the theorem. For the sake of concreteness, I will write the Harsanyi aggregation theorem in this form:

Theorem 4.2 (Weymark 1991, Theorem 8). *Let R^h, $h = 1, \ldots, H$, be a preference order of individual h over L, let R be a "social" preference order over L, and let all these preference orders satisfy the von Neumann–Morgenstern axioms. Let R^h be represented by the von Neumann–Morgenstern utility u^{*h}.*

(a) If Pareto indifference is satisfied (that is, $p I^h q$ for all $h \Rightarrow p I q$, where I^h and I are the indifference relations associated with R^h and R) then there exist numbers $a^h \in \mathbf{R}$ such that R is represented by the functional $W(u) = \sum a^h u^{*h}$.

(b) If Strong Pareto is satisfied (that is, $p R^h q$ for all h, and $p P^h q$ for some h implies $p P q$, where P^h and P are the strict preference relations associated with R^h and R), then the a^h may all be chosen to be positive.

(c) If Independent Prospects is also satisfied (see below), then the $\{a^h\}$ are unique up to a positive factor of proportionality.

Definition 4.1. A profile $(R^1, \ldots, R^H)$ and a set of lotteries L satisfies *independent prospects* iff for each h there exists a pair of lotteries $p^h, q^h \in L$ such that $p^h I^j q^h$ for all $j \neq h$ and $p^h P^h q^h$.

Independent Prospects is satisfied if, for any individual h, there are two prizes (or social outcomes) that differ only in what individual h receives or experiences, and assuming as always that individuals' preferences are self-regarding.

Theorem 4.2 has an attractive feature that the social choice theorems we have discussed thus far lack: it does not require an unrestricted domain of utility profiles. It is what is called a single-profile result, as it postulates just one profile. As I remarked in §2.1, the unrestricted domain axioms of Arrovian social choice theory and Nash bargaining theory are philosophically questionable, for they require the consideration of an infinitude of possible worlds, most of which will never exist. To put the point more pragmatically, if we view a social choice theorem as an instruction to a planner, then its prescription is only convincing if the planner believes that she might encounter a distribution problem that takes the form of any problem in the domain. But it would then appear that the unrestricted domain axiom is far too strong an axiom. Without pursuing this issue further, we may simply observe that Harsanyi's theorem is immune to the implied criticism.

Theorem 4.2 is surely an interesting, and surprising, mathematical result. But there are two criticisms of it as an argument for utilitarianism. The first is due to Diamond (1967), who argues that even if individuals' preferences over L obey the von Neumann–Morgenstern axioms, it is unreasonable to assume that society's preferences should. To see this, let H consist of two individuals, and L consist of lotteries over two prizes, denoted $(A, 0)$ and $(0, A)$. We may think of there being one indivisible object, A: in $(A, 0)$, the first person gets it, and in $(0, A)$, the second person does. Now L consists of the set of probability vectors $p = (p^1, p^2)$: the lottery p is one in which the prize A goes to the first person with probability p^1 and to the second with probability p^2. Let us suppose that from a social viewpoint, the outcomes $(A, 0)$ and $(0, A)$ are equally good—society plays no favorites. We write $(A, 0) \sim (0, A)$, where $\sim$ stands for social indifference. A "mixture" $\alpha p + (1 - \alpha)q$ means the lottery $(\alpha p^1 + (1 - \alpha)q^1, \alpha p^2 + (1 - \alpha)q^2)$. To use a notation that may be more transparent, let us write $pX + qY$ for the lottery "with probability p, X is the social state and with probability q, Y is the social state." Now by the independence axiom of von Neumann and Morgenstern, we must have

$$\tfrac{1}{2}(A, 0) + \tfrac{1}{2}(0, A) \sim \tfrac{1}{2}(A, 0) + \tfrac{1}{2}(A, 0) = (A, 0).$$

But this means that society is indifferent between flipping a fair coin to decide who gets the object A (the left-hand lottery in the above mathematical statement) and giving the object A for sure to the first person, an unpleasant conclusion! Indeed, fairness dictates that society should prefer the allocation of the object by a fair coin toss, to allocating it for sure to individual one.

In my opinion, Diamond has presented a knockdown argument against the ethical attractiveness of Theorem 4.2. Epstein and Segal (1992) ask the question: what happens if we require only that social preferences satisfy an axiom which is weaker than the von Neumann–Morgenstern independence axiom, one which will prevent Diamond's example from occurring? They propose two axioms to replace independence, called Mixture Symmetry and Randomization Preference. We return to the notation in which a lottery in L is a probability vector p. In the following, R, P, and I denote the social preference order, its strict subrelation, and its indifference subrelation.

Axiom of Mixture Symmetry (MS).   If pIq then for any $\alpha \in [0, 1]$, $(\alpha p + (1 - \alpha)q)I((1 - \alpha)p + \alpha q)$.

Axiom of Randomization Preference (RP).   If pIq and if there exist individuals h, j such that pP^hq and qP^jp, then $\left(\frac{1}{2}p + \frac{1}{2}q\right)Pp$.

Notice that MS and RP are both attractive axioms in the Diamond example: in fact, RP tells us that the mixture $\frac{1}{2}(1, 0) + \frac{1}{2}(0, 1)$ is strictly socially preferred to $(1, 0)$ or $(0, 1)$, which I said should be the case.

Define a Bergson-Samuelson social welfare function on $\mathbf{R}^H$ to be *quadratic* iff $W(\bar{u}^1, \ldots, \bar{u}^H) = \sum_{h=1}^H \sum_{j=1}^H a_{hj}\bar{u}_h\bar{u}_j + \sum_{h=1}^H b_n\bar{u}_h$, where a_{hj} and b_h are real numbers and for all h, j, $a_{hj} = a_{jh}$. We then have the remarkable:

Theorem 4.3 (Epstein and Segal 1992).   *Let individual preferences R^h on L satisfy the von Neumann–Morgenstern axioms; let social preference R on L satisfy Strong Pareto, Continuity,*[4] *MS, and RP. Then R is represented by a quadratic, strictly increasing, quasi-concave Bergson-Samuelson social welfare function.*

The proof of Theorem 4.3 uses a representation theorem for quadratic preferences presented in Chew, Epstein, and Segal (1991). Theorem 4.3 is an appealing resolution of the Diamond challenge—but, of course, it is no longer an argument for utilitarianism.

There is, however, a second objection to both Theorems 4.2 and 4.3, whose upshot is that neither theorem can be interpreted as making a meaningful statement in the language of classical utilitarianism.[5] To render this objection comprehensible, it is advisable briefly to review what von

---

4. Recall that Continuity requires the upper and lower contour sets under the preference order of a given lottery to be closed.

5. This issue was first raised, though not in exactly this form, in an exchange of papers between Harsanyi (1975, 1977b) and Sen (1976, 1977, 1986). Blackorby, Donaldson, and Weymark (1980) argue that Harsanyi's utilitarianism cannot be identified with classical utilitarianism. The issue in something like the present form is discussed in Weymark (1991).

Neumann–Morgenstern utility functions are. We begin with a set of lotteries L over a set of prizes M; each individual is postulated to have an *ordinal ranking* of these lotteries. Denote the prizes $x^1, \ldots, x^n$. Fix an order of L, call it R. If R can be represented by a utility function, then there is a large infinitude of utility functions that represent it—if u is such a utility function and φ is any strictly monotone mapping of the real numbers into itself, then $\varphi \circ u$ is an equally good utility representation of R. Now suppose that the preference order R on L satisfies several axioms known as the von Neumann–Morgenstern axioms. It can then be proved that there is a special utility representation u^* of R with the following linearity property: for any lottery p,

$$
(4.7) \quad
\begin{aligned}
u^*(p) = {}& p^1 u^*(1, 0, \ldots, 0) \\
& + p^2 u^*(0, 1, 0, \ldots, 0) + \ldots + p^n u^*(0, 0, \ldots, 0, 1).
\end{aligned}
$$

That is, the utility of a lottery p is just equal to the probability-weighted average of the utilities of the "sure prospects," where a sure prospect just chooses one of the n prizes (or outcomes) for sure. Indeed, it can be proved that, up to affine transformation, the function u^* is unique. Now the function u^* is a very convenient one to use in analyzing choice behavior, because we know that it is completely characterized by n numbers, the values of u^* on the n sure prospects. Alternatively put, if the von Neumann–Morgenstern axioms characterize choice under uncertainty, then preferences are of a particularly simple type: they are completely determined by a choice of n numbers.

The salient point for our purposes is that von Neumann–Morgenstern utility functions are representations of *ordinal* preference over lotteries only. The original preference order R provides no information about intensity of preference. Moreover, if we have a population of individuals, each of whom has a preference order R^h over lotteries, and we are given no information allowing us to make interpersonal comparisons of welfare, then the von Neumann–Morgenstern preferences can give us no meaningful way of making interpersonal comparisons—if the conception of utility does not include a way of comparing welfare levels interpersonally, there is no way we can deduce such interpersonal comparability by mathematical manipulation. The information simply is not there to be had.

Now suppose that we do have a conception of the welfare that persons derive from lotteries that is interpersonally comparable. That is, there is a choice of profile $u = (u^1, \ldots, u^H)$ of utility functions of individuals on the space of lotteries L which it is meaningful to sum. By Proposition 4.1, we know that, for utilitarianism to be meaningful, these representations must be unique up to transformation by some group G contained in G^{CUC}. Let $CUC(u)$ be the set of profiles consisting of all CUC-transformations of u— this is the largest set of profiles that can possibly represent utility in a sense that is meaningful to sum. If individual preferences over lotteries obey the von Neumann–Morgenstern axioms as well, then we know there is also a choice of profile $u^* = (u^{*1}, \ldots, u^{*H})$ representing individuals' preferences that is unique up to transformations in the group G^{CNC} and whose component functions enjoy the expected-utility property [that is, they obey equation (4.7) above]. Let $CNC(u^*)$ be the set of CNC-transformations of u^*. Now *there may exist no utility profile contained in both CUC(u) and CNC(u*)*. Indeed, these two families of profiles are each "extremely small" in the entire family of ordinal utility representations of the given preferences. In particular, this means that the representation $\sum a^h u^{*h}$ of Theorem 4.2, which is a sum of utility functions in $CNC(u^*)$, is almost surely not ordinally equivalent to a sum $\sum v^h$ of utility functions v^h in $CUC(u)$. In other words, the lottery which maximizes $\sum a^h u^{*h}$ is not maximizing a *meaningful* sum of individual utilities—a sum, that is, of some measure of welfare which we have initially posited to be interpersonally comparable and summable. To summarize, Harsanyi's aggregation theorem is not a theorem about utilitarianism; it is, rather, a quite different result about the representation of social preferences in terms of individual von Neumann–Morgenstern utilities.

Because this point is not well understood in the literature, it is perhaps worth elaborating upon it with an example. Suppose society has 65 units of a good to divide between two persons. It must choose between two possible outcomes or "prizes": the first outcome is $x_1 = (1, 64)$ in which the first person gets 1 unit and the rest goes to the second person; the second outcome is $x_2 = (64, 1)$, in which the first person gets 64 units and the rest goes to person two. (Perhaps these are the only possible ways of dividing the 65 units of the good.) The two individuals have von Neumann–Morgenstern preferences R^1 and R^2 over amounts of the good determined by utility functions $v^{*1}(x) = x^{1/2}$ and $v^{*2}(x) = x^{1/3}$, where x is the amount of the good. We have specified the utility functions v^{*i} over amounts of the good received for sure; but by the expected utility property, we can represent the utility of individual i derived from a lottery $p = (p^1, p^2)$ over prizes x_1 and x_2 by a function $u^{*i}(p) = p^1 v^{*i}(x_{1i}) + p^2 v^{*i}(x_{2i})$, where $x_1 = (x_{11}, x_{12})$ and $x_2 = (x_{21}, x_{22})$, and so x_{ij} is the amount of the good person j receives if the outcome is prize i. Thus, u^{*1} and u^{*2} are defined on lotteries over the two prizes. The functions u^{*1} and u^{*2} are simply special representations of the *ordinal* preferences of the individuals over lotteries L.

Now suppose that we have a prior conception of *interpersonally comparable* satisfaction that the two individuals derive from lotteries—say, the satisfaction level of individual one at a lottery p is given by $u^1(p) = (p^1 x_{11}^{1/2} + p^2 x_{21}^{1/2})^2$ and the satisfaction level of individual two at a lottery p is given by $u^2(p) = (p^1 x_{12}^{1/3} + p^2 x_{22}^{1/3})^3$. There is only one thing we must check for these satisfaction functions to be possible—that they each represent the ordinal preferences R^i. We know that u^{*i} is a representation of preference order R^i on L, and note that u^i is just a strictly monotonic transformation of u^{*i}— for $i = 1$, use $\varphi^1(z) = z^2$, and for $i = 2$, use $\varphi^2(z) = z^3$—and so, indeed, the functions $u^i(p)$ are representations of R^i. Let us suppose, for the sake of simplicity, that the utility functions u^1 and u^2 are absolutely measurable and comparable—thus $u^i(p)$ is a specific quantity of satisfaction in meaningful units that we cannot tamper with. Then there is a *unique* utilitarian social choice function, which represents the total amount of satisfaction these two individuals derive from lotteries, given by $U(p) = (p^1 x_{11}^{1/2} + p^2 x_{21}^{1/2})^2 + (p^1 x_{12}^{1/3} + p^2 x_{22}^{1/3})^3$. Now in our problem $x_{11} = 1$, $x_{12} = 64$, $x_{21} = 64$, and $x_{22} = 1$; furthermore, we can write $p^2 = 1 - p^1$. This allows us to write the function $U(p)$ as a function $\tilde{U}$ of p^1 only, and we compute that:

$$(4.8a) \qquad \tilde{U}(p^1) = (8 - 7p^1)^2 + 3(1 + 3p^1)^3.$$

Now consider the Harsanyi representation $\sum a^h u^{*h}$. By Strong Pareto, a^1 and a^2 may be chosen to be positive; without loss of generality we may choose $a^1 = 1$, and call a^2 simply a. Then the representation $\sum a^h u^{*h}$ becomes $U^*(p; a) = (p^1 x_{11}^{1/2} + p^2 x_{21}^{1/2}) + a(p^1 x_{12}^{1/3} + p^2 x_{22}^{1/3})$, which again can be represented as a function $\tilde{U}^*(p^1)$, which we can compute to be:

$$(4.8b) \qquad \tilde{U}^*(p^1; a) = 8 + a + (3a - 7)p^1.$$

$\tilde{U}(p^1)$ defines a specific social preference order on the feasible space of lotteries; and for each a, so does $\tilde{U}^*(p^1; a)$. I claim that *for no positive number a are the orders $\tilde{U}$ and $\tilde{U}^*(\cdot, a)$ the same*. The proof is simple. First case: suppose $a \geq \frac{7}{3}$. Then $\tilde{U}^*(\cdot, a)$ is (weakly) monotone increasing in p^1. We may compute the derivative of $\tilde{U}$: $d\tilde{U}/dp^1 = -14(8 - 7p^1) + 9(1 + 3p^1)^2$. For p^1 close to 0, we see that $\tilde{U}$ is *strictly decreasing* in p^1. Thus $\tilde{U}$ and $\tilde{U}(\cdot, a)$ are different preference orders. Second case: suppose $a < \frac{7}{3}$. Then

$\tilde{U}^*$ is strictly monotone decreasing in p^1; but for p^1 near 1, $\tilde{U}$ is strictly increasing in p^1. Thus the claim italicized just above is proved.

This example demonstrates concretely why Theorem 4.2 cannot be interpreted as a theorem about utilitarianism in the philosophically meaningful sense. We cannot derive any kind of meaningful interpersonal comparability given only the fact that each individual has ordinal preferences over lotteries satisfying the von Neumann–Morgenstern axioms. If we *can* independently make such comparisons, the utility functions which make comparability possible will have only this in common with the von Neumann–Morgenstern utilities: they each are ordinal representations of the underlying preference orders over lotteries. The view that Harsanyi's aggregation theorem has anything to do with the idea that society should maximize the total well-being of its members is wrong by virtue of a confusion concerning the representation of orders by cardinal utility functions. Note that Harsanyi's theorem was presented in 1955, twenty years before economists formulated the ideas of measurability and comparability in a satisfactorily precise manner. The continuing interest in Harsanyi's aggregation theorem among economists, I believe, is only sustained by an incomplete understanding of these ideas.

Similar observations apply to Theorem 4.3. The premises of that theorem respond to the Diamond criticism, and so the theorem is an ethically more powerful argument for adopting a quadratic social choice functional than the Harsanyi theorem is for adopting a utilitarian one. But again, it is incorrect to view Theorem 4.3 as saying that society should maximize some quadratic function of the well-beings of its members. When is it meaningful to maximize some quadratic function of the "utilities" of individuals? Only when we have a prior conception of utility that is at most ratio-scale comparable—that is, quadratic social welfare requires a conception of utility in which transformations by some group G which is a subgroup of G^{RFC} are allowed.[6] But if we have a profile $u = (u^1, \ldots, u^H)$ that is specified up to RFC transformations and that measures the degree of satisfaction of persons, there is no reason that quadratic functions of profiles in RFC(u) will give the same ordering over lotteries as quadratic functions of CNC(u^*), where u^* is a profile of von Neumann–Morgenstern preferences. Thus Epstein and Segal (1992, p. 693) are incorrect when they write "[our theorem

---

6. I do not prove this assertion here: to do so would require an argument of the sort presented in Proposition 4.1.

shows that] given suitable Pareto and continuity conditions, the moral view that fairness of the social choice process matters is properly represented (only) by the adoption of a strictly quasi-concave, quadratic social welfare function," *if* they have in mind the *standard* moral view, which states that society must take into account the degrees or levels of welfare that different distributions of resources engender among society's members. The kind of utility for which quadratic social welfare is morally meaningful can only be utility specified up to ratio and difference comparability, or some stricter invariance condition, and the von Neumann–Morgenstern utility functions to which Theorem 4.3 applies are not of that type.

Finally, we turn to a characterization theorem of Myerson (1981). Let S and T be two convex sets in $\mathbf{R}^H$, and λ a number in the interval $[0, 1]$. We define the set $\lambda S + (1 - \lambda)T = \{y \in \mathbf{R}^H \mid y = \lambda s + (1 - \lambda)t$ for some $s \in S, t \in T\}$. Let S be a set of convex, comprehensive sets in $\mathbf{R}^H$; we say S is a *convex collection* if $S, T \in S$ implies $\lambda S + (1 - \lambda)T \in S$. Let $F : S \to \mathbf{R}^H$ be a *solution:* that is, for all $S \in S$, $F(S) \in S$. We say a solution defined on a convex collection is *linear* if for all $S, T \in S$ and $\lambda \in [0, 1]$, $F(\lambda S + (1 - \lambda)T) = \lambda F(S) + (1 - \lambda)F(T)$. What is the interpretation of linearity? Suppose there is uncertainty as to what the resource endowment of society will be next year. We have a fixed population of H individuals (with their fixed von Neumann–Morgenstern utility functions); with probability λ, next year's aggregate endowment will be one that will engender the utility possibilities set S for these individuals, and with probability $(1 - \lambda)$, the resource endowment will be such that the utility possibilities set engendered is T. Today society must choose what the allocation of resources will be next year in either state: thus society must choose an expected utility in the set $\lambda S + (1 - \lambda)T$. Linearity says that the solution F has this property: the expected utility of each individual will be the same whether we choose the contingent allocation today, or we wait until next year and then choose the allocation (according to F) from whatever resource bundle becomes available.

A solution F is *weighted utilitarian on* S if there exists a vector $p = (p^1, \ldots, p^H) \geq 0$ such that for all $S \in S$, $p \cdot F(S) = \max_{s \in S} p \cdot s$. That is, $F(S)$ maximizes the sum of weighted utilities $p \cdot s$. We have:

Theorem 4.4 (Myerson 1981). *Let S be a convex collection of convex, comprehensive sets in R^H, and let F be a weakly Pareto optimal, linear solution on S. Then F is weighted utilitarian.*

The proof involves a separating hyperplane argument.

As a theorem about distributive justice, 4.4 has three flaws. First is its welfarist character. The motivation for the linearity postulate comes from an appeal to underlying economic environments which do not appear in the model. Therefore the criticisms raised against Nash-type bargaining theory in Chapter 2 apply. In particular, the linearity axiom is too strong: it enforces a restriction on F when none can be justified—when, indeed, there are three "environments" generating utility possibilities sets S, T, and Q and $Q = \lambda S + (1 - \lambda)T$, but Q cannot be interpreted as the expected utilities of agents who may face S or T tomorrow, with the appropriate probabilities. Second, the weights p come out in the wash; if the theorem were stated on economic environments, then it would say that there is a particular choice of von Neumann–Morgenstern utility function for each individual such that F maximizes the sum of those von Neumann–Morgenstern utilities. (Indeed, this is not quite accurate, for some of the p^h may be zero. So some individuals may be ignored in the weighted utilitarian calculus.) But there is no interpretation for those particular choices having to do with any kind of comparability across persons—here, the arguments given above concerning the "utilitarianism" of Theorem 4.2 apply. Third, exactly those arguments apply more generally: we cannot interpret the utilitarianism of Theorem 4.4 as having anything to do with philosophical utilitarianism, that is, maximizing the sum of some kind of interpersonally comparable utility.

Thus Theorem 4.4 is, like Theorems 4.2 and 4.3, an interesting representation result. But it has nothing to do with utilitarianism as a theory of distributive justice.

4.4 Utilitarianism from behind the Veil of Ignorance

Harsanyi (1953, 1977a) has also proposed a second and completely different argument for utilitarianism, based upon what social state a soul behind a veil of ignorance would choose. Suppose there is a set of states X (say, possible distributions of income) each of which may be chosen for a society of H types of person. The members of each type are identical, and the fraction (frequency) of type h in the population is π^h. Each type has preferences over lotteries of X satisfying the von Neumann–Morgenstern axioms; let u^h be a von Neumann–Morgenstern utility function for type h. Harsanyi argues that society should choose that state x that a soul would choose who knew that it had a probability of π^h of being born as a type h person. Thus the soul faces a decision problem behind a veil of ignorance, where it knows the probability distribution of types in the actual world, but not which person it shall become in the birth lottery.

From the soul's viewpoint, it faces "extended prospects" of the form (h, x) where h is a type and $x \in X$: that is, it could be embodied in a person of type h in state x, for any h and x. Let $\mathcal{L}$ be the set of lotteries on objects (h, x). Harsanyi posits that the soul has preferences over these lotteries that obey the von Neumann–Morgenstern axioms. (We shall presently inquire where these preferences come from.) They can be represented by a von Neumann–Morgenstern utility function Φ on $\mathcal{L}$. Let us denote by $\pi(x)$ the lottery in $\mathcal{L}$ which gives probability π^h of the outcome (h, x). Then, by the expected utility property, we can write:

$$(4.9) \qquad \Phi(\pi(x)) = \sum \pi^h \Phi((h, x)).$$

Now Harsanyi argues that, over lotteries whose prizes are all of the form (h, x) for fixed h (and varying x), it is reasonable to suppose that the soul has the same von Neumann–Morgenstern preferences as type h: that is, the soul should have the same preferences over lotteries on X as type h does, when it is imagining itself fixed as a type h person. Harsanyi calls this the "principle of acceptance." Thus for all h, and for some (a^h, b^h), with $a^h > 0$, the following should hold:

$$(4.10) \qquad \Phi((h, x)) = a^h u^h(x) + b^h.$$

(Since Φ is fixed and the u^h are fixed, the choice of (a^h, b^h) is completely determined.) Substituting from (4.10) into (4.9) yields:

$$\Phi(\pi(x)) = \sum \pi^h a^h u^h(x) + K,$$

where K is a constant. Since the soul's decision problem is to choose x to maximize $\Phi(\pi(x))$, the constant K is irrelevant, and we conclude that the soul maximizes a function of the form $\sum \pi^h a^h u^h(x)$. More explicitly, there are von Neumann–Morgenstern utility functions $\tilde{u}^h$ for the types—namely, $\tilde{u}^h(x) = a^h u^h(x)$—such that the soul chooses x to maximize $\sum \pi^h \tilde{u}^h(x)$. But this, Harsanyi says, is the utilitarian objective: the soul chooses x to maximize average utility in the society. Weymark (1991, p. 293) calls this argument Harsanyi's Impartial Observer Theorem.

The argument, however, is flawed for the same reason that the interpretation of Theorem 4.2 as an argument for utilitarianism is flawed, namely, there is no sense in which the summation $\sum \pi^h \tilde{u}^h(x)$ can be interpreted as the sum of some kind of well-being across persons. Let us return to the first step in Harsanyi's argument, that the soul has preferences over the set of lotteries $\mathcal{L}$. In particular, the soul must have preferences over the set of extended prospects (the prizes in $\mathcal{L}$), $\{(h, x) \mid h \in H, x \in X\}$. Now how can the soul decide whether it is better to have the prize (h, x) than the prize (j, y)—that is, that it is better to be a person of type h in state x than a person of type j in state y? There are, it seems, only two possibilities: either it must be capable of making an interpersonal comparison of the welfare levels of person h in state x and person j in state y, or it has some *perfectionist* view, that the life of a person of type h in state x is more worthwhile than that of a person of type j in state y, independently of how these persons themselves evaluate their lives. In the second case, we would have to justify why the soul should hold such a perfectionist view. It is, I think, much simpler to suppose that the first possibility holds, namely, that the soul has an ordinal-level comparable utility function, call it Ψ, defined on the set of extended prospects. Thus the statement $\Psi((h, x)) > \Psi((j, y))$ is meaningful—it means that the soul would prefer to be a type h in state x than a type j in state y, and this precisely because a type h person in state x is better off than a type j person in state y. Let us move into our old notation of preference profiles: then we will represent the utility function Ψ as a profile $\psi = (\psi^1, \ldots, \psi^H)$, where $\psi^h(x) \equiv \Psi((h, x))$. Now to speak of average welfare in the society, one would like to take sums of the form $\sum_h \pi^h \psi^h(x)$—this, however, is not meaningful unless the profile ψ is defined up to cardinal-unit-comparable transformations. Thus the profile Ψ must be both ordinal level comparable and cardinal unit comparable, which means that we can permit transformations only of the form $\varphi(z) = (az + b, az + b, \ldots, az + b)$, for $a > 0$ and b real. That is, the profile Ψ must be fully measurable and comparable (FC).

We have not yet shown that Harsanyi's Impartial Observer Theorem has nothing to do with utilitarianism: to do so, we must show that there exists no function of the form $F(x) = \sum_h \pi^h a^h u^h(x)$ which gives the same ordering of states in X as a function of the form $G(x) = a \sum_h \pi^h \psi^h(x) + b$, for $a > 0$, where the u^h are the initially chosen von Neumann–Morgenstern utilities and the ψ^h are fully measurable and comparable utilities. We proceed to show this by example. Let $H = \{1, 2\}$, suppose there is one person of each type, and suppose the states X consist of all possible divisions of one dollar between the two persons. Represent by $\tilde{x}$ the state in which individual 1 gets x dollars and individual 2 gets $1 - x$ dollars. Let

$u^1(\tilde{x}) = x^{1/2}$, $u^2(\tilde{x}) = (1-x)^{1/2}$, and let $\psi^1(\tilde{x}) = d^1 x$ and $\psi^2(\tilde{x}) = d^2(1-x)$, where $d^1 > d^2$. There is no inconsistency in saying that the von Neumann–Morgenstern utility of individual h is u^h and the degree of fully measurable and comparable utility is given by ψ^h. Further, suppose that $\pi^1 = \pi^2 = \frac{1}{2}$. Then any function $G(x)$ that represents a meaningful average of utility of this society is ordinally equivalent to $\frac{1}{2}(\psi^1(\tilde{x}) + \psi^2(\tilde{x})) = \frac{1}{2}(d^1 x + d^2(1-x))$. This defines a strictly monotone increasing order on x in $[0, 1]$, since $d^1 > d^2$. In particular, if this society were to maximize average utility, it would give the whole dollar to individual 1. Next we examine functions of the form $F(\tilde{x}) = \sum_h \pi^h a^h u^h(\tilde{x}) = a^1 x^{1/2} + a^2(1-x)^{1/2}$. Without loss of generality, since we are only concerned with the order on states that F generates, and a^1, a^2 are both positive, we may choose $a^1 = 1$. Thus $F(\tilde{x}) = x^{1/2} + a^2(1-x)^{1/2}$. The derivative of this function w.r.t x is $\frac{1}{2}\left(x^{-1/2} - a^2(1-x)^{-1/2}\right)$. Note that, for any positive number a^2, and for all x sufficiently close to 1, this quantity is negative. Hence it is never socially optimal to give the whole dollar to person 1, if F is the social objective. We have shown that no weighted sum of von Neumann–Morgenstern utilities gives the true utilitarian ordering of states in X, that given by G.

Hence Harsanyi's Impartial Observer Theorem does not justify the view that society should choose that state that maximizes the average utility of society's members. The Impartial Observer Theorem is a representation theorem, and that is all.

4.5 An Implication for the Interpretation of Individual Optimization under Uncertainty

There is a rather striking implication of the reasoning just given for the interpretation of individual optimization for a person with von Neumann–Morgenstern preferences: her expected utility is not the same thing as her average utility! Consider an insurance problem for a population of identical individuals. There are s states of the world; with probability π^s any individual will receive an income of x^s. Suppose all persons have the same concave, von Neumann–Morgenstern utility function u over lotteries on money prizes. The optimal insurance problem for any individual consists in choosing a vector $(M^1, M^2, \ldots, M^s)$ to

$$\text{maximize} \quad \sum_s \pi^s u(x^s + M^s)$$

(4.11)

$$\text{subject to} \quad \sum_s \pi^s M^s = 0.$$

Since u is concave, this program implies complete consumption smoothing: that is, $M^s = \bar{x} - x^s$, where $\bar{x} = \sum_s \pi^s x^s$. We can say that the individual maximizes her expected utility subject to constraint by arranging to consume average income in each state.

Now the utility function u is a representation of ordinal preferences only over lotteries on income, and averages of a function representing ordinal preferences have no interpretation in terms of averages of some underlying quantity associated with those states. That is to say, the individual may well have a cardinal-unit-comparable representation ψ of the satisfaction or utility she enjoys in consuming different amounts of income—any positive affine transformation of ψ will do just as well. We can then say that her (meaningful) average utility, if she consumes $x^s + M^s$ in state s, is $\sum_s \pi^s \psi(x^s + M^s)$, where we have used weights π^s in computing the average. Since the individuals in this society are identical, we may interpret this sum as the average utility in a fully insured society in which the frequency of incomes of x^s is just π^s.

If ψ is also concave, then the solution of the problem "maximize average utility in this society" will also be to pool income, to arrange that every individual consume exactly $\bar{x}$. Thus maximizing expected utility and average utility will lead to the same outcome. There is, however, no reason that u and ψ should be both concave or both convex. For example, it is not hard to imagine persons for whom ψ is concave (they get decreasing marginal satisfaction from each unit of incremental consumption), but for whom u is convex (they enjoy gambling). These persons may choose not to insure, but their average satisfaction over states (not lotteries) is maximized with complete consumption smoothing. The opposite situation can also be imagined, of people who do not enjoy the uncertainty of lotteries—because, for instance, planning is made difficult—but they have increasing marginal satisfaction in income, at least over a range, perhaps because there is a "fixed cost" component in consumption.

Perhaps a somewhat different example will make the point more sharply. Imagine that there is just one person; on each day of a decade, there is a probability of π^s that her income will be x^s, for $s = 1, \ldots, S$, and these events are independently distributed (across days). She can arrange to save on days when her income is high and to consume from her inventory on days when it is low, but she wishes neither to have excess savings on average nor to be consistently in debt to an outside creditor. Suppose she has von Neumann–Morgenstern preferences over the income lottery she faces, represented by u. Then her optimal savings program will be given by the solution to program (4.11) above. Now the intertemporally comparable satisfaction that she gets from consuming an income x may well be given by another cardinal utility function ψ. By the law of large numbers, her average satisfaction over the decade, if she arranges to consume $x^s + M^s$ when her income is x^s, will be very close to $\sum_s \pi^s \psi(x^s + M^s)$: this average is meaningful only because ψ is an intertemporally comparable measure of satisfaction. As I have argued, if ψ and u are not both concave or convex in the appropriate region, the savings program that maximizes her average satisfaction will differ from the program that maximizes her expected utility.

What *should* she maximize? I am not sure, but I think the answer depends on whether she derives satisfaction or dissatisfaction from looking back, and what her preferences over lotteries take into account. If she has no memory of past satisfaction, then the correct path is surely to maximize expected utility: for each day she should choose the lottery that she most prefers, and hindsight is irrelevant. If, however, she looks back on her choices and her consumption ex post, she must consider that, from the vantage point of hindsight, she may well want to have lived in a way that maximized her average satisfaction over the decade. Now we might add that her preferences over lotteries actually take into account how she expects to feel with hindsight when she looks back on the lottery she chose, and on her consequent consumption. In this case she should maximize expected utility. But note that it is precisely this kind of hindsight that appears to cause people, in actual experiments, to appear not to have von Neumann–Morgenstern preferences! I refer to the interpretation of the Allais paradox having to do with individuals' fears of regret, which are just fears having to do with hindsight. (See Loomes and Sugden 1982.) So it seems that if we view a person's preferences over lotteries as reflecting, inter alia, her expected satisfaction upon viewing her choices with hindsight, then we are ill advised to assume that her preferences over lotteries obey the von Neumann–Morgenstern axioms! But if we take her preferences over lotteries as not taking hindsight into consideration, then it is not clear that she should maximize her lottery preferences; rather, she must take into consideration both her lottery preferences and her expected hindsight views. More could be said, but I will leave the problem here.

The upshot of this discussion is that it is incorrect to view optimization under uncertainty by an agent with von Neumann–Morgenstern preferences over lotteries as resulting in a kind of intra-personal utilitarianism.

A number of authors, I believe, have been guilty of this error, including myself.[7]

4.6 Optimal Population Size

The question of what is the best population size for the world is not, strictly speaking, one of distributive justice, for given any population size, there should exist a just distribution of resources. If the distribution is just in each of two worlds with different population sizes, I do not think we can further say that one world is more *just* than another, by virtue of a difference in their population sizes and/or aggregate resource endowments. Nevertheless, we may think that one world is *better* than another by virtue of both its population size and how resources are distributed among its population. Classical utilitarianism asserts that the best (if not most just) world is the one which maximizes total utility. There may be no such world. Suppose utility is absolutely measurable and comparable, and the utility function of every person is $u(x) = x^{1/2}$, where x is the amount of a single good. Suppose there is one unit of the good. According to classical utilitarianism, there is no optimal population: the more people, the better, even though as the number n of people gets large, each consumes only an extremely small fraction of the resource. [The total utility $n(\frac{1}{n})^{1/2} = n^{1/2}$ goes to infinity with n.]

Suppose we define a social state as a complete history of the world, including the specification of all the people who will have lived in that world, the resources they consumed, and the utility they enjoyed. Assume that this utility is absolutely measurable and comparable. Let us identify a utility of zero as characteristic of a person who evaluates his life as neither better nor worse than not having lived. Doing so requires an assumption, that all lives which are "neutral" in this sense are associated with the same utility level. Assume that we have an ordering of such states, R, and that it is welfarist: that is, we need only know the utilities of every person who lived in two states to say which state is better according to R. Here, a person's utility is identified with her lifetime utility. Note that, which will emerge as important later, we do not begin with a profile of individual orders over states, as

---

7. See Roemer (1985), in which I characterized various insurance problems as implementing "sectional utilitarianism." On the basis of the present discussion, I retract this statement, and hence the implication I drew that Dworkin's insurance proposal (discussed in Chapter 7 of this book) is closer to utilitarianism than he would like.

in Chapter 1. The individuals here derive utility from the worlds they live in, but they do not have preference orders over states. The "social" profile R is here rather disembodied: perhaps it reflects our own views of what kind of a world is a good one.

That R is welfarist, it should be noted, rules out social discounting of lives lived later in history, for the dates at which a person is alive are non-welfare information. Individual discounting of later periods in a person's life is permitted, however, for in this model there is no formulation of how a person's lifetime utility is computed.

R induces, in particular, an ordering R_n over all states in which exactly n persons lived. Let us suppose that each R_n is utilitarian: that is, R_n is represented by the Bergson-Samuelson social welfare function $W(\bar{u}^1, \ldots, \bar{u}^n) = \sum \bar{u}^n$. Thus R is what Blackorby and Donaldson (1984) call "same-numbers utilitarianism": if two worlds have the same numbers of people, then the one with greater total utility is better. This alone does not tell us anything about how R compares two worlds in which different numbers of people will have lived—that is, we cannot deduce that R is classical utilitarianism just from information about the orderings R_n. The following axiom, however, enables us to deduce classical utilitarianism.

Pareto Population Principle (PP).   For any positive integer n, and any vector $\bar{u} \in \mathbf{R}^n$, $(\bar{u}, 0) I u$, where I is the indifference subrelation of R.

PP says that if a person whose life is neutral is added to a world with n persons, then the new world is judged indifferent to the old one.

Same-numbers utilitarianism plus PP immediately imply classical utilitarianism. For let $\bar{u} \in \mathbf{R}^n$ and $\bar{\bar{u}} \in \mathbf{R}^m$ be the utility vectors for two states where $m = n + 1$. Let $\bar{v} = \frac{1}{n} \sum u^h$ and $\bar{\bar{v}} = \frac{1}{m} \sum \bar{\bar{u}}^h$ be average utility in the two states, and suppose that $n\bar{v} \geq m\bar{\bar{v}}$. Let us now denote a state by $(n, \bar{u})$, where n is the number of persons who lived in that state and $\bar{u}$ is their vector of experienced utilities. Let 1_n be the vector in $\mathbf{R}^n$ all of whose components are one. Then we have $(n, \bar{u}) I_n (n, \bar{v} 1_n) I (m, (\bar{v} 1_n, 0)) R(m, \bar{\bar{v}} 1_{n+1}) I_n (m, \bar{\bar{u}})$, where the first indifference is due to R_n being utilitarian, the second is due to PP, and the last two orders are due to R_m being utilitarian. By transitivity of R, we conclude $(n, \bar{u}) R(m, \bar{\bar{u}})$. By induction, we can extend this reasoning to show that R ranks any two states, with arbitrary n and m, according to the classical utilitarian formula.

Let us now drop the assumption that R_n is utilitarian and assume that for each n, R_n is represented by a strictly quasi-concave, strictly monotonic Bergson-Samuelson social welfare function: thus for any n and vector $\bar{u} \in$

$\mathbf{R}^n$ not all of whose components are equal, the world $(n, \bar{v}1_n)$ is judged better than the world $(n, \bar{u})$, where $\bar{v}$ is the average utility of $\bar{u}$. Suppose that PP holds. Let ε be any (small) positive number. Then

$$\left(n+1, \frac{n\bar{v}+\varepsilon}{n+1}1_{n+1}\right) P(n+1, (\bar{v}1_n, \varepsilon)) P(n+1, (\bar{v}1_n, 0)) I(n, \bar{v}1_n).$$

By induction, for any integer m, we have that

$$\left(n+m, \frac{n\bar{v}+m\varepsilon}{n+m}1_{n+m}\right) P(n, \bar{v}1_n).$$

But we can choose m large enough and ε small enough so that $(n\bar{v} + m\varepsilon)/(n+m)$ is arbitrarily close to zero. This means that there is always a world with huge numbers of people, each of whom is only incrementally better off than having not lived, which is preferable to the world $(n, \bar{v}1_n)$ which we may take to be a world in which everyone's life is well worth living! This is what Parfit (1984) calls the repugnant conclusion. To be precise, we will say that the *repugnant conclusion* holds if and only if, given any state x, and any (small) positive number $\delta > 0$, there is a state y preferred to x where no person experiences a utility greater than δ.

Blackorby and Donaldson (1984) and Blackorby, Bossert, and Donaldson (1993) are concerned with finding an ethically appealing way of avoiding the repugnant conclusion. They begin with an ordering R of the states X described above. For any vector $\bar{u} \in \mathbf{R}^n$, describing the lifetime utilities of n people who are alive in a given state, they define the "equally-distributed-equivalent utility" as the number $\bar{v}$ such that $\bar{v}1_n I_n \bar{u}$, where I_n is the indifference subrelation of R_n. (If R_n is same-numbers utilitarianism, $\bar{v}$ is just the average of the components of $\bar{u}$, as above.) Define the function $\bar{v} = \Upsilon^n(\bar{u})$ which assigns the equally-distributed-equivalent utility to any vector of utilities $\bar{u} \in \mathbf{R}^n$.

Theorem 4.5 (Blackorby and Donaldson 1984). *If R is anonymous and welfarist, and R_n is continuous, then there exists a function $W : \mathbf{Z}_{++} \times \mathbf{R} \to \mathbf{R}$, increasing in its second component, such that for all $\bar{u} \in \mathbf{R}^n$ and $\bar{\bar{u}} \in \mathbf{R}^m$, $\bar{u} R \bar{\bar{u}} \Longleftrightarrow W(n, \bar{v}) \geq W(m, \bar{\bar{v}})$, where $\bar{v} = \Upsilon^n(\bar{u})$ and $\bar{\bar{v}} = \Upsilon^m(\bar{\bar{u}})$. ($\mathbf{Z}_{++}$ is the set of positive integers.)*

W is called a "social evaluation function." Theorem 4.5 says that R has a particularly simple representation: we need only know the numbers of people in two states and the equally-distributed-equivalent utility in the states to rank them according to R.

Blackorby and Donaldson (1984) introduce two additional axioms. The first is a kind of separability axiom. Let N be a subgroup of a set of persons M who exist in a state x. Let $\bar{u} = (\bar{u}^1, \ldots, \bar{u}^n, \bar{u}^{n+1}, \ldots, \bar{u}^m)$ be the utilities of all persons in a state x, where, by anonymity, we may assume that the subgroup N consists of the persons $1, \ldots, n$. Let $\bar{v} = \Upsilon^n(\bar{u}^1, \ldots, \bar{u}^n)$. Then $(\bar{v}1_n, \bar{u}^{n+1}, \ldots, \bar{u}^m) I \bar{u}$. This axiom is called the *Population Substitution principle* (PS). The second axiom is a generalization of the Pareto Population principle:

Critical-Level Population Principle (CLP).   There is a number α such that, for all $n \in \mathbf{Z}_{++}$ and $\bar{u} \in \mathbf{R}^n$, $(\bar{u}, \alpha) I \bar{u}$.

We can see at once that CLP, combined with same-numbers utilitarianism, prevents the repugnant conclusion, if $\alpha > 0$. For suppose R_n is represented by the utilitarian Bergson-Samuelson social welfare function $\sum_{i=1}^n \bar{u}^h$, and let ε be a (small) positive number. Then, using the same reasoning that we employed several paragraphs above, we have

$$\left(n + 1, \frac{nv + \alpha + \varepsilon}{n + 1} 1_{n+1} \right) I_{n+1}(n + 1, (v1_n, \alpha + \varepsilon)) P(n, v1_n).$$

By induction, we have, for any positive integer m and positive ε,

$$\left(n + m, \frac{nv + m(\alpha + \varepsilon)}{n + m} 1_{n+m} \right) P(n, v1_n).$$

But as m goes to infinity, the utility in the state on the left-hand side of the last mathematical statement does not approach zero. It is, in fact, bounded below by α.

We have:

Theorem 4.6 (Blackorby and Donaldson 1984).   *Let the premises of Theorem 4.5 hold, and in addition, let PS, CLP, and Strong Pareto hold. Then there is a strictly increasing, continuous function g with $g(0) = 0$ such that the social evaluation function $W(n, \bar{v})$ is ordinally equivalent to $n(g(\bar{v}) - g(\alpha)) = \sum_{i=1}^n (g(\bar{u}^i) - g(\alpha))$.*

If g is the identity function, and $\alpha = 0$, then the ordering R is classical utilitarian. If $\alpha > 0$ (and g is the identity), then R_n is utilitarian for each n, but

R is called "critical-level utilitarian." We have seen that critical-level utilitarianism (when $\alpha > 0$) avoids the repugnant conclusion. In the general case of Theorem 4.6, Blackorby and Donaldson call R "critical-level generalized utilitarianism."

In Blackorby, Bossert, and Donaldson (1993), the authors extend the work just described in several ways. They work on a domain of states which contain more information than the states just described. Let M be a matrix whose columns are time periods and whose rows are associated with persons. The element m_{ij} of M gives the utility of person i in time period j; if person i was not alive at time period j, then m_{ij} is left blank. Here is an example:

	1	2	3	4	5	6
Alan	10	-2	3	1		
Betsy			2	2	-5	17
Charlie		4	0	-1		
Dick	14	10	-5			
Elaine		3	0			

In this matrix, no person lives more than four periods. The set of states, $\mathcal{M}$, consists of all matrices M with a finite number of rows and columns, where the nonblank elements in any row consist of contiguous strings of not more than T elements. (The maximum feasible lifetime is T periods.) It is assumed that an ordering R of $\mathcal{M}$ is given. In addition, each person i who exists in a state M is endowed with an absolutely measurable and comparable utility function u_l^i defined on vectors in $\mathbf{R}^l$. $u_l^i(\bar{u})$ is the utility that person i derives from experiencing a life of l periods, in which the single-period utilities are given by the vector $\bar{u}$. Note that this lifetime utility does not depend on when i lives. The welfarist assumption that the authors use is that the ordering R of $\mathcal{M}$ depends only on the lifetime utilities of the persons who live (at some time) in that state. In particular, this rules out social discounting of utilities of persons who live late in history, but not individual discounting.

The key axiom introduced is *independence of utilities of the dead* (IUD). The dead in state M at period t consist of all persons whose life has ended before period t (that is, their rows are blank from period t on). Given two states M^1 and M^2, let N^1 and N^2 be the list of persons who exist in each state. Define $D_t(M^1, M^2)$ as the members of $N^1 \cap N^2$ who are dead by period t. Consider new matrices, called M_t^1 and M_t^2, constructed by removing the rows of M^1 and M^2 associated with the members of the set $D_t(M^1, M^2)$. The axiom IUD says that if each member of $D_t(M^1, M^2)$ has the same lifetime utility in both M^1 and M^2, then the matrices M^1 and M^2 should be ranked by R in the same way that R ranks the matrices M_t^1 and M_t^2. This must hold for all t. Thus if in two histories of the world M^1 and M^2 the dead at time t experienced equivalent lives, then they can be ignored in ranking M^1 and M^2.

The remarkable result is that, by postulating the axiom IUD, the authors reproduce the conclusion of Theorem 4.5 without recourse to either of the axioms PS or CLP:

Theorem 4.7 (Blackorby, Bossert, and Donaldson 1993). *The ordering R of $\mathcal{M}$ satisfies Strong Pareto, Anonymity, Continuity, and IUD iff it is characterized by a social evaluation function $W(n, \bar{v})$ which is ordinally equivalent to $n(g(\bar{v}) - g(\alpha)) = \sum_{i \in N}(g(\bar{u}^i) - g(\alpha))$, where g is a continuous, increasing function with $g(0) = 0$.*

(Here $\bar{u}^i$ is the lifetime utility of individual i, and $\bar{v}$ the equally-distributed-equivalent utility of the state M with n persons whose lifetime utilities are given by $\{\bar{u}^i\}$.)

Thus critical-level generalized utilitarianism is characterized by "lifetime welfarism" and the axioms listed. As a corollary, it follows that the repugnant conclusion is avoided if and only if $\alpha > 0$.

Although CLP is not a premise of Theorem 4.7, it immediately follows that the axioms of the theorem imply CLP. Therefore the repugnant conclusion is avoided only if we agree that the CLP axiom is a good one, for $\alpha > 0$. It is, however, not obvious that this is an ethically appealing postulate. Sikora (1978), for one, advocates the Pareto Population principle. And I think an argument can be made for the Pareto Population principle as follows, by introducing individual preferences over states. (Recall the caveat of the second paragraph of this section.) Consider two states $x = (\bar{u}^1, \ldots, \bar{u}^n)$ and $y = (\bar{u}^1, \ldots, \bar{u}^n, \varepsilon)$, where ε is positive and small. Without loss of generality, we may assume, by anonymity, that the first n individuals in both states are the same, and there is an additional individual, call him Adam, in state y who experiences a lifetime utility of ε. If we asked Adam to choose between x and y, he would choose y: I take it this is what it means for a utility ε to signify a life that is worth living for Adam. Now all the other individuals concerned are indifferent between states x and y, for they receive the same utility in both states. (Note that this does not imply that they receive the same *consumption* in both states: for the utilities of the first n persons in state y may well incorporate the disutility they experience from living in a world with a person whose life is just barely worth living! "Individual" welfarism does not require self-regarding preferences.) Therefore the social ordering should prefer y to x, if it obeys a Pareto axiom with respect to individual preferences over states.[8] (This does not follow from Strong Pareto, because the sets of individuals who are alive in states x and y differ.) If the social ordering is continuous, this means, taking the limit as ε goes to zero, that the state $z = (\bar{u}^1, \ldots, \bar{u}^n, 0)$ should be socially at least as good as x. Now using the same argument, but beginning with $y' = (\bar{u}^1, \ldots, \bar{u}^n, -\varepsilon)$, we can conclude that x is socially at least as good as z. Hence x and z are socially indifferent, which is just the Pareto Population principle; in addition, the axioms of Theorem 4.7 imply the repugnant conclusion.

Thus I am not convinced that the "repugnant conclusion" deserves that name. In the analysis of Blackorby and Donaldson (1984) and of Blackorby, Bossert, and Donaldson (1993), as I have said, the "social" ordering R of states does not come from "aggregating" the preferences of individuals over states. Individuals (who may or may not be alive in certain states) are not endowed with preferences over states. In the above paragraph I have suggested that perhaps they should be and, further, that, if they are, the "social" order R should reflect those preferences in the sense I have outlined. If so, then the Pareto Population principle is justified, and it along with the axioms of Theorem 4.7 implies that R must be generalized utilitarianism, that is, $\alpha = 0$. Utilitarianism, *tout court,* does not follow, for no argument has been given that g should be the identity function.

A final note: I think that "no social discounting of utilities of persons who live late in history" is ethically correct. This does not imply that, in our own planning, we should not discount the utilities of persons in the future: such discounting may be justified, but only because future lives are uncertain. In the models discussed in this section, uncertainty is not an issue. It would be worthwhile to apply social choice techniques to study the decision problem of a society that must choose among alternative plans, each one of which induces, from the viewpoint of the present, a probability distribution over future possible worlds.

---

8. To be precise, I must also add an axiom stipulating that the preferences of individuals who are not alive in either state must be ignored in comparing x and y.

4.7 Conclusion

I have argued that, when the population is fixed, the most compelling argument for utilitarianism is Theorem 4.1. Although that theorem concerns an abstract set of social states, we may derive an analogous result on a domain of economic environments using the methods of §1.5. Thus we can think of the premises of Theorem 4.1, along with the COAD axiom, as implying that society should distribute its resources in that way that maximizes the total utility of its citizens. As one can see from the proof of Theorem 4.1, the axioms U*, SP*, I*, AN, CONT, and EL show that the social ordering must be "generalized utilitarianism," in the Blackorby-Donaldson sense: that is, F must be representable by a Bergson-Samuelson social welfare function of the form $\sum g(\bar{u}^h)$, where $\bar{u}^h = u^h(x)$ and g is a strictly monotone increasing function. It is the invariance assumption of full measurability and comparability which then forces g to be linear and utilitarianism to result. As we have seen, if utility is ratio-scale fully comparable, then social choice functions which are highly averse to inequality—as utilitarianism is not—are admissible, namely, those that order states according to $\sum (\bar{u}^h)^{1/r}$, where r is a large positive number. Thus we may say that the six axioms listed above suffice to characterize utilitarianism only because the information available about utility is not sufficiently informative. Note, for instance, that with only full measurability and comparability, we cannot identify anyone as living below the poverty line or living a life of misery. For such an identification, in a welfarist theory, must be made by associating a certain utility level with poverty or misery. The general utility level, however, has no meaning when utilities are fully measurable and comparable. If we cannot identify poverty and misery, the fact that utilitarianism is insensitive to inequality of utility is much less bothersome.

As I have said, perhaps the most powerful ethical criticism of utilitarianism is that it is insensitive to inequality of utility among individuals—for instance, with two persons, the utility pairs $(1, 99)$ and $(50, 50)$ are socially indifferent. This indeed is disturbing if utilities are absolutely measurable and comparable. For then the two distributions just described could refer, on the one hand, to a situation in which one person is almost starving (say, a utility of zero is associated with starvation) while the other is as rich as Croesus, and, on the other hand, to a situation in which both persons are moderately prosperous. With utilities that only carry cardinal-unit-comparable information, no such identification is possible—indeed, we cannot even say that, in the $(1, 99)$ state, the first person is worse off than the second. Thus an inequality-averse observer has no reason to be disturbed by Theorems 1.4 and 1.8. She may have, however, some reason to be disturbed by Theorem 4.1, although her strongest aversions to inequality cause no reason to be alarmed by that theorem, because it does not contain a prescription to look only at the sum of utilities when issues of misery or poverty are being discussed. Indeed no theorem in this chapter would require our inequality-averse observer to use utilitarianism, when she consents to a set of reasonable axioms and when utility information is sufficiently fine-grained to enable notions of misery and poverty to be represented. Some egalitarians, myself included, regard equality not as the most fundamental ethical goal, but as a method for sharing scarcity of resources fairly, when the aggregate resource endowment is insufficient to enable everyone to reach a certain minimal level of functioning or opportunity.[9] Once this level is reached by all, the commandment to distribute remaining resources equally is much less compelling. Since the utilitarianism of Theorem 4.1 does not recognize absolute utility levels of any kind, it is not inconsistent with this "instrumental egalitarian" view.

Having said this, it is useful to remark that even an inequality-averse observer might advocate utilitarianism in some instances, even when utilities are absolutely measurable and comparable. Consider the following example, discussed in detail in Roemer (1993a). The set of *individuals* consists of different countries; the set of *states* consists of different distributions of an international agency's health service resources to countries; the *utility function* for an individual reports the rate of infant survival (one minus the rate of infant mortality) in that country as a function of health resources it receives from the agency. The utility functions are absolutely measurable and comparable in this case. Let us compare leximin and birth-population-weighted utilitarianism, the ordering induced by $\sum p^h u^h(x)$ where p^h is the number of births in country h, in this problem.[10] Leximin instructs the agency to distribute its health resources in such a way as to minimize the highest infant mortality rate across countries. Birth-population-weighted utilitarianism, however, instructs the agency to distribute its re-

---

9. In axiom CLP, it might be appealing to set α at the level of well-being at which this minimal level of functioning obtains.

10. Birth-population-weighted utilitarianism is not a welfarist social choice rule; it depends on the number of births in countries, numbers which are not recoverable from the utility numbers that describe states.

sources in that way which minimizes the number of infant deaths in the world. A misery-averse ethical observer should, I think, prefer the latter to the former.

We may put the point of the last two paragraphs quite succinctly. Utilitarianism is criticized by egalitarians for ignoring the boundaries between individuals, for it cares only about total utility and not at all about how that utility is distributed among individuals. But there are times when, for egalitarians, the boundaries between "individuals" *should* be ignored—for instance, when those boundaries create morally arbitrary distinctions between individuals. This may well be the case when the "individuals" are countries. Thus whether or not one favors utilitarianism depends on what the *names* of the individuals, utility functions, and social states of the model are.

I have also argued, along with Sen, Blackorby, Donaldson, and Weymark, that Harsanyi's theorems on utilitarianism have nothing to do with the ethically contentious doctrine of utilitarianism. Harsanyi's aggregation theorem remains a notable mathematical result, and his impartial observer theorem is important as a pre-Rawlsian formulation of a veil-of-ignorance approach to ethics and distributive justice.

Finally, Blackorby, Donaldson, and Bossert have suggested a way—critical-level generalized utilitarianism—of escaping Parfit's repugnant conclusion. They have, furthermore, shown that, given a set of reasonable axioms for restricting preference orders over worlds with different numbers of people, their suggestion exhausts the class of admissible preference orders. Thus we now have a precise characterization of how to avoid the repugnant conclusion—by choosing a value of α greater than zero in Theorem 4.7. I have, however, offered a skeptical view, suggesting that choosing α equal to zero is ethically preferred, which would, if correct, require us to challenge Parfit's intuition about worlds with many people each of whose lives was barely worth living.

5

Primary Goods, Fundamental Preferences, and Functionings

5.1 Countering Utilitarianism

John Rawls (1971, 1975, 1980, 1982, 1985) and Amartya Sen (1980, 1985, 1987, 1992, 1993) have each put forth theories which are best understood as responses, on the one hand, to utilitarianism, and on the other, to theories that view formal equality of opportunity as necessary and sufficient for distributive justice. By formal equality of opportunity, I mean the condition that there is no legal bar to access to education, to all positions and jobs, and that all hiring is meritocratic.

Rawls believes that the "conceptions of the good" held by different persons are so various as to be incommensurable. In our language, relevant utility is not interpersonally comparable. He says, however, that there are certain "primary social goods" that a person needs no matter what his conception of the good is, and these it is possible to compare. In particular, he asserts there is an index of vectors of primary social goods with which we can compare the "amounts" of these goods enjoyed by different individuals. One mandate of justice is to adopt those institutions which will maximize the amount (index) of primary social goods enjoyed by the individual or group who receives least of them: that is, to maximize, over all possible economic regimes, the minimum, over all persons, of the bundle of primary social goods. He calls this moral mandate the "difference principle."[1]

---

1. Equal liberty, however, is a Rawlsian mandate of justice which is lexically prior to the operation of the difference principle

Sen's view is that Rawls has not focused on the right maximandum. It is not certain *goods* as such that are important for all conceptions of welfare or the good, but rather what goods can *do* for people. Goods enable people to function in various ways: to move around, to be healthy, to be literate, and so on. Sen believes that the mandate of justice is to "equalize" at the highest possible level, over all economic regimes, the sets of vectors of *functionings* that are available to persons. Sen calls the set of functionings available to a person his *capability*; thus his theory is summarized as "equality of capabilities." For this view to be well defined, one must have an order over sets of vectors of functionings.

These two theories have four characteristics in common, which make them, in my view, first cousins in the family of proposals for distributive justice. (1) Both views are nonwelfarist. The maximandum is not utility, but rather some "objective" standard—in one case, primary social goods, in another, capabilities. (2) Both views are egalitarian. (3) Neither theory advocates a distribution of final outcomes; both primary goods and functionings are inputs into what a person can accomplish by his own volition. Thus both theories reserve a space for personal responsibility. If one person makes judicious use of her resources and opportunities once primary social goods, or functionings, have been equalized, while another squanders his, the unequal outcomes are not compensable at the bar of justice. (4) Both views invoke a notion of equality of opportunity that is more radical than formal equality of opportunity. It is not sufficient to forbid legal bars to access to education and jobs, for persons differ by virtue of a variety of traits whose distribution is morally arbitrary: the nations and families into which they are born, and their natural abilities, talents, and handicaps. Real equality of opportunity requires compensating persons for these differences. For Rawls, this equalization is carried out by equalizing primary social goods; for Sen, by equalizing capabilities.

These views differ from utilitarianism on the first three points. Utilitarianism is a welfarist, nonegalitarian view. Conventional utilitiarianism would maximize the sum of final utilities, in violation of point (3). This marks the first appearance of the issue of personal responsibility in our study, an idea that will become increasingly prominent and focused in the remaining chapters: if one idea must be singled out as the most prominent in contemporary theories of distributive justice, it is that personal responsibility justifiably restricts the degree of outcome equality.

I shall also briefly present the egalitarian theory of Kolm (1972), who, independently of Rawls, arrived at the conclusion that the socially optimal allocation is the one that renders the worst-off person as well off as possible. Kolm, however, reserved the adjective "just" for allocations that render persons completely equal in condition. Yet Kolm's work did not share the features that I have enumerated (1), (3), and (4). In fact, Kolm proposed, as we shall see, a fundamentally different solution to the problem of finding a common core of needs for all persons with respect to which one could measure equality of condition.[2]

5.2   Primary Goods, Welfare, and Equality

In *A Theory of Justice*, Rawls lists the primary social goods, in broad categories, as rights and liberties, opportunities and powers, and income and wealth (Rawls 1971, p. 92). Later (1982, p. 162), he specifies five primary goods, or categories of such goods: (a) basic liberties, including freedom of association, liberty, and so on, (b) freedom of movement and choice of occupation, (c) powers and prerogatives of offices and positions of responsibility, (d) income and wealth, and (e) the social bases of self-respect. This last is defined to be "those aspects of basic institutions that are normally essential if citizens are to have a lively sense of their own worth as moral persons and to be able to realise their highest-order interests and advance their ends with self-confidence" (1982, p. 166). Rawls states that the equalization of goods listed under (a) and (b) must be complete and is lexically prior to the distribution of the other primary social goods; that is, he advocates first choosing a politico-economic system that maximizes the degree to which (a) and (b) can be provided to all citizens on an equal basis, and then choosing the distribution of economic resources and the forms of economic and political institutions that will maximize an index of the remaining three primary social goods going to the least well-off group (well-off, that is, as measured by that index).

One should first note that there is a distinction between primary social goods and economic resources and commodities. The only primary good that is a conventional private good is income (and wealth). I think that the primary social goods (c) and (e) are best viewed as local public

---

2. Kolm's monograph has unfortunately received far less attention in Anglo-American social science than it deserves, because, until now, it has been available only in French.

goods. Any set of economic and political institutions will provide varying degrees of power, prerogatives, and a sense of self-worth to office- and job-holders in various positions. These "goods" are not distributed to citizens as private goods, but are embodied in the institutions. Individuals come to "consume" these goods as they take their place in these institutions. Let us denote a *set of political and economic institutions* for society by I, and the class of feasible sets of institutions by $\mathcal{T}$. A *location* $l \in I$ is a specification of the positions in institutions an individual might hold. Thus l might be "holds a position on the city council, is president of the local PTA, and works as a tool-and-die maker in a factory." Locations in I are denoted $l_1, l_2, \ldots, l_N$. Associated with each location is a vector $q^I(l)$ that specifies the relevant nonincome attributes that location l embodies, by which I mean the powers and prerogatives of those positions, the degree of autonomy the position provides to its holder, and so forth. This vector is independent of the person who holds the position.

I think we are faithful to Rawls if we say that, as far as a person is concerned, the primary social goods encompassed in (c), (d), and (e) are $q^I(l)$ and income. Further, persons are free to choose their occupations and positions, subject to the filling of these positions by a meritocratic procedure, and to choose the amount of time they work. Thus the primary social goods "consumed" by a person will be a function of his job and labor choice, for the job choice defines (at least part of) his location l, and the job and labor choice will at least in part determine his income.

Rawls is unfortunately vague on the relationship between labor choice and primary goods. He clearly states that the free choice of occupation, and presumably of the amount of time worked, is guaranteed by primary social good (b). But this does not preclude society from designing tax schedules that induce people to work inordinately large amounts, and this it might do in order to generate tax revenue to be redistributed to the worst-off. Moreover, if society does not treat labor or leisure as a primary good, then it arguably *must* announce that kind of tax schedule. (For an elaboration, see Howe and Roemer [1981].) Furthermore, Rawls must acknowledge that in any complex society labor markets are necessary, from which it follows that a person's income will depend on his job and labor choices and, of course, on the tax schedule. Therefore one cannot even define the vector of primary social goods enjoyed by a person without knowing his labor contribution. Hence I will assume that labor should be counted as a primary good and that an index of primary social goods is one aggregating $q^I(l)$, m, and L, where m is income and L is labor. I will denote by x the generic vector $(q^1(l), m, L)$, where we must remember that m will be some function of L and l, determined by some combination of markets and tax schedules.[3]

Finding an index is a problem that Rawls does not solve, and although many have glossed over the issue, I agree with Arneson (1990b) that it is a key problem in Rawls's theory, for on it hangs Rawls's claim that his theory is nonwelfarist. Arneson argues that either the index must be based on some perfectionist view—that there is one right way to add up these primary social goods, on the basis of their contribution to some objective measure of what is good for people—or it must be based on how primary goods facilitate the accomplishment of individual life plans, in which case the index must differ for different people and be linked to individual conceptions of welfare. Arneson argues that Rawls could never intend the first option, for he situates his theory of justice as an instance of toleration of diverse conceptions of the good—it would be foreign to such a view to advocate any kind of perfectionism. But if the second option is taken, then welfarism creeps back in, for the amount of primary social goods a person has will be measured by the extent to which the achievement of his life plan is enhanced by the possession of those goods. I will argue that Arneson's criticism of Rawls is mainly correct, but it does not follow, as he believes, that Rawls's theory must be welfarist.

I think that Rawls's views of happiness, of the relationship between primary goods and the achievement of life plans, and of the existence of an "objective" index of primary goods are inconsistent, although it does not follow that the index of primary goods must be equivalent to welfare. On the relationship between primary goods and the achievement of life plans, it is worthwhile to quote Rawls in full:

> Now primary goods, as I have already remarked, are things which it is supposed a rational man wants whatever else he wants. Regardless of what

---

3. Cohen (1995a) remarks on Rawls's lexical priority for occupational choice and criticizes Howe and Roemer (1981) for not taking it into account. But Cohen fails to appreciate that, unless the value of leisure is taken into account, society can design tax schedules that induce people to work too hard even given free choice of job and labor. Alternatively put, if labor-leisure is not a primary good, but is important for fulfilling life plans, then the amount of primary goods a person enjoys will not be monotonically related to the degree of his life-plan fulfillment. I argue below that Rawls clearly intends that this relation be monotonic.

an individual's rational plans are in detail, it is assumed that there are various things which he would prefer more of rather than less. With more of these goods men can generally be assured of greater success in carrying out their intentions and in advancing their ends, whatever these ends may be.   (1971, p. 92)

On happiness, Rawls writes:

a person is happy when he is in the way of a successful execution (more or less) of a rational plan of life drawn up under (more or less) favorable conditions, and he is reasonably confident that his intentions can be carried through. Thus we are happy when our rational plans are going well, our more important aims being fulfilled, and we are with reason quite sure that our good fortunes will continue.   (1971, p. 548)

From the second quotation, I believe it is consistent to say that the utility function, for Rawls, measures happiness or, equivalently, that it measures the degree or extent to which one's life plan is being carried out. (I shall be more specific about this below.) Now suppose this degree or extent is measured by a function $u^h(q^I(l), m, L)$—that is, the extent to which one's life plan will be fulfilled is a function of the three primary social goods (c), (d), and (e), and of the labor or leisure one chooses. (I ignore primary goods (a) and (b), as their levels have already been set, because of their lexical priority, and therefore do not concern us.) Rawls, of course, does not propose to maximin the values of the functions u^h, but only of some index of the primary social goods. Let us postulate the general case, that the index of $(q^I(l), m, L)$ depends on the person: call it $\mu^h(q^I(l), m, L)$. Now suppose that there were two vectors of primary goods x and x' such that $\mu^h(x) \geq \mu^h(x')$ and $u^h(x) < u^h(x')$. This would mean that at x, individual h enjoys a bundle of primary goods at least as large as at x', but his life plan achievement is going better at x' than at x. I claim that this is in violation of the last sentence of the first Rawls quotation above. Therefore it must be the case that

(5.1)   for all x, x', $\hat{\mu}^h(x) \geq \hat{\mu}^h(x') \Rightarrow u^h(x) \geq u^h(x')$.

The converse of (5.1) must also be true, by reference to the last sentence in the first quotation. Hence the function μ^h is ordinally equivalent to the function u^h—there exists an increasing function $\varphi^h : \mathbf{R} \to \mathbf{R}$ such that $u^h = \varphi^h \circ \mu^h$. Now in general there is no reason to suppose that, for two individuals j and h, u^h and u^j are ordinally equivalent—persons have very different life plans, and presumably they are variously satisfied by inputs of primary social goods. It therefore follows that the indices μ^j and μ^h are not ordinally equivalent. For suppose they were, that is, suppose there were a monotone function φ such that $\varphi \circ \mu^j = \mu^h$. Then

$$u^h = \varphi^h \circ \mu^h = \varphi^h \circ \varphi \circ \mu^j = \varphi^h \circ \varphi \circ (\varphi^j)^{-1} \circ \varphi^j \circ \mu^j$$
$$= \varphi^h \circ \varphi \circ (\varphi^j)^{-1} \circ u^j,$$

which shows that u^h and u^j are ordinally equivalent, contrary to hypothesis.

We have shown that each individual's index of primary goods is ordinally equivalent to his measure of happiness, and that these indices are themselves not generally ordinally equivalent. In particular, the indices are different across persons. It is therefore not consistent for Rawls to claim that a single index of primary goods can be used.

Rawls only requires that the indices of primary goods be ordinally measurable and fully comparable. I shall call $\mu = (\mu^1, ..., \mu^H)$ a *generalized index of primary goods*. Rawls requires statements of the form "$\mu^h(x) > \mu^j(y)$" to have meaning: that is, h has more primary goods in distribution x than j does in distribution y. Thus μ is just as good an index if all of its component functions are transformed by the same monotone function. We cannot, however, conclude that μ^h can be replaced by u^h. We can, of course, write $\mu = ((\varphi^1)^{-1} \circ u^1, \ldots, (\varphi^H)^{-1} \circ u^H)$, and so μ *depends* on the notions of happiness of the individuals. But this does not render Rawls's theory welfarist, for it depends on information *other* than that provided by utility numbers: in particular, to calculate Rawls's maximin allocation we need to know the profile $\varphi = (\varphi^1, \ldots, \varphi^H)$ as well as the profile u. Thus Rawls's views are not consistent, nor is Arneson's conclusion correct. The truth lies in between: Rawls's notion of primary goods must depend on the conceptions of the good that individuals have, but it cannot be recovered solely by knowing those conceptions.

I will next propose what the utility functions, the measures of happiness u^h, might be. Suppose that a given life plan can, by the end of one's life, be fulfilled in various degrees, where "degree" takes on values between zero and one. Let us denote the degree of life-plan fulfillment by δ. Given a set of institutions I and a distribution of the relevant "resources," it is still uncertain to what extent one's plan of life will be fulfilled. Let us suppose there is a probability measure $\Pi^h(\cdot; x)$ defined on the sample space $[0, 1]$

which specifies this uncertainty: that is, for D a measurable subset of $[0, 1]$, $\Pi^h(D; x)$ is the probability that with a primary social good "allocation" x, h's life plan will be fulfilled to some degree $\delta \in D$. Thus, the *expected degree of life-plan fulfillment of person h*, as a function of his primary good consumption (including labor or effort expended) is given by

$$E^h(x) = \int_0^1 \delta \pi^h(\delta; x) d\delta,$$

where I have assumed that $\Pi^h(\cdot; x)$ has a density function $\pi^h(\delta; x)$. Now $E^h(x)$ is not yet individual h's utility, for h has attitudes toward risk that have not yet been considered. In particular, h has preferences over lotteries, where lotteries are represented by probability measures, and utility is represented, say, by a function $v^h(\Pi)$. (There is no reason to suppose that these preferences satisfy the von Neumann–Morgenstern axioms.) I maintain that it is reasonable to say that h's (Rawlsian) utility function is given by

$$u^h(x) = v^h(\Pi^h(\cdot; x)).$$

In the case where v^h satisfies the von Neumann–Morgenstern axioms, we can write:

$$u^h(x) = \int_0^1 v^h(\delta) \pi^h(\delta; x) d\delta.$$

Let us take the special case that all individuals have von Neumann–Morgenstern preferences over lotteries and are risk neutral. Then it follows from the above that $u^h(x) = E^h(x)$: a person's happiness at an allocation x is the expected degree of fulfillment of her life plan. Now it would not be friendly to Rawls to assume that $\mu^h = u^h$, for if so, then equalizing primary goods would mean equalizing the expected degree to which persons fulfill their life plans. But Rawls is clear that some persons will choose more expensive or ambitious life plans than others, that these persons are responsible for doing so, and that it therefore follows that society has no Rawlsian obligation to give these ambitious life-plan choosers as high an expected degree of life-plan fulfillment as it gives to those who adopt less ambitious goals.[4] What we do know, in this case, is that $\mu^h(x)$ must be ordinally equivalent to $E^h(x)$, that there exists a monotone φ^h such that $E^h(x) = \varphi^h(\mu^h(x))$. Before the Rawlsian theory is well defined, it must contain a rule for specifying the profile $\varphi = (\varphi^1, \ldots, \varphi^H)$.

To review the matter: Rawls believes that society's responsibility is to equalize primary social goods, not degrees of life-plan fulfillment, because individuals must be held responsible for their choice of life plan. Thus someone who chooses a life plan that requires a very large income to fulfill should not on that account receive more income in his primary-good allocation than another whose life plan requires less income. Indeed, Rawls says that a complement of primary social goods enables persons to *choose* their life plans, an element of the theory that I have not modeled here. (I have, rather, taken individuals' life plans as given.) We have shown that if primary social goods are to advance every person's degree of expected fulfillment of her life plan, a Rawlsian requirement, then the needed indices of primary social goods must be ordinally equivalent to their utility (life-plan) functions. Rawls's proposal is incomplete, because he has not provided a determination of the profile, φ, of monotone functions that is necessary to define the generalized indices of primary goods. Contrary to a prevalent view, the choice of an index (or, as I have argued, a profile of indices) of primary goods is not just an unresolved footnote of the theory. Arneson is right to push Rawls on this point, but not right to conclude that the Rawlsian view must dissolve into welfarism—in particular, into equalizing (or maximinning) welfare. There may be room for a theory which chooses indices of primary goods which are ordinally equivalent to welfare or, as I have argued, ordinally equivalent to the expected degree of life-plan fulfillment, which is not the same as welfare if individuals are other than risk neutral. Such a theory would not be welfarist, as these indices need not be recoverable from information on welfare levels. The task for a Rawlsian must be to find such indices which are justifiable without appeal to a per-

---

4. For instance, Rawls writes: "The third respect in which citizens are regarded as free is that they are regarded as capable of taking responsibility for their ends and this affects how their various claims are assessed . . . citizens are thought capable of adjusting their aims and aspirations in the light of what they can reasonably expect to provide for" (Rawls 1985, p. 243). And: "citizens and associations accept the responsibility for revising and adjusting their ends and aspirations in view of the all-purpose means they can expect" (Rawls 1982, p. 170).

fectionist standard or to the inherent superiority of some life plans over others.

5.3   Rawls's Arguments for Maximin (the Difference Principle)

Rawls puts forth two arguments for the difference principle. The first attempts to show that only an allocation of resources which maximizes the index of primary goods going to the worst-off group is fair. The second is a particular attempt to formalize this view by invoking the veil of ignorance and the original position.

The first argument is clearly summarized by Barry (1989, pp. 213–234). Rawls proceeds by progressively deepening the notion of equality of opportunity. In "the system of natural liberty," which is a regime of private property rights in which everyone is entitled to benefit by virtue of exchanging his property with others, only formal equality of opportunity is guaranteed. People are allowed to benefit by virtue of all endowments they acquire through birth, including inherited wealth. Presumably, however, discrimination is not permitted. In a regime of "liberal equality," individuals may benefit by virtue of their native talents, but not by virtue of inherited income and wealth. Thus all persons with the same native talents should face the same prospects. Rawls calls this "fair equality of opportunity." In a regime of "democratic equality," an individual may benefit neither on account of inherited wealth, nor on account of the family into which he is born, nor by virtue of his natural talents or luck. All of these characteristics, including the endowment of natural talents and handicaps, are morally arbitrary. Rawls asserts that it follows that equality of the index of primary goods is called for. Perhaps, however, a regime of equality of primary goods is not efficient, in the Pareto sense that there may exist an allocation of resources that delivers a distribution of primary goods that gives everyone a higher index of those goods than at the equal distribution. In this way Rawls passes from equality to the set of maximin allocations. Among the maximin allocations, he at one point picks out the leximin allocations (Rawls 1971, p. 83) as most preferred.

There are (at least) three points at which the argument is weak, apart from the already discussed issue of choosing the index (or, as I have argued, indices) of primary goods. The first is the implicit assumption that the "natural" distribution of primary goods—that is, the one that would occur were there to be no Rawlsian redistribution—is the consequence of characteristics and endowments of persons all of which are morally arbitrary. Although we may agree that family background, natural talents, and inherited wealth are all morally arbitrary, perhaps there is such a thing as freely chosen effort which is not. Rawls must, it seems, argue either that there is no such thing as freely chosen effort—effort which a person expends on his own hook, and for which he is morally responsible—or that such effort only comes into play in moving from the distribution of primary goods to the fulfillment of life plans. Some claim (for instance, Barry [1989, p. 225]) that Rawls views everything, including effort, as morally arbitrary (for example, effort is determined by familial, cultural, and genetic influences which are themselves morally arbitrary). But if this is so, it is not clear why the Rawlsian maximandum is an index of primary goods instead of happiness, that is, the degree of fulfillment of life plans. If everything, including the choice of one's life plan, is morally arbitrary in the sense of being determined wholly by forces beyond one's control, then it would seem that the just distribution of resources is that which equalizes (or maximins or leximins) the degrees of life-plan fulfillment. Thus consistency seems to require Rawls to argue that "effort" and responsible volition only come into play in the move from the primary goods allocation to the achievement of life plans (this, of course, includes the choice of life plan).

The second weak point is the move from the moral arbitrariness of all characteristics of individuals to *equality* of primary goods. Here I mean the emphasis to be on equality, not on primary goods—equality of welfare would do just as well. I think the only argument Rawls puts forth for this move is the one based on the original position, which I will come to presently. But our own analysis can help Rawls here: in particular, Theorems 1.7 and 1.9 provide arguments for maximin that may well be consistent with Rawls's intentions. Recall that these theorems apply to economic environments, where the distribution of resources is at issue. The axioms of Theorem 1.7, in addition to a minimal equity axiom, imply maximin, and Theorem 1.9 as it stands is an argument for maximin.

In citing these theorems in *amicus curiae* for Rawls's case, one must interpret the profile u of utility functions as a generalized index of primary goods (see §5.2). There are two differences between the argument via Theorem 1.7 and via Theorem 1.9. The former theorem requires invariance of social choice with respect to all ordinal-level comparable transformations of the profile u, while Theorem 1.9 does not, and hence 1.9 applies to an index u that is absolutely measurable and comparable; and the argument of 1.7 uses a minimal equity axiom, while the argument of 1.9 uses resource monotonicity. Both theorems, however, similarly rely on the COAD axiom.

Although Rawls himself says that an ordinal-level comparable profile of primary goods indices is all that is needed, I prefer Theorem 1.9, as it deduces maximin even with the assumption of an absolutely measurable and fully comparable (AFC) profile of such indices. Furthermore, the price to be paid for using an AFC generalized index of primary goods is replacement of a minimal equity axiom by resource monotonicity (RMON). I find RMON unobjectionable from a Rawlsian viewpoint: if in two worlds the individuals are identical, but the resource endowment in one world dominates component-wise the resource endowment in the other, then all individuals should enjoy indices of primary goods at least as large in the world with the greater resource endowments.

Thus the argument for maximin via Theorem 1.9 requires only a justification of COAD (I consider the other axioms to be unobjectionable, with the possible exception of continuity, which, as we know, rules out leximin). Now COAD may be interpreted as modeling the requirement that the social choice rule should take account of the morally arbitrary distribution of natural talents and familial and cultural environments in prescribing its allocation of conventional and exchangeable resources, as follows. Let us say that an individual h's circumstances, by which I mean the genetic and environmental influences just listed, can be represented by a vector $r^h \in \mathbf{R}^n$, and that the primary goods a person enjoys are a function both of the conventional resources she receives, denoted as a vector $x^h \in \mathbf{R}^m$, and of her vector of circumstantial resources, r^h. In particular, her index of primary goods is a function $u^h(x^h, r^h)$. Now the Rawlsian social choice rule F should take into account the entire vector (x^h, r^h), or for the whole society the vector (x, r), in the sense that it must distinguish between the morally arbitrary characteristics r^h and the life-plan conceptions, which Rawls assumes are the responsibility of individuals. In actuality, the "resources" r^h cannot be redistributed among individuals, if we assume that Rawls would not consider an amendment to his theory friendly were it to advocate the destruction of conventional families and so on and assuming that genetically engineered alterations or redistributions of talents are not possible. Thus the Rawlsian planner must in fact think of holding the vector r fixed, in which case her job is to consider the "reduced" problem in which only conventional resources are distributed and in which the "reduced form" indices of primary goods are given by $\hat{u}^h(x^h) \equiv u^h(x^h, r^h)$. COAD says that the planner will order two distributions of conventional resources, x and y, in the same way when considering the reduced problem with the profile $\hat{u}$ as she would order the distributions (x, r) and (y, r) in the "extended" problem with the profile u. COAD therefore guarantees that the planner's ordering of distributions of transferable resources will necessarily be the same whether or not she explicitly takes into account the vector of circumstantial resources.

I should add that the COAD axiom does more than this, because the goods are not *named* in the environments to which it applies—we have no way of distinguishing resources which represent genetic and familial influences from conventional resources. COAD enforces dimensional consistency in all cases, whether the "r" resources are circumstantial or conventional. For Theorem 1.9 to be a tight argument for maximin, we must also accept dimensional consistency when the vector of resources referred to by the vector r are conventional ones, and we take the distribution $r = (r^1, \ldots, r^H)$ to be the Rawlsian one when the space of resources is $\mathbf{R}^{m+n}$. COAD is then interpreted as an axiom that implements informational simplicity, for it says that if we know that some primary goods are already distributed in the Rawlsian way (say, educational services, through a well-financed system of schools and universities), then we can ignore education in deciding what the Rawlsian distribution of the other primary goods should be.

The third point on which Rawls's first argument has been challenged will be the subject of §5.4.

We now turn to Rawls's second argument for the difference principle, via the original position. While the first argument attempts to establish the difference principle as an instance of justice as impartiality, in Barry's terminology, the second tries to establish it as an instance of justice as mutual advantage. The idea is that the just distribution of resources is that which would be chosen in a social contract among individuals who are shielded from knowledge of what position (and location) they (will) in fact hold in actual society. Thus individuals should make this social contract when they know the actual distribution of circumstantial and genetic traits among persons in society, but none knows what person he shall become. Here again there is a problem, for Rawls also assumes that individuals do not know their life plans behind the veil of ignorance, although we may suppose they know the joint distributions of such life plans and all other resources. But if life plans are not morally arbitrary, then why should individuals in the morally correct posture for making the social contract not know them? And why should they not know their propensities to expend effort or, rather, that part of effort for which individuals are morally responsible? After all, the veil of ignorance is only supposed to shield individuals from knowledge of their morally arbitrary features. I do not think that these questions have satisfactory answers in Rawls: it is in the more recent political philosophy (of Ronald Dworkin, Richard Arneson, and G. A. Cohen) that is the topic of Chapters 7 and 8 that the distinction between morally arbitrary and nonarbitrary characteristics of persons comes fully into play.

Rawls's veil-of-ignorance argument is not simply an effort to render his argument for justice as fairness rigorous, for it depends upon another ingredient, namely, the supposition that justice is embodied in some kind of social contract agreed to by individuals who are to some large extent self-regarding. I agree with Barry (1989) that this is the wrong tack for Rawls. One can make the argument for equality rigorous in ways other than appealing to social contracts behind the veil of ignorance, as I have indicated above, and I believe that path is more consistent with Rawls's encompassing view of fairness.

Let us, nevertheless, focus for the remainder of this section on the contractarian approach, and ask how the difference principle might emerge in such a setting. Let us furthermore focus on the "maximin" aspect of the Rawlsian recommendation, and not on the putative inconsistency in supposing that individuals are shielded from knowledge of their life plans by the veil of ignorance. I have argued in Chapter 4 that Harsanyi is incorrect to claim that behind the veil individuals would choose the utilitarian distribution of resources. But what could justify their choice of the maximin distribution?

The first observation is simple but powerful. All souls are identically placed in Rawls's original position: there is no difference among them. But a social contract among a set of agents who are identical is trivial in this sense: it is simply the choice (of distribution, or of economic system) which is optimal for the generic such agent. That is, as Rawls has constructed the original position, the problem of social contracting dissolves into a decision problem, an optimization problem for the individual, representative soul.

I will study a particular example of a society which will, I hope, be sufficient to upset Rawls's claim that the difference principle would emerge as an optimal decision by a representative soul in the original position. I will suppose that the actual society consists of a continuum of individuals who are characterized as having different abilities to produce income (a consumption good). There are just two goods that matter to people, leisure and the produceable consumption good. We may represent the differential abilities of persons by their real wages w, where w is the amount of the consumption good a person can produce with one unit of labor (say, an hour of work). I assume that the consumption good is produced by labor alone, and that a person's utility function over bundles of the good and labor (or leisure) can vary with her ability: the utility function can be represented as $u(y, L; w)$, where y is the amount of consumption good and L is the amount of labor expended, and u is continuous in all three arguments. Actual abilities (that is, real wages) are distributed according to a probability measure G on a compact interval of real numbers Ω. (Thus for a measurable subset W of Ω, $G(W)$ is the fraction of persons in the actual society with $w \in W$.)

We may view the pair (u, G) as defining the profile of utility functions. I assume that this profile is defined up to at least ordinal-level comparability: that is, it makes sense to say $u(y^1, L^1; w^1) > u(y^2, L^2; w^2)$. I have argued in §4.4 that the choice of distribution from behind a veil of ignorance is impossible unless utility is at least ordinal-level comparable. I am willing to say that $u(y, L; w)$ measures the degree or expected degree of life-plan fulfillment, but not, as Rawls must, that u is an index of primary goods. That might be justifiable if, behind the veil, souls knew nothing about the distribution of life plans individuals in actual society have, but I see no reason that the morally correct posture (that is, the original position) should shield them from that knowledge. Souls who "represent" the interests of self-regarding persons will be concerned with life-plan fulfillment, not only with primary goods.

The only transferable resource in the model I have just defined is the consumption good. Let us say, then, that behind the veil of ignorance, the problem is to choose a tax schedule τ. I shall further assume that τ can depend only on the income a person earns, that is, the amount of the consumption good she produces. (All these simplifications merely mean we are studying a special case.) The tax a person pays, who produces output y, if the tax schedule is τ, is $\tau(y)$. Once a tax schedule τ has been announced, an individual, who can be represented by his real wage w, will, in the actual world, choose a labor supply L to maximize his utility, that is to maximize $u(wL - \tau(wL), L; w)$. Define $L(\tau; w)$ as the solution to this maximization problem. Then we may define individual w's indirect utility at the tax schedule τ as

(5.2) $v(\tau; w) = u(wL(\tau; w) - \tau(wL(\tau; w)), L(\tau; w); w).$

The set of feasible tax schedules τ may be defined as the set T of schedules, taken from some larger prespecified set, that are purely redistributive, or for which the government's budget balances, that is for which:

(5.3) $$\int_{\Omega} \tau(wL(\tau; w))dG(w) = 0.$$

Consider the subset of feasible tax schedules τ with these four properties:

(i) there is a number $\bar{u}$ such that $\{w \mid v(\tau; w) < \bar{u}\}$ has G-measure zero,

(ii) for all numbers $\bar{\bar{u}} > \bar{u}$, the set $\{w \mid v(\tau; w) < \bar{\bar{u}}\}$ has positive G-measure,

(iii) the G-measure of the set $\{w \mid v(\tau; w) \leq \bar{u}\}$ is as small as possible for schedules satisfying (i) and (ii), and

(iv) $\bar{u}$ is the largest number with properties (i)–(iii).

Let us assume enough topological structure on the universal set of tax schedules that at least one feasible tax schedule satisfying (i)–(iv) exists: call the set of schedules satisfying (i)–(iv), T^*. These are the Rawlsian tax schedules, for they make the worst-off group as well off as possible, and among those schedules that make the worst-off group as well off as possible they make the worst-off group as small as possible.

The virtue of the measure-theoretic approach is that it allows us to ignore groups of citizens which are "small," in the precise sense that they are sets of measure zero. Rawls states that he intends the worst-off group to be of nontrivial size—he mentions that we might conceive of this group as all those whose income is less than half of median income (Rawls 1971, p. 98). With the measure-theoretic approach, sets of individuals of measure zero are ignored. At a Rawlsian tax schedule, there may be individuals whose welfare is lower than $\bar{u}$, but they are a "small" group and are ignored.

Each $\tau \in T$ induces a probability measure on the real line that specifies probabilities for welfare for souls behind the veil of ignorance. To be explicit, we define for any $\tau \in T$ and for any real number s, the set $W(s; \tau) = \{w \mid v(\tau; w) = s\}$. Now for any Lebesgue-measurable set S on the real line, define

$$\gamma(S; \tau) = G\left(\bigcup_{s \in S} W(s; \tau)\right).$$

$\gamma(\cdot;\tau)$ defines a probability measure on the real line; for any measurable set S of real numbers, $\gamma(S;\tau)$ is the fraction of society that will end up with welfare levels in S when τ is the chosen tax scheme. From the point of view of a soul behind the veil, $\gamma(S;\tau)$ is the probability that it will end up being embodied in a person with a welfare level in S if τ is the chosen schedule.

Thus any τ induces a lottery from the viewpoint of a soul behind the veil, represented by the probability measure $\gamma(\cdot;\tau)$. The decision problem of the soul consists in choosing one of these lotteries. To so choose, the soul must have a preference order over these lotteries. If the soul is to choose a lottery associated with a Rawlsian τ^*, then it must weakly prefer the lotteries $\gamma(\cdot;\tau^*)$ to all other lotteries. This means the soul would have to be extremely risk averse (I will amplify this below). Rawls gives no convincing argument that the soul should have such risk-averse preferences, nor can I provide one.

It is certainly possible for the soul to have preferences, and even von Neumann–Morgenstern preferences, that will induce choice of the maximin tax schedules. For example, let the soul's preferences be defined as follows. It is indifferent among all Rawlsian tax schedules, and indifferent among all other tax schedules, and it prefers the former to the latter. Define a function ρ on lotteries by $\rho(\gamma(\cdot;\tau)) = 1$ if $\tau \in T^*$ and $\rho(\gamma(\cdot;\tau)) = 0$ if $\tau \notin T^*$, and for any number p between 0 and 1, and where $p\gamma(\cdot;\tau^1) + (1-p)\gamma(\cdot;\tau^2)$ is a lottery between $\gamma(\cdot;\tau^1)$ and $\gamma(\cdot;\tau^2)$, define $\rho(p\gamma(\cdot;\tau^1) + (1-p)\gamma(\cdot;\tau^2)) = p\rho(\gamma(\cdot;\tau^1)) + (1-p)\rho(\gamma(\cdot;\tau^2))$. Then ρ is a utility function on lotteries, representing preferences over lotteries obeying the von Neumann–Morgenstern axioms, which will induce a choice of the Rawlsian tax schedules.

The usual definition of agent rationality in economic theory presupposes that the agent possesses preferences over the objects to be chosen. The rationality assumption does not tell us what preferences (over lotteries) the agent should have. One might, as another case, suppose that, behind the veil, the soul is risk neutral. Thus the soul will want to maximize the expected value of the lottery for welfare; that is, its utility function over tax schedules will be:

(5.4) $\qquad \rho(\tau) = \int s \, d\gamma(s;\tau).$

The τ that maximizes $\rho(\tau)$ will not, of course, generally be the Rawlsian tax schedule.

Example. It is perhaps worthwhile to work out an example to make this point as concretely as possible. Suppose that $u(y, L; w) = y - L^2/2$ (in this case, utility does not depend on w), and that w is uniformly distributed on the interval $[0, 1]$. Suppose the set of possible tax schedules are linear, $\tau(y) = cy + d$, with $0 \leq c \leq 1$. Faced with a tax schedule $cy + d$, the individual with real wage w will maximize utility by choosing a labor supply of $\hat{L} = w(1 - c)$. Invoking the feasiblity constraint (5.3), we calculate that $d = -(c(1 - c)/3)$. Thus balanced-budget tax schedules are of the form $cy - (c(1 - c)/3)$; we may therefore identify a feasible tax schedule by its parameter c. Using these facts, one can write down the problem of choosing the tax schedule that makes the person with lowest utility as well off as possible as:

(5.5)
$$\max_c \min_w \left\{ w^2(1 - c) - \left[c(w^2(1 - c)) - \frac{c(1 - c)}{3} \right] - \frac{w^2(1 - c)^2}{2} \right\}.$$

Solving (5.5), we get that the optimal tax schedule is $\hat{c} = \frac{1}{2}$. That is, the Rawlsian tax schedule for this society, given the restriction to linear tax rules, would be to set the marginal tax rate at 50%.

Let us now compute what tax schedule would be chosen by a soul behind the veil who is risk neutral. Representing τ by c, we compute the indirect utility function:

$$v(c, w) = \frac{w^2(1 - c)^2}{2} + \frac{c(1 - c)}{3},$$

and hence expected utility is

$$\int_0^1 v(c, w)dw = \frac{1 - c^2}{6},$$

which is maximized at $c = 0$. Thus the risk-neutral soul would choose to have no redistribution at all.

I am not asserting that the soul behind the veil should be risk neutral; I wish only to illustrate the arbitrariness of assuming it is so risk averse as to choose the Rawlsian lottery. The assumption of rationality is insufficient to enable us to determine the soul's preferences over lotteries. Recall that Harsanyi's impartial observer theorem (§4.4) faced a similar problem (although this was not the major problem with Harsanyi's utilitarian claim): we have no way, on the basis of rationality alone, of choosing the constants a^h and b^h in Equation (4.4).

To summarize. Either the life plan of a person and her propensity to expend effort are morally arbitrary features or they are not. If they are, then souls should be shielded from knowledge of them in the original position, though not shielded from knowledge of how they are distributed in society. But then all souls are identically placed, and the social contract dissolves into an individual optimization problem of a representative soul. The choice, by such a soul, of a Rawlsian tax scheme is hardly justified by rationality, for there seems no good reason to endow the soul with preferences that are, essentially, infinitely risk averse. On the other hand, if a person's life-plan and effort choices fall within the orbit of what a person is morally responsible for, then souls behind the veil of ignorance should know the life plans and effort propensities of the persons they shall become, but not the knowledge of what other resources, whose distribution is morally arbitrary, they shall come to have. This is essentially the way that Dworkin sets up the problem of distributive justice, which is the subject of Chapter 7.

There is one other way of generating a choice of the Rawlsian tax scheme from behind the veil, and this is to postulate that the representative soul faces a decision problem under ignorance, that it does not know the probability distribution of traits in actual society. There is a literature on decision under ignorance which advocates the choice of an alternative that maximizes the minimum possible utility (see Milnor [1954] and Maskin [1979], for instance). But this move is surely inappropriate here, for there is no reason to shield souls in the original position from knowledge of what the distribution of circumstances and life plans is in actual society. Moreover, the claim that maximin is the rational strategy for the decision problem under ignorance is not uncontested (see Nehring [1995]).

Final remarks on the issue of individual responsibility are in order, for on this issue, I believe, rests the coherence of the Rawlsian system. The expected degree of life-plan fulfillment, as modeled above in §5.2, depends upon actions taken by individual h, her choice of location l and labor or effort L. Rawls clearly wishes to reserve a space for responsible choice, as he explicitly declares in regard to the choice of life plans. His first argument for equalizing primary social goods hinges on the determinants of those goods being morally arbitrary. But if Rawls views the choice of life plan as within the realm of a person's responsible choice, then it seems only consistent to extend this responsibility to the choice of occupation and labor or effort expended—or, more precisely, to admit that to some extent those choices must be not morally arbitrary, but due to responsible volition.[5] But then the distribution of primary social goods cannot be considered to be morally arbitrary, and hence the rationale for equalizing them across persons dissolves. The alternative would seem to be not to include labor and occupation as influencing the consumption of primary social goods. In the case of labor, I have argued (in §5.2) that this leads to Rawlsian tax schedules which are punitive, and in the case of occupation, that Rawls's explicit definition of primary social good (b) is contradicted.

For these reasons I think the Rawlsian system is inconsistent and cannot be coherently reconstructed while preserving its major elements. These major elements are: (1) the index of primary goods must be such that its increase enhances the prospects of realizing a person's life plan, (2) the choice of a person's life plan is her responsibility, (3) the primary goods a person enjoys are due to social choices (tax schedules) and to morally arbitrary features of persons, and (4) equalization of the consequences of morally arbitrary features, but not of the consequences of features that are not morally arbitrary, is required for justice. From (2), (3), and (4), we conclude: (5) justice requires equalizing primary social goods but not the expected degrees of life-plan fulfillment. Element (1) is not needed for the syllogism, but on account of Rawlsian neutrality: the conception of primary goods must be consistent with the advancement of all life plans. Relevant minor elements of the system, which can be altered without shaking its foundation, are whether the index of primary goods is personalized or the same for all, and whether labor is a primary good. I have argued that preserving major element (1) requires the primary-goods index to be personalized and also requires that labor-leisure be a primary good. But if freedom of occupational choice and labor-leisure are primary goods, then the only way to preserve (3) is to argue that occupation and labor-leisure choices are not the responsibility of persons, that they are determined by features whose distribution is morally arbitrary. But this, I maintain, is in-

---

5. Cohen (1989) raises this point.

consistent with (2). The inconsistency is not displayed by the above syllogism, but becomes apparent if one tries to explain how life-plan choices could be in the realm of personal responsibility of a person while occupation and labor choices were not. Are not occupation and labor choices among the most important ingredients in life-plan fulfillment, for many (most?) life-plan conceptions? And if these choices do not involve an element of personal volition, then what choices do?

5.4 The Cohen Criticism

This putative inconsistency in the Rawlsian system ignores the distinction between equality of primary social goods and the maximin distribution of such. Cohen (1995a) has recently argued that the move by which Rawls proceeds from equality to maximin is flawed. That argument was reproduced at the beginning of §5.3: first, mandated equality of primary goods was deduced from their moral arbitrariness, and then maximin was deduced from the claim that Pareto-improving moves from any allocation must be approved. In Chapter 1, I have indeed suggested that Pareto optimality is a requisite of justice: for should not citizens be free to propose Pareto improvements of a proposed social alternative? Cohen disagrees. While the distinction between equality and maximin might appear to be a small point, Cohen shows that it is not. Indeed, he argues that there are deep issues of the conception of justice involved. In this section, I shall put aside the concerns of the last section and concentrate only on Cohen's point.

The argument hinges on the distinction between two sets of allocations. The first, which I continue to call X, is the set of feasible allocations for the society. By feasible, we here mean physically and technologically possible. To render this notion precise, think of X as the set of allocations a planner could implement if she were omniscient and omnipotent: she would know precisely the capabilities of every person and technology, and could force every person to do anything of which he was capable. The second set of allocations, Y, is the set of allocations that are in fact available to a society: it is, of course, a subset of X, constrained by the knowledge of the planner (government), the power of the planner, the necessity of using markets to decentralize economic activity, the limitations of feasible taxation-redistribution schemes that society may legislate to protect the privacy and self-esteem of individuals (for example, a society might say a person's tax liability should not depend on his IQ, because persons of low IQ would suffer loss of self-esteem from receiving a subsidy on that account), and other limitations necessary to ensure the other primary goods (free choice of occupation, freedom of association, and so on). Finally, and this is key, let us assume that Y is determined by self-regarding actions that individuals take when facing the government's taxation schedule. We may assume that each person calculates his occupational and labor choice to maximize his expected degree of life-plan fulfillment, given the tax schedule.

There is an allocation x^* in X that maximizes the index of primary goods of the worst-off group, and there is a tax schedule τ^*, among the socially acceptable ones, that maximizes the index of primary goods going to the worst-off group, at some allocation y^* in Y. (For instance, we calculated τ^* in the example of the last section.) Rawls views y^* as the just allocation. Cohen argues that Rawls can only consistently view x^* as the just allocation.

In particular, the achievement of y^* will in general depend on giving talented people incentives to engage their valuable abilities in the social interest. These incentives will usually entail their receiving a larger index of primary goods than the worst-off, perhaps a considerably larger index. Rawls finds this difference morally all right: in fact he states clearly that differences in income are just when they improve the condition of the least well-off. This is, indeed, the difference principle. In particular, those who possess certain traits whose distribution is morally arbitrary, such as innate ability or certain family backgrounds, will receive more income and primary social goods in y^* than others who are less fortunate. Cohen insists that declaring such a distribution just contradicts the initial claim of the argument, that the arbitrariness of the talent distribution means that justice requires equality of primary goods. Moreover, the talented, high-income persons at y^* are not themselves embracing the condition of justice, which is that society should endeavor to engender arrangements to the greatest benefit of the least well-off. At y^*, these talented persons (among others) are maximizing their own utility. Justice requires them to take those actions which render the least well-off as well off as possible: otherwise, they are consenting to enjoy a greater bundle of primary goods than others by virtue of characteristics which they possess by morally arbitrary good luck. While Cohen would presumably advise the government to choose τ^*, and therefore settle for y^*, he does not call that allocation just—at least, he does not grant that Rawls has demonstrated it is just.

In the allocation x^*, there is no incentive pay. If some end up with more primary goods than others, it is solely because there is no way of arranging institutions, even given selfless behavior on the parts of individuals, to generate a greater index of primary goods for the worst-off. Thus some persons may have more after-tax income than others at x^* because they must consume more to sustain their talents or labor power. The key point is that x^* will be considerably more egalitarian than y^*.

For Cohen, self-regarding behavior is inconsistent with Rawlsian justice, for justice requires a (Rawlsian) fraternity among citizens that cannot exist if the talented willingly choose to be well off in the face of poverty of others that is owing to morally arbitrary features. The talented highly paid people cannot say to low-talent, poor people, "If society raises the tax rate on my income by 10%, I will work so much less that your income from transfer payments will fall. Therefore, you shouldn't raise my tax rate," and simultaneously claim to be their brothers. But such fraternity, or community, is a necessary part of Rawlsian justice (Cohen 1992).

5.5 Kolm's Fundamental Preferences

Approximately contemporaneously with Rawls, Serge-Christophe Kolm (1972) published his egalitarian theory of justice. He began the third part of his book, entitled "Justice," with the sentence: "Fundamentally, all individuals have the same needs, the same tastes, and the same desires. Doubtless, this assertion demands an explanation" (1972, p. 79). The viewpoint is not dissimilar to that of Rawls, which asserts that all individuals share a common core of need for primary goods. But Kolm develops his view in a far more Cartesian (some would say "reductionist") manner than Rawls. He says that if two persons have preferences which appear different, there is a reason for it; there is something which renders them different. Let us make this "something" an object of preference, thus expanding the dimension of the space on which preferences are defined. If their newly extended preferences are still different, there must be something that renders them so. Add this "something" to the "commodity" space. Kolm asserts that, by continuing in this way, we eventually can represent the preferences of the two persons as identical, on an extended space of "goods" of high dimension. No proof of this assertion is offered.

There is a mathematical sense in which Kolm is right. Howe (1987) proves the following theorem: if a set of H persons have concave, monotone, continuous non-negative utility functions on a commodity space with n goods, then each utility function can be expressed as a projection of a *single* concave, monotone, continuous utility function defined on a space of $n + H$ goods.[6] In fact, Howe's representation theorem does both more and less than Kolm proposes. It does more in representing each of the H persons as consuming one unit of a personalized good, and it is precisely that good which characterizes the person's preferences as being what they are in the lower dimensional space $\mathbf{R}^n$. (See note 6; the unit vector e^h gives individual h one unit of the hth personalized good.) It does less than Kolm proposes in that the additional "goods" that are added to the original commodity space are entirely abstract. We cannot describe these goods as "synaptic connections, endorphins, French culture," and so on.

Note that, while Rawls retreats to primary goods in part because of the incommensurability of different life plans, Kolm argues that differences between persons are ephemeral and that, in truth, apparently different conceptions of the good are completely commensurable, if one goes "all the way down."

Kolm defines a distribution of resources as *just* if all individuals' consumption vectors in the space on which the fundamental preferences are defined (in $\mathbf{R}^{n+H}$, if we use Howe's representation theorem) lie on the same indifference surface of the fundamental preference order. This is a definition, not a theorem; its appeal must come from the inherent sameness of all individuals. From this, it would probably be fair to say that Kolm advocates equality of welfare. But the justification for that egalitarian mandate is not that all persons should be equally happy, or have their life plans fulfilled to equal degrees on account of some sense of fairness, but rather that all persons are really the same person deep down. Thus equality of condition is a kind of justice-as-impartiality, but an impartiality that relies on a notion of symmetry, that identical individuals should be treated identically. Kolm asserts that utility becomes interpersonally comparable at the level of fundamental preferences, since all persons become, in fact, the same at that level (1972, p. 123).

Kolm does not raise the issues of responsibility for life plans and the moral arbitrariness of personal circumstances that are important in the Rawlsian analysis.

---

6. Let $\{u^h \mid h = 1, \ldots, H\}$ be a set of continuous, concave, non-negative, increasing (CCNI) functions mapping $\mathbf{R}^n_+$ into $\mathbf{R}$, and satisfying Condition (3.1). Then there exists a CCNI function $v : \mathbf{R}^{n+H}_+ \to \mathbf{R}$ such that, for $h = 1, \ldots, H$ and all $x \in \mathbf{R}^{n+H}$, $u^h(x) = v(x, e^h)$, where e^h is the hth unit vector in $\mathbf{R}^H$.

Kolm's treatment of justice and Pareto efficiency shares aspects of Cohen's criticism (§5.4) of Rawls. An allocation (of transferable goods) which puts all individuals on the same indifference surface of the fundamental preferences (that is, equalizes utility), and only such an allocation, is just. Kolm writes that there may be no feasible, just allocations, or there may be a best feasible just allocation, which is nevertheless inefficient (in the Pareto sense). He writes, "Justice may be impossible, and life necessarily unjust," and "justice may be inefficient, and efficiency necessarily unjust" (1972, p. 83).

Because there may exist no feasible just allocation, or the best just allocation may be inefficient, Kolm defines *practical justice* (1972, p. 115). An allocation is practically just exactly when it is the leximin allocation! Thus Kolm distinguishes between just allocations and social optima. The social optimum (the leximin allocation) may not be just, even though just allocations exist. Kolm makes precisely the distinction that Cohen would have Rawls make between justice (as complete equality of condition) and social optimality (as leximin).

John Broome (1993) has raised a telling objection against Kolm's "fundamental preferences." One must distinguish, he argues, between objects of preference and causes of preference. Let us say the space of commodities (objects of preference) is $\mathbf{R}^n$; we have a set of H individuals, and the preferences of individual h may be written over commodity vectors $x \in \mathbf{R}^n$ as $u(x; \eta^h)$, where η^h is a vector in $\mathbf{R}^m$, for all h; thus u is Kolm's fundamental utility function. η^h is a vector of h's personal characteristics which cause her to have preferences over commodity bundles x represented by the utility function $u^h := u(\cdot; \eta^h)$. Broome observes that it is wrong to think of u as representing everyone's preference order over the "commodity space" $\mathbf{R}^{n+m}$. Thus suppose for concreteness that $m = 3$, and that these three dimensions are "culture, health, and endocrine balance": that is, a person's culture, her health status, and her endocrine balance determine her preference order over the commodity space $\mathbf{R}^n$. Now person h may very well *have* a preference order over the "extended" commodity space $\mathbf{R}^{n+m}$, where the last three components measure culture, health, and endocrine balance, respectively, but that preference order will not be given by u. For instance, h might prefer to "consume" (x, η^1) to (x', η^2)—she might prefer to have characteristics η^1 and consume x than have characteristics η^2 and consume x'—but that is an entirely different statement from saying that a person with characteristics η^1 has preferences over x given by $u(x; \eta^1)$. Indeed, knowing just that $u^h(\cdot) = u(\cdot; \eta^h)$ does not tell us anything about h's preferences over the extended commodity space $\mathbf{R}^{n+m}$.

The fact that $\{u^h\}$ can be represented as above by the function u does not mean that all individuals involved have the same preferences over extended bundles. Furthermore, from the fact that $u(x; \eta^1) = u(x'; \eta^2)$ it does not follow that individual 1 is as well-off consuming x as individual 2 is consuming x': we can garner no information about interpersonal comparisons of well-being from the representation u. To this point, Kolm could, perhaps, respond that a person's *degree* of well-being is in fact measured by his fundamental utility function u—this, I think, is not an unreasonable claim—and hence u can be endowed with interpersonal comparability, although a theorem like Howe's alone does not allow us to deduce interpersonal comparability from nothing. That is, one could maintain that a person's circumstances (η) determine the degree of well-being she receives from commodities (x).

Regardless of whether or not u measures interpersonally comparable well-being, Kolm's justification of the equal-utility distribution of commodities as just is incorrect. As Broome has shown, the symmetry that Kolm invokes (that all persons have the same preferences on the extended space) is in fact not there. Whether, because any person with circumstances η *would* have well-being $u(x; \eta)$ when consuming x, it should follow that well-being should be equalized, is a different question. Equality of well-being may well be appealing, but it appears that Kolm has not produced an additional argument for it.

5.6   Functionings and Capability

Sen (1980) argued that, in reacting against welfarism, Rawls went too far in the other direction. Rawls objected to welfarism for three reasons: some people derive welfare from "offensive tastes" (for example, deriving pleasure from another's suffering), some people have "expensive tastes," and conceptions of welfare are so diverse as to be incommensurable. The first two reasons are ones for society's not unequivocally trying to maximize a social welfare function which is increasing in the welfares of its members, and the third reason says that it is futile to try to compare welfare levels across persons. Sen did not disagree, but claimed that primary goods were not the appropriate maximanda. The focus should be on what goods do for people, and they do things for people short of providing idiosyncratic welfare: they enable people to escape morbidity, to be adequately nourished, to have mobility, to achieve self-respect, to take part in the life of the community, and to be happy (Sen 1993, p. 36).[7] These "doings and beings" Sen calls *functionings*. Rawls's theory suffers from a "fetishist handicap" (Sen 1980) in focusing on goods as such. If the various institutional primary goods were being equally supplied (prerogatives and powers, the social bases of self-respect), then Rawls would call for equalizing the remaining one, income: but, Sen says, that is wrong. Incomes should be not equalized, but distributed in such manner as to equalize the functionings that persons can achieve. A handicapped person will generally require more income than an able-bodied one, an inequality that Rawls's approach will not assent to.

Cohen (1993) has dubbed the thing one enjoys from one's functionings *midfare*, something which is midway between goods and welfare. Midfare, like Rawlsian primary goods, is something which everyone wants, which is arguably an input into any life-plan conception. Sen's proposal is that distributive justice entails equalizing midfare levels across persons.

There are, however, several ways in which Sen's proposal differs from Rawls's apart from the shift in the maximandum. Before discussing these, it should be remarked that, from the analysis in §5.2, we have at hand a way of resolving the dispute between Sen and Rawls. As we saw, Rawls's two views that life-plan conceptions are incommensurable, and that primary goods advance the achievement of all life plans, together require the existence of a generalized index of primary goods $\mu = (\mu^1, \dots, \mu^H)$. We can simply take μ^h to be the function that converts resource vectors into an index of functionings for person h. Then the maximandum for Rawls becomes an interpersonally comparable index of functionings! This is not to say that discovering the function μ^h is easy: for some functionings, the relationship between goods and functionings is reasonably straightforward, but for others, there is a subjective element (happiness, self-respect). In principle, though, this resolution allows Rawls's theory to take Sen's critique on board.

This resolution, however, does not exhaust Sen's differences with Rawls, for there is for Sen an importance in "freedom" which we do not find so explicitly in Rawls. Sen defines a person's *capability* as the set of vectors of functionings which are available to him. View each person as having a cer-

---

7. Sen does not share Rawls's concept of happiness, which is the state a person enjoys when she is fulfilling her life plan. For Sen, happiness is a feeling of pleasure.

tain income or wealth. The person can convert this income into various vectors of functionings; the set of all such vectors is his capability. Sen does not call for equalizing an index of functionings, *tout court*, but rather for equalizing these *sets* across persons. He leaves the problem open of specifying the equivalence relation on capability sets. Consider two persons: Andrea has just one vector of functionings available to her, and Bob has available a capability consisting of many functioning vectors, the best one of which (for him) is exactly the same as Andrea's one vector. Sen might well consider Bob to be better off.[8] Why? By virtue of the enhanced freedom Bob has to choose different options. The ability to choose among options has a value for Sen other than the instrumental one (that choosing enables the person to get the thing he most prefers), and this value is reflected in the range of options in a person's capability. In this way, Sen's position is similar to Scanlon's (1988), who argues that choice has noninstrumental value for people (his so-called "demonstrative" and "symbolic" values of choice). To illustrate the difference between a concern for a person's capability and his achieved vector of functionings, consider the contrast between a rich person on a hunger strike and a poor one who is starving for lack of money to buy food. These two may have the same level of nourishment, but the capability of the former is greater than that of the latter. It is capability that matters.

Thus far I have presented Sen's theory as an attempt to provide a better common denominator for different "conceptions of the good" than Rawlsian primary goods. But Sen goes farther. He is concerned not only with offensive and expensive tastes but with tastes that are formed under conditions of truncated opportunity: to wit, those of "the battered slave, the tamed housewife, the broken unemployed, the hopeless destitute" (Sen 1987, p. 11). These types form plans of life that are too modest—they are too easily pleased—and hence counting only their self-conceived senses of welfare in the social calculus would give them too little. Thus Sen is concerned with those who have "cheap tastes," when those tastes are formed in reaction to conditions of deprivation.[9] A focus on functionings will go a

---

8. I say "might," because one possibility is to consider two capabilities equivalent if their "best vectors" are the same.

9. This concern was introduced by Elster (1979), in his discussion of endogenous taste formation.

long way to giving these types a fair deal, even though it may be more than they dreamed they were entitled to. Cohen (1993) gives the case of Dickens's character Tiny Tim in point: Tim, who couldn't walk, was blessed with a sunny disposition. To realize his life plan, or to be happy, he needed very little. But Sen would argue that Tim should get a wheelchair from the Ministry of Justice, even though it might render him much happier than others with their quota. (There is some problem for Sen here, deriving from the inclusion of "happiness" as a functioning. Arguably, because of that inclusion, Tim should not get the wheelchair, for it would boost his functioning or capability index above the index of others. I will return to this below.)

Sen thinks that the human condition can be measured in a variety of ways, and that there is no unique best way. He differentiates among the terms well-being, standard of living, happiness, agency achievement, and opulence. The simplest of these is opulence, or wealth, and Sen is critical of it for being a fetishist measure. Well-being is measured by the functioning vector a person enjoys. Standard of living is measured not by wealth, but by some of the functionings. Sen writes that if political prisoners are freed in a distant country, my well-being may be improved, but not my standard of living. I am not sure which of one's functionings would improve with the release of these prisoners, but the suggestion is that well-being includes some other-regarding features of one's preferences, while standard of living does not. Happiness for Sen is a less exalted state than for Rawls, and is associated with feelings of pleasure. A person's "agency goals" are what she wishes to accomplish; this is the synonym for Rawlsian life plans, the achievement of which, for Rawls, is indexed by happiness.

Because of these multiple measures of human advantage, Sen claims there is no single recipe for distributive justice. Specifically, he argues that there are at least four goals the Ministry of Justice might have. One can distinguish between well-being and agency goals, on one dimension, and between achievement and freedom to achieve on another. The "Cartesian product" of these two dimensions produces four possible equalisanda: achievement of well-being, freedom to achieve agency goals, and so forth. Sen does not claim that an aggregation of these four social concerns can be found, but rather that, for practical purposes, we can often partially order alternative social states on the basis of the degrees/levels of equalization they provide of these four equalisanda.

I shall raise five criticisms of Sen's theory. As I noted above, (1) including happiness as one of the functionings weakens the extent to which an index of functionings will be independent of self-conceived notions of welfare. This is not necessarily bad, but note that we jeopardize Tiny Tim's receiving a wheelchair by including happiness as a functioning. The pleasure that I receive from satisfying my offensive and expensive tastes will also generate happiness, and this weakens the detour around these kinds of taste that focusing on functionings was supposed to facilitate. (2) Sen has not provided an index of functionings; if an increase in one's (index of) functionings should never decrease the possibility of achieving one's agency goals, then we can deduce, as we did in the case of Rawlsian primary goods, that the functioning index for a person must be a monotone transform of the utility function that represents her agency-goal preferences. Thus there will be a "generalized index" of functionings, and the functioning indices for different individuals will be different. Again, the functioning index loses its independence from agency-goal preferences, as it did with Rawls. (3) Even given functioning indices, Sen provides no equivalence relation on the class of capability sets which would enable us to say when one person's capability is better or richer than another's. He rightly points out that, for many social policy questions, the partial ordering provided by set inclusion will suffice (that is, if S and T are two capabilities, and $S \subset T$, then T is the richer capability). But we do not always have set inclusion, especially, perhaps, when the two individuals concerned come from very different cultures. An antiegalitarian relativist could claim that it is impossible to say which of two capabilities is richer. ("Who are you, Justice Commissar, to say the Bengali beggar's capability is less rich than the Princeton professor's?") The larger the equivalence classes of capabilities, the less radical are the egalitarian prescriptions of the theory. (4) Sen criticizes Rawls for his "extremism of giving total priority to the interests of the worst off" (Sen 1992, p. 146), but offers no explicit social objective in his own theory. He speaks of equalizing capabilities, but does not discuss the equalization objective so precisely as would force him to face the issues of maximin and leximin. If Sen would not maximin, but would trade off an increase in welfare of the worst-off from some other objective, then he should inform us what the other objective is, and how he would judge the trade-off. (5) The treatment of agent responsibility is essentially Rawlsian and, from the hindsight of more recent writings of Arneson and Cohen on the question (see Chapter 8), inadequate. Individuals are implicitly viewed as not responsible for their opportunities, as measured by their capabilities, but responsible for their choice of functioning vector and their agency goals (life plans). But it may be the case, in reality, that a person's agency goals are socially determined in a way that precludes her having responsibility over them. And, conversely, a person may have responsibility in part over the functioning vectors in her capability, especially, for example, if happiness and self-respect are included as functionings.[10] (*In re* self-respect, might not an individual set unrealistically demanding conditions for its achievement?)

Sen explicitly defends himself against the charges in the second and third points above; he argues that partial orderings (of functioning vectors and of capabilities) are really all that we can make, and that it is a foolish Cartesianism that seeks completion of the theory in the sense of providing complete orders of these objects. To continue the metaphor, Sen would view himself as the Heisenberg of distributive justice theory, in the sense that he maintains there is no universally correct or unique answer to the distribution question. He may be right, but, in my estimation, the assertion is unproved. One feels that Sen often tries to make a virtue of necessity when he writes that certain hard questions have no right answers. The alternative, in science, is to admit that there are answers, but we do not have them yet. I do not think the theory of distributive justice is as yet so advanced that we should reject this hypothesis.

5.7   Equality of Functionings or Primary Goods:
An Alternative Approach

It is natural, when speaking of equalizing or maximinning primary goods or capabilities, to suppose one has a profile of indices of primary goods or capabilities that is ordinally measurable and fully comparable (OFC). In this section I propose an alternative in which no explicit indices of primary goods or capabilities are computed, but information from utility functions is used to calculate how needy a person is with respect to the

---

10. Cohen (1993) has raised another criticism of Sen's theory, that as stated, there is an ambiguity in his use of the term "capability." Cohen argues that capability has an "athletic" connotation, of what a person can achieve by virtue of exercising his will and taking action, which is different from the passive notion of some of the functionings. A baby can be well nourished, warm, and sheltered although it is not "capable" of nourishing, clothing, or sheltering itself. Moreover, Cohen maintains that Sen uses capability in both its "athletic" and passive senses. Sen (1993) has responded to Cohen's charge of inconsistency. I have tried to avoid the dispute by using capability in the way that Sen (1993) defines it, and using "freedom," as Sen uses it, to refer to the capacity of a person to take action.

resources that engender primary goods and functionings. The approach I shall present requires only ordinal noncomparable information on preferences. There are costs to working with ordinal noncomparable preferences only, of course, but I argue that we may be able to go a considerable distance toward "equalizing capability" without recourse to interpersonally comparable indices.

I shall from now on refer to functionings, as I think the model below fits that interpretation somewhat better than "primary goods." Suppose that there are R functionings, where the rth is denoted Y_r. We further suppose that there are two kinds of resource: those which affect the functionings, and those which do not. Thus, perhaps housing space, health services, and educational services have an effect on functionings, but yachts, diamond rings, and scotch whiskey do not. Let us call the first kind of resource "primary" and the second kind "secondary," and partition the resource space into an n-dimensional space of primary resources and an m-dimensional space of secondary resources. I will continue to write the set of feasible resource distributions as $X \subset \mathbf{R}^{H(m+n)}$ (there are H individuals) and will represent the generic element of X as (x, y) where $x \in \mathbf{R}^{Hn}$ is the distribution of primary resources and $y \in \mathbf{R}^{Hm}$ is the vector of secondary resources. Define $Y_r^h = F_r^h(x)$ as the functional relationship between (primary) resources and functionings. It is important to note that the partition of the set of resources into primary and secondary is the same for all persons. The secondary resources may be viewed as ones that contribute to fulfillment of some life plans or agency goals, but not all life plans, or as ones that a person would rather have more of than less, although they do not contribute to fulfilling her life plan.

I will next suppose that each individual h has preferences over bundles of resources (x^h, y^h) she may receive, which reflect the degree to which her life plan will be achieved with these resource bundles. There are several restrictions on these preferences. First, they do not depend on the whole vector (x, y) but only on (x^h, y^h); in other words, preferences are self-regarding. This requires a narrower conception of functionings than Sen's, for "self-respect" and "being able to appear comfortably in public" may well be functionings that depend on what others in the society are capable of achieving. Second, I will suppose that individual h's preferences can be represented by a separable utility function of the form $u^h(x^h, y^h) = v^h(x^h) + w^h(y^h)$. The functions u^h are ordinal noncomparable representations of preferences: any monotonic transformations of these functions will do just as well, but representing preferences in this separable form will be useful for analysis. We may think of v^h as the contribution to happiness (in the sense of Rawls, see §5.2) from the consumption of basic necessities and w^h as the idiosyncratic contribution to happiness. We could also view v^h as a reduced form of a utility function whose arguments are functionings, $\tilde{v}^h(Y_1, \ldots, Y_R)$, where $v^h(x) = \tilde{v}^h(F_1^h(x), \ldots, F_R^h(x))$. Note that this division of resources corresponds to the practice of welfare states, which are concerned with guaranteeing each person a minimal consumption of housing, education, nutrition, and health. One might even argue that the functions v^h are the same for all persons, but I shall not need to do so.

Let x_i and x_{-i} stand for the ith component of a vector $x \in R^n$ and the $(n-1)$-dimensional vector consisting of x absent x_i, respectively. For what follows, I shall assume that:

for all h, v^h is strictly concave, strictly monotonic, and C^2,

(5.6)   and if $x_{-i} \neq 0$, then $\lim_{x_i \to 0} v_i^h(x) = \infty$,

where v_i^h is the ith derivative of v^h,

and that

w^h is concave, C^1, monotonic, and $w_j^h(0)$ is finite for all j,

(5.7)   where w_j^h is the jth derivative of w^h.

In particular, consider the marginal rate of substitution $m_{ij}^h(x, y) = v_i^h(x)/w_j^h(y)$ of a primary resource against a secondary resource. Let $M^h(x, y)$ be the matrix $(m_{ij}^h(x, y))$. As x_i approaches zero, $m_{ij}^h(x)$ becomes infinite, by (5.6) and (5.7). This expresses the idea that primary resources are primary in the sense that a person is willing to trade off arbitrarily large amounts of any secondary resource to get very small amounts of a primary resource as the amount of that primary resource goes to zero. Why might this be so? Perhaps if any primary resource is zero, then some functioning is zero (for example, zero housing services implies no shelter from the elements), and if any functioning is zero, the person cannot survive or do anything. These resources are, then, truly needed. Strictly speaking, of course, one cannot separate needs from wants at the abstract level of general preferences. I am asserting that, if we know a priori which are the primary resources and which the secondary, then the marginal rates of substitution will have this property. (I am not admitting nonconvexities—that a person may require some threshhold amount of primary resource before it is of any use to her.)

It is natural to say that a person's needs for primary resources have been met when he starts devoting income to the purchase of secondary resources. More specifically, we might measure the extent to which a person suffers deprivation from lack of primary resources (or functioning deprivation) by his marginal rates of substitution of primary resources against secondary resources at an allocation. Let $\| \ \|$ be a norm on $\mathbf{R}^n$. Let $M_j^h(x, y)$ be the jth column of the matrix $M^h(x, y)$. Let $\mu^h(x, y) = \min_j \|M_j^h(x, y)\|$. The above remarks suggest that $\mu^h(x, y)$ is a measure of the extent of deprivation from lack of primary resources of a person with utility function $v^h(x) + w^h(y)$ when he consumes (x, y). It is a summary measure of the magnitude of the trade-offs he is willing to make of the secondary resource he values most highly against all the primary resources.

Definition 5.1. Let the set of feasible allocations be X. An allocation $(x, y) \in X$, $((x^1, y^1), (x^2, y^2), \ldots, (x^H, y^H))$, is *acceptable* iff it is Pareto optimal and it solves

$$\min_{(x,y)\in X} \max_{h\in H} \mu^h(x^h, y^h).$$

Thus the worst-off person is said to be the one whose index of deprivation from lack of primary resources (μ^h) is largest, and an acceptable allocation makes that person as well off as possible (in the sense of minimizing μ^h).

Note that, although I have limited the domain of preferences by imposing the separable representation and conditions (5.6) and (5.7), the concept of an acceptable allocation is a purely ordinal one: it depends only on marginal rates of substitution, which are properties of indifference curves only. Furthermore, welfares are not assumed to be interpersonally comparable.

For the theorems below it is useful to impose some conditions on the norm, namely:

(5.8a)   Let $v^1, v^2 \in \mathbf{R}^n$ and $v^1 \geq v^2$. Then $\|v^1\| > \|v^2\|$.

(5.8b)   Let v^k be a sequence of vectors such that $v_i^k \to \infty$ for some component i. Then $\|v^k\| \to \infty$.

Both conditions are satisfied, for instance, by the Euclidean norm [but the "sup" norm, for instance, violates (5.8a), and a norm that ignored a particular component would violate (5.8b)].

I further specialize the environment by assuming there is a fixed amount, say, unity, of some all-purpose production input, which can be used to produce any of the $m + n$ consumption resources according to the linear production functions $x_i = r$ and $y_j = r$, where r is the amount of the input used. It follows that the Pareto optimal allocations are completely characterized as follows: allocate the entire amount of the production input to the citizens in any way, say, $\mathbf{r} = (r^1, \ldots, r^H)$, and allow each citizen to choose how to use his input to produce consumption resources. Thus citizen h solves the program:

$$\max v^h(x) + w^h(y)$$
(5.9)
$$\text{s.t. } \sum_i x_i + \sum_j y_j \leq r^h$$

The resulting allocation is Pareto optimal, and all Pareto optimal allocations arise in this way, by the linearity of the production functions. We will henceforth denote the individually optimal solution of agent h, who has the input resource in amount r, $(x^h(r), y^h(r))$.

Lemma 5.1. *For any $r^* > 0$, and any function v satisfying property (5.6), there is a unique solution $(x_1, \ldots, x_n, \lambda^*)$ to the following $n + 1$ equations:*

$$v_i(x) = \lambda, \qquad i = 1, \ldots, n$$
$$\sum_i x_i = r^*.$$

The functions $x_i(r)$ and $\lambda(r)$ so defined, as we vary the endowment of the input resource, are differentiable, and $\lambda'(r) < 0$.

Proof:

1. Consider the maximization problem

$$\max v(x)$$
$$\text{s.t. } \sum_i x_i \leq r^*.$$

By continuity of v and compactness of the domain, it has a solution, and the solution is unique by strict concavity of v.

2. At the solution x^*, by the Kuhn-Tucker theorem, there is a non-negative number λ^* such that

$$v_i(x^*) - \lambda^* \le 0 \qquad \text{for } i = 1, \ldots, n$$

$$x_i^*(v_i(x^*) - \lambda^*) = 0 \quad \text{for all } i = 1, \ldots, n.$$

If, for some i, we had $x_i^* = 0$, then one of the inequalities of the first type would be violated, since $v_i(x^*)$ would be infinite. Hence $x^* > 0$, and it follows that $v_i(x^*) = \lambda^*$ for all i. This shows that the equations under study have a solution; it must be unique, since any solution to these equations is associated with a solution of the maximization program in step 1, using again the Kuhn-Tucker theorem and concavity of v, and we know there is a unique solution to that program.

3. Thus (x^*, λ^*, r^*) is a solution to the following set of $n + 1$ equations in the $(n + 2)$ variables (x, λ, r):

$$
\begin{aligned}
v_1(x) - \lambda &= 0 \\
v_2(x) - \lambda &= 0 \\
\cdots & \\
v_n(x) - \lambda &= 0 \\
x_1 + \ldots + x_n &= r.
\end{aligned}
$$

By the implicit function theorem, there are unique, differentiable functions $x(r)$ and $\lambda(r)$ solving these equations in a neighborhood of r^* if the following Jacobian is nonsingular:

$$
J = \begin{bmatrix}
v_{11} & v_{12} & \cdots & v_{1n} & -1 \\
v_{21} & v_{22} & \cdots & v_{2n} & -1 \\
\cdots & & & & \\
v_{n1} & v_{n2} & \cdots & v_{nn} & -1 \\
1 & 1 & \cdots & 1 & 0
\end{bmatrix}.
$$

4. We may write, using the obvious notation,

$$
J = \begin{bmatrix} H & -\vec{1} \\ \vec{1} & 0 \end{bmatrix},
$$

where H is the Hessian matrix of v. Recall that H is negative definite, by the strict concavity of v. But:

$$(x', y) \begin{bmatrix} H & -\overrightarrow{1} \\ \overrightarrow{1} & 0 \end{bmatrix} \begin{pmatrix} x \\ y \end{pmatrix}$$

$$= (x'H + y \cdot \overrightarrow{1}, -x' \cdot \overrightarrow{1}) \begin{pmatrix} x \\ y \end{pmatrix}$$

$$= x'Hx + yx \cdot \overrightarrow{1} - yx \cdot \overrightarrow{1} = x'Hx < 0,$$

and hence J is negative definite; a fortiori, it is nonsingular. Thus the differentiable functions $x(r)$ and $\lambda(r)$ exist.

5. Note the value function $V(r^*)$ of the program in step 1 is strictly concave. Since the solution (x, λ) is unique it follows that V is differentiable and $V'(r) = \lambda$. Since λ is differentiable, V is twice differentiable, and $V''(r) = \lambda'(r)$. The strict concavity of V finally allows us to conclude that $\lambda'(r) < 0$. (We can also show $\lambda'(r) < 0$ by differentiating the system of equations in step 3 w.r.t r and using the negative definiteness of H.) ∎

Let $\mathbf{1}$ denote the vector $(1, 1, \ldots, 1)$ in R^n. Let $\delta = \|\mathbf{1}\|$.

Lemma 5.2. *Let r be the amount of the input resource allocated to an individual with utility function $u^h(x, y)$ satisfying conditions (5.6), (5.7). Then $\mu^h(x^h(r), y^h(r))$ is strictly decreasing in r until it reaches its minimum value of δ, at some number $\bar{r}^h$.*

Proof: For small values of r, the solution to program (5.9) is associated with a large Lagrangian multiplier $\lambda(r)$. Indeed, by (5.6), $\lambda(r)$ approaches infinity as r approaches 0. Hence, for sufficiently small r, by (5.7), $y^h(r) = 0$, for as r increases, $\lambda(r)$ decreases by Lemma 5.1, until a value $\bar{r}^h$ is reached at which $\lambda(\bar{r}^h) = \max_j w_j^h(0)$. For $r \leq \bar{r}^h$, $y^h(r) = 0$. For $r > \bar{r}^h$, $y^h(r) \neq 0$, and by the Kuhn-Tucker conditions for program (5.9), some column vector of the matrix $M^h(x^h(r), y^h(r))$ is the vector $\mathbf{1}$ for $r \geq \bar{r}^h$. It follows that $\mu^h(x^h(r), y^h(r)) = \delta$ for $r \geq \bar{r}^h$. ∎

Lemma 5.3. *Let $(r^1, \ldots, r^H)$ be the distribution of the input resource among H agents. The associated allocation is acceptable if $r^h \geq \bar{r}^h$ for all h.*

Proof: If $r^h \geq \bar{r}^h$ for all h, then $\mu^h(x^h(r^h), y^h(r^h)) = \delta$ for all h. It follows from Lemma 5.2 that the associated allocation is acceptable. ∎

Theorem 5.1. *Let society consist of H citizens with preferences represented by separable utility functions u^h satisfying (5.6) and (5.7), and let $\| \ \|$ be a norm satisfying (5.8). Let the amount of resource available be unity. Then:*

(a) If there exists a Pareto efficient allocation where all individuals consume at least one secondary resource, then all allocations at which every individual consumes at least one secondary resource are acceptable. Almost all other allocations are not acceptable.

(b) If there exists no Pareto efficient allocation at which all individuals consume some secondary resource, then only one acceptable allocation exists, and in it no secondary goods are consumed. This allocation is independent of the choice of norm.

Proof:
Part (a). Let the amount of the input resource being used by person h be r^h. (This is the amount of resource embodied in his consumption bundle.) At an allocation at which all persons consume some secondary resource, $\max_h \mu^h(x^h, y^h) = \delta$. By Lemma 5.2, no μ^h is ever smaller than δ, so the allocation is acceptable. Indeed, the acceptable allocations are precisely those at which, for all h, $r^h \geq \bar{r}^h$. The only ones of these which are acceptable but at which some person consumes no secondary resource are those for which $r^h = \bar{r}^h$, some h. But these allocations constitute a set of measure zero within the set of acceptable allocations (with the uniform measure on vectors $\mathbf{r} = (r^1, \ldots, r^H)$ on the $(H-1)$-simplex in $\mathbf{R}^H$).

Part (b). We know $\sum \bar{r}^h \geq 1$, for otherwise there would exist Pareto optimal allocations at which every person consumes a secondary resource. Therefore, unless $\sum \bar{r}^h = 1$, any allocation involves $r^h < \bar{r}^h$ for some h. We now assume $\sum \bar{r}^h > 1$. It follows from Lemma 5.2 that, if $r^h < \bar{r}^h$, $\mu^h(x^h(r^h), y^h(r^h)) > \delta$. Therefore, at any allocation, $\max \mu^h > \delta$.

Suppose we are at an allocation (x, y) at which the numbers μ^h are not all equal. Then let $k^* = \text{argmax}_h \mu^h$ and $k_* = \text{argmin}_h \mu^h$. In particular, we know $\mu^{k^*} > \delta$. If a small amount of resource is transferred from k_* to k^*, μ^{k^*} will decrease: this follows from Lemma 5.1 (the fact that λ^{k^*} is strictly decreasing in r, since k^* is consuming no secondary resource), and condition (5.8a) on the norm. Hence the allocation (x, y) is not acceptable.

Therefore, any acceptable allocation must equalize the numbers μ^h in this case, and those numbers can only be equalized at a number μ greater than δ. We prove that a unique such allocation exists by induction on the number of individuals in the society. Suppose $H = 2$. If we allocate virtually all the input resource to individual 1, then $\|\mu^1\| < \|\mu^2\|$. (This uses condition (5.8b).) By contrast, if we allocate virtually all the input resource to individual 2, then this inequality is reversed. It follows by the continuity of the μ^h in r that there exists an allocation at which $\|\mu^1\| = \|\mu^2\|$. This allocation is unique by Lemma 5.1 (the strict monotonicity of μ^h in r in the appropriate region). Thus assume that a μ-equalizing allocation exists in a society of H persons. We must prove such an allocation exists in a society of $H + 1$ persons. In such a society, allocate r amount of the input resource to the first person and $1 - r$ to the others in aggregate. By the induction hypothesis, there exists a unique allocation of the resource endowment $(1 - r)$ among those H agents which equalizes the numbers $\mu^2, \mu^3, \ldots, \mu^{H+1}$. Call that common value $\hat{\mu}(1 - r)$, since it is a function of the amount of resource given to them. The first person's μ-value is $\mu^1(r)$. We know that $\mu^1(r)$ approaches infinity as r approaches 0, and $\hat{\mu}(1 - r)$ approaches infinity as r approaches 1. It follows, as before, that there exists a value of r at which $\mu^1(r) = \hat{\mu}(1 - r)$, and that common value must be greater than δ, in this case. By Lemma 5.1, that value of r is unique.

Finally, we return to the case where $\sum \bar{r}^h = 1$. Here the acceptable allocation is unique: it requires $r^h = \bar{r}^h$ for all h. For suppose $r^1 < \bar{r}^1$ but $r^2 > \bar{r}^2$. Then we know $\|\mu^2\| = \delta < \|\mu^1\|$, and this is not acceptable, as an allocation exists at which, for all h, $\|\mu^h\| = \delta$. ∎

Theorem 5.1 shows that "acceptable" allocations are ones that would be advocated by the "instrumental egalitarian" of §4.7, for whom equality is only a compelling goal when not everyone can feasibly have "enough." The theorem is, I think, consistent with the intentions of Rawls and Sen, who are concerned not with the distribution of resources in general, but only that, in a world in which resources are too scarce to supply all with a vector of functionings/primary goods sufficient to enable each to make meaningful choices among different life plans, primary resources should be distributed as equally as possible—or, in my parlance, in such a way as to equalize the deprivation owing to insufficient amounts of them. A person is viewed as having a sufficient amount of primary resources if she chooses to use some of her input resource to produce (or purchase) secondary resources. The theorem says there are two possibilities: either we live in a world of abundance (Part a), in which it is possible for everyone to consume secondary resources, or we do not (Part b). In the first case, any allocation of the input resource which induces all to consume secondary resources is acceptable—even though, among those allocations, there may be quite nontrivial variations in utility (life-plan achievement or agency-goal achievement), and in particular, in the utility of the person with lowest utility. These utility variations, though, are not of Rawlsian/Senian concern. When, however, the input resource is scarce in the sense that there is no distribution of it that will induce all to consume secondary resources, then there is only one allocation of the resource which is acceptable, and in it, no one consumes any secondary resource. None shall consume luxuries while deprivation for others continues to exist.

Finally, I note some ways in which the above model is an inadequate or unfaithful representation of Sen's views. It is surely inadequate by virtue of the assumption of separability on utility. It is unfaithful in not representing the capability set, except insofar as each individual chooses a vector of functionings to produce with his input resource. The individuals are modeled as pursuing agency goals; the model does not represent Sen's concern with agency freedom, as opposed to agency-goal achievement. How about offensive tastes, expensive tastes, and overly modest tastes of the "tamed housewife and hopeless destitute"? I have assumed preferences are self-regarding, and so have simply ignored offensive tastes. But I would argue that the model deals passably well with expensive tastes and overly modest tastes, because it never requires any judgment involving *levels* of utility. Expensive tastes are a problem when the level of an individual's utility is low compared with the levels of others' utilities if she consumes the same bundle of goods they do; a similar statement (with "low" replaced by "high") applies to the tamed housewife (cheap tastes). But levels of utility play no role in the above analysis.

5.8 Conclusion

I have treated the theories of Rawls and Sen as first cousins because they share the four attributes listed in §5.1. In turn, they differ from the egalitarian theories of Dworkin, Arneson, and Cohen that follow them (chronologically) principally in their less focused, and I would say less consistent, treatment of agent responsibility. Rawls's book (1971) remains the most significant intervention in twentieth-century Anglo-American political philosophy, for it served to place the question of distributive justice within the jurisdiction of analytical philosophy and social science. It must be added that Kolm (1972) took a methodologically similar approach, one with more mathematical and less philosophical sophistication than Rawls's. (Indeed, the first section of Kolm's monograph is entitled "Toward a Formal Ethics.") After Rawls and Kolm, it becomes natural to discuss the problem of distributive justice axiomatically, and because of this, differences in "values" can be reduced to differences in quite primitive postulates. Rawls pioneered a method in political philosophy, as did Arrow in social choice theory and Nash in bargaining theory, and their methods remain of lasting value even if their particular conclusions (the argument for egalitarianism from the original position, the impossibility of social choice, and the Nash solution to the bargaining problem, respectively) do not seem so convincing upon further analysis. More particularly, Rawls provided the first grand attempt at deriving egalitarianism from a series of apparently acceptable postulates.

Sen improved upon Rawls's theory, I believe, by locating a kind of human advantage that lies between the access to goods and welfare. The usefulness of Sen's innovation of "well-being" or "midfare" for social policy can be seen, for instance, in the annual *Human Development Reports* issued by the United Nations Development Program (UNDP), in which an index of functionings per capita is computed for every country in the world. The objective nature of most functionings makes this statistical task feasible, and the ranking of countries according to their "human development index," as the UNDP calls it, is significantly different from their ranking according to gross national product (GNP) per capita, the latter being what Sen would describe as a fetishist index. Moreover, the human development index is, as Sen has taught us, arguably a better measure of economic development than GNP per capita.

The criticisms of the theories of Rawls, Kolm, and Sen that I have raised should not overshadow their importance in laying the foundation of the science of egalitarianism.

6

Neo-Lockeanism and Self-Ownership

6.1 Nozick's Theory of Distributive Justice

Robert Nozick (1974, chap. 7) proposed a theory of distributive justice which differs from those discussed thus far in that the justice of a distribution depends overwhelmingly on how the distribution came about. First, Nozick requires a definition of "justice in acquisition": what conditions must an acquisition satisfy to be just? Second, he requires a definition of "justice in transfer": what conditions must a transfer between persons satisfy in order to be just? Nozick (1974, p. 151) relates these notions to the notion of entitlement as follows:

1. A person who acquires a holding in accordance with the principle of justice in acquisition is entitled to that holding.

2. A person who acquires a holding in accordance with the principle of justice in transfer, from someone else entitled to the holding, is entitled to the holding.

He adds:

3. No one is entitled to a holding except by (repeated) applications of 1. and 2.

Finally, a distribution is just if and only if everyone is entitled to his holdings.

Everything, of course, hinges on how one defines "justice in transfer" and "justice in acquisition." Let us suppose, as Nozick does, that gift giving is an instance of just transfer and robbery at gunpoint is not. Then we see that the same distribution may be just or unjust, depending on how it came about. (If I give you a large sum of money to which I am entitled, then you justly own it, but if you take it from me at gunpoint, you do not.)

Nozick, in fact, later relaxes his claim (3), by admitting that it may be possible to undo past unjust acts by an act of retribution. Thus a just distribution need not have as its antecedents a sequence of distributions all of which are just [as (3) would seem to imply]. It might be possible for the U.S. government today to compensate the living descendants of the original Native Americans in such a way as to make up for the injustices done to their ancestors by the European settlers in the United States. The process of constructing the counterfactuals one would need to arrive at just retribution would be extremely complex.

It hardly need be observed that Nozick's approach is orthogonal to the other approaches to justice that we have studied. Nozick is not interested in maximizing social welfare functions: whether a utilitarian distribution is just or unjust would depend on how it came about. Nozick discusses at some length the "unpatterned" nature of his concept of justice. Justice does not entail equalizing anything, be it primary goods or opportunities or marginal utilities, or distributing according to a maxim of the form "from each according to his X, to each according to his Y." For him, the principles of justice in acquisition and justice in transfer are intended to place certain restrictions on individual freedom; subject to those restrictions, anything goes.

To my knowledge, there has been no careful analysis of Nozick's general proposal, as summarized in (1)–(3) above. The critical literature has instead focused on the particular proposal Nozick has made for what constitutes "justice in acquisition," with much less discussion of his notion of "justice in transfer." Nozick begins with Locke's statement that a person is entitled to appropriate part of the natural world, which is not yet privately owned, as his own, as long as he leaves "enough and as good in common for others." This is a severe proviso, which denies anyone the right to appropriate scarce natural resources. Nozick therefore amends it in a way that seems consistent with Locke's intention, but allows considerably more freedom to appropriate: an appropriation of part of the unowned natural world is just as long as it leaves no one worse off than she would have been had that part remained unowned. In particular, if I appropriate some unowned natural material and use it to produce a drug that no one else knows how to make, selling it to others at a price that makes them better off than had they not purchased the drug, then the appropriation is just. If voluntary markets are an instance of justice in transfer, then Nozick's proposal for "justice in acquisition" clearly licenses the possibility of just, highly unequal distributions. In particular, one can imagine how a world in which no natural resources remain unowned, and in which the distribution of assets, income, and welfare is highly unequal, can come about through a sequence of Nozickian-just moves. (For this, one needs to know that Nozick considers gifting, and hence inheritance, an instance of just acquisition.) It does not matter that there are no natural resources left for members of the present generation to appropriate, for they are arguably better off than they would have been had past appropriations been forbidden. Thus Nozick has constructed what appears to be a powerful justification for a highly unequal capitalism: not that actual capitalisms are just, replete as their histories are with episodes of robbery, genocide, and slavery, but that the distributions we see in those capitalisms are not a priori unjust. Capitalism as such (where I exclude robbery, genocide, and slavery as inessential to capitalism per se) does not lead to unjust distributions. Indeed, Nozick would defend pure capitalism with fewer constraints than exist in actual capitalism. Monopoly would not be against the law, there would be no redistributive taxation unless all agreed to it, and discrimination in hiring would not a priori be forbidden (as an owner could choose what workers should have access to his physical productive assets).

The minimal role of the state follows, for Nozick, from the view that involuntary appropriation by others of my entitlement is unjust. Thus I cannot be forced to pay taxes, which finance transfers or public goods. It does not matter if I benefit from the public goods so provided.[1] Of course, if all agree to pay taxes, no one's rights are abrogated: a person can legitimately decide not to enforce a right he holds.

Before proceeding to the critical literature, note that Nozick's rule for justice in acquisition is indeed quite different from Locke's, so Nozick's intended improvement on Locke is contestable. Nozick's appropriation proviso is very similar to the maxim "first come, first served." Consider a society with two persons, A and B, each of whom shall live for many periods. There is one unit of a resource in the external world, which is unowned at the

---

1. Arneson (1991) has noticed the apparent inconsistency of this view and Nozick's appropriation proviso. I may coercively deny you access to a piece of land that formerly you had access to if I render you better off by so doing, but the state may not coerce you to pay taxes, even if you are rendered better off by the public goods thereby provided. See also Cohen (1986).

beginning. Let us suppose that each period, A and B awake anew with different talents. Specifically, in all the odd-numbered periods, only A has a talent for transforming the resource into a good that provides welfare for both A and B, and in the even-numbered periods, only B possesses that talent. If the resource remains unused, both A and B have a welfare level of zero. Let us suppose that in period 1, A appropriates the resource and distributes the produced good between B and himself so that B receives utility ε and he receives utility $1 - \varepsilon$, where ε is a small positive number, for period 1 and all periods thereafter. According to Nozick, this appropriation by A is just, for if the resource had remained unowned, B's utility would have been 0. Had "history" started at date 2, instead, then only B would have been able to transform the resource into the good, and she could have appropriated it and given ε to A, retaining $1 - \varepsilon$ for herself, for all periods thereafter. This also would be Nozick-just. Locke's proviso, by contrast, does not permit either individual to appropriate the object. This does not mean that it would remain unused, but rather that A and B have to come to some agreement about the disposition of the product. Nozick's proviso countenances "first come, first served"; Locke's does not.

6.2   Challenges to Nozick

G. A. Cohen has coined the term "self-ownership" to describe Nozick's view of the rights of persons over themselves:

> Each person is the morally rightful owner of himself. He possesses over himself, as a matter of moral right, all those rights a slaveholder has over a complete chattel slave as a matter of legal right, and he is entitled, morally speaking, to dispose over himself in the way a slaveholder is entitled, legally speaking, to dispose over his slave.   (Cohen, 1986, p. 109)

In particular, the self-ownership postulate says that a person has a moral right to use her powers to benefit herself, as long as she does no harm to others. What kinds of use, by a person, of a resource external to herself and not owned by anyone else, satisfy the no-harm principle? Nozick has defined the no-harm "baseline" for this problem as what the welfare of others would have been if the resource had remained unowned, or in common use. A. Gibbard (1976), Cohen (1986, 1995b), and J. O. Grunebaum (1987) have all argued that Nozick's choice of baseline is arbitrary and not compelling, if not demonstrably incorrect.

Gibbard (1976) proposes what he calls the "hard libertarian position," that everyone has an equal right to use all things. No one has, a priori, a right to exclude others from using things that she has produced. With no social contract establishing property rights, this situation engenders, Gibbard says, "miserable lives." No one will have an incentive to clear land and grow grain. Presumably, a farmer cannot even morally prevent others from entering the field she cleared to take the grain, as others have a right to the grain, too. Gibbard argues that, in such a situation, members of society will enter into a bargain which will establish some kinds of property rights. Because everyone has a right to the use of all things before the establishment of such property rights, he argues that "something resembling a welfare state" will emerge from this bargaining game. The handicapped— those who, by themselves, cannot transform the external world into goods they need—will not assent to a system of property rights in the external world that would leave them unable to get what they need. Some kind of redistributive taxation would then follow, according to Gibbard, from "hard libertarian rights."

Gibbard states that the Locke-Nozick view that "one has a right to do anything that will benefit oneself without worsening the position of anyone else" is not defensible, essentially because it mixes up "rights" and "welfare." An appropriation (of a piece of unowned land) is not relevantly an act that changes the physical world, but rather one that alters the rights of others, for it means others cease to have the right to use the appropriated thing. Thus such an appropriation is morally permissible only if others agree to give up that right. If everyone has a right to take unowned land, then no one has a right to take it without the approval of others.

Thus, according to Gibbard, either "hard libertarian rights" or Lockean rights lead to a relationship between persons and the external world that can be described as one of joint ownership: no individual can appropriate a part of the external world without the consent of others.

Cohen (1986, 1995b) reaches a similar conclusion, but not by deducing it from self-ownership, as Gibbard putatively does. Cohen argues, rather, that Nozick's assumption that the external world, before becoming privately owned, was, morally speaking, unowned, is arbitrary. After all, we are considering not the legal status of the external world, but its moral status, just as persons, in a natural state, were morally self-owned, according to Locke, not legally self-owned. Why not assume that the external world is jointly owned by all, rather than unowned?

Cohen (1995b, chap. 3) also points out that Nozick transforms Locke's proviso in two ways. The first is to substitute "leaving others at least as well off" for "leaving enough and as good for others," a move Cohen agrees is a friendly amendment to Locke. The second, however, considerably weakens Locke, and that is to take the baseline as how well people would have been if the external resource had remained unowned, rather than being used in some other reasonable way. Indeed, Cohen surmises that the appropriate generalization of the Lockean proviso to conditions where external resources are scarce may be something like "an appropriation of part of the external world is just only if it leaves no one worse off than he would have been in some unignorable alternative." He then notes that, under this proviso, almost no economic system will be just, as there will almost always be an unignorable alternative that leaves any particular individual better off. He concludes that the Lockean approach to justifying property rights will not work.

Essentially the same objections to Nozick's baseline that Cohen (1986) posed are posed by Grunebaum (1987, pp. 80–85). Why not, he says, view the external world as being communally owned before any private appropriation takes place? Grunebaum gives the example of a shipwrecked sailor who lands on an unpopulated island and develops it. Later, a group of explorers comes upon the island. Although the sailor may be due some compensation for having developed the island, there is no reason, Grunebaum says, that he should have acquired permanent, bequeathable rights to it.

The challenges to Nozick that I have reviewed here are all conservative in the sense that none questions the postulate of self-ownership: rather, they challenge Nozick's view on the private appropriation of external resources, either as being arbitrary (Cohen and Grunebaum) or as inconsistent with self-ownership (Gibbard). Cohen points out that this kind of challenge may be sufficient to justify massive redistribution, for it calls into question the legitimate property rights that individuals have over almost all things—for every thing was produced by something that was produced by something . . . that was (far enough back) produced by something that was appropriated from a (legally) unowned part of the external world. Gibbard's method of deducing the redistributive welfare state from hard libertarian rights is novel; certainly, the more usual way is, following Rawls, to deny the moral attractiveness of self-ownership on the grounds that the distribution of personal characteristics is in large part morally arbitrary, and hence to justify redistribution directly. In §6.5, I will briefly take up the issue of the morality of the self-ownership postulate.

There is a large literature on neo-Lockean distributive justice, to which these two short sections can hardly do justice: the interested reader would do well to consult Waldron (1988) and Steiner (1994).

6.3 Joint Ownership of the External World

If the correct generalization of the Lockean proviso to situations in which external resources are scarce is joint ownership of the external world, or if that postulate is independently appealing, then, as Gibbard and Cohen both note, the distribution problem becomes a bargaining problem. It may be worthwhile to note, as the following example shows, that joint ownership can then nullify any kind of self-ownership. Consider a two-person world, in which a single consumption good, x, can be produced from labor and an external technology,[2] according to the production function $x = sL$, where L is the amount of labor used and s is the skill level of the worker. (Thus, more generally, $x = \sum s^i L^i$, where L^i is the amount of labor expended by workers with skill level s^i.) The technology is, in this example, a feature of the external world that is jointly owned. The two persons each have a unit endowment of labor, and they have skill levels s^1 and s^2. Suppose that, in the absence of an agreement on how to distribute the proceeds from production, no good is produced, and each consumes nothing. Let us take the two as having the same von Neumann–Morgenstern utility functions, $x^{1/2}(1 - L)^{1/2}$, in the good and in leisure. If we take the Nash solution as the solution of the bargaining problem, for the sake of concreteness, then the solution will be the same whether or not we view the individuals as owners of their skills: it will be that allocation that maximizes the product of utilities (since the threat point awards them each a utility of zero). My claim that the result is the same even if their labor is jointly, rather than privately, owned only holds if the individuals derive no utility from self-ownership per se, as is the case in this bare, typically economic, formulation.

We may compute the Nash solution for this problem as follows. Maximizing the product of the utilities from the threat point means to choose x, L^1, and L^2 to

$$\max x^{1/2}(s^1 L^1 + s^2 L^2 - x)^{1/2}(1 - L^1)^{1/2}(1 - L^2)^{1/2}$$

$$\text{s.t.} \quad L^1 \leq 1 \quad \text{and} \quad L^2 \leq 1.$$

---

2. Alternatively, think of production as requiring a tract of land which is jointly owned, but which does not appear in the production function.

It is clear that, for any choice of L^1 and L^2, we must choose

$$x = \frac{s^1 L^1 + s^2 L^2}{2}.$$

Making this substitution, and taking derivatives of the objective function with respect to L^1 and L^2 gives two linear equations which can be solved to give:

$$L^1 = \frac{3s^1 - s^2}{4s^1}, \quad \text{and} \quad L^2 = \frac{3s^2 - s^1}{4s^2},$$

as long as this labor allocation is an interior one. Suppose, now, that $s^1 \leq s^2$. It is always the case that the less-skilled individual works less than the more skilled one. Indeed, if $s^1 < s^2/3$, then the solution entails that the less-skilled individual not work at all. But we know that output is shared equally. This is the welfare state, with a vengeance.

For a society with many individuals, bargaining theory is of little help. (We do not have compelling solutions to the n-person noncooperative bargaining problem.) The core concept is also of little help: if the external world is jointly owned, then when a coalition of players withdraws from the game, it takes with it only the labor of its members, with which it can do nothing. It follows that the core is huge.

An alternative to the bargaining approach is to take an axiomatic approach in the style of Chapters 2 and 3. The axioms would attempt to capture not the essence of bargaining, but rather some minimal properties of what "self-ownership" and "joint ownership" should entail. Hervé Moulin and I (1989) attempted this, as follows. Consider a class of economic environments of the form $e = \langle u, f, s^1, s^2 \rangle$. f is a production function that transforms efficiency units of labor $(s^1 L^1 + s^2 L^2)$ into a single consumption good, x. u is a utility function defined on bundles of the good and leisure. It is assumed that both individuals' utilities are measured by u, and that the individuals have skill levels given by s^1 and s^2. A *mechanism* is a mapping that associates to any economic environment a feasible allocation for that environment. Let $\mathcal{D}$ be the class of environments where u is increasing in x and decreasing in L, s^1 and s^2 are arbitrary non-negative numbers, and f exhibits nonincreasing returns to scale in efficiency units of labor (that is, if L is labor in efficiency units, then $f(L)/L$ is nonincreasing). We proposed the following restrictions on the mechanism F's behavior, where $F^i(e)$ is the allocation of labor and the good to individual i under F:

Domain (D). F is defined on $\mathcal{D}$.

Pareto (P). F is Pareto optimal.

Self-Ownership (SO).   If $s^1 \geq s^2$ then $u(F^1(e)) \geq u(F^2(e))$.

Technological Monotonicity (TM).   Let $e = \langle u, f, s^1, s^2 \rangle$ and $e^* = \langle u, g, s^1, s^2 \rangle$, where $g \geq f$. Then $(u(F^1(e^*)), u(F^2(e^*))) \geq (u(F^1(e)), u(F^2(e)))$.

Protection of Infirm (PrI).   Let $e = \langle u, f, s^1, s^2 \rangle$, $e^* = \langle u, f, s^1, s^1 \rangle$, and $s^2 \geq s^1$. Then $u(F^1(e)) \geq u(F^1(e^*))$.

   The interpretation of utility that I prefer in this model is as a kind of welfare that is absolutely measurable and comparable. In particular, the result that is derived below needs nothing more than this. Axiom SO says, under this interpretation, that the more skilled individual receives (weakly) higher welfare than the less skilled. Alternatively, if we think of u as representing ordinal preferences, with no interpersonal comparability assumed, then SO can be interpreted as saying that the more-skilled individual does not envy the less-skilled individual at the solution.[3]
   Axiom SO is intended not as fully capturing what self-ownership entails, but as a necessary condition of self-ownership. Axiom TM is arguably a requirement of joint ownership. Whatever joint ownership means on this domain, it should entail what TM says—that if one world is more abundant than another, but the individuals in the two worlds are the same, then no one should end up worse off in the more abundant world. This clearly cannot be taken to be a *general* requirement of joint ownership of the external world. Suppose in one world there is an individual Adam who has a very scarce talent to transform grains of sand into penicillin, while in a second world all the individuals are the same as in the first, but penicillin is an abundant natural resource. It is not unreasonable to suppose that, whatever joint ownership entails, Adam will be worse off in the more abundant second world. I therefore make the more restrictive statement that, on the domain of economic environments $\mathcal{D}$, TM is arguably reasonable.

---

3. I thank Carmen Beviá for this point.

Finally, the axiom PrI states that the weaker agent (Infirm, to borrow from Cohen's parables concerning Able and Infirm) should not suffer by virtue of living in a world with one who is more able than she. That is, under F's action, she is rendered at least as well off as she would have been had the other individual been precisely as able as she. I cannot justify PrI either on account of self-ownership or joint ownership of the external world, but it may be independently morally attractive to others, as it is to me.

Let $\mathcal{D}(u)$ be the subclass of $\mathcal{D}$ whose environments all have the given "u" as their utility function. We denote by $D(u)$ the domain axiom "F is defined on $\mathcal{D}(u)$." We have:

Theorem 6.1. *For any u, there is a unique mechanism satisfying axioms $D(u)$, P, SO, TM, and PrI: it is the egalitarian mechanism, that equalizes the utilities of the individuals at the highest feasible level.*

Proof:

1. Fix s^1 and s^2, and let $\mathcal{D}(u, s^1, s^2)$ be the class of environments with the components (u, s^1, s^2) fixed. We first show that F must be a monotone utility path mechanism on $\mathcal{D}(u, s^1, s^2)$ (see Definition 2.3). Let $e^1 = \langle u, f^1, s^1, s^2 \rangle$ and $e^2 = \langle u, f^2, s^1, s^2 \rangle$ be two environments in this class, and define $f = \max(f^1, f^2)$. Note that f also enjoys nonincreasing returns to scale, so $e = \langle u, f, s^1, s^2 \rangle$ is an environment in $\mathcal{D}(u, s^1, s^2)$. By TM, $u(F^j(e)) \geq u(F^j(e^i))$ for $i, j = 1, 2$, since $f \geq f^i$. But $F(e)$ is a feasible allocation in either e^1 or e^2 (since every allocation in e is feasible in either e^1 or e^2). Say $F(e)$ is feasible in e^1. Then P, together with the inequality stated three sentences ago, requires that $u(F^j(e)) = u(F^j(e^1))$, for $j = 1, 2$. Hence $u(F^j(e^1)) \geq u(F^j(e^2))$, for $j = 1, 2$, showing that F is a monotone utility path on $\mathcal{D}(u, s^1, s^2)$.

2. Let $f_\alpha(L) := \alpha$ for all L, and note that f_α enjoys decreasing returns to scale (for all non-negative α). (Think of the technology f_α as "manna from heaven.") By SO and P, it follows that $F(\langle u, f_\alpha, s^1, s^1 \rangle) = ((\alpha/2, 0), (\alpha/2, 0))$. Now let $s^2 > s^1$. Neither agent ever expends labor at a Pareto optimal allocation when f_α is the production function. By PrI, it follows that $F(\langle u, f_\alpha, s^1, s^2 \rangle)$ must give at least $\alpha/2$ units of the good to the first individual. By SO, the second agent must therefore get at least $\alpha/2$ units of the good in $\langle u, f_\alpha, s^1, s^2 \rangle$. It therefore follows that $F(\langle u, f_\alpha, s^1, s^2 \rangle) = ((\alpha/2, 0), (\alpha/2, 0))$. Thus if we fix s^1 and s^2, then on the class of environments $\mathcal{D}^M(u, s^1, s^2) = \{\langle u, f_\alpha, s^1, s^2 \rangle \mid \alpha \geq 0\}$, F is the equal-utility mechanism.

3. But $\mathcal{D}^M(u, s^1, s^2) \subset \mathcal{D}(u, s^1, s^2)$, and we have shown that the subclass on the left of this set inequality defines a monotone utility path, namely, the equal-utility path. Since F is MUP on $\mathcal{D}(u, s^1, s^2)$, the mechanism is determined on that domain as the equal-utility mechanism. ∎

Remarks

1. A slightly more elaborate proof demonstrates the result on a domain where the production function exhibits nondecreasing returns to scale (see Moulin and Roemer 1989). The theorem also remains true if we add the restriction that $f(0) = 0$: thus, we need not, as the above proof does, assume that a "manna from heaven" technology exists. The given proof does not work, however, on a domain where the production functions are restricted to be concave, for the domain of concave functions is not closed under the "max" operation of step 1 of the proof. The domain of functions with nonincreasing returns to scale is strictly larger than the domain of concave functions.

2. One might think it is a restriction to work on a class of environments where both individuals have the same utility function. But it is not. The theorem says that, even if F is defined on a larger domain, as long as it must satisfy the listed axioms on the subdomain where both individuals have the same utility function u, then on that subdomain it must equalize utilities. Thus on that subdomain, a higher skill level does not translate into higher utility. This suffices to show that joint ownership plus PrI "trumps" self-ownership.

3. Theorem 6.1 postulates certain weak requirements for self-ownership and joint ownership of the external world. If one wished to add stronger requirements, then one might well generate an impossibility. For instance, if we strengthen SO to state that the more skilled agent should receive (strictly) greater utility in the solution, then there is no allocation mechanism satisfying the axioms.

4. The theorem can be generalized to environments with many individuals (see Moulin and Roemer 1989).

6.4 Generalizations of Locke on Economic Environments

Gibbard, Cohen, and Grunebaum (among others, for instance, Arneson [1991]) have argued that Nozick's generalization of the Lockean proviso to situations where resources in the external world are scarce is inadequate. These writers all argue against Locke's proviso as well: for joint ownership of the external world, which they (except Cohen[4]) advocate, does not permit an individual to appropriate part of it even if he leaves "enough and as good in common for others." Imagine a world with an infinite amount of some natural resource, and two persons, one of whom is incapable of using the resource to produce welfare (Infirm). Under joint ownership, he can forbid the other one (Able) from using any of the resource unless he is fed. Under the Lockean proviso, of course, this is not the case.

We may ask: Are there natural ways of generalizing Locke's proviso to worlds in which resources are scarce, but that are more egalitarian in consequence than Nozick's generalization of Locke, and in which the right of self-ownership is more potent than it apparently becomes when the external world is jointly owned? The Nozickian critics of §6.2 were radical in the sense of posing joint ownership of the external world as the alternative to an unowned external world. Perhaps there are other allocation mechanisms that generalize Locke (as those proposals do not) but not so radically (in the other direction) as Nozick does.

To study this question, we shall work on a class of economic environments of the form $\langle u^1, \ldots, u^H, s^1, \ldots, s^H, f \rangle$ where there is one good produced from labor, measured in efficiency units, using the technology f and the external world. Individual h is endowed with one unit of labor (therefore s^h units of labor in efficiency units), and utility is defined over bundles of the good and leisure. We may think of the external resource as a lake, and f as the technology of fishing. Some fishers catch more fish per hour than others—this is summarized in their different "skill" levels.

There is one set of cases in which Locke's proviso can be met: when f exhibits constant or increasing returns to scale (in labor efficiency units). In the case of constant returns, one person's ability to catch fish is unaffected by how much others are fishing; in the case of increasing returns, a given person's catch will be increased if others are fishing too. In the case where f exhibits constant returns (that is, f is a linear function of labor in efficiency units), there is a natural Lockean solution: let each fisher fish as much as she wishes on the lake. If utility is strictly quasi-concave for each fisher, this yields a unique solution, which is Pareto efficient. Each leaves enough and as good for others, and does the best for himself. Indeed, any other Pareto efficient allocation will make some individual worse off

---

4. Cohen rejects joint ownership because it would forbid individuals to appropriate parts of the external world, without the consent of others, which they need to stay alive.

than she is under the stated allocation, so we may argue that the stated allocation is the unique Lockean allocation.

Let the class of environments of the form $\langle u^1, \ldots, u^H, s^1, \ldots, s^H, f \rangle$, where the u^h are quasi-concave, increasing in x and decreasing in L, and f is concave, be denoted $\mathcal{D}$ for the duration of this section.

Suppose that f is strictly concave. When a fisher uses the lake, she does not leave enough and as good for others. There is a natural notion of equilibrium in this case: it is the Nash equilibrium in the game where each fisher's strategy is the amount of labor she expends on the lake. Let us state this precisely. Let $L = (L^1, \ldots, L^H)$ be the amounts of labor expended by the H fishers; then total labor in efficiency units is $s \cdot L \equiv \sum s^i L^i$. The total catch is $f(s \cdot L)$, and the amount of fish going to fisher i is $(s^i L^i f(s \cdot L))/(s \cdot L)$—that is, we assume that each fisher is equally likely to catch a fish with the expending of a unit of labor in efficiency units. Define $(s \cdot L)_{-i} = \sum_{j \neq i} s^j L^j$. Then we may define:

Definition 6.1. An *equilibrium under unrestricted common ownership* for the environment $\langle u^1, \ldots, u^H, s^1, \ldots, s^H, f \rangle$ is an allocation $((\bar{x}^1, \bar{L}^1), \ldots, (\bar{x}^H, \bar{L}^H))$ such that, for all h:

1. $\bar{L}^h$ solves the problem $\quad \max_L u^h \left(\dfrac{s^h L f((s \cdot \bar{L})_{-h} + s^h L)}{(s \cdot \bar{L})_{-h} + s^h L}, L \right)$, and

2. $\bar{x}^h = \dfrac{s^h \bar{L}^h f(s \cdot \bar{L})}{s \cdot \bar{L}}$.

Condition (1) states that, given the actions of all individuals but h, h's choice of labor maximizes her utility. I call this an equilibrium under *unrestricted common ownership*, since when a resource is held in unrestricted common ownership, as opposed to *jointly*, every participant may use it as much as he pleases.[5]

If f is concave and u is quasi-concave, then an unrestricted common ownership equilibrium always exists. (This follows directly from the standard theorem for the existence of a Nash equilibrium when best response functions are quasi-concave.) If f is strictly concave, then the equilibrium is not Pareto efficient: we may view this as an instance of the "tragedy of the commons." Common owners of a scarce resource will tend to overuse it, in

---

5. Below I will introduce a distinction between "unrestricted common" and "common" ownership.

the sense that all could be better off if they exploited the resource less, in an organized way. There are many examples, in real life, of "unrestricted common" property passing into "common" property (see Ostrom 1990). The common owners of the resource agree to regulate its use to achieve an allocation that is Pareto superior to the common ownership equilibrium: in other words, to put certain restrictions on access to the resource. One simple way to do this is to privatize the "lake," giving each fisher a share in the firm that operates the lake equal to her share of labor (in efficiency units) in the unrestricted common ownership equilibrium. The next proposition shows that the Walrasian equilibrium for the private ownership economy with these property rights Pareto dominates the unrestricted common ownership equilibrium.

Theorem 6.2. Let $(\bar{x}, \bar{L}) = ((\bar{x}^1, \bar{L}^1), \dots, (\bar{x}^H, \bar{L}^H))$ be an unrestricted common ownership equilibrium for the environment $\langle u^1, \dots, u^H, s^1, \dots, s^H, f \rangle$, where f is concave. Define a private ownership economy with one private firm whose technology is f, in which fisher h owns a share equal to $s^h \bar{L}^h / s \cdot \bar{L}$. Let $(\hat{x}, \hat{L})$ be a Walrasian equilibrium of this economy. Then for all h, $u^h(\hat{x}^h, \hat{L}^h) \geq u^h(\bar{x}^h, \bar{L}^h)$.

Proof:

1. Let $\bar{X}$ be total output at the given equilibrium under common ownership, and $\hat{X}$ be total output in the Walrasian equilibrium. We know that, in the common ownership equilibrium, labor in efficiency units is proportional to the amount of fish received, which implies:

(1) $$\frac{\bar{x}^h}{\bar{X}} = \frac{s^h \bar{L}^h}{s \cdot \bar{L}}.$$

Let p be the price of the good in the Walrasian equilibrium, when the wage rate in efficiency units of labor is normalized at one. Multiplying both sides of (1) by p, subtracting $s^h \bar{L}^h$ from both sides, and rearranging gives:

(2) $$-s^h \bar{L}^h + p\bar{x}^h = \frac{s^h \bar{L}^h}{s \cdot \bar{L}}(p\bar{X} - s \cdot \bar{L}).$$

2. Since the firm is maximizing profits at the Walrasian equilibrium, we know that $p\hat{X} - s \cdot \hat{L} \geq p\bar{X} - s \cdot \bar{L}$. It follows from (2) that:

(3) $$p\bar{x}^h \leq s^h \bar{L}^h + \frac{s^h \bar{L}^h}{s \cdot \bar{L}}(p\hat{X} - s \cdot \hat{L}).$$

The second term on the right-hand side of (3) is just the share of profits going to individual h at the Walrasian equilibrium. Hence equation (3) is just the statement that $(\bar{x}^h, \bar{L}^h)$ is a feasible choice for h at the Walrasian prices (that is, it satisfies her budget constraint).

3. It therefore follows that $u^h(\hat{x}^h, \hat{L}^h) \geq u^h(\bar{x}^h, \bar{L}^h)$. ∎

Thus privatizing the lake and giving each fisher a share of the firm equal to her "historical" share of labor (in efficiency units) expended under unrestricted common ownership produces a Pareto efficient allocation that renders everyone at least as well off as she was under unrestricted common ownership.

We can thus define a mechanism F^{ND} on $\mathcal{D}$: F^{ND} assigns to an environment the set of Walrasian allocations associated with firm ownership shares $s^h \bar{L}^h / s \cdot \bar{L}$, where $\bar{L}$ is the labor vector associated with any Nash equilibrium under common ownership. F^{ND} is called the *Nash dominator* mechanism.[6] F^{ND} is one way of generalizing the Lockean solution (of the constant returns case) to the general case of a concave technology. (It is immediately evident that, if f exhibits constant returns, then F^{ND} is the free-access solution.)

Joaquim Silvestre and I (1989) proposed three other possible solutions to the problem of generalizing the Lockean solution to the domain $\mathcal{D}$. The requirements for such solutions are that (1) they coincide with the free access solution on linear economies, and (2) they be Pareto efficient. I state the first of these conditions as an axiom, for convenience:

Free Access on Linear Economies (FALE).   The mechanism F coincides with the free access (or Lockean) solution when f is linear.

We call these three solutions F^{EB} (equal benefits), F^P (proportional), and F^{CRE} (constant returns equivalent).

The *equal-benefits solution* is the Walrasian equilibrium in the fish economy associated with equal distribution of the profits of the firm that runs the lake. Thus the lake is again privatized, but each citizen receives an equal share of the firm, not, as in the Nash-dominator solution, a share equal to her "historical" labor share. We call this "equal benefits" for the following reason. Let $(\bar{x}, \bar{L})$ be a Walrasian equilibrium with equal shares,

---

6. The Nash dominator mechanism was first proposed in Roemer (1989).

where p is the equilibrium price vector, and the wage for one efficiency unit of labor is unity. Equivalently, we may say that the wage for one unit of labor (not efficiency) of individual h is s^h. Hence, at equilibrium prices, the value of individual h's consumption bundle of fish and leisure is $p\bar{x}^h + s^h(1 - \bar{L}^h)$. Before production began, individual h possessed a bundle consisting just of s^h units of labor (and no fish). Hence her *gain* at the equilibrium is $p\bar{x}^h + s^h(1 - \bar{L}^h) - s^h = p\bar{x}^h - s\bar{L}^h$. But her budget constraint (at the Walrasian equilibrium) can be written $p\bar{x}^h - s\bar{L}^h = \frac{1}{H}\bar{\Pi}$, where $\bar{\Pi}$ is the firm's equilibrium profits. Thus the gain for all individuals is equal (measured at the Walrasian prices)—hence, equal benefits. Thus we define F^{EB} as the mechanism that associates to any environment in $\mathcal{D}$ all the Walrasian allocations associated with private ownership of labor and equal per capita ownership of the firm operating the lake. Of course, F^{EB} is Pareto efficient and satisfies FALE.

Moulin (1990) has established an interesting characterization of the equal-benefits solution. Recall, from §3.2, that a correspondence F, mapping economic environments into feasible allocations, is said to be *full* iff whenever $z \in F(e)$ and z' is Pareto indifferent to z then $z' \in F(e)$. Moulin's theorem uses the next two axioms as well:

Unanimity Lower Bound (ULB). Let $e = \langle u, s, f \rangle$ and $(\bar{x}, \bar{L}) \in F(e)$. Then $u^i(\bar{x}, \bar{L}) \geq \max_{L^i} u^i\left(\frac{1}{H}f(Hs^iL^i), L^i\right)$.

Suppose, momentarily, that all individuals were identical to individual i: then the symmetric, Pareto optimal solution would entail each receiving the allocation (x^i, L^i) where $L^i = \max_{L^i} u^i\left(\frac{1}{H}f(Hs^iL^i), L^i\right)$. ULB therefore says that each person should do at least as well in e under F as if he were in a "symmetric" equilibrium of an economy composed of H individuals just like himself. Thus each should (weakly) benefit from the "preference externality," that is, the welfare surplus available in e by virtue of the fact that individuals have different preferences. Gevers (1986) initially introduced this concept under the name of "full individual rationality."

Technological Contraction Consistency (TCC). Let $e = \langle u, s, f \rangle, e' = \langle u, s, g \rangle, g \geq f$. A solution F satisfies TCC iff $(z \in F(e'), z$ feasible in $e) \Rightarrow z \in F(e)$.

TCC (which Moulin calls "IIA") is a version of Nash's contraction consistency axiom (see §2.2). Note that the utility possibilities set of e' contains the utility possibilities set of e.

Theorem 6.3 [essentially Moulin (1990), Theorem 1]. *Let F be a full so-lution on $\mathcal{D}$ satisfying ULB and TCC. Then, for all $e \in \mathcal{D}$, $F^{EB}(e) \subseteq F(e)$. Furthermore, F^{EB} is full and satisfies ULB and TCC.*

ULB is arguably an ethically attractive property, and fullness (Pareto indifference) is a weak version of welfarism. TCC has no obvious ethical justification. The theorem states that F^{EB} is the "smallest" allocation mechanism on $\mathcal{D}$ satisfying these axioms.

Proof of Theorem 6.3:

1. Let $\bar{z} = (\bar{x}, \bar{L}), \bar{z} \in F^{EB}(e)$, where $e = \langle u, s, f \rangle$. Let F be a full solution satisfying ULB and TCC. We must show $\bar{z} \in F(e)$.

2. Let $\bar{z}$ be supported by the Walrasian real wage for efficiency labor, w, where the price of output (fish) is one; let Π^* be profits of the firm at the equal division equilibrium. Define the production function $g(\ell) := w\ell + \Pi^*$, where ℓ is labor in efficiency units. Note that $f \leqq g$, since Π^* is maximum profits at the Walrasian prices (that is, $f(\ell) - w(\ell) \leq \Pi^*$ for all ℓ). Define the environment $e' = \langle u, s, g \rangle$.

3. Note that $\frac{1}{H}g(H\ell) = w\ell + \frac{1}{H}\Pi^*$. Since $(\bar{x}^i, \bar{L}^i)$ maximizes $u(x^i, L^i)$ subject to $x^i \leq ws^i L^i + \frac{1}{H}\Pi^*$ (by definition of the equal division equilibrium), we write $u^i(\bar{x}^i, \bar{L}^i) = \max_{L^i}\{u^i(x^i, L^i) \mid x^i \leq \frac{1}{H}g(Hs^i L^i)\}$.

4. Let $z' \in F(e')$. By ULB, it follows that

$$u^i(x'^i, L'^i) \geq \max_{L^i} u^i\left(\frac{1}{H}g(Hs^i L^i), L^i\right), \quad \text{for all } i.$$

From step 3, we therefore have

$$u^i(x'^i, L'^i) \geq u^i(\bar{x}^i, \bar{L}^i), \quad \text{for all } i.$$

5. Note that $\bar{z}$ is indeed feasible in e': for

$$g\left(\sum s^i \bar{L}_i\right) = w\sum s^i \bar{L}_i + \Pi^* = f\left(\sum s^i \bar{L}^i\right) = \sum \bar{x}^i,$$

since $\Pi^* = f\left(\sum s^i \bar{L}^i\right) - w\sum s^i \bar{L}^i$. Furthermore, $\bar{z}$ is indeed an equal division Walrasian allocation in e' at prices $(1, w)$. To see this, note first that profits are identically equal to Π^* with technology g and prices $(1, w)$. Hence the budget of individual i at labor supply L^i in e' at prices $(1, w)$, if there is equal division of profits, is $ws^i L^i + \frac{1}{H}\Pi^*$, the same as in e, and it follows that $\bar{z}$ is Walrasian in e'. Hence $\bar{z}$ is Pareto optimal in e'.

6. It therefore follows, from step 4, that indeed

$$u^i(x'^i, L'^i) = u^i(\bar{x}^i, \bar{L}^i), \quad \text{for all } i.$$

That is, $\bar{z}$ is Pareto indifferent to z'; it follows by fullness of F that $\bar{z} \in F(e')$.

7. But since $\bar{z}$ is feasible in e, it follows by TCC that $\bar{z} \in F(e)$. This proves $F^{EB}(e) \subseteq F(e)$.

8. That F^{EB} satisfies the axioms is left as an exercise for the reader. ∎

Remark. Moulin (1993) does not assume F is full. Instead, he assumes that the u^i are strictly quasi-concave. Then Pareto indifference of $\bar{z}$ and z' (step 6 above) enables him to conclude that $\bar{z} = z'$, and so $\bar{z} \in F(e')$.

To motivate the *proportional solution* (F^P), notice that at the Lockean solution in constant-returns economies, the efficiency units of labor expended by fishers are proportional to the amount of fish they catch. Question: Can this proportionality feature of the allocation be preserved on $\mathcal{D}$ along with Pareto efficiency? The answer, perhaps surprisingly, is yes.

Theorem 6.4 (Roemer and Silvestre 1989, 1993). *For every environment in $\mathcal{D}$, there exists a Pareto efficient allocation $(\hat{x}, \hat{L})$ such that for all h, j:*

$$\frac{s^h \hat{L}^h}{\hat{x}^h} = \frac{s^j \hat{L}^j}{\hat{x}^j}.$$

The proof of this theorem in the general case will not be reproduced here; we shall, instead, be content with the next, much simpler result. Let $\tilde{\mathcal{D}}$ be the subclass of $\mathcal{D}$ consisting of environments in which, for any distribution of shares of the firm operating the lake, the Walrasian equilibrium is unique. We shall prove:

Theorem 6.4*. *For every environment in $\tilde{\mathcal{D}}$, there exists a Pareto efficient allocation $(\hat{x}, \hat{L})$ such that for all h, j:*

$$\frac{s^h \hat{L}^h}{\hat{x}^h} = \frac{s^j \hat{L}^j}{\hat{x}^j}.$$

Proof:

1. Let $e \in \tilde{\mathcal{D}}$ be given. Let $\theta = (\theta^1, \dots, \theta^H)$ be any distribution of share ownership of the firm which operates the lake. By assumption, there exists

a unique Walrasian equilibrium associated with this share distribution: call the Walrasian allocation $(x(\theta), L(\theta))$. Define $\eta^h = (s^h L^h(\theta))/(s \cdot L(\theta))$. Define the mapping ζ from the S^{H-1} simplex[7] into itself by $\zeta(\theta) = \eta$. ζ is a continuous mapping of S^{H-1} into itself, and by Brouwer's theorem, it has a fixed point: call it $\bar{\theta}$.

2. I claim that the Walrasian equilibrium allocation associated with initial shares in the firm $\bar{\theta}$ indeed has the proportional property. Let $(\bar{x}, \bar{L})$ be that allocation, and p the equilibrium price of fish. Then the budget constraint of individual h at the equilibrium allocation reads:

$$(1) \qquad p\bar{x}^h + s^h(1 - \bar{L}^h) = \bar{\theta}^h(pX - s \cdot \bar{L}) + s^h = \frac{s^h \bar{L}^h}{s \cdot \bar{L}}(pX - s \cdot \bar{L}) + s^h$$

which reduces to

$$\frac{\bar{x}^h}{s^h \bar{L}^h} = \frac{X}{s \cdot \bar{L}},$$

and the theorem is proved. The key step, which is the second equality in (1), follows from the definition of $\bar{\theta}$ as the fixed point of ζ.[8] ∎

The *constant-returns-equivalent solution*, F^{CRE}, is less easy to define analytically: its appeal comes from the next theorem. For this result we must work on the larger domain $\mathcal{D}^+$, consisting of environments where f exhibits nonincreasing returns to scale.

Theorem 6.5.   *There is a unique mechanism on $\mathcal{D}^+$ satisfying FALE, Pareto, and Technological Monotonicity.*

Proof:

1. Fix the profile $(u, s) = (u^1, \ldots, u^H, s^1, \ldots, s^H)$, and consider the subclass of environments $\mathcal{D}^+(u, s)$ gotten by attaching to (u, s) any nonincreasing-returns-to-scale production function f. By the argument of

---

7. The S^{n-1} simplex is $\{p \in \mathbf{R}^n_+ \mid \Sigma_i p_i = 1\}$.

8. Unfortunately, this proof does not generalize to the class of convex economies where multiple Walrasian equilibria exist, because the analogous correspondence ζ does not in general possess a continuous selection. A more delicate argument (Roemer and Silvestre 1993) is required.

step 1, Theorem 6.1, F must be a monotone utility path mechanism on $\mathcal{D}^+(u, s)$.

2. Now consider the subclass $\mathcal{D}^{+,L}(u, s)$ of $\mathcal{D}^+(u, s)$ consisting of environments with linear production functions. By FALE, F must be the free-access solution on $\mathcal{D}^{+,L}(u, s)$. But this generates a monotone utility path on $\mathcal{D}^{+,L}(u, s)$. Therefore the mechanism is entirely determined on $\mathcal{D}^+(u, s)$. ∎

Thus, by step 2 of the proof, we may define $F^{CRE}(e)$, for any $e \in \mathcal{D}$, as follows. If $e = \langle u, s, f \rangle$, consider the class of linear economies $\{\langle u, s, \beta \rangle \mid \beta \geq 0\}$, where "$\beta$" stands for the linear production function $f(L) = \beta L$. There is exactly one of these linear economies in which the free-access allocation produces a utility allocation that lies on the Pareto frontier of the utility possibilities set of e. Define $F^{CRE}(e)$ as the allocation(s) in e that generate(s) that point.

The discovery of the CRE mechanism is due to Mas-Colell (1980). A characterization theorem similar to 6.5 was first proved by Moulin (1987).

I have motivated the introduction of the four mechanisms F^{ND}, F^{EB}, F^P, and F^{CRE} as efficiency-preserving generalizations of the free-access (Lockean) solution on linear economies. The free-access solution on linear economies enjoys all four of these properties: it (weakly) Pareto dominates the Nash solution (in fact, it coincides with it), all citizens enjoy equal benefits in it, fish consumed by fishers are proportional to efficiency units of labor expended in it, and it is itself a linear economy (and so, trivially, the allocation is constant-returns-equivalent, as defined). The second, third, and fourth properties each characterize a unique solution on the domain $\mathcal{D}$ (or $\mathcal{D}^+$); there are other solutions besides F^{ND} that share the first property, but F^{ND} has a particular historical motivation that may be politically compelling in some actual situations.

I have not argued that these mechanisms are candidates for ways of implementing *joint* ownership of the external world in conjunction with private ownership of labor (self-ownership), for we have noted that, if the lake is jointly owned, then an individual whose skill level is zero will still be able to bargain for some fish income from the lake. And once property rights are given, then an individual is entitled, under those rights, to whatever bargaining can bring him. Among these four mechanisms, only equal benefits would deliver fish to such an "infirm" individual. But I think each of these mechanisms has a claim to being a reasonable solution to the problem of *common* ownership of a world with scarce resources in conjunction with self-ownership.[9] F^{ND} is an efficient mechanism that improves on the voluntary, unregulated free-access solution (that is, equilibrium under unrestricted common ownership) for all. F^{EB} gives each person equal gain over her pretrade allocation, measured in efficiency prices; alternatively, it views citizenship as bestowing a right to a per capita share of the surplus from operating the community's commonly owned asset in a market economy. F^P implements the "socialist" dictum, "from each according to his ability, to each according to his work": for under it, the value of an individual's income (in fish) is proportional to the value of the labor she expended (at efficiency prices). Finally, under F^{CRE}, each receives exactly the utility that he would have received in a certain linear economy, under the free-access solution; alternatively, F^{CRE} is the unique mechanism satisfying the two basic properties (FALE and Pareto), which also satisfies an attractive postulate for common ownership of the lake, technological monotonicity. Unfortunately, none of these mechanisms "contains" another: that is, for any two mechanisms F^i and F^j of these four, there exist environments e such that $F^i(e) \not\subset F^j(e)$.

Recall, as well, that F^{ND}, F^{EB}, and F^P can each be conveniently characterized as Walrasian allocations following from certain specific assignments of property rights in the lake, when each fisher owns her own labor. In F^{ND}, shares in the lake are distributed according to "historical" labor shares from the period of unrestricted common ownership; in F^{EB}, citizenship is viewed as conferring an equal share in the lake to all citizens; in F^P, shares in the lake's surplus are set equal to *current* labor shares. There is no convenient characterization of F^{CRE} in terms of shares in the lake.

There is, finally, a characterization of the proportional mechanism that displays one of its arguably attractive properties. Suppose an allocation $y = (x, L)$ has been proposed to the community of fishers. Some fishers would like to increase (or perhaps decrease) their labor supply, providing they would receive the same share of total output as they do at y (of course, total output will change if one fisher increases his labor supply and all others remain fixed). But if one fisher increases his labor, then it

---

9. This is a slight modification of the view expounded in Roemer and Silvestre (1989).

is only fair to allow others to do so as well. This motivates the following definition:

Definition 6.2.   An allocation $y = (x, L)$ is *Kantian-stable* iff for all ε (positive or negative) for which $L(1 + \varepsilon)$ is a feasible labor allocation, no individual h prefers the allocation $(\bar{x}, L(1 + \varepsilon))$ to y, where $\bar{x}^h = (x^h/X) f(s \cdot L(1 + \varepsilon))$.

Thus no fisher prefers an allocation in which *all* increase or decrease their labor supplies by the same fraction, maintaining the same shares of output as at y. The invocation of Kant comes from the categorical imperative: perform an action only if you would be willing to have others do likewise.

We have:

Theorem 6.6.   *Let e be an environment where f is concave and differentiable and the profile u is quasi-concave and differentiable. Then $F^P(e)$ consists exactly in the Pareto efficient Kantian-stable allocations of the environment e.*

Proof:

1. We first prove that any allocation $(x, L) \in F^P(e)$ is Kantian-stable. Since (x, L) is proportional, if all fishers increase or decrease their labor supply by fraction ε, the new allocation for individual h is $\bar{x}^h = (s^h L^h/(s \cdot L)) f((1 + \varepsilon)s \cdot L)$, $\bar{L}^h = L^h(1 + \varepsilon)$. We know (x, L) is a Walrasian allocation associated with shares in the firm $\theta^h = s^h L^h/(s \cdot L)$. Let the Walrasian price of fish be p in that allocation.

2. To show $u^h(\bar{x}^h, \bar{L}^h) \leq u^h(x^h, L^h)$, it suffices to show that the bundle $(\bar{x}^h, \bar{L}^h)$ is affordable by h at the prices holding in that Walrasian equilibrium. That is, it suffices to show:

(1) $\qquad p\left(\dfrac{s^h L^h}{s \cdot L} f((1 + \varepsilon)s \cdot L)\right) \leq \dfrac{s^h L^h}{s \cdot L}(pf(s \cdot L) - s \cdot L) + s^h L^h(1 + \varepsilon).$

By profit maximization in the Walrasian equilibrium, we have $pf'(s \cdot L) = 1$, or

(2) $\qquad p = \dfrac{1}{f'(s \cdot L)}.$

Substituting from (2) into (1) and simplifying shows that (1) is equivalent to:

(3) $$\frac{f((1+\varepsilon)s \cdot L) - f(s \cdot L)}{s \cdot L} \leq \varepsilon f'(s \cdot L).$$

Case (i): $\varepsilon > 0$.
   In this case, (3) is equivalent to:

(3′) $$\frac{f((1+\varepsilon)s \cdot L) - f(s \cdot L)}{\varepsilon s \cdot L} \leq f'(s \cdot L).$$

But (3′) is true for any concave function: it says the derivative of f at a point $(s \cdot L)$ is at least as large as the slope of the chord between $f(s \cdot L)$ and $f((1+\varepsilon)s \cdot L)$.

   Case (ii): $\varepsilon < 0$.
   In this case, (3) is equivalent to:

(3″) $$\frac{f((1+\varepsilon)s \cdot L) - f(s \cdot L)}{\varepsilon s \cdot L} \geq f'(s \cdot L),$$

a fact which is similarly true for any concave function.
   This proves the first direction of the theorem.

   3. We will prove the converse with the help of Figure 6.1. It is convenient to work with utility functions whose arguments are fish (x) and *efficiency units* of labor. Thus, let ℓ be an amount of labor in efficiency units and

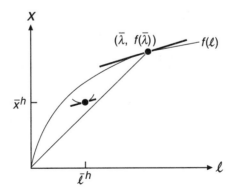

Figure 6.1

define $v^h(x, \ell) = u^h(x, \ell/s^h)$. Then v^h is also a utility function representing h's preferences.

Suppose $(\bar{\ell}, \bar{x})$ is an efficient Kantian-stable allocation that does not lie in $F^P(e)$. Then there is an h such that $(\bar{\ell}^h, \bar{x}^h)$ does not lie on the line segment connecting the origin to the point $(\bar{x}, f(\bar{\lambda}))$, where $\bar{\lambda} = \sum \bar{\ell}^h$ is total efficiency units of labor expended at $(\bar{\ell}, \bar{x})$, as illustrated in Figure 6.1. Note that, since $(\bar{\ell}, \bar{x})$ is efficient, the two tangent lines drawn in the figure are parallel (MRS = MRT in efficiency labor). The indifference curve at $(\bar{\ell}^h, \bar{x}^h)$ in the figure is associated with v^h.

4. We shall show that $(\bar{\ell}, \bar{x})$ is not Kantian-stable by showing that there exists a small positive ε that individual h would advocate increasing all labor supplies by. If all labor supplies were increased by fraction ε from $(\bar{\ell}, \bar{x})$, then in the experiment that defines Kantian-stability, h's new allocation would be

$$\tilde{x}^h = \frac{\bar{x}^h}{\bar{X}}(\bar{X} + \varepsilon\bar{\lambda} f'(\bar{\lambda})), \qquad \tilde{\ell}^h = (1+\varepsilon)\bar{\ell}^h,$$

where the equation for $\tilde{x}^h$ is a first-order approximation. (Recall that $\bar{X} = \sum \bar{x}^h$.) Hence

$$\Delta x^h \equiv \tilde{x}^h - \bar{x}^h = \frac{\bar{x}^h}{\bar{X}}(\bar{X} + \varepsilon\bar{\lambda} f'(\bar{\lambda})) - \bar{x}^h,$$

and $\Delta \ell^h = \tilde{\ell}^h - \bar{\ell}^h = \varepsilon\bar{\ell}^h$.

If, for small ε, we can show that $\Delta x^h/\Delta \ell^h > f'(\bar{\lambda})$, then at the ˜ allocation, h will be above her indifference curve at $(\bar{\ell}^h, \bar{x}^h)$ illustrated in the figure, a contradiction to the supposition that $(\bar{\ell}, \bar{x})$ is Kantian-stable. This conclusion requires that v^h be differentiable at $(\bar{\ell}^h, \bar{x}^h)$, as illustrated.

5. Thus we need only show that, for small $\varepsilon > 0$:

(4) $$\frac{\bar{x}^h}{\bar{X}^h}(\bar{X} + \varepsilon\bar{\lambda} f'(\bar{\lambda})) - \bar{x}^h > \varepsilon\bar{\ell}^h f'(\bar{\lambda}).$$

Inequality (4) is easily shown to be equivalent to:

(4') $$\frac{\bar{x}^h}{\bar{\ell}^h} > \frac{\bar{X}}{\bar{\lambda}}.$$

But $(4')$ is true (see Figure 6.1). Hence, in the case of Figure 6.1, the theorem is proved. The other case, when $\bar{x}^h / \bar{\ell}^h < \bar{X} / \bar{\lambda}$, is similarly proved (by choice of $\varepsilon < 0$). ∎

If the hypothetical experiment proposed in the test for Kantian stability embodies an attractive kind of fairness, then an allocation which is Kantian-stable is an equilibrium in a game whose agents are behaving morally. No one will recommend a change from a Kantian-stable allocation in which all would be permitted the same change in their actions (labor supplies) as she wishes to make. We could, that is, define a *Kantian equilibrium* as we do a Nash equilibrium, except substituting a different hypothetical counterfactual from Nash's. When a player examines whether or not to change his labor supply from a given allocation, he does not assume that the others hold their supplies fixed at the allocation in question (Nash), but that they change their labor supplies by the same fraction that he would change his by (Kant). Then the proportional solutions for suitably differentiable environments are just their Kantian equilibria.

Moulin (1990) gives an axiomatic characterization of F^P which differs from that of Theorem 6.5; the axioms, however, do not have the kind of ethical interpretation that Kantian stability does, and so I do not reproduce his theorem here.

6.5 Implementation

In social choice theory, there is a large literature studying when a social choice rule can be decentralized. The notion of decentralization, originally due to Maskin (1977, 1985), is that the allocations prescribed by the rule should be achievable as the equilibrium of a game played among the individuals of society, in the following sense. Let F be a social choice rule— in our case, a mechanism assigning a set of feasible allocations to each economic environment in $\mathcal{D}$. Let us fix $(s, f) = (s^1, \ldots, s^H, f)$—we shall presently think of varying the profile u. Given (s, f), the set of feasible allocations of the environment is determined (independent of u). Define a *game form* as a collection $\gamma = (T^1, \ldots, T^H, \varphi)$ where φ is a function mapping $T^1 \times T^2 \times \ldots \times T^H$ into this set of feasible allocations. The T^h are abstract sets, with no restrictions on their structure. Now view T^h as the strategy set of individual h in the following game. When each player proposes a strategy $t^h \in T^h$, a strategy vector $t = (t^1, \ldots, t^H)$ is determined, and hence a feasible allocation $\varphi(t)$ is determined. This in turn generates a utility $u^h(\varphi^h(t))$ for each individual h. Thus, in game-theoretic language, we have a payoff function π^h for each individual h defined on the strategy space $T = T^1 \times \ldots \times T^H$, given by $\pi^h(t^1, \ldots, t^H) = u^h(\varphi^h(t^1, \ldots, t^H))$. Thus $(T^1, \ldots, T^H, \varphi, u)$ defines a noncooperative game. We say that the game form $(T^1, \ldots, T^H, \varphi)$ *Nash-implements* the mechanism F iff, for all profiles u, the Nash equilibria of the game $(T^1, \ldots, T^H, \varphi, u)$ consist precisely in the allocations $F((u, s, f))$.

Suppose that there is a game form γ that implements a given mechanism F. Then we can think of γ as decentralizing the mechanism F in the following sense: a planner announces γ and stipulates that each individual h must announce a strategy in T^h, with the consequence that the allocation chosen shall be $\varphi(t)$. Let us assume that players will announce a set of strategies that make up a Nash equilibrium of the induced game. Then the allocation $F((u, s, f))$ is implemented. The "decentralization" point is that the planner need not know the profile u to carry out the implementation of F.

There are two kinds of generalization of the concept of Nash implementation. The first consists in using some other concept than Nash equilibrium, for example, dominant-strategy equilibrium. Implementation in dominant-strategies is a much more compelling concept of decentralizability than implementation in Nash equilibrium, for an equilibrium in dominant strategies will naturally occur (each player simply announces his best strategy, which is independent of what the others announce), whereas it will be difficult for players to find a Nash equilibrium unless each knows the preferences of the others. The second generalization consists in positing game forms with more information than the strategic form, in particular, games in extensive form. One then can require implementation in subgame perfect Nash equilibrium, or in the various refinements of that equilibrium concept. The basic result of implementation theory, crudely stated, is that very few mechanisms can be implemented in dominant-strategy equilibrium, quite a few can be implemented in Nash equilibrium, and almost all mechanisms can be implemented as subgame perfect Nash equilibria of extensive form games.

I will report some results about the implementability of the four mechanisms discussed in §6.3, without proof. F^{EB} and F^P can be implemented in Nash equilibrium; F^{ND} and F^{CRE} cannot be. Moulin shows that F^{CRE}

can be implemented in subgame perfect Nash equilibrium in a two-stage game.[10]

There is a stronger result concerning F^{ND}:

Theorem 6.7 (Roemer 1988). *There is no efficient mechanism on $\mathcal{D}$ that Pareto-dominates the common ownership equilibrium and that can be implemented in Nash equilibrium.*

This theorem can be viewed as damaging for Nozick's (1974) conjoined views of distributive justice and the ethical requirement of a minimal state. According to Nozick, a fisher can legitimately privatize the lake, formerly used in common by the fishers, as long as he guarantees each of the other fishers that she will be at least as well off as she was when the lake was held in common. This means that the allocation rule determined by the privatization must be describable as a mechanism F that Pareto-dominates equilibrium under unrestricted common ownership. If that mechanism is also Pareto optimal, then the theorem asserts it cannot be decentralized in the sense of Nash implementation. If we view the kind of intervention represented by the insistence of a state that society's members "play" a game form as of a minimal kind, then something more than a minimal state is needed to see to it that private appropriations of the lake are Nozickian-just.

This conclusion, however, must be tempered by the observation that, if the "historical" labor shares that different citizens have expended on the lake while it was under common ownership are publicly known, then there is an easy way for the state to supervise private appropriation of the lake— it simply requires that each fisher be given a share in the firm that runs the lake equal to his historical share of labor expended on the lake in efficiency units. The problem is that the planner designing the game form in the Nash implementation story does not know those historical shares.

The final result I shall report concerns implementation on "large" environments, ones with a continuum of citizens. It is based upon theorems of Makowski and Ostroy (1992), in which allocation mechanisms on finite-type economies which are Pareto efficient and which can be implemented in dominant strategies are characterized. It can be shown that, on a domain of "fisher" economies analogous to $\mathcal{D}$ but with a continuum of fishers, of a finite number of types, the only mechanism that can be implemented in

---

10. In personal correspondence with the author, April 4, 1994.

dominant strategies is the equal-benefit mechanism (see Roemer [1987a] for proof).

I have reported the material in this section in a cursory way because I do not find the theory of implementation, as it currently stands, a compelling theory of decentralizability. First, the games that members of society are required to play in order to "implement" social choice rules are often highly complex: one cannot realistically suppose that these games could ever be used to implement allocations in actual, large societies. Second, actual governments and "planners" usually have much more information about individuals which they can use in "implementing" distribution rules than they are endowed with in the abstract theory. For instance, even if planners do not know what preferences and endowment each individual has, they generally know the distribution of preferences and endowments in a population—at least, they can often observe demand and supply curves. On these two counts, implementation in actual societies will be both harder (on count one) and easier (on count two) than in the theory.

6.6   The Morality of Self-Ownership

Cohen distinguishes between the *concept* of self-ownership, which is defined here at the beginning of §6.2, and the *thesis* of self-ownership, the claim that self-ownership is morally correct. The writers cited in this chapter who are critical of neo-Lockeanism do not challenge that thesis (at least, in the arguments presented thus far), but impeach Nozick's inegalitarian conclusion by challenging his "principle of justice in acquisition." The outstanding example in contemporary political philosophy of a challenge to the thesis of self-ownership is Rawls's work, in which the right to derive income from personal attributes is denied when those attributes are due to luck, whether of the genetic or the environmental variety. Nozick includes luck as a legitimate means of acquiring assets. Inheritance is therefore a just means of acquiring assets (it being an instance of luck from the point of view of the receiver and an exercise of the right of self-ownership from the point of view of the donor). Thus highly unequal opportunities of a real sort for the generation of young heirs are condoned by Nozick.

Although the moral arbitrariness of genetic and environmental luck may convince some that the thesis of self-ownership is unsound, many are not persuaded of that position by virtue of hypothetical situations involving the coercive transfer of bodily parts. Consider a lottery run by the state, with compulsory participation by all citizens with two good eyes, in which the chosen would be compelled to donate one eye for transplantation into the head of a blind person. Many people are repelled by such a lottery, and this repulsion is taken as implying support for the thesis of self-ownership.

There are, however, several responses to this visceral argument for self-ownership. First, a denial of the thesis of self-ownership need not imply the acceptance of eye lotteries. Perhaps that denial would only deny the right to keep all of one's income (that is, the denial would only permit taxation). If the thesis of self-ownership states that the concept of self-ownership is morally correct, then it states that it is morally correct that a person have all the rights over himself that a slaveholder has over a chattel slave. The negation of this statement is that it is not morally correct "that a person have all the rights . . . " This does not imply that it is morally correct "that a person have *none* of the rights that a slaveholder has over a chattel slave." In particular, it is consistent with the negation of the thesis of self-ownership that a person have *some* of the rights that a slaveholder has over a chattel slave, in particular, the rights to dispose as he wishes of his bodily parts.[11]

What I have just said can be construed as the "logical reply" to the claim that general repulsion at eye lotteries implies the (moral) truth of the thesis of self-ownership. The "radical reply" is the Rawlsian thesis that a person has no moral right to two good eyes while others have none, by virtue of the moral arbitrariness of luck.[12] (I am, then, imagining a case where the unsighted person became so by virtue of no fault of his own.) Cohen (1995b, chap. 10) presents an argument that differs from both the logical reply and the radical reply: it does not challenge the repulsiveness of the eye lottery (as the radical reply does), but instead argues that what is repulsive about the lottery is not the incursion against one's ownership of one's eyes, but something else. Imagine, says Cohen, a world in which no one is born with eyes, but the state implants in all infants two artificial eyes. Some persons become blind, as adults, through no fault of their own. It is, however, impossible to implant new artificial eyes in adults—only implantations of eyes that have matured in another person can be successfully implanted in another adult. Therefore, the state conducts an eye lottery for the sake of blinded adults. Cohen says that if one is repelled by the eye lottery in the

---

11. Slaveholders did not, in fact, always have the right to such disposal of the slave's bodily parts, as the murder of slaves was not generally permitted.

12. I do not claim that Rawls himself supports this view, but rather that it follows from some things he writes.

world where people are born with natural eyes, one will probably also be repelled by this second eye lottery. But in the second case, the repulsion cannot be due to self-ownership, for the state may well maintain ownership of all artificial eyes, even when they are implanted in people, and if so, that would hardly change one's feeling about the eye lottery. Cohen believes that this example shows that the basis of the feeling of repulsion at eye lotteries may be not a belief in the thesis of self-ownership, but rather a reaction against "interference of a catastrophic kind in someone's life." Consider also the fact that many people who are repelled by the eye lottery would also consider it horrendous for persons to sell one of their good eyes (a fortiori, both of them) to someone else, and might well support legislation against such sales. But would not such legislation deny that persons are the rightful owners of their eyes?

It will not have escaped the reader (as Cohen also points out) that our own laws concerning rape and prostitution constitute a somewhat less fanciful example than the eye lottery, with similar implications. That we view rape (the coercive borrowing of sexual organs) as morally wrong suggests that we view persons as the rightful owners of their sexual organs, but the illegality of prostitution suggests that we do not view persons as the rightful owners of themselves. The analogy between eyes and sexual parts is imperfect, owing to possible negative externalities that may be associated with prostitution that have no correlate in an eye market: to wit, prostitution may engender a social view that women are objects in a way that the eye market would not engender a parallel view of eye sellers. This disanalogy, however, does not disturb the claim that our treatment of rape and prostitution shows the consistency of denying self-ownership yet affirming bodily integrity.

6.7   Conclusion

I have focused on two criticisms of Nozick's theory of justice. First, his theory of justice in acquisition acquires its moral attractiveness from the premise that, before individual property rights are established with respect to resources in the external world, these resources should be viewed, morally speaking, as unowned. But one might equally well argue that pristine natural resources are, morally speaking, jointly owned by all, or owned in common. Second, one may challenge the thesis of self-ownership.

Locke's proviso is far stronger than Nozick's, that is, it approves of private appropriations of pristine external resources in many fewer situations than Nozick's would. In the economy of fishers, Locke's proviso only approves individuals' claims to fish precisely as much as they wish when the lake is effectively of infinite size. The economic analysis of this chapter studied how Locke's ethical theory of resource allocation could be generalized to cases in which the lake is of finite size (that is, when there are decreasing returns to fishing on the lake). Four resource allocation mechanisms were described, each of which is a generalization of Locke's proposal in the precise sense that each prescribes Locke's allocation ("free access in linear economies") when there is always enough and as good of the lake left for others, and, as well, each is Pareto efficient. Each of these four mechanisms has one additional attractive property, also shared by the free access allocation mechanism on linear economies. All four of these mechanisms will typically deliver more equality of condition than Nozick's theory would countenance, for his would allow the appropriation of the lake by a first comer, who would then hire the other fishers as wage laborers, keeping the profits for herself. I have not shown that this private-appropriation mechanism would indeed be worse for every fisher than each of the four mechanisms defined earlier—or would it? This is left as a useful exercise for the reader. (Assume that the lake's owner and the fishers are all price takers, so the mechanism assigns the Walrasian equilibrium in which one outsider owns the lake.)

None of the four mechanisms described challenges self-ownership—indeed, the FALE axiom embodies self-ownership. Yet the thesis of self-ownership may very plausibly be challenged, as Rawls has. Finally, it is important to note Cohen's argument about eye lotteries, which shows that the popular view that denying self-ownership is equivalent to licensing coercive lotteries for bodily parts is incorrect.

7

Equality of Welfare versus Equality of Resources

7.1 Introduction

In the early 1980s, Ronald Dworkin (1981a, 1981b) produced the next (after Nozick's) major contribution to the theory of distributive justice, which was to remain the most important intervention in the debate until near the end of that decade. Dworkin began by supposing that justice requires equal treatment of individuals, and asking in what dimension that treatment should be measured. He considers two classes of possibility for the equalisandum: welfare and resources. I say "classes," because welfare can be conceived in a variety of ways, as can resources. In the first essay Dworkin attempts, first, to argue that equality of welfare, as usually conceived, is ethically unattractive, and second, to argue that an attempt to modify the usual conception to render it more attractive finally shows it to be an incoherent concept. In the second essay, Dworkin proposes a way of conceiving of equality of resources, and argues that such equality is the right way of defining distributive justice.

Dworkin's work brought into much sharper focus an important issue that was germinal in the work of Rawls and Sen, personal responsibility. Dworkin argues that justice requires compensating individuals for aspects of their situations for which they are not responsible and which hamper their achievement of whatever is valuable in life, but only for those aspects. Differences between aspects of the situations of individuals owing to acts/beliefs for which they are responsible are of no concern for justice. Moreover, Dworkin takes the view that individuals are responsible for their preferences, as long as they identify with those pref-

237

erences.[1] His antipathy to equality of welfare and his explicit proposal for
what equality of resources entails both depend intimately on this view. As
I tried to show in Chapter 5, the idea of allowing a space for personal responsibility occurs in Rawls and Sen, but it is incompletely developed. It
is Dworkin's originality in attempting a thorough treatment of the role
of responsibility in distributive justice which marks the significance of his
contribution.

In what follows, I shall first review Dworkin's arguments against equality
of welfare and then offer a partial rebuttal. I then present his proposal for
equality of resources and criticize it. Finally, I offer a critique of my own
criticism.

7.2   Dworkin on Equality of Welfare

Dworkin begins with an example. Suppose a parent has four children: one
is blind, another a playboy with expensive tastes, a third a poet with humble needs, and a fourth a sculptor who requires expensive materials. How
should the parent divide her estate among them? Equality of welfare might
require giving the largest fraction to the playboy. But this doesn't seem
right. The example forces us to think about several questions: to wit, the
extent to which welfare reflects needs versus desires, the extent to which
expensive tastes which are voluntarily cultivated deserve consideration, and
the inherent value in different conceptions of the good (sculpting versus
playing). Dworkin takes the example as demonstrating that equality of welfare, at least naively conceived, is not an attractive principle of distributive
justice. The parent should not divide her estate so as to render each child
equally well-off (in the sense of well-being).

There are, in particular, at least two important problems with equality of
welfare as a prescription for distributive justice, even assuming that welfare
is interpersonally comparable (its incomparability would, of course, immediately render equality of welfare an incoherent notion). These are the
problems of "cheap tastes"—the "battered slave" and "tamed housewife,"
to recall Sen's examples—and expensive tastes. The two problems are not
two sides of the same coin, for cheap tastes are a problem only when they
are involuntarily cultivated, and expensive tastes are a problem only when
they are voluntarily cultivated. To see this, imagine that the only individuals

---

1. This excludes cravings and addictions, which one wishes one did not have.

with cheap tastes have cultivated them voluntarily, and the only individuals with expensive tastes have had those tastes irresistibly impressed on them by their environments. If we hold people responsible for those tastes and only those tastes which are voluntarily cultivated, then in the society just defined, distributing resources to engender equality of welfare would not be so obviously unappealing.

But if some have taken on cheap tastes as a survival strategy (the tamed housewife) and some have deliberately trained themselves to have expensive tastes, then equality of welfare would seem to be doubly unfair.

Dworkin's strategy is, next, to try and modify the unadorned equality-of-welfare prescription to resolve these two problems. He concludes that his attempt fails, and conjectures (admittedly without proof) that any such attempt must fail. This constitutes his full argument against equality of welfare.

There are various conceptions of welfare considered by Dworkin: I shall concentrate on two of them, which seem to me to be most reasonable conceptions, and indeed the ones that I have often considered in this study. These are what Dworkin calls "relative success" and "overall success." The former is the degree to which one's life's plan is being fulfilled. The latter is the degree to which one's life is, overall, a success. To distinguish between the two, imagine that a person adopts a plan to be a music teacher; he would rather be a concert pianist, but realistically assesses that he lacks the talent to be a good one. In the event, he becomes a fine music teacher who produces many an accomplished student. This individual has a high degree of relative success, but perhaps a low degree of overall success. Given his chosen plan of being a music teacher, he succeeded admirably; but his achievement was low measured against what he would have liked to have been. Dworkin's relative and overall success measures constitute a refinement of what I have earlier called the degree to which one's life plan is being fulfilled. One virtue of such measures, as I have noted, is that they provide an absolutely measurable and comparable measure of welfare.

Choosing one of these success measures does not resolve the problems of cheap and expensive tastes. Perhaps the "poet with humble needs" will consider his life to be a great success, on either a relative or overall basis, with a small fraction of his parent's estate, while the "playboy with expensive tastes" will consider it to be a failure, also on both grounds, with a larger fraction of the estate. Would this be grounds for transferring yet more resources from the poet to the playboy? Let us assume that both tastes are voluntarily cultivated. Dworkin says clearly not. He then proposes the following solution. A person, he says, has cause to believe his life is of little success compared with another's if and only if he has more cause *reasonably to regret* his situation than the other does (Dworkin 1981a, p. 216). The proposal sounds right, but, of course, it rides on the possibility of providing an independent measure of reasonable regret. The intuition is that if, let us say, the poet and the playboy each received the same inheritance from their parent, neither would have cause reasonably to regret his situation—or, more weakly, neither would have cause reasonably to regret his situation more than his sibling has. How can we make this precise?

Dworkin observes that, in calculating whether one's regret is reasonable, one must compare one's situation with the situation of others: in particular, Jill has cause for reasonable regret if no defensible account can be given of why she does not have Jack's abundant resources. To say that a defensible account can be given of the resource distribution is to say that distribution is fair. Thus, to paraphrase, no one has cause for reasonable regret if and only if the distribution of resources is fair. To give an account of what constitutes reasonable regret requires having a prior notion of fair distributions of resources; hence, it is impossible to use the notion of reasonable regret as *defining* a just distribution of resources! And, claims Dworkin, there is no other way of trying to modify equality of welfare into an acceptable ethical view except by using the notion of reasonable regret. Thus, Dworkin says, the attempt to define a cogent equality-of-welfare view is circular, or incoherent. It is perhaps worth quoting Dworkin in full on this point, as it is the central argument of his first essay:

> Any proposed account of equality of overall success that does not make the idea of reasonable regret (or some similar idea) pivotal in this way is irrelevant to a sensible theory of equality in distribution. . . . But any proposed account that does make this idea pivotal must include, within its description of equality of overall success, assumptions about what a fair distribution would be, and that means that equality of overall success cannot be used to justify or constitute a theory of fair distribution.   (Dworkin 1981a, p. 217)

This is not Dworkin's final attempt to impugn equality of welfare. Later in the essay he supposes, for the sake of argument, that the just described "proof" of the incoherence of equality of welfare is false, and that there is a coherent definition of what equality of relative or absolute success consists in. At that point (1981a, pp. 228–240) he attempts to provide another argument against equality of welfare based on voluntarily cultivated expensive tastes. For example, Dworkin describes the case of Louis, an individual in a society in which equality of welfare has been, by supposition, achieved with a certain distribution of resources. Louis has, at present, modest tastes. Now Louis entertains the possibility of cultivating expensive tastes. Dworkin writes that Louis should have two alternatives: to keep his present tastes, or to alter his tastes but keep the same resources he was given, thus perhaps having a lower rate of relative success (and perhaps absolute success as well, as his conception of what constitutes a worthwhile life will arguably change along with his tastes). "It is quite unfair," Dworkin writes, "that he should have a third choice, that he should be able, at the expense of others, to lead a life that is more expensive than theirs at no sacrifice of enjoyment to himself just because he would, quite naturally, consider *that* life a more successful life overall than either of the other two" (1981a, p. 237).

It may be noted that if society adopts that distribution of resources which equalizes degrees of overall success (assuming, for the sake of argument, that the idea can be made coherent), then no individual would have an incentive to adopt expensive tastes. For having done so, and after resources have been distributed in the correct manner, such an individual would end up with, presumably, a lower degree of overall success than before. This follows because the same total resource endowment (here, we assume a fixed such endowment) would have to be distributed among a set of citizens one of whom is harder to satisfy than before, and so the new level at which the degrees of overall success would be equalized (or leximinned) would be lower than before. So those who do voluntarily cultivate expensive tastes in a society ruled by the equality of degree of overall success principle either do so irrationally or because, with expensive tastes, their lives are better (or they believe that they will be better) in some way not captured by the degree of overall success. But this latter possibility seems to contradict the definition of overall success in a life. So it must be that it is irrational to cultivate expensive tastes in such a society. While many economists prefer to postulate that individuals are not prone to such irrationality, it would be unwise to construct a theory of distributive justice on that assumption, and so the problem of voluntarily cultivated expensive tastes, and involuntarily cultivated cheap tastes, remains important.

7.3   Countering Dworkin's Central Argument against Equality of Welfare

I will accept, for the sake of argument, Dworkin's claim that a theory of equality of welfare requires a theory of reasonable regret, but I will argue against his claim that a theory of reasonable regret requires a priori a theory of fair distribution of resources and hence cannot itself lead to a theory of fair distribution. My argument consists in proposing a particular distribution of resources which, I claim, will give no individual a cause for reasonable regret. This section prefigures Chapter 8.

Imagine the following procedure. Let us assume that we know (as a matter of biological and social science) what circumstances are influential in the formation of a person's conceptions of life plans, or conceptions of a successful life: these might include a person's family background (education and wealth thereof, number of siblings), her ethnic, national, and cultural background, her health (physical and mental), and her intelligence or talent (assuming these terms have a meaning independent of the circumstances I have already mentioned). The word "circumstance" is used in the sense of Chapter 5—a person's circumstances are the environment, external and internal, over which he arguably has no control, but that influence his behavior and beliefs. Once this list has been compiled, every individual in society can be represented by a vector of circumstances, a list of numerical values that describe his circumstances, so defined.

The next step in the procedure is to partition society into *classes* of individuals, where each class consists of persons who share the same (or approximately the same) vectors of circumstances. Let us assume, for the sake of argument, that this can be done so that there are many fewer classes than persons—in particular, so that each class consists of a large number of persons. Thus one class, in U.S. society, might consist of black, Protestant individuals who grew up in working-class families, with parents who had only an elementary school education, who had three or more siblings, who are healthy, mentally and physically, and whose IQ's measure between 95 and 105. This will be a large class. Let us call these classes $T^1, T^2, \ldots, T^N$.

We must consider the important fact, which Dworkin emphasizes, that the conceptions of overall and relative success a person adopts are endogenous, in the sense of being influenced by the resources that constitute his environment. (This, indeed, is the problem of the tamed housewife and battered slave.) I will consider the class of external resource distributions such that all members of any class T^n receive the same allotment. Call this set of distributions Δ; its generic element can be represented by a vector $x = (x^1, \ldots, x^N)$, where x^n is a vector of resources in the appropriate commodity space. Any allocation $x \in \Delta$ induces a distribution of conceptions of overall success in each class T^n, and, I will assume, a corollary distribution of degrees of overall success in each class that can be achieved with the resources allotted to members of that class. I shall call the set of conceptions of overall success in a class its set of *types*. Thus, associated with class T^n and distribution x is a set of types $\{t_x^{n1}, t_x^{n2}, \ldots, t_x^{nM^n}\}$, where there are M^n types in class T^n. The degree of overall success that type t_x^{nh} in class n achieves under the distribution x will be denoted $d^{nh}(x)$. (For the sake of simplicity, I here telescope the period of one's life between the receipt of resources and the achievement of some degree of success. The action, in this model, is over once one has "chosen" one's conception of a successful life.) The types within a class are endogenous—they depend on the resources members of that class receive, as noted in this paragraph's opening sentence. To be perfectly general, I should write M^n as a function of x also, but I do not for simplicity's sake.

Also associated with a given class n and a given x is a *distribution* of types; thus, let $\pi^n(x) = (\pi^{n1}(x), \ldots, \pi^{nM^n}(x))$, where $\pi^{nh}(x)$ is the fraction of type h in class n under distribution x. The mean degree of overall success of members of T^n under distribution x is $\sum_h \pi^{nh} d^{nh}(x) \equiv d^n(x)$. We may take $d^n(x)$ to be the expected degree of overall success a person of class n will achieve at x, where we view the assignment of types to individuals in a class as a stochastic process.

Suppose there is an allocation $x^* \in \Delta$ so that $d^n(x^*)$ is equal across all classes n. I shall argue that this distribution is one that gives no individual reasonable cause for regret.

Fix an individual, Adam. I shall first argue that Adam has no cause reasonably to regret his life in comparison with the lives of others in his class. For the list of circumstances, which define the classes, has been chosen so that all circumstances which are not within the individual's jurisdiction of responsibility have been accounted for. Thus the differences of conceptions of life plan/success *within a class* are entirely the responsibility of individuals: these differences are due solely to the voluntary choices of persons. All individuals in the same class began with the same external resource bundle, and hence the differences among the numbers $\{d^{n1}(x), d^{n2}(x), \ldots, d^{nM^n}(x)\}$ are entirely due to voluntary personal choices. Thus the only basis on which Adam could reasonably regret his life in comparison with Eve, another in his class, because his achieved degree of overall success is less than Eve's, is by arguing that the original list of circumstances has not included an important circumstantial difference between him and Eve. People can certainly regret that certain items are not included in the list, but I say that they cannot reasonably regret such a fact, for the list was chosen using the best available scientific knowledge.

Next we must ask whether Adam has cause for reasonable regret by comparing his life with the life of someone in another class. As I have just argued that Adam has no cause reasonably to regret his life in comparison with other members of his own class, I shall suppose the question just posed is equivalent to asking whether, on account of the allocation x^*, Adam has cause reasonably to regret how his class was treated under x^* compared with how another class—say class m—was treated. But the expected degree of overall success of a person of class m at x^* is just $d^m(x^*)$. By hypothesis, $d^m(x^*) = d^n(x^*)$. I conclude that no member of class n has a cause reasonably to regret how his class was treated in comparison to class m.

Briefly to recap: a person has no cause reasonably to regret not being treated like another in her own class, because all members of her own class receive the same bundle of external resources, and the other differences between her and her class sisters are, by virtue of how the list of circumstances was constructed, either irrelevant to her conception of a life plan or are her own responsibility. A person has no cause to regret her class's treatment vis-à-vis another class's, as the expected degrees of success of all classes are, at x^*, equal.

I have, in this construction, ignored something that arguably should not be ignored: individuals may have reason to regret not being in another class not only by virtue of what the mean degree of overall success of persons in that class is, but by virtue of what the other features of the distribution (for example, the variance) of degrees of overall success are for another class. Implicitly, I have assumed that persons care only about *expected* relative success when facing uncertainty, which is equivalent to their having risk-neutral von Neumann–Morgenstern preferences over relative success. One could, alternatively, avoid this issue, by making the adverb "reasonably" carry even more baggage: namely, by asserting that members of one class have no cause reasonably to regret not being in another class as long as the expected degrees of relative success are the same in the two classes.

The provided construction deals adequately, I think, with the problem of voluntarily acquired expensive tastes, but not with the problem of involuntarily acquired cheap tastes. The former is the case of a person who has a lower degree of overall success than others in his class with the given resource bundle by virtue of having voluntarily adopted more expensive tastes than others in the class: as I have argued above, he has no cause for reasonable regret. To see, however, that cheap tastes remain a problem, we need only note that the construction does not preclude the possibility that one class consists of "tamed housewives" who achieve the same (average) degree of overall success in their lives as other classes do by virtue of adopting truncated conceptions of success. Having made this observation, we can finally note that some persons may unfairly suffer for appearing to have expensive tastes when, indeed, they do not. Consider, within the class of "tamed housewives," the subclass of persons who, on their own, manage to overcome the modesty characteristic of their class and form untruncated conceptions of overall success. Their achieved degree of overall success, under the distribution x^*, will be less than the average of their class, and hence less than the social average. Formally, they appear as individuals with expensive tastes, but this is so only because they are compared with others who have cheap tastes. Put in terms of reasonable regret, we can say that members of the class of "tamed housewives" do, intuitively speaking, have cause for reasonable regret, although the formal test does not produce this verdict.

What I claim to have rebutted by this section's construction is Dworkin's claim that no coherent concept of equality of overall success can be defined because of the circularity ostensibly involved in trying to define the notion of reasonable regret. But as the last paragraph demonstrates, the conception of reasonable regret produced here, though coherent, is not thoroughly ethically attractive by virtue of the problem of truncated conceptions of success. The problem of endogenous conceptions of success— that those conceptions are determined inter alia by the resources one receives or expects to receive—remains the Achilles' heel, I believe, of any welfarist approach to distributive justice, if a person's welfare is measured by her own evaluation.

7.4   Dworkin's Definition of Equality of Resources

Dworkin's second essay is devoted to articulating a definition of equality of resources, which is appealing as a solution to the problem of distributive justice. Both Rawls's difference principle and Sen's equality of capabilities can be considered theories of equality of resources, where resources are defined as things that help people realize their plans of life or achieve success. For Rawls, equality of resources has been attained when the bundles of primary social goods obtained by persons are equal, and for Sen it has been attained when the sets of vectors of functionings are "equal." Both Rawls and Sen emphasize the distinction between their definitions of resource equality and equality of welfare or success in achieving life plans or, in Sen's terminology, agency goals. This they have in common with Dworkin. Dworkin's innovation is to distinguish, more carefully than Rawls and Sen do, between a person's circumstances and his tastes and ambitions. His theory moves to center stage the issue of responsibility, which appears only embryonically in the work of Rawls and Sen.

The essential problem in producing an appealing conception of resource equality is the following. If all individuals in society were identical—they were siblings produced from the same zygote, with the same parents, growing up in identical conditions—then an attractive conception of resource equality would be to give each an equal share of society's external resources. In reality, people are far from identical, and they differ on account of having different circumstances (which include, to recall, different environments, both genetic and social) and different preferences and ambitions. One might take the view that the differences across persons in preferences and ambitions are completely determined by their different circumstances, and if so, then all aspects of a person belong in the category of "circumstances." But I shall assume, at least for now, following Dworkin, that differential circumstances do not completely explain the differences among individuals, and so there is a "residual" category, here labeled "preferences and ambitions." A person's circumstances may be considered a part of his resource endowment—they consist of attributes of his environment which affect his ability to achieve his life plan or to satisfy his preferences. Dworkin's central point is that an attractive conception of resource equality must implement an equalization across persons of the comprehensive bundles of resources, consisting of both conventional external resources and "circumstantial" resources. But many circumstantial resources cannot be easily transferred from person to person, such as genes, parents, handicaps, and talents. The problem thus becomes: What distribution of transferable, external resources will count as bringing about equality of comprehensive resource bundles, or, what distribution of external resources appropriately compensates persons for their differential bundles of circumstantial resources?

Let us first consider the simple case of an exchange economy: there is a fixed aggregate endowment of goods and a society of individuals with different preferences over those goods. A first pass at defining equality of resources would be to define it as the equal division allocation, in which each receives a per capita share of all external resources. This is unappealing, however, by virtue of generally not being Pareto efficient. A second pass is to say that equality of resources consists in any Walrasian allocation arrived at from an equal initial distribution of resources. I have earlier called this an "equal division Walrasian equilibrium (EDWE) allocation" or, in §6.3, the equal-benefits solution. (Dworkin's second pass at defining resource equality is indeed the set of EDWE allocations, which he describes by a colorful story about shipwrecked immigrants on an island, who divide up its resources by an auction in which each bids for resources with an initially equal endowment of "clamshell" money.) But this conception is unattractive if, as Dworkin cogently argues, handicaps should be thought of as resource deficits, for those deficits are ignored at EDWE allocations. In this pure exchange environment, let us think of a handicap as something that prevents a person from efficiently transforming external resources into welfare or into the ingredients of a successful life.

The third pass, to take handicaps into account, involves the construction of a hypothetical insurance market. Suppose it were possible meaningfully to distinguish between a person's tastes and her handicaps. Suppose we imagine all individuals as situated behind a "thin" veil of ignorance, where each knows his preferences (conceptions of overall success, or of life plans) but not his handicaps. (This veil is thin in contrast to Rawls's, behind which souls do not know their preferences.) All do know, however, the distribution of handicaps in the actual world (but not the joint distribution of handicaps and preferences). Behind this veil, each can purchase external resources using an initial equal allotment of clamshells (units of account), but also can purchase insurance against being born with a handicap. There will be an equilibrium in this market economy with markets for contingent claims, in which people purchase insurance contracts promising them compensation with varying bundles of external resources should they, in the actual world, turn out to be persons who suffer handicaps of various sorts. In particular, the equilibrium in the market economy behind the thin veil of ignorance will induce a distribution of external resources in the actual world, where the actual world is simply one possible future state of the world envisioned behind the veil of ignorance. Dworkin defines that actual distribution as implementing equality of resources, where handicaps are acknowledged as being resources, and have been taken into account.[2]

One can understand the sense in which Dworkin views the described distribution as constituting a fair distribution of resources (or what he calls an "equal" one) by noting his views toward two kinds of luck, which he calls "option" and "brute." Option luck is the outcome of a gamble explicitly taken, while brute luck is an outcome in which no gamble was entered into. Being struck by lightning when no insurance was available against that calamity is brute luck; being struck by lightning, if insurance was available, whether or not you were insured, is a matter of option luck. (Not having purchased insurance when it is available is taking a gamble of a certain kind.) Thus the presence of insurance markets transforms events of brute luck into events of option luck. Dworkin's view is that it is fair for persons to suffer the consequences of option luck, for persons decide how much to insure against those kinds of event. Brute luck, however, is a morally arbitrary (and hence unfair) way of distributing resources. Thus handicaps which cannot be insured against, and for which no compensation is otherwise forthcoming, are events of brute luck and unfair. The hypothetical insurance market converts that brute luck into option luck for the "souls" behind the veil. Dworkin defines fair compensation for those in the actual society who suffer handicaps as the contingent compensation they would have purchased, knowing the risks of becoming handicapped, had insurance been available.

Dworkin's equality-of-resources proposal involves a more intimate dependence on individual preferences than Rawls's and Sen's approaches do. In particular, Dworkin makes an explicit distinction between preferences, which (except in a case to be described momentarily) cannot be insured against, and circumstances, which can be. All individuals have the same opportunity, behind the thin veil of ignorance, to purchase identical insur-

---

2. This summary of Dworkin's insurance market is surely less complex, and far more succinct, than the proposal as he makes it. I do not, however, believe I have misrepresented his attempt. The somewhat Byzantine complexity of Dworkin's presentation of an insurance market behind the veil is the product of a clever but economically untrained philosopher struggling to rediscover a subtle economic idea, namely, of an equilibrium in an economy with a set of markets for contingent claims. I should also add that Dworkin does not use the "veil of ignorance" terminology, and even has objections to it. But I think the term conveniently communicates his proposal.

ance policies, for each has the same initial allotment of units of account, and each knows the true distribution of handicaps in the actual world. Differences in insurance coverage are due only to preferences, and persons are viewed as responsible for their preferences (assuming they identify with those preferences).

There are two points at which I shall press Dworkin's conception. The first concerns his placing of "tastes and ambitions" in the category of things for which a person should be held responsible. Dworkin summarizes his view by saying that outcomes should be ambition-sensitive but not endowment-sensitive, where endowment is the bundle of resources and circumstances, and ambition stands for voluntary choice guided by preference. Dworkin does, indeed, agree that there is one category of preference a person should be viewed as not responsible for: cravings. A craving, as Dworkin defines it, is a desire one would rather not have. It is, in that sense, separate from the essence of the person. Behind the thin veil, there will be markets in which persons can purchase insurance against cravings. Except for cravings, however, a person is considered to be responsible for his tastes, regardless of whether they were voluntarily or involuntarily cultivated, *because they are tastes he is glad that he has.*

But this italicized criterion for responsibility is certainly a questionable one. Indeed, as Dworkin carefully pointed out in the first essay, the conceptions of success that individuals adopt are influenced (if not determined) by the resources and circumstances they have. If one is not responsible for one's circumstances, should one be responsible for the preferences that have been adopted because of them? Consider the tamed housewife who is glad she has her overly modest ambitions. Dworkin would hold her responsible for the consequences of those preferences. Is this sensible?

Thomas Scanlon (1986) gives a related example where it appears to be sensible. Consider the person who adopts a religion that requires he live with only a minimal complement of worldly goods. He adopted the religion because his parents chose it and instilled its beliefs in him at an early age. Now he identifies with these beliefs, is glad he has them. Surely it would be wrong for the Ministry of Justice to give him more resources, as large a bundle as others receive.

But I do not think we can generalize from Scanlon's convincing example to Dworkin's view that a person should be held responsible for the consequences of her tastes as long as she is glad she has them or identifies with them. There are important differences between the religious man and the tamed housewife: if we give him a large bundle of resources, it will not increase the degree of overall success he rates his life as having, whereas if we give her a similar bundle, it will increase the degree of overall success she rates her life as having, "far more than I deserve." Indeed, because of his tastes, there is very little the Ministry of Justice can do to increase the degree of overall success of the religious man's life.

The second point concerns the adequacy of the insurance mechanism for equalizing resources comprehensively (when both external and circumstantial resources are included) even if we accept Dworkin's cut between preferences and circumstances. Assuming with Dworkin that people are responsible for their preferences, I think it does follow that if one person chooses to insure against a handicap and the other does not, in the hypothetical insurance market, and both end up having the handicap in the actual state of the world, then they have been equally treated. The hard case, however, is another one. Compare the situations of two persons with identical preferences, and who insure identically against handicaps, but one ends up handicapped and the other able. The insurance contract will, of course, entail a payment from the able one to the disabled one (that is, the first pays a net premium and the second receives a net payout), which, in the actual world, will take the form of a tax and transfer. It is, however, not obvious to me that resources have been appropriately equalized between these two. After all, they have identical preferences and took identical actions. Is the *difference* in their final states not a matter of brute luck, is it not a difference which is morally arbitrary? Indeed, since their conceptions of overall success are identical, and the actions they have taken to reach their goals are identical, is this not a case where equality of the degree of overall success of their lives *is* the right kind of equality to ask for? The arguments impugning equality of overall success as the right kind of equality to seek all derived their power from the fact that people have different conceptions of overall success, some easy to fulfill and some hard. But that difference does not exist in this case. Should not, then, equality of resources entail equality of overall success in actual lives for persons who have identical conceptions of success and take identical actions to achieve it? If so, the insurance mechanism does not implement an appealing kind of equality of resources.

We turn, finally, to the issue of differential talent. We could simply view a talent as the inverse of a handicap. But Dworkin does not, for he writes, "the connection between talents and ambitions . . . is much closer than that between ambitions and handicaps" (1981b, p. 316). Ambitions, recall, are desires associated with the person, whereas talents and handicaps are to be viewed as resources. Dworkin is saying that a person's plan of life is more influenced by the talents he has than by his handicaps, a questionable psychological claim. The upshot, at any rate, is that, while Dworkin considers it acceptable to separate preferences from handicaps in constructing the thin veil of ignorance, he does not consider it similarly acceptable to separate talents from preferences. So in the hypothetical insurance market, persons cannot insure themselves against lacking certain talents. Everyone knows his talents behind the veil. How, then, can the inequality in talents, which are admittedly resources, be compensated? Dworkin proposes that, although persons know their talents behind the veil, they will be assumed not to know what income those talents will bring. To put this in economic language, the wages associated with talented labor are state-contingent; they depend on what state of the world is realized. What persons *can* insure against is having a low income.

Although it admittedly strains credibility to conceive of a person's goals in life independently of his talents, I do not find the strain much worse than what had to be borne in separating handicaps from life goals. Moreover, there is a serious issue of inequality arising in Dworkin's formulation. As I wrote, one models the idea that a person is uncertain about what wages her talents will bring by postulating that there is a probability distribution over states of the world, and wages are state-contingent. Now consider two persons, one with an endowment of talents that dominates the other's: Andrea has much more of every talent than Bob. Assume as well that Andrea and Bob have the same preferences. Now Andrea will insure herself less (against having a low income) than Bob: for in every state of the world, she will be able to earn more than Bob, and they have the same preferences (toward risk, in particular). Thus Bob will have fewer "clamshells" (units of account behind the veil) to spend on other things. Bob, therefore, is unambiguously worse off than Andrea—he's worse off in every possible state of the world. But this is not on account of differential preferences or ambitions, it is on account of having a bad deal in resources. The insurance mechanism, however, is supposed to "equalize resources."

The example of Bob and Andrea is not an eccentric one: indeed, it is perhaps the central example of inequality of talents that a resource-egalitarian ethic should address. Some individuals, in reality, have talents that, regardless of the state of the world, will earn them more income than others can earn with their talents. If these talents are due to genetic or environmental influences for which they are not responsible, a resource-egalitarian ethic should rectify that inequality. But if talents are included as part of the person behind Dworkin's veil, his insurance mechanism will not carry out this rectification.

One might propose a solution to talent inequality which is, in a sense, the polar opposite of Dworkin's: allow people to purchase property rights in the talents of others. Thus behind the thin veil of ignorance, persons know their talents but they do not own them: anyone's talented labor power can be purchased with the initial clamshell endowment. This is equivalent to equal division of talents in the initial endowment, in the sense that each owns a per capita share of everyone else's talented labor. Dworkin calls this regime the "slavery of the talented," and rejects it on those grounds. I do not automatically reject it on those grounds, for the slavery label is a misnomer: in such a regime, each has a property right in the income others are capable of earning, not in their bodily persons. Such property rights induce a kind of taxation that is not a priori repulsive.

Despite my disagreement with Dworkin that the above distribution of property rights should be described as enslaving the talented, Dworkin and I agree that such a distribution does not implement "equality of resources," as follows. Consider Karl and Adam, who have identical preferences over leisure and goods (or conceptions of overall success which depend on their consumption of leisure and goods), but Adam possesses highly talented labor while Karl's talent is run-of-the-mill. In the market, Adam's labor will command a higher wage than Karl's. Now if Adam wants to expend leisure, he must purchase it—that is, he must buy the right to use some of his potential labor power as he wishes—for that commodity is up for auction. Thus Adam is precisely in the shoes of a person with an involuntary expensive taste, a taste for his own leisure. He will, therefore, end up worse off than Karl, who can purchase his leisure more cheaply. But if Karl and Adam differ only in their resource endowment (in which talents are included), then equality of resources should deliver them the same welfare—so equal division of talents is not a proposal for implementing that ideal.

7.5 An Axiomatic Approach to Equality of Resources

If I have shown, in §7.4, that Dworkin's proposal fails in satisfactorily rectifying inequalities in circumstantial resources while continuing to hold people responsible for their preferences, we should now ask whether there is a better proposal. In this section, I shall apply the methods of Chapter 3 to study this question.[3]

We shall work on the domain of problems $\hat{\Gamma}^P$: this is the subdomain of $\hat{\Gamma}$, as defined in §3.2, whose utility functions are taken from $\hat{\mathcal{U}}^P$ (see §3.3). Thus a typical element of the domain is $\langle n, \bar{x}, u, v \rangle$ where u and v can be viewed as measuring the degree of overall success of a life, a number between 0 and 1, achieved as a function of resources consumed. The resource vector $\bar{x}$ must now be thought of as including both external and internal resources. This is a domain of environments without production, so with it we are only capable of studying the problem of resource egalitarianism in pure exchange economies. (We shall shortly see how handicaps can be modeled on this domain.)

Our problem is to discover an allocation mechanism F, which assigns to each $\mathcal{E} \in \hat{\Gamma}^P$, a resource allocation (or set of such allocations) that, we can argue, implements comprehensive equality of resources. We shall assume, following Chapter 3, that F is a full correspondence that is essentially a function. This assumption is not harmless: as I pointed out in Chapter 3, fullness is the assumption of Pareto indifference, that if two allocations give the same pair of utilities to the individuals and one is chosen by F, then they both are chosen by F. There is, then, a weak element of welfarism in the fullness assumption.

I should at once warn the reader that Dworkin's insurance mechanism is *not* a definable mechanism on the domain $\hat{\Gamma}^P$, and for this reason, this section is not, strictly speaking, an attempt to generalize Dworkin's project. To do so, we would have to work on a domain whose environments contained utility functions expressing persons' preferences over lotteries of resources. But I have stated that the functions u and v are to be viewed as (absolutely measurable and comparable) measures of the degree of life-plan fulfillment or overall success. That is, to include Dworkin's insurance mechanism as a special case, I would have to work with environments of the form $e = \langle n, \bar{x}, u, U, v, V, \Pi \rangle$ where u and v are as above, U and V are representations of the individuals' preferences over lotteries of the resources $\bar{x}$, and Π is a set of states of the world and a probability distribution over such states, where each state consists of a particular distribution of the resources between the per-

---

3. Following Roemer (1986a, 1987b).

sons. On that kind of environment, the insurance mechanism can be defined.[4]

With the next example, I shall display an unattractive feature of the insurance mechanism. Suppose we have an environment with one good, call it corn, available in one unit; let us suppose that the two individuals, Andrea and Bob, have identical von Neumann–Morgenstern preferences over lotteries of corn represented by $U(x) = x^{1/2}$. There are no handicaps here—just preferences (which Bob and Andrea are responsible for) and corn. Suppose there are two possible states of the world: either Andrea will get all the corn or Bob will get it all, each occurring with probability $\frac{1}{2}$: this describes Π. Given their concave risk preferences, Andrea and Bob will fully insure in this case; they will write a contract entailing that each will end up, after the actual world is revealed, with $\frac{1}{2}$ unit of corn. Formally, let F^D be Dworkin's insurance mechanism. No matter what the functions u and v are, we have $F^D(e) = \left(\frac{1}{2}, \frac{1}{2}\right)$, where $e = \langle 1, 1, U, u, U, v, \Pi \rangle$.

Now suppose we discover that, in fact, the above formulation misrepresents the actual environment. Andrea's and Bob's risk preferences appear to be U, but actually they each have preferences defined over two goods: corn and an internal resource, endorphins. In fact, if we view endorphins as a resource, then Andrea and Bob have identical risk preferences over corn-endorphin bundles, of the form $W(x, E) = x^{1/2}E^{1/2}$. Andrea is endowed with 4 units of endorphins, and Bob with 1 ($\bar{E}^A = 4$, $\bar{E}^B = 1$). This generates the risk preferences U for each of them when only corn lotteries are considered. Comprehensively to equalize resources (of corn and endorphins) requires us to consider an environment in which there are two resources, corn and endorphins, and in which the distribution of endorphins, as well as corn, in the actual world is unknown. Let us suppose, since this is a two-person world, that all four events are equally likely: that is each has a 50% chance of ending up with all the corn, as above, and from behind the veil, each has a 50% chance of ending up with the larger endorphin allotment, and these events are independently distributed. Thus there are four states of the world, where each state occurs with probability $\frac{1}{4}$. If we denote an allocation in a state as $((x^A, E^A), (x^B, E^B))$ where x^j and E^j are, respectively, the corn and endorphin allotment that j receives in

---

4. In my original work on this topic in the articles just referenced, I had not fully comprehended the point that to model the insurance mechanism and overall success would require two different utility functions.

the birth lottery, then the four equally likely states (in terms of their initial allocations) are:

state 1 $((1, 4), (0, 1))$,
state 2 $((1, 1), (0, 4))$,
state 3 $((0, 4), (1, 1))$,   and
state 4 $((0, 1), (1, 4))$.

Thus we can represent this environment as $e^* = \langle 2, (1, 5), u, W, v, W, \Pi^* \rangle$, where Π^* denotes the four states, each occurring with probability one-fourth. To calculate the action of F^D on e^*, we must compute the insurance contract that Andrea and Bob will write, facing the lottery Π^*. Now the only resource that can be transferred between the two of them in the actual world after the true state is revealed is corn—each will be stuck with his endorphins at that point. Each person is identically placed behind the veil, so we can write the insurance problem as a decision problem for that generic agent, who must choose how to allocate the corn in each of the four states so as to maximize "its" expected utility. Thus the decision variable can be written (x^1, x^2, x^3, x^4), where x^i is Andrea's consumption of corn if state i occurs. Since preferences obey the von Neumann–Morgenstern axioms, the problem for Andrea behind the veil is to choose (x^1, x^2, x^3, x^4) to

$$\text{maximize} \quad \tfrac{1}{4} W(x^1, 4) + \tfrac{1}{4} W(x^2, 1) + \tfrac{1}{4} W(x^3, 4) + \tfrac{1}{4} W(x^4, 1)$$

$$\text{s.t.} \quad x^1 + x^4 = 1$$

$$x^2 + x^3 = 1.$$

Note, by considering the equilibrium condition, that the constraints must take the above form. States 1 and 4 simply permute the two individuals, as do states 2 and 3. Thus, in equilibrium, the corn Andrea ends up consuming in state 4 must be the corn that Bob ends up consuming in state 1, with an analogous statement for states 2 and 3.

We can rewrite this decision problem as:

$$\text{choose } x^1, x^2 \quad \text{to} \quad \max \ 2(x^1)^{1/2} + (1 - x^1)^{1/2}$$

$$+ (x^2)^{1/2} + 2(1 - x^2)^{1/2}$$

$$\text{s.t.} \quad 0 \le x^i \le 1, \quad \text{for } i = 1, 2.$$

The solution to the program is $x^1 = \frac{4}{5}$, $x^2 = \frac{1}{5}$, and therefore $x^3 = \frac{4}{5}$ and $x^4 = \frac{1}{5}$. This means that whoever ends up with the larger endorphin bundle (which in the actual state of the world will be Andrea) will also get four-fifths of the corn under the Dworkin insurance mechanism! Thus the insurance mechanism renders the "handicapped" person, Bob, worse off than he would have been had we not tried to "compensate" him for his handicap—for in that case, we noted that he would receive one-half of the corn.[5] The intuition behind this result derives from the fact that the soul behind the veil, in maximizing its expected utility, equalizes the marginal utility of the various persons it might become. Since Bob's marginal utility at consumption x is $1/2\sqrt{x}$ and Andrea's marginal utility at consumption y is $1/\sqrt{y}$, Andrea must receive more corn than Bob.

I believe this example constitutes a fatal blow to the view that the insurance mechanism implements an attractive kind of resource egalitarianism.[6] One should note that the example is far from perverse: we have assumed that both persons have identical Cobb-Douglas von Neumann–Morgenstern preferences over lotteries, hardly an eccentric choice. Whatever resource egalitarianism means, it should at least entail assigning as much corn to Bob in the environment e^* as he gets in the environment e: for in e, Bob was being held responsible for a preference that later, in e^*, is shown to be due to a handicap requiring compensation. But F^D assigns Bob *more* of the transferable resource, corn, in e than in e^*.

---

5. One must here recall Broome's (1993) admonition to distinguish between a cause and an object of preference (see §5.5). I have described the Andrea-Bob example so that endorphins are an *object* of preference, not simply a cause of particular corn preferences. In my initial presentation of this example (Roemer 1986), I failed to make this distinction. If endorphins are viewed merely as a cause of corn preferences, then we could not view the Andrea/Bob soul behind the veil of ignorance as having a preference order over the four states enumerated above: it would not be capable of ranking corn-endorphin bundles involving different levels of endorphins.

6. Van Parijs (1995, chap. 3) criticizes my attack on the insurance mechanism by arguing that individuals should not be modeled as expected utility maximizers; rather, they would behave in the extremely risk-averse fashion of maximinners behind a Dworkinian veil of ignorance. Van Parijs fails, in fact, to make the distinction between risk aversity and extreme risk aversion: an individual with a concave von Neumann–Morgenstern utility function is risk averse and, indeed, can be very risk averse. Thus the expected-utility assumption (that is, the von Neumann–Morgenstern axioms) allows the modeler to endow individuals with arbitrarily high degrees of risk aversion. If, for example, we

Let us now return to the domain of environments $\hat{\Gamma}^P$, and ask what resource egalitarianism on that domain should entail. On $\hat{\Gamma}^P$, we lose the ability to discuss lotteries. How, then, might internal resources like endorphins be represented? We can use the following trick. Let us retell the story of Andrea and Bob with their differential endorphin levels. Suppose that $u(x) > v(x)$ for all $x > 0$: for any given positive level of corn, Andrea's life has a higher degree of overall success than Bob's does at that level. We have the environment $\mathcal{E} = \langle 1, 1, u, v \rangle$. Now it is revealed that Bob's apparently less successful life is a consequence of being handicapped by a low endorphin level. Andrea has 4 units of endorphins and Bob 1. We will represent the new environment as one in which individuals have preferences over *three* resources: corn (x), Andrea's endorphins (E^A), and Bob's endorphins (E^B). Thus Andrea's success function, which displays its dependence on endorphins, is $w^A(x, E^A, E^B)$, and Bob's is $w^B(x, E^A, E^B)$. Furthermore, we may stipulate that there is a function w defined on $\mathbf{R}^2$ such that $w^A(x, E^A, E^B) = w(x, E^A)$ and $w^B(x, E^A, E^B) = w(x, E^B)$, and in fact $u(x) = w(x, 4)$ and $v(x) = w(x, 1)$—that is, the success functions u and v defined on corn are really derived from success functions defined on the corn-endorphin domain. Thus Andrea and Bob each have the "same" success function w, in terms of corn and endorphins—but he cannot effectively consume her endorphins nor can she effectively consume his. Thus, we can represent the new environment as $\mathcal{E}^* = \langle 3, (1, 4, 1), w^A, w^B \rangle$. In $\mathcal{E}^*$ there are three goods—corn, Andrea's endorphins, and Bob's endorphins—given by the endowment vector (1,4,1)—with preferences over these goods given by w^A and w^B. If we insist that the allocation mechanism F be Pareto optimal, then it must assign all of Andrea's endorphins to Andrea and all of Bob's endorphins to Bob, since Andrea gets no utility from Bob's endorphins nor he any from hers. But the mechanism can certainly also be required to take account (in some way not yet specified) of

---

stipulated that the Andrea-Bob von Neumann–Morgenstern preferences over bundles of corn and endorphins were of the form $w(x, E) = X^{1/n}E^{1/n}$, where n is large, then Andrea-Bob would be very risk averse, although the perverse result that Bob ends up with less corn under the insurance mechanism than Andrea still holds. Nevertheless, one must remark that there is a large empirical literature critical of the von Neumann–Morgenstern independence axiom. Van Parijs offers his own criticisms of Dworkin, and his own positive proposal of justice as undominated diversity, which I discuss in the Appendix.

that fact that Andrea is getting a big allotment of A-endorphins and Bob a small allotment of B-endorphins by adjusting appropriately how the corn is distributed between them.

This, then, is the trick for modeling internal resources: they will be represented as resources that only one person likes in the precise sense of Definition 3.1. An internal resource (in this case, a consumption talent) can only be enjoyably "consumed" by one person, and hence, if Pareto efficiency is required, will surely be assigned in its entirety to that person by the mechanism.

Let us, then, first require of a resource-egalitarian mechanism that it be Pareto efficient.

Second, I maintain that, whatever resource-egalitarianism means, it should at least mean the following: that if the persons are *identical* as far as the distribution problem is concerned—that is, u and v are the same function—then each should receive exactly half of the resource bundle. Note this is just the economic symmetry axiom Sy (§3.3). Andrea and Bob are not identical in $\mathcal{E}^*$ above: they have different preferences w^A and w^B. In particular, if in $\mathcal{E}$ the two persons are identical, that means there are no internal resources at issue—for then, as I have explained, the two would not have identical preferences. The Sy axiom is not vacuous—for instance, it will apply when persons have identical talents and handicaps and identical preferences. We might, in such a case, just ignore the internal resources and represent their preferences as defined over external goods only: then symmetry requires the mechanism to split the external resources equally. Since the domain assumption requires the "utility" functions to be concave, this is a Pareto optimal allocation. As I argued in §7.4, when individuals are identical, equality of overall success is surely what resource egalitarianism should entail.

Third, I maintain that, whatever resource egalitarianism means, it should at least entail resource monotonicity (RMON). If we compare two worlds in which the two sets of persons have the same profile of overall success functions, and in world 1 the resource vector (weakly) dominates the resource vector in world 2, then resource egalitarianism should require that no one have a lower degree of overall success in world 1 than her counterpart does in world 2. This, of course, applies to increases in "internal" resources as well. Thus if Andrea's endorphins are more plentiful in world 1 than in world 2, but Andrea's and Bob's preferences are the same in the two worlds as are Bob's endorphins, then Bob should get at least as much corn in world 1 as he does in world 2. This is a strong axiom, but it is arguably consistent with what resource egalitarianism should mean. Note that RMON is a weaker axiom than one which would require that every person get at least as much of every *resource* in world 1 as in world 2.

Finally, I will propose that F satisfy CONRAD. This is the most complex proposal to justify: it is justified by reference to the Andrea-Bob tale. I will show that CONRAD prevents the perversity from occurring which I showed earlier is characteristic of the insurance mechanism (of rendering Bob worse off when endorphins are considered within the jurisdiction of resources than when only corn is a resource). Consider, again, the two environments $\mathcal{E} = \langle 1, 1, u, v \rangle$ and $\mathcal{E}^* = \langle 3, (1, \bar{E}^A, \bar{E}^B), w^A, w^B \rangle$ defined several paragraphs above. By Pareto, we know that F must assign all of $\bar{E}^A$ to Andrea and all of $\bar{E}^B$ to Bob; so we can write $F(\mathcal{E}^*) = ((\hat{x}, \bar{E}^A, 0), (1 - \hat{x}, 0, \bar{E}^B))$, where $\hat{x}$ is the amount of corn assigned to Andrea, which we have not as yet determined. Now each of the two endorphins is liked by at most one person. We can there consider the CONRAD-restricted environment, gotten by holding fixed the endorphin allocation just displayed, and calculating the restricted utility functions. But since $w^A(x, \bar{E}^A, 0) = w(x, \bar{E}^A) = u(x)$ and $w^B(x, 0, \bar{E}^B) = w(x, \bar{E}^B) = v(x)$, the CONRAD restriction of $\mathcal{E}^*$ (gotten by fixing the endorphin levels) is exactly the environment $\langle 1, 1, u, v \rangle$, that is, $\mathcal{E}$. CONRAD therefore requires the distribution of corn to be the same in $\mathcal{E}$ as in $\mathcal{E}^*$—that is, $F(\mathcal{E}) = (\hat{x}, 1 - \hat{x})$. In particular, Andrea and Bob will each fare exactly as well in $\mathcal{E}$ as they do in $\mathcal{E}^*$. Perhaps this is going too far—I will return to this point below. For the moment, let us simply note that CONRAD prevents the perversity from occurring: a mechanism F that satisfies CONRAD will not hurt handicapped persons when their handicaps are included within the jurisdiction of resource equalization, as the insurance mechanism may.

We now invoke Theorem 3.2: if F satisfies the above axioms, then F must be the allocation mechanism that equalizes utilities (degrees of overall success). (Recall the Remark at Chapter 3, p. 115, noting that Theorem 3.2 remains true on the domain $\hat{\Gamma}^P$.) Thus I have argued that any appealing conception of resource egalitarianism must dissolve into welfare egalitarianism.

Scanlon (1986) has provided a critique of this argument (that is, the application of Theorem 3.2 to the problem of equality of resources) that I find, in large part, convincing. His critique consists essentially of two points. The first point is that the assumptions of Pareto efficiency and resource monotonicity impose a "welfarist" conception of what equality of resources should mean. Pareto efficiency says that one allocation is better than another if it delivers everyone more utility: but why, Scanlon says, if one is a resource egalitarian, should one measure betterness in terms of utility? Resource monotonicity says that if resources are more abundant in one world than another, everyone should get more utility in the first world—but why, says Scanlon, take the metric of resource "size" as the utility it delivers? Perhaps there is some more appropriate measure of a resource bundle's size than the utility it engenders.

I will, indeed, propose what that more appropriate measure might be. A resource egalitarian is not unconcerned with welfare: she believes, however, that justice need only concern itself with "part" of welfare, namely, the part that is, so to speak, morally arbitrary. Dworkin has proposed a way of "equalizing" that part, loosely speaking, while allowing interpersonal welfares to differ insofar as they are due to non-morally-arbitrary features and actions of persons. Thus the measure of the "size" of a resource bundle should be the degree of that "morally arbitrary part" of welfare that it engenders. That could be, for instance, the vector of functionings it delivers to a person, or the vector of primary goods it delivers. If, for example, we chose the former, then we could consider the utility functions in an environment to measure the degree of functioning of a person (assuming that could be represented by a number). If the axioms were appropriately reinterpreted, then Theorem 3.2 would say that resource egalitarianism requires equalizing the degrees of functioning of all persons.

Scanlon's second point concerns the CONRAD axiom. In the statement of CONRAD (§3.3), let us call $\mathcal{E}^*$ the original environment and $\mathcal{E}$ the extended environment. As Scanlon correctly notes, a given original environment has many extended environments, but there is no reason to assert that the "new resources" which appear in one of these extended environments actually are hidden resources (as in the endorphin story I told above) in the original environment. Yet CONRAD forces "consistency" between resource allocation in the original environment and any of its extensions, regardless of whether or not the "new resources" are actually hidden in the original environment. Thus CONRAD enforces more consistency in resource allocation than the Andrea-Bob story justifies. I agree with this criticism. Indeed, it is a criticism of precisely the same kind that I made against Nash-type axiomatic bargaining theory in §2.5. The CONRAD axiom enforces more consistency than the motivating intuition warrants.

What Scanlon's second criticism would require is that we model which goods are "actually hidden" in the original environment, and then formulate a weaker version of the CONRAD axiom that would require consistency only between an original environment and its extension if the "new resources" in the extension were actually hidden in the original. I have, indeed, described how to do this (Roemer 1987); the upshot is that Theorem 3.2 is not preserved.

I should add that Scanlon also insists, again I think rightly, that distributive justice should be discussed on environments where goods are named. (Indeed, he writes that "argument about justice involves names 'all the way down' " (Scanlon 1986, p. 117).) In particular, to know that the "new resources" in an extended environment are indeed the same as the "hidden resources" in the original environment, we must know the names of the goods. But as I have argued at the end of §3.6, if we require our domain of environments to be sufficiently realistic, in respect of representing the names of goods and other characteristics, then it is questionable whether we can retain any of the axiomatic characterizations presented in Chapter 3. Scanlon's general position is that discussion of justice requires great specificity ("names all the way down"); this can be interpreted as rejecting the strong domain assumptions required of axiomatic theory and hence the simple conclusions of that theory, in the sense that §3.6, I hope, clarified.

One can also argue, as I indicated above, that CONRAD is too strong an assumption for preventing the perversity of the insurance mechanism, because it requires Bob to be exactly as well off in the "original" environment and its extension under F, rather than being at least as well off in the extension. In Roemer (1994, pp. 177–178), I have shown that, if we replace CONRAD with an axiom that models just this, then we lose the conclusion of Theorem 3.2 as well.

7.6   Conclusion

Dworkin's 1981 articles advanced the conceptions of egalitarianism put forth by Rawls and Sen by focusing more clearly on the issue of responsibility. The general conception of egalitarianism he advocated would attempt to compensate persons for inequalities in their circumstances (aspects of their situations for which they are not responsible) but not to compensate them for inequalities for which they are responsible, which include, contestably, inequalities resulting from the exercise of preferences which they are glad they have. His hypothetical insurance market is a device for implementing this proposal. As we have seen, however, the insurance market does not do what a Dworkinian resource egalitarian requires.

I offered an axiomatic approach as an attempt to discover a good resource egalitarian mechanism and concluded that resource egalitarianism dissolves into welfare egalitarianism, a result that Dworkin, who rejects welfare egalitarianism, would find repellent. But Scanlon offered a salient critique of my attempt: indeed, it falls prey to the same error which, I argued earlier, characterizes the application of Nash-type bargaining theory to distributive justice.

We are left, at this point, with no mechanism that implements a Dworkinian kind of resource egalitarianism. But rather than try further to refine Dworkin's approach in the hope of finding one, we shall turn to critiques made of Dworkin's position in the late 1980s and early 1990s, which again advanced the debate to a new stage.

8

Equality of Opportunity
for Welfare

8.1 Relocating Dworkin's Cut, 1

Dworkin placed the boundary between what a person is responsible for and what he is not to separate his preferences from his resources or, as Dworkin says, his ambitions from his endowments.[1] As I remarked, this requires an apparently peculiar conception of responsibility, for that term usually denotes an aspect of a person's situation associated with actions over which she has had control, and one may not be responsible for one's preferences under this construal. Preferences could have been (and usually are) in large part embedded in one by one's environment before one could reasonably be said to have had control over the process. Dworkin would not disagree, but he nevertheless holds a person responsible for those preferences, as long as she is glad she has them. At the end of the decade, Arneson (1989, 1990a) and Cohen (1989) proposed similar revisions to Dworkin's cut, with the intention of separating more cleanly these two aspects of a person's situation. Each proposal shares with Dworkin's the general view that distributive justice consists in a restricted kind of egalitarianism: persons should be rendered equal in condition insofar as their condition results from circumstances over which they cannot be held responsible, but differences in condition are admissible when those differences are due to actions/beliefs for which they are responsible.

---

1. This section's title is borrowed from section IV of Cohen (1989).

Before discussing their proposals, I should reiterate that Dworkin's decision to place preferences within the jurisdiction of a person's responsibility is not undefended. He shares with Scanlon (1986, 1988) the view that one should be held responsible for one's preferences as long as one identifies with them, is glad one has them. (Recall Scanlon's example of the religious person in §7.4.) This view is probably justified in something like the following way. A person's preferences, assuming she identifies with them, are intimately related to, may even constitute, her conception of herself. Not to consider her responsible for them would, if this is so, degrade her in the sense of holding her not accountable for actions (choices) that she considers to be expressive of herself. Scanlon (1988) argues that the act of making choices has value for people for noninstrumental reasons,[2] that choices signal to others the kind of person one is (Scanlon's "symbolic" and "demonstrative" values of choice). If that signal is to be meaningful, he argues, a person must be held responsible by society for his choices, assuming they follow from preferences with which he wishes to be identified.

Arneson, however, advocates the more conventional conception of responsibility, the one which takes as central the control the person has or had over the action/belief in question. His proposal moves both "forward" and "backward" from Dworkin's: forward in proposing a new cut between those aspects of a person's situation she is responsible for and those she is not, and backward in taking welfare or utility as the equalisandum, suitably modified, rather than resources. He dubs his proposal "equal opportunity for welfare." Imagine a "decision tree" with many paths or branches, all beginning at the present (the root). Each branch describes the utility that the person would derive were he to choose a particular set of preferences and make various decisions at critical points in his life. Wherever there are various states of the world that may unfold after a particular time on a given path, the path branches into several subsidiary branches, each describing what happens to the person should a particular state of the world be realized. Arneson writes:

> We then add up the preference satisfaction expectation for each possible life history. In doing this we take into account the preferences that people have regarding being confronted with the particular range of options given at each decision point. Equal opportunity for welfare obtains among persons when all of them face equivalent decision trees—the

---

2. The instrumental value of choice is in achieving the alternative one most desires.

expected value of each person's best (= most prudent) choice of options, second-best, . . . n^{th} best is the same. The opportunities persons
encounter are ranked by the prospects for welfare they afford.   (Arneson
1989, pp. 85–86)

Let us try to state this idea precisely using choice-theoretic language. In
the second sentence, Arneson is clearly referring to preferences over lotteries; in the next sentence he considers two decision trees "equivalent" if the
expected "values" along the branches are equal. What Arneson needs is an
assumption that individuals' utilities over lotteries are interpersonally comparable; then the trees of Adam and Eve will be "equivalent" if there is an
isomorphism between their branches such that the utility of each branch
on Adam's tree, evaluated from the present time, is equal to the utility
of the corresponding branch of Eve's tree. The utility function (over lotteries), however, that is used to evaluate the branches itself changes (in
general) with the branch being evaluated, for different branches may entail adopting different preferences and, in particular, different risk preferences.

We may summarize this as follows, making certain simplifying assumptions along the way. A decision tree consists of a set of paths (to use game-
theoretic language), each beginning at the root and ending at a terminus.
Let us suppose that the number of distinct paths at the root is n, and let
us further suppose that these paths represent distinct choices of life plan
and preference, after which all further branching is determined by nature (thus we simplify by assuming that a person chooses her life plan only
once, and after that it unfolds according to randomly distributed states of
nature). Each of these n initial paths is associated with a utility function
defined over lotteries. (The utility function of the ith initial path is used
to evaluate the compound lottery represented by the developments along
that path.) These utility functions are interpersonally comparable. Two decision trees are *equivalent* if each has the same number of initial paths, and
there is a one-to-one mapping between these sets of n paths such that the
utility of each path on one tree is equal to the utility of "that" path on the
other tree. (The evaluation of utility along one of the initial paths will generally involve computing the utility of a very complex compound lottery.)

Opportunities for welfare, however, are not yet equal, even if the decision trees are equivalent. For it might be that Adam and Eve are differentially aware of the existence of some paths on their trees, or it might
require great self-control, will power, or strength of character for Adam

to choose his third path, while Eve can choose her third path with ease. So Arneson refines the definition to consider two decision trees *effectively equivalent* if and only if they are equivalent, each is fully aware (let us say) of the definition of his tree, and each path is as accessible to Adam as the corresponding path is to Eve. (Arneson does not use the word "accessible"; I use it as prefiguring Cohen's conception of egalitarianism, to be described presently.) Further philosophical analysis may, of course, be necessary to decide when two paths are equally accessible.

Arneson says that equality of opportunity for welfare has been equalized if transferable resources have been distributed so that the decision trees of any two individuals are effectively equivalent. (Let us not, for the present, worry about whether such a distribution of resources exists.) He argues that none of the criticisms that Rawls and Dworkin have registered against equality of welfare holds against equality of opportunity for welfare, so conceived. When equality of opportunity for welfare is equalized, it will generally be the case that Adam and Eve will choose "different" paths (meaning a pair of paths that are not mapped into each other by the isomorphism): they have, according to Arneson's view, no claim at the bar of justice for the unequal welfares which they then achieve.

As I have thus far described Arneson's position, it is almost welfarist. Almost all we need know about the world is the set of vectors of utility numbers associated with a given distribution of resources, where each vector lists the utilities along the n initial paths of the decision trees of the individuals under that distribution. The nonutility information required is that the various paths are equally accessible to individuals. We can immediately see that, because of this (almost) welfarism, the proposal as it stands is incapable of dealing with the "tamed housewife" problem. It may be that the resource distribution gives Eve a very small bundle of resources and Adam a great quantity, and given this distribution, Eve conceives of various possibilities for her life, each of which involves some variation of "tamed housewife," Adam conceives of various possibilities of "playboy," and their utilities are appropriately isomorphic. Surely this cannot do. So Arneson further refines the definition of equality of opportunity for welfare by placing a condition on the environment in which individuals conceive of their preferences and hence decision trees. He writes:

> The preferences that most plausibly serve as the measure of the individual's welfare are hypothetical preferences. Consider the familiar account: The extent to which a person's life goes well is the degree to

which his ideally considered preferences are satisfied. My ideally considered preferences are those I would have if I were to engage in thoroughgoing deliberation about my preferences with full pertinent information, in a calm mood, while thinking clearly and making no reasoning errors. (We can also call these ideally considered preferences "rational preferences.")   (Arneson 1989, pp. 82–83)

There is yet one more stipulation. Arneson distinguishes between "first-best" and "second-best" ideally considered preferences. The distinction takes account of the fact that, when thinking about his preferences, the individual already has some preferences. Suppose that Eve has been, for some years, a music teacher. Her first-best preference might be to be a concert pianist; but she has already become accustomed to a style of life with a certain steady income from teaching piano. Were she now to undertake the career of a concert pianist, she would for some years have to live from hand to mouth. Thus, taking into account the costs of preference change, Eve would now prefer to remain a music teacher. There was a time, however, earlier on, that she would have chosen to be a concert pianist, had she had the opportunity. Eve's second-best ideally considered preferences are her music-teacher preferences.

Arneson's fully articulated view, I believe, is that equality of opportunity for welfare is achieved when the decision trees of all individuals are effectively equivalent, and each of the n initial paths on a person's tree corresponds to an ideally considered second-best preference, that is, to a kind of life one might pursue and its associated welfare, given the fact that one is already imprinted with preferences from the pre-equality world.

In my opinion, Arneson has been too ambitious in trying at once to solve the problems of future inequalities and past inequalities—past inequalities necessitating the distinction between first- and second-best ideally considered preferences. From a conceptual viewpoint, my modeling strategy would have been to imagine that the resource distribution is carried out so that it provides "children" (that is, persons whose preferences have not yet been formed) with the opportunity "to engage in thoroughgoing deliberation about [their] preferences with full pertinent information, in a calm mood, while thinking clearly and making no reasoning errors." Then we would need only consider Arneson's first-best preferences. I will consider this a friendly amendment to Arneson's proposal, for I think the second-best move fails, but Arneson will have achieved a great deal if even the so-amended proposal, which is easier to defend, works.

The second-best move fails for the following reason. The process of forming "tamed housewife" preferences is one of cognitive dissonance: Eve learns to be content, or enjoy, her truncated situation, because to do otherwise would be unbearable. Given that she has successfully done so, the options of becoming instead a senator or a lawyer strike Eve as outlandish. Eve has come to believe deeply that a woman's place is in the home. Hence her second-best ideally considered preferences will all be some variant of "tamed housewife," for example, perhaps with the daring addition that she have a night out on the town with her own friends each month. If this is so, clearly the second-best move does not succeed in bringing about equal opportunity in an adequate sense. For Arneson to counter by saying that the Eve I have depicted is not "engaging in thoroughgoing deliberation about [her] preferences" is to have his cake and eat it too: if he wants seriously to consider the problem that people enter into these deliberations with their preferences already formed under conditions of unequal opportunity, he cannot simultaneously endow them with a freedom of thought which is inconsistent with who they are now.

I proceed, then, to consider the proposal as amended. Let me remind the reader that the stipulation of ideally considered preferences (or something similar to it) is critical to Arneson's claim that equality of opportunity for welfare escapes the Rawlsian, Senian, and Dworkinian criticisms of equality of welfare, for without it, as I have noted, the "tamed housewife" problem is not solved. But under that stipulation, nobody becomes a "tamed" housewife, although many may become housewives by choice. For each will have considered many other options under the stipulation.

How is the problem of expensive tastes dealt with? Expensive tastes are ones that, with a given resource bundle, engender lower welfare than one would have were one to have cheaper tastes. With the distribution of resources that renders decision trees effectively equivalent, some will choose expensive tastes, putting them on paths associated with relatively low welfares, and others will choose paths corresponding to cheap tastes, with relatively high welfares. This inequality of welfare is not compensable.

The problem of offensive tastes (that some may derive utility from the pain of others) is, as far as I can see, not addressed by Arneson's proposal.

Let us continue with the choice-theoretic analysis of the proposal, which is surely consistent with Arneson's modeling of the problem of "rational preferences"—he is endowing individuals with a superlative ability to deliberate about choice. How do individuals choose among the various paths of their decision trees? They must have preferences over these paths. (If they lacked such preferences, but merely chose their paths randomly, that would hardly be a process the results following from which people should be held responsible for. If persons are deemed to be responsible for the path they choose, as Arneson intends, it must be by virtue of having deliberated about the choice which gave rise to following that path.) These are not the same as the preferences already associated with *given* paths. Now I have already assumed that the utilities of paths are interpersonally comparable, and I mean them also to be intrapersonally, interpath comparable. (Thus it makes sense to say that individual i gets more utility in following path p than individual j gets in following path q, for any i, j, p, and q.) Does this not define, for each person, a preference order over paths? Why, in other words, doesn't every individual choose the path associated with the "cheapest tastes"?

Let us first state this precisely. Denote the preferences of individual i associated with taking path p as u^{ip}. Of course if i chooses path p, it is possible to evaluate what his utility would have been along a different path $q(u^{ip}(q))$, but that utility will never be available to him, for taking the path q also entails having preferences u^{iq}. (Thus I maintain that it is coherent for the music teacher to ask herself how she would like the life of a concert pianist [p = music teacher path, q = concert pianist path].) We can state the equivalence of the decision trees of individuals i and j with this notation as follows. There exists a one-to-one mapping φ of the set of i's initial paths onto the set of j's initial paths such that for all p in i's initial path set, $u^{ip}(p) = u^{j\varphi(p)}(\varphi(p))$. I now stipulate that each individual i has a preference order over paths represented by a utility function U^i, and the choice of path is governed by U^i. Furthermore, it is not required that $U^i(p)$ be ordinally equivalent to the function V^i defined by $V^i(p) \equiv u^{ip}(p)$.

What preferences, then, could U^i represent, if they differ from the preferences defined by V^i? Here Dworkin's distinction between overall and relative success of a life comes into play. u^{ip} could be the *relative* success one rates one's life as having if one chooses the life corresponding to path p. Thus $u^{ip}(p)$ is the expected relative success of choosing the path p. U^i is a measure of overall success. How might "$U^i(q) > U^i(p)$" and "$u^{ip}(p) > u^{iq}(q)$" be consistent? This is the case of a person who will rate her life as having been better if she chooses the concert-pianist path (q) rather than the music-teacher path (p), although she expects to achieve more as a music teacher than she would as a concert pianist, with respect to the standards of success in those two endeavors. I therefore believe it is coherent, not just logically possible, for the preferences defined by U^i and V^i to differ.

Thus we shall assume that the individuals in Arneson's world choose the path p to maximize $U^i(p)$. Even though persons, in the state of equality of opportunity for welfare, face effectively equivalent decision trees, they generally have different (ordinal) preferences U^i. These preferences they are held responsible for, in the sense that society does not indemnify them against the choices they make according to U^i. It is not necessary to assume that the U^i are interpersonally comparable. For Arneson's proposal to be philosophically appealing, it must be the case that persons are deemed as having control over the formation of the preferences U^i, or are responsible for them for some other reason. I think that whatever conditions create the ambience for "ideal consideration of preference" can also be assumed to engender "autonomous" formation of the conceptions of overall success, U^i.

Cohen (1989) suggests (although not using this notation) another reason why persons who have identical decision trees may choose different paths. A person might choose one path over another not because it affords him a higher welfare or expected success in his life but because it is better for other reasons—it is more altruistic, or moral on some other grounds. Thus persons may differ in their U preferences while having the same decision trees. Society should not compensate people for their choice of path because it owes persons no compensation on account of their moral views (reflected, in this case, in the U preferences). On this account, it matters not whether the U preferences were formed autonomously or not.

I now raise an old and a new criticism of Arneson's proposal as amended, short of raising the existence question. The old criticism centers on there being two different ways in which states of the world come about as one proceeds "down" an individual's decision tree (I here linguistically follow the practice in game theory of placing the root of the extensive form game at the top of the page). The first is by the choices of the individual, the second is by the choices of nature. Arneson wants to hold individuals responsible for their choices: but there is no obvious reason they should be responsible for nature's choices, in the sense of not being indemnified against bad outcomes of natural lotteries. Thus Eve and Ellen both choose to become music teachers, face the same lifetime lotteries as music teachers, and have the same expected utilities, but Eve suffers bad luck and Ellen does not. Under Arneson's proposal, no compensation is forthcoming for Eve. I raised this criticism against Dworkin's insurance scheme in §7.4, and also raised it in §4.5 when discussing ex ante versus ex post utility. Arneson's choice to consider only ex ante utility is certainly the conventional choice, but it may not be the choice that accords best with what equality of opportunity for welfare should require.

The new criticism involves the experiment conceived to define ideally considered preferences. I am now considering the experiment of providing an ambience for all "children" to form first-best ideally considered preferences. I do not wish to raise the point that it is impossible to provide the resources to all children to allow them to deliberate in the autonomous way that Arneson requires. Rather, my claim is that the formation of preferences can never be autonomous, in the Arnesonian sense. Preferences are necessarily in large part imprinted in persons from their environments, in particular from looking at the preferences of other people in their social environments. The experiment which Arneson requires for the definition of first-best ideally considered preferences is biologically/psychologically an impossible one.

One move to amend Arneson's amended proposal, in light of the new criticism, is to use the decision trees that people construct *given* the resources provided them in the Ministry of Justice's allocation. Thus a distribution of resources would be said to equalize the opportunity for welfare if, under that distribution, persons form decision trees that are effectively equivalent. But this definition fails adequately to deal with the problem of the tamed housewife: the argument has already been given earlier in this section, and in the penultimate paragraph of §7.3. To recap briefly, equality of opportunity for welfare may be achieved, under the new definition, when some individuals receive very few resources and construct decision trees all of whose paths are variants of tamed-housewife preferences and life plans.

I therefore conclude that Arneson's approach, which admirably (in my view) attempts to relocate Dworkin's cut, in the end does not completely succeed. The critical failure lies in the attempt to construct preferences under conditions of ample opportunity. Ideally considered preferences are a chimera: to have the kind of autonomy that would be required for Arnesonian equality of opportunity, would individuals not have to deliberate in an institution-free environment, obviously an impossibility? Having now analyzed Arneson's proposal, and having been driven to the present conclusion, the reader may be retroactively more impressed with Dworkin's proposal, which avoids the central problems of Arneson's equality of opportunity for welfare, as here described, by adopting the

Scanlonian view of responsibility and using actual preferences with the insurance mechanism.

8.2   Relocating Dworkin's Cut, 2

Cohen writes:

> Dworkin has, in effect, performed for egalitarianism the considerable service of incorporating within it the most powerful idea in the arsenal of the anti-egalitarian right: the idea of choice and responsibility. But that supreme effect of his contribution needs to be rendered more explicit.   (Cohen 1989, p. 933)

And Cohen proposes that "the right cut is between responsibility and bad luck, not between preferences and resources" (Cohen 1989, p. 921). Cohen thus describes the distinction between his and Arneson's views and Dworkin's views somewhat differently than I have described it. I have characterized Dworkin also as believing that "the right cut is between responsibility and bad luck," but as taking a Scanlonian view of responsibility. Cohen, however, reserves "responsibility" as following exactly from having control over one's actions, and hence says that Dworkin's cut is not between responsibility and bad luck. This is, as far as I can see, a semantic distinction with little importance for the present inquiry.

The view that Arneson and Cohen share, and which allies them in opposition to Dworkin, is that the right cut is between bad luck and the actions one could have chosen not to have done. They differ, however, on how further to articulate that view. Cohen advocates a view that he calls "equality of access to advantage," which signals the two ways in which he differs with Arneson, in preferring "access" to "opportunity" and "advantage" to "welfare."

Let us take up the advantage-welfare distinction first. Cohen's key example that challenges "welfare" as the relevant kind of advantage is Tiny Tim. Tim is paralyzed, but has a sunny disposition. Even without a wheelchair, his welfare level is higher than that of normally cheerful able people. On grounds of equality of opportunity for welfare, Tim should get no wheelchair. But Cohen takes it as self-evident that justice requires that Tim be assigned a wheelchair. This would suggest that egalitarians consider resources or functionings important, not just welfare.

Now Arneson, it seems, could bite the bullet and object that Cohen's intuition is wrong. Maybe Cohen's egalitarians are just unschooled, and after considering the merits of equality of opportunity for welfare, they should agree that Tim's claim on a wheelchair comes after others' (including able persons') claims for welfare-augmenting resources. Cohen rests his case on an intuition.

Cohen, however, thinks welfare counts, too. The key example here is of a man who is perfectly able to move his arms, but *after* moving them, suffers intense pain. This pain can be prevented by taking an expensive medication. The man, Cohen says, suffers no resource deficiency: he can do with his arms whatever others can do with theirs. What he suffers is an involuntary welfare deficiency. This man has a claim against society at Cohen's bar of justice for the money to purchase the medication. Cohen foresees that a resource egalitarian might respond by saying that "compensation is in order here because the man lacks the resource of being able to avoid pain," but he says this is but a thin disguise for invoking the idea of equality of opportunity for welfare.

So both welfare and resources of certain kinds must be included in whatever it is the opportunities for which should be equalized. Cohen calls that thing "advantage," and puts off its further articulation to another time. ("One hopes that there is a currency more fundamental than either resources or welfare in which the various egalitarian responses which motivated my proposal can be expressed" [Cohen 1989, p. 921].)

Cohen discusses another case, which he believes points to "advantage" rather than "welfare" as the right kind of condition. The case concerns Jude, a character in one of Dworkin's stories. Jude initially has very modest desires, and with a small amount of money, say M_1, is as happy as the average person. But then he reads Hemingway, and cultivates a desire to attend bullfights in Spain. He now requires M_2, more than M_1, to reach the average welfare level, but still less than the average person needs, M_3, to achieve that level of welfare. Cohen claims that, according to equality of opportunity for welfare, Jude should not receive the bullfighting stipend, since he voluntarily cultivated the relatively expensive taste. But, since Jude's new bullfighting tastes require less than the average ($M_2 < M_3$), Cohen thinks Jude should receive M_2.

In fact, the Jude example is not sufficiently specified to permit us to decide whether Cohen's intuition contradicts equality of opportunity for welfare, for we need to know Jude's entire decision tree, not just how much welfare he gets from attending bullfights. Suppose the pre-Hemingway and post-Hemingway Jude have the same Arnesonian decision tree—Jude simply decides to choose another path after reading Hemingway. Formally,

Jude changes his U-function after reading; in this case, society owes him no compensation: in particular, it does not owe him an increase of stipend from M_1 to M_2. Then Cohen's objection stands: it may indeed be intuitively implausible that Jude should be denied the increased stipend, since his new choice of path still would cost society less than others' choices cost society. But suppose that, as a result of reading Hemingway, Jude's preferences along some paths change: in particular, he now understands that watching bullfights would increase his welfare more than he formerly thought. In this case, Jude's initial preferences were not "ideally considered," and his pre-Hemingway decision tree was not the right one. Here the Arnesonian ethic does require increasing the stipend to Jude and decreasing the stipends to all others a little bit to achieve equality of opportunity for welfare.

I conclude that, of the two examples Cohen offers to prosecute his claim that Arneson's welfare must be broadened to include something else (Tiny Tim and Jude), one rests on an undefended intuition and the other is correct in one possible reading of the Jude story. Cohen may be right on both counts: that is, perhaps Tiny Tim should (under an equal-opportunity ethic) receive the wheelchair, and perhaps Jude should receive the extra stipend even if his decision tree has not changed after reading Hemingway. Cohen has not, unfortunately and thus far, provided us with tools for transforming these intuitions into knockdown arguments.

Next we turn to Cohen's preference for "access" over "opportunity." As far as I can see, this is a semantic, not a substantive, distinction. Cohen writes that one does not regard meager personal capacity (owing, for instance, to low intelligence) as detracting from opportunity. "Access," however, is reduced by meager personal capacity. But certainly, if this distinction is correct, then Arneson would be willing to substitute "access" for "opportunity" in his proposal. For in requiring decision trees to be *effectively* equivalent, he addresses precisely this point, and therefore his conception of "opportunity" is in fact Cohen's "access." There is no disagreement between Arneson and Cohen on this point.

Cohen does not address what I have claimed is the key weakness in Arneson's proposal, namely, the infeasibility of the experiment required to endow persons with the "right" preferences for the determination of justice. Nor does Cohen propose a precise definition of his proposal, in the sense of Arneson's decision-tree construction or of Dworkin's insurance mechanism. I conclude that Cohen may have a case for broadening welfare to advantage, but it is unproved.

Cohen furthermore amends his own proposal after considering the views of Scanlon. Scanlon (1975) argues that some of a person's interests deserve more consideration than others at the bar of justice by virtue of being more urgent, where that urgency may be defined by an objective standard, not one that is necessarily reflected in the person's own preferences. Thus a deeply religious person might prefer to use a meager income to build a monument to his god, not to purchase food. Justice, however, may prescribe that society give him food stamps, not money that could be spent on religious monuments. Cohen is not, in principle, opposed to this prescription, for his "advantage" may well include nonwelfare elements, for example, being well nourished. It is, rather, another Scanlonian (1986) example, of the religious man, discussed in §7.4, that troubles Cohen. That man, I should add, suffers from a sense of guilt on account of his religion, a kind of illfare. Not only should he not receive more resources than his penurious lifestyle requires (this was the point in §7.4), but neither should he receive the resources that a welfare-equalizing theory would require. Cohen agrees with Scanlon on this, and on that basis amends his proposal so it would only "compensate for disadvantages which are not traceable to the subject's choice *and* which the subject would choose not to suffer from." Unfortunately, this amendment goes too far: for it would direct society not to redress the situation of the tamed housewife. As stated, the amendment inadvertently denies compensation to those whose "sour grape" preferences cause them (falsely, we would say) to deny the attraction of more highly resourced lives.

Cohen points out that two other strategies remain for addressing the case of Scanlon's guilt-ridden believer. The first is "to argue that it is because the burdens of religion so manifestly reflect choice that compensation for them is out of the question," and the second is "to argue that it is not as odd as Scanlon maintains to compensate a person for those burdens" (Cohen 1989, p. 936). My preference would be to articulate something like the first of these strategies. The essential distinction, I think, between the guilt-ridden believer and the tamed housewife is that the former's beliefs, though not voluntarily taken on, were not adopted precisely because opportunities were objectively lacking, while the tamed housewife's preferences (also not voluntarily taken on) were adopted for that reason. To make this precise, of course, requires a noncircular way of deciding when opportunities were objectively lacking. And if we can solve that problem, there is yet a further troubling example: of the guilt-ridden and/or ascetic believer who adopts his religion because of an objective

poverty (in the resource sense). Some have argued that the depth of ad-
herence to an ascetic religion among Tibetans is explained in this way.
Such beliefs/preferences are quite arguably an instance of sour grapes, yet
their adherents may identify with those beliefs far more intimately than the
fox identified with his dispreference for grapes. Because of this, the policy
question whether to provide resources to such people is subtle. (Parenthet-
ically, I should remark that I am not convinced that Tibetans would reject
those resources, although they apparently do reject the dissolution of their
religious institutions by the Chinese state.)

8.3   Equality of Opportunity: An Example

In this section I shall bracket the problem of finding ideally considered
preferences or, more generally, of finding the kind of advantage that the
just society should equalize opportunities for (whether it be welfare associated with ideally considered preferences or expected degree of life-plan
fulfillment or aggregate level of functioning or midfare), and concentrate
instead on how we might implement "equality of opportunity for advantage
X." In particular, I shall argue that there is a method superior to the construction of Arnesonian decision trees, for in general there will exist no
distribution of resources that renders the decision trees of all individuals
effectively equivalent.

The problem of defining a way of implementing the equality-of-access/
opportunity view of distributive justice that has been discussed in this chapter can be phrased as follows. Individuals take actions (where I include
choosing a preference order as an action) which lead to welfare in varying degrees (interpersonal comparability is always assumed). These actions
are determined jointly by circumstances beyond their control and by their
own free volition. (One who believes in hard determinism can still agree
with this statement: she simply says the second category is empty.) We wish
to find a distribution of social resources which renders persons equal in advantage insofar as they face similar circumstances, but allows inequality of
advantage insofar as the freely chosen aspects of their behaviors differ: call
this the Equality of Opportunity principle (EOp). The reader will note the
similarity of what follows to the construction of §7.3.

Consider the problem of compensating persons for lung cancer acquired as a result of smoking. Here the relevant action is "choosing to
smoke" or "not to smoke." The choice a person makes is in part determined by his circumstances—say, his economic class, his ethnicity, whether

his parents smoked, and his level of education—and is in part a matter of voluntary choice. (One might question whether "economic class" and "level of education" are properly part of circumstances, since there is an aspect of volition in determining them. I shall assume that, for the purposes of analyzing the smoking problem, these are circumstances, if a person should not be held responsible for failing to consider the effect of his "choice" of economic class and level of education on whether or not he will come to smoke.) Society must first make a list of the factors beyond a person's control which it views as influencing the decision whether or not to smoke, as described above. Second, society is partitioned into equivalence classes according to individuals' vectors of these factors (that is, a given equivalence class consists of all persons whose vectors of factors are approximately equal). For example, if the vector of circumstances is ⟨gender, ethnicity, occupation, age⟩, then one equivalence class will consist of sixty-year-old white, female college professors and another of sixty-year-old black, male steelworkers. I call a given vector of circumstances, or its associated equivalence class, a *type*.

Society wishes to decide the compensation a person should receive if he contracts lung cancer. (The relevant advantage for which opportunities are to be equalized could be either welfare or freedom from disease, a kind of functioning.) Assume that the probability of contracting the disease is an increasing function of the number of years the person has smoked. Within each type, there is a distribution of years smoked. This distribution is a *characteristic of the type*, not of any individual. We view the different locations of sixty-year-old black steelworkers in this distribution as due to their responsible choice, for their *circumstances* have already been normalized by type, and similarly for sixty-year-old white female college professors. That one is much more likely to have smoked for thirty years, say, if one is a black male steelworker than if one is a white female college professor is not due to the responsible choice of individuals, but to type. Thus the distribution of years smoked within a type provides us with a way of calibrating the degree of access, in Cohen's sense, to the action of "not smoking" that members of a given type have. To take an extreme case, if all sixty-year-old steelworkers smoked for thirty years, we would say that the choice of "not smoking" is not accessible to steelworkers: as a steelworker, one would have had no effective opportunity but to smoke for thirty years. Given the type, certain choices are *effectively*, in the sense of Arneson, barred.

How, then, might one equalize the opportunity/access to welfare/freedom from disease in this example? I propose that we seek a distribution of

money (if that is the transferable resource to be allocated) which equalizes across types the "advantage" of all those who exercised a "comparable
degree of responsibility" in regard to the choice of smoking behavior. To
be specific, consider, for example, the college professor and steelworker
who each have smoked the median number of years for their types—
suppose these two have smoked ten and thirty years, respectively. I view
these two as having exercised comparable degrees of responsibility. Alternatively phrased, the act of smoking ten years conditional upon being a
college professor and the act of smoking thirty years conditional upon being a steelworker are equally accessible. The plausibility of this claim rests
on there being a large number of persons of each type. Then the frequency
of years smoked within a type can be viewed as the probability distribution
that governs the number of years a member of a type will smoke. Thus,
for example, I say that if 30% of individuals of type one smoked less than
seven years, and 32% of individuals of type two smoked less than five years,
then smoking less than five years is a more accessible action for a type-two
person than smoking less than seven years is for a type-one person, and this
because the probability that a type-one person will smoke less than seven
years is .3, while the probability that a type-two person will smoke less than
five years is .32.

This approach directs us to equalize the advantage not only of the "median" smokers across types, but of all smokers across types at any centile
of the smoking distributions. This will generally be impossible. In the next
section I shall propose a second-best approach. But here I want to emphasize the main point of the proposal, which is to calibrate the "degree of
responsibility" a person has by virtue of his "voluntary" choice via a two-step
procedure. First, factor out all aspects of (what society considers to be) circumstances beyond a person's control which affect choice, by partitioning
individuals into equivalence classes as described, and second, decide upon
the accessibility of various options to individuals by examining the empirical distribution of the choice of those options for each type.

The proposal I have outlined in this section[3] is "political" rather than
"metaphysical," to borrow a distinction of Rawls (1985). For I here advocate no particular set of criteria for factoring causes of choice into ones
beyond a person's control and ones within it. This set of criteria is envi-

---

3. The proposal was first presented, with some additional elaboration, in Roemer
(1993b) and is reprinted in Roemer (1994).

sioned to be, for each society, a subject of political debate. Thus the procedure outlined in this section, and made more precise below, is designed to implement a conception of equality of opportunity for advantage consistent with each society's conception of personal responsibility. As a theory of justice, then, the present proposal is lacking, unless one believes—as I do not—that distributive justice is a concept which depends upon particular social conceptions of responsibility. To put the matter slightly differently, the proposal of this section constitutes a theory of distributive justice (as equality of opportunity for advantage) which leaves two issues unresolved: what advantage consists in, and how to distinguish causes of behavior that are within, as opposed to beyond, a person's control.[4]

8.4 Equality of Opportunity: A Formalization

8.4.1 The Environment

There is a continuum of individuals.[5] Each individual is completely described by a *vector of traits* $s \in \bar{S}$, where $\bar{S}$ is a sample space, perhaps in $\mathbf{R}^n$, for some large n, endowed with the probability measure H. If $S \subset \bar{S}$ is measurable, then $H(S)$ is the fraction of society whose trait vector lies in S. One should think of "s" as being a complete list of the circumstances and behavioral propensities describing a person. There is an *advantage function* $u(x, e, s)$ that gives the advantage (say, health) enjoyed by an individual with traits s, who receives x units of the resource to be allocated (say, health services), and who expends effort e (say, abstaining from smoking for a certain number of years). We fix one kind of advantage for the discussion. It will usually be assumed that u is monotone increasing in x and e; in such cases, advantage is different from "utility," if utility is associated with choice behavior, for effort normally enters as a cost in utility.

Suppose a planner, who has a fixed supply of the resource available, offers to distribute it to individuals according to a transfer rule $\varphi(e)$: if an

---

4. A number of scholars have commented upon the present proposal in the *Boston Review* 20, April/May 1995 (R. Solow, T. M. Scanlon, R. Epstein, S. L. Hurley, N. Rosenblum, E. Fox-Genovese, S. Scheffler, E. Maskin, and A. Ripstein). My response to their comments is also published there.

5. Note that §8.4*, which follows the present section, presents the material that follows without the notation of probability measures, but in a condensed fashion. I urge the reader who is uncomfortable with the notation of probability measures to read both sections.

individual expends effort e, she shall receive $\varphi(e)$ units of the resource. I shall, for the remainder of this section, assume that all such transfer rules are linear, of the form $\varphi(e) = \gamma e$, for some non-negative γ. We suppose that, associated with each trait s, is an *effort response function* $e^s(\gamma)$. Perhaps this response is the result of some utility-maximization process; we will inquire no further into what causes the response. An *environment* is fully specified by the data $(u, \bar{S}, H, e^s(\cdot))$.

8.4.2   Societies

A society is derived from an environment. The society has at its disposal ω units per capita of the resource, to be allocated among its members. There is, as well, a given measurable, finite partition of $\bar{S}$ into $S^1 \cup S^2 \ldots \cup S^r$. The individuals whose s lies in S^i constitute the ith *type*. In the last section, I described the partition as being the consequence of a social decision about what constituted a person's circumstances, over which he had no control. Thus, informally, all members of a given type have approximately the same vector of such circumstances.

The social welfare agency never observes the environment. It does, however, calculate an advantage function for each type, using some sampling procedure; if the sample is representative, and its measurement of the advantage functions of individuals in the sample is accurate, then the advantage function it assigns to type i, denoted $u^i(x, e)$, will be approximately, for a large sample size:

$$u^i(x, e) = \int_{S^i} u(x, e, s) dH(s) / H(S^i).$$

In other words, the advantage for individuals of type i, used by the planner, is the average of the (true) advantage functions of individuals of that type. The planner also knows the aggregate effort responses of each type to any given transfer rule $\varphi(e) = \gamma e$: facing transfer rule φ^i, she observes a distribution of efforts in type i characterized by a probability measure F^i_φ on the set of possible effort levels. Just as we derived the advantage function u^i from the underlying environment, we could derive the measures F^i_φ from the underlying effort response functions e^s. But for the planner, the data $\{F^i_\varphi\}$ are the primitives.

Thus the data characterizing a *society* are $(\omega, u^1, \ldots, u^r, S^1, \ldots, S^r, H, \{F^i_\varphi\})$.

Let $p^i = H(S^i)$. The planner can distribute the resource to individuals via a *transfer rule*, a vector of transfer functions, one for each type, $\varphi = (\varphi^1, \varphi^2, \ldots, \varphi^r)$. We thus restrict the planner to treating all members of a type identically (that is, exposing them to the same transfer rule), but allow her to treat different types differently. A transfer rule is *admissible* if and only if the following budget constraint is satisfied:

$$(8.1) \qquad \sum_i p^i \int_E \varphi^i(e) dF_\varphi^i(e) \leq \omega.$$

Thus, for any society, there is a set Φ of admissible transfer rules. I will further assume that every type contains a continuum of individuals, and that the probability measures F_φ^i are absolutely continuous with respect to Lebesgue measure; thus F_φ^i can be represented by a density function f_φ^i. (This property follows from suitable assumptions about the function $e^s(\cdot)$.)

An *allocation mechanism* is a mapping $\mathcal{F}$ that associates to each society (in some domain) a transfer rule. We proceed to define three allocation mechanisms.

8.4.3   The Equality of Opportunity (EOp) Mechanism

Let $e^i(\pi, \varphi)$ be the effort level expended by the individual at the πth centile of the effort distribution of type i under the admissible transfer rule φ. $e^i(\pi, \varphi)$ is defined by the equation:

$$(8.2) \qquad \pi = \int_{\underline{e}}^{e^i(\pi,\varphi)} f_\varphi^i(e) de.$$

As I explained in the last section, our task is to choose a transfer rule φ that equalizes advantage across types, for each given π.

More precisely, we want to equalize advantage at the highest possible level. More conventionally, we want, for each π, to maximize over Φ the minimum over i of the advantage u^i. Let us define the "indirect advantage function" v^i by:

$$v^i(\pi, \varphi^i) = u^i(\varphi^i(e^i(\pi, \varphi^i)), e^i(\pi, \varphi^i)).$$

$v^i(\pi, \varphi^i)$ is the advantage of the individual of type i at the πth centile of the "effort" distribution under the admissible transfer rule φ. For a *given* π, the decision problem would be to choose φ to

$$\sup_{\varphi} \min_{i} v^i(\pi, \varphi^i).$$

Call the solution to this maximization problem φ_π—this is the admissible allocation that "maximins" the advantage of all those who expended the "π^{th} degree of effort" across types.

If φ_π were the same transfer rule for all π, then that rule would be the perfect choice to equalize opportunities for advantage u. Unfortunately, this will not generally be the case: we cannot expect an infinite number of maximization problems to yield a common solution. Some compromise is therefore needed. We must, so to speak, aggregate the different rules φ_π across all π. I propose to do so by giving a weight to the interests of the πth quantile individuals equal to their frequency in the population, which I call $n(\pi, \varphi)$. Then I propose to choose φ to:

$$\sup_{\varphi} \int_0^1 \min_{i} v^i(\pi, \varphi^i) n(\pi, \varphi) d\pi.$$

Let $N(\pi, \varphi)$ be the fraction of individuals at the πth quantile or lower of their effort distributions under φ. By definition, $N(\pi, \varphi) = \pi$. But N is just the cumulative distribution function of the density function n, so it follows that $n(\pi, \varphi) = 1$, and we can write the solution of the last maximization problem as:

$$(8.3) \qquad \varphi^E = \arg\sup_{\varphi} \int_0^1 \min_{i} v^i(\pi, \varphi^i) d\pi,$$

where φ^E is the transfer rule that equalizes opportunities for u.

It will be instructive to compare the equality-of-opportunity approach to the Rawlsian difference principle and to utilitarianism, always taking the advantage measured by u to be the maximandum. I shall interpret Rawlsian justice as calling for the maximizing the advantage of the worst-off. There is no issue of responsibility. Nevertheless, we can represent the Rawlsian allocation using quantiles as:

(8.4) $\varphi^R = \arg \sup\limits_{\varphi} \min\limits_{\pi, j} v^j(\pi, \varphi^j).$

Utilitarianism also ignores the issue of responsibility. Each person's advantage should receive equal weight in the utilitarian calculation. Thus, the average advantage of all persons at quantile π of the effort distribution is $\sum_i p^i v^i(\pi, \varphi^i)$. Further, every quantile gets equal weight in the social average; so it follows that:

(8.5) $\varphi^U = \arg \sup\limits_{\varphi} \displaystyle\int_0^1 \sum_{i=1}^r p^i v^i(\pi, \varphi^i) d\pi.$

In the next section I shall compute these three solutions in several examples. The procedure defining the EOp mechanism arguably provides an appealing way of separating the influence of a person's circumstances and of his responsible behavior on the effort level chosen, of equalizing advantage to the extent that persons differ only by circumstance, and of allowing differential advantage insofar as people have similar circumstances but choose different efforts. It is possible to extend the definition to the case in which the choice variable (e) is multidimensional, although I will not do so here.

We can ask: Will equality of opportunity ever render those who expend more effort worse off in advantage (u) than those who expend less, holding type constant? (This would be rather perverse.) As long as the components of the transfer rule φ are increasing functions of effort, this cannot occur, since those who expend more effort will receive more of the resource. If advantage is a monotonic function of effort and resource consumed, those who expend more effort will end up with greater advantage.

8.4*   A Discrete Formulation of Equality of Opportunity

Some readers may be uncomfortable with the continuous formulation just provided; this section presents a discrete formulation of the problem. Let there be r types, where the fraction of type i individuals in the population is p^i. The advantage function of type i persons is $u^i(x, e)$. Let ω be the per capita social endowment of the resource to be allocated. Facing a transfer rule $\varphi^i(e)$, the individuals of type i respond with various efforts. Instead of measuring effort (and advantage) continuously, as in §8.4, we only observe quantiles. Suppose the number of quantiles is J (for example, if we calculate responses for effort deciles of the type, then $J = 10$). Let e^i_j be the average effort expended by individuals in the jth effort quantile of type i when facing transfer rule φ^i. Then those individuals receive, on average, $\varphi^i(e^i_j)$ amount of the resource. The level of advantage of individuals of quantile j in type i facing φ^i is, therefore on average, $u^i(\varphi^i(e^i_j), e^i_j)$, which we define to be $v^i(j, \varphi^i)$. Thus the *admissible* transfer rules $\varphi = (\varphi^1, \ldots, \varphi^r)$ are those for which the following budget constraint holds:

$$(8.1^*) \qquad \sum_i \sum_j p^i \varphi^i(e^i_j) \leq \omega.$$

If we were only concerned with equalizing advantage, across types, for persons at the jth quantile of their type-effort distribution, we would choose φ to

$$\max_\varphi \min_i v^i(j, \varphi^i).$$

Call the solution to this problem φ_j. If φ_j were the same rule for all j, then that rule would be the unambiguous equality-of-opportunity rule for the society. In general, however, φ_j will vary with j. Hence, we define an overall equality-of-opportunity rule by averaging the j different objectives suggested by the last maximization problem, that is:

$$(8.2^*) \qquad \varphi^E = \arg\sup_\varphi \frac{1}{J} \sum_{j=1}^J \min_i v^i(j, \varphi^i).$$

In (8.2^*), each quantile has a weight in the objective function equal to its fraction in the population. (8.2^*) is the discrete analogue of (8.3).

Similarly the discrete analogues of the Rawlsian and utilitarian mechanisms are:

$$(8.3^*) \qquad \varphi^R = \arg\sup_\varphi \min_{i,j} v^i(j, \varphi^i).$$

and

$$(8.4^*) \qquad \varphi^U = \arg\sup_\varphi \sum_i \sum_j p^i v^i(j, \varphi^i).$$

For a given transfer vector φ, define the $I \times J$ matrix $V(\varphi)$ to have, as its ij^{th} element, $v^i(j, \varphi^i)$. The data needed to calculate the three mechanisms consist in the family of matrices $\{V(\varphi) \mid \varphi \text{ admissible}\}$. In applications, the data usually come in this discrete form—for example, income-distribution data are generally available in discrete quantile form, not in continuous density-function form. Nevertheless, in the examples that follow, we formulate problems in the continuous form, for simplicity of computation.

8.5 Examples of the EOp Mechanism

8.5.1 An Example in a Pure Exchange Economy

In this example, we study how the EOp mechanism changes as society changes its conception of type in a way that holds individuals decreasingly responsible for their characteristic.

There is a continuum of individuals, represented by the interval $A = [1, 2]$ and distributed uniformly on the interval. The generic individual is denoted α. The *advantage* of α is given by $u(x, e, \alpha) = \alpha x^{1/2} e^{1/2}$, where x is a good to be allocated and e is the "effort" expended by α. Advantage is interpersonally comparable. α's *preferences* are represented by the utility function $w^\alpha(x, e) = x^{\alpha/2}(2 - e)^{1-\alpha/2}$. Thus effort involves a disutility. We can think of e as "years abstained from eating high cholesterol foods" and u as a measure of health.

Society has a per capita endowment $\omega = 1$ of the good, to be distributed among its members. Suppose it partitions A into $A^1 \cup A^2$, where $A^1 = \left[1, \frac{3}{2}\right]$, $A^2 = \left[\frac{3}{2}, 2\right]$. These are the two *types*. (I shall interpret this partition in a moment.) An *allocation* of the good is a feasible way of assigning it to individuals. Suppose that society is constrained to choosing allocation functions that are linear in effort. It will choose one allocation function of the form $\varphi^i(e) = \gamma^i e$ for each type i.

Thus society has decided that individuals are of either the "high" or the "low" type with respect to the trait α. It makes no finer distinction than that. It wishes not to hold individuals responsible for their health outcome (advantage) insofar as that outcome is due to being of a "high" or "low" type; but individuals are to be held responsible for their "effort to protect health" within type. (Perhaps those individuals with α in A^2 come from homes with well-educated parents, and those with α in A^1 come from other homes. Individuals are not to be held responsible for their family background, but are held responsible for their preferences conditional on family background.) I assume that the planner is able to assign exact advantage functions to each person: she is able to observe α. Note that this assumption is in contrast to what I assumed in the abstract model of §8.4.2, where the planner assigns an average advantage function to each type.

Facing an effort function of the form "$\varphi(e) = \gamma e$," α chooses e to maximize $(\gamma e)^{\alpha/2}(2 - e)^{1-\alpha/2}$. The solution is easily seen to be $e(\gamma, \alpha) = \alpha$, which is independent of γ due to the Cobb-Douglas formulation. Thus we can readily write down the distribution of effort in A^1 as a response to a linear allocation rate: it is given by

$$e^1(\pi, \gamma) = 1 + \frac{\pi}{2},$$

where π is the effort quantile, which takes on values from 0 to 1. In the notation of the last section, F_γ^1 is the uniform distribution on $\left[1, \frac{3}{2}\right)$. Similarly $e^2(\pi, \gamma) = \frac{3}{2} + \frac{\pi}{2}$. F_γ^1 is the uniform distribution on $\left[\frac{3}{2}, 2\right]$.

We may now write the advantage functions in terms of π as

(8.6)
$$v^1(\pi, \gamma) = \left(1 + \frac{\pi}{2}\right)\left(\gamma\left(1 + \frac{\pi}{2}\right)\right)^{1/2}\left(1 + \frac{\pi}{2}\right)^{1/2} = \left(\frac{2 + \pi}{2}\right)^2\sqrt{\gamma}$$

$$v^2(\pi, \gamma) = \left(\frac{3 + \pi}{2}\right)^2\sqrt{\gamma}.$$

Recall that $v^i(\pi, \gamma)$ is the advantage accruing to the individual in A^i whose effort response to "$\varphi(e) = \gamma e$" is at the πth quantile of effort responses of all those in A^i. Hence Equation (8.3) becomes

(8.7a)
$$\varphi^E = \arg\sup_{\gamma^1, \gamma^2} \int_0^1 \min\left(\left(\frac{2 + \pi}{2}\right)^2\sqrt{\gamma_1}, \left(\frac{3 + \pi}{2}\right)^2\sqrt{\gamma_2}\right) d\pi.$$

The feasibility constraint, that per capita "income" (x) not exceed ω, is $\int_1^{3/2} \gamma_1\alpha d\alpha + \int_{3/2}^2 \gamma_2\alpha d\alpha = \omega$, or

(8.7b) $5\gamma_1 + 7\gamma_2 = 8.$

Thus, our problem is to find (γ_1, γ_2) to maximize the integral in (8.7a) subject to (8.7b).

Note that

$$\left(\frac{2+\pi}{2}\right)^2 \sqrt{\gamma_1} \leq \left(\frac{3+\pi}{2}\right)^2 \sqrt{\gamma_2} \quad \text{iff} \quad \frac{2+\pi}{3+\pi} \leq \left(\frac{\gamma_2}{\gamma_1}\right)^{1/4}.$$

Let $k \equiv (\gamma_2/\gamma_1)^{1/4}$. It follows that $v^1(\pi, \gamma_1) \leq v^2(\pi, \gamma_2)$ if and only if:

(8.8)
$$\pi \leq \frac{3k-2}{1-k} \quad \text{when } k < 1$$

$$\pi \geq \frac{3k-2}{1-k} \quad \text{when } k > 1$$

There are six cases to consider.

Case (i). $k < 1, 3k \leq 2$.
   Then $v^1(\pi, \gamma_1)$ is only less than $v^2(\pi, \gamma_2)$ when $\pi < 0$. This never occurs, and so (8.7a) may be written

$$\sup_\gamma \int_0^1 \left(\frac{3+\pi}{2}\right)^2 \sqrt{\gamma_2}\, d\pi.$$

Case (ii). $k < 1, 0 < 3k - 2$, and $(3k - 2)/(1 - k) < 1$.
   In this case, according to (8.8), (8.7a) becomes

$$\sup_\gamma \int_0^{\frac{3k-2}{1-k}} \left(\frac{2+\pi}{2}\right)^2 \sqrt{\gamma_1}\, d\pi + \int_{\frac{3k-2}{1-k}}^1 \left(\frac{3+\pi}{2}\right)^2 \sqrt{\gamma_2}\, d\pi.$$

Case (iii). $k < 1, 3k - 2 > 0$, and $(3k - 2)/(1 - k) \geq 1$.
   In this case, according to (8.8), $v^1(\pi, \gamma_1) \leq v^2(\pi, \gamma_2)$ for all π, and (8.7a) becomes:

$$\sup_\gamma \int_0^1 \left(\frac{2+\pi}{2}\right)^2 \sqrt{\gamma_1}\, d\pi.$$

Case (iv). $k > 1, 3k \geq 2$.

In this case, we have $v^1(\pi, \gamma_1) \leq v^2(\pi, \gamma_2)$ for all π, and (8.7a) becomes:

$$\sup_\gamma \int_0^1 \left(\frac{2 + \pi}{2}\right)^2 \sqrt{\gamma_1} \, d\pi.$$

Case (v). $k > 1, 3k < 2$, and $(3k - 2)/(1 - k) \leq 1$.

This case is impossible: $k > 1$ implies $3k > 2$.

Case (vi). $k > 1, 3k < 2$, and $(3k - 2)/(1 - k) \geq 1$.

This case is likewise impossible.

We must next solve the first four cases. The one which gives the largest value for the objective is the global solution.

Case (i).

The integral computes to $\frac{37}{12}\sqrt{\gamma_2}$. Hence we must solve the program, to choose γ^1, γ^2 to

$$\max \quad \frac{37}{12}\sqrt{\gamma_2}$$

$$\text{s.t.} \quad \gamma_2 \leq \gamma_1$$

$$\gamma_2 \leq \frac{16}{81}\gamma_1$$

$$5\gamma_1 + 7\gamma_2 = 8$$

$$\gamma_1, \gamma_2 \geq 0.$$

The first constraint is "$k \leq 1$"; the second constraint is "$3k \leq 2$"; the third constraint is feasibility. Clearly the first constraint is not binding. Graphing the other constraints in the $\gamma_1 \times \gamma_2$ plane, and noting that the objective is equivalent to "max γ_2," we see that the solution occurs at the intersection of the lines $\gamma_2 = \frac{16}{81}\gamma_1$ and $5\gamma_1 + 7\gamma_2 = 8$, that is, $\hat{\gamma}_2 = 0.248$.

Hence the value of the objective, $\frac{37}{12}\sqrt{\hat{\gamma}_2}$, is 1.53.

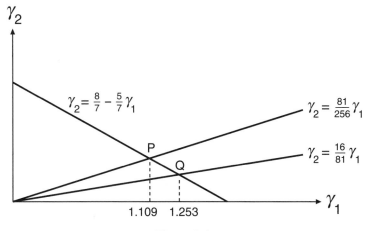

Figure 8.1

Case (ii).

The constraints are

$$\gamma_2 \le \gamma_1 \qquad (k \le 1)$$

$$\gamma_2 \ge \tfrac{16}{81}\gamma_1 \qquad (0 \le 3k - 2)$$

$$\gamma_2 \le \tfrac{81}{256}\gamma_1 \qquad (3k - 2 \le 1 - k)$$

$$5\gamma_1 + 7\gamma_2 = 8 \quad \text{(feasibility).}$$

The feasible set is the line segment $\overline{PQ}$ in Figure 8.1. Thus we may write the feasible set as

$$(8.9) \qquad \gamma_1 \in [1.109, 1.253], \qquad \gamma_2 = \frac{8 - 5\gamma_1}{7}.$$

Integrating the objective gives

$$\sup_{\gamma}\left\{ \left(\frac{2}{3}\left(\frac{2 + \frac{3k-2}{1-k}}{2} \right)^3 - \frac{2}{3} \right)\sqrt{\gamma_1} \right.$$

$$\left. + \left(\frac{2}{3}\left(\frac{5}{2} \right)^2 - \frac{2}{3}\left(\frac{3 + \frac{3k-2}{1-k}}{2} \right)^3 \right)\sqrt{\gamma_2} \right\},$$

which must be maximized subject to (8.9). This is a nice problem for *Mathematica*; the solution is $\gamma_1 = 1.168$, $\gamma_2 = 0.309$, and the objective's value is 1.106.

Case (iii).

Here, the problem is

$$\max_{\gamma} \quad \frac{19}{12}\sqrt{\gamma_1}$$

$$\text{s.t.} \quad \gamma_2 \leq \gamma_1 \qquad (k \leq 1)$$

$$\gamma_2 \geq \frac{16}{81}\gamma_1 \qquad (3k \geq 2)$$

$$\gamma_2 \geq \frac{81}{256}\gamma_1 \qquad \left(\frac{3k-2}{1-k} \geq 1\right)$$

$$\gamma_2 = \frac{8 - 5\gamma_1}{7} \qquad \text{(feasibility)}$$

$$\gamma_1, \gamma_2 \geq 0.$$

Graphing shows the solution is at $\gamma_1 = 1.109$, and the objective's value is 1.667.

Case (iv).

Here, the problem is

$$\max_{\gamma} \quad \frac{19}{12}\sqrt{\gamma_1}$$

$$\text{s.t.} \quad \gamma_2 \leq \gamma_1 \qquad (k \leq 1)$$

$$\gamma_2 \geq \frac{16}{81}\gamma_1 \qquad (3k - 2 \geq 0)$$

$$\gamma_2 = \frac{8 - 5\gamma_1}{7}$$

$$\gamma_1, \gamma_2 \geq 0.$$

Graphing shows that the solution occurs at $\gamma_1 = \frac{2}{3}$. Since the objective is the same as in Case (iii), the solution here is dominated by Case (iii) (that is, $\frac{19}{12}\sqrt{\frac{2}{3}} < 1.667$).

Reviewing the four cases, we see the solution to the maximization problem occurs in Case (iii), when $\gamma_1 = 1.109$ and $\gamma_2 = 0.351$. One may compute that these values give rise to levels of advantage in the interval $[2.37, 3.23]$ for individuals in A^1, and to levels of advantage in the interval $[3.0, 3.70]$ for individuals in A^2. So the best-off, in terms of advantage, are the high-effort persons of type 2. Note that high-effort persons of type 1 do better (always in terms of advantage) than do low-effort persons of type 2.

Let us call the solution just computed $\varphi^{E,2}$: it is associated with the partition of the society A into two intervals of equal measure (recall the distribution of α is uniform on A). Denote by $\varphi^{E,n}$ the solution where A is divided into n intervals of equal length. The next exercise is to ask: What mechanism does $\varphi^{E,n}$ converge to (if any), as $n \to \infty$? As the partition becomes ever finer, society is holding individuals less and less responsible for their α value, but is continuing to hold them responsible for their effort, conditional upon being in a small interval in A.

Let us set up the problem for $n = 3$. The intervals are $A^1 = \left[1, \frac{4}{3}\right)$, $A^2 = \left[\frac{4}{3}, \frac{5}{3}\right)$, $A^3 = \left[\frac{5}{3}, 2\right]$. Again, the effort response is given by $e(\alpha, \gamma) = \alpha$. We may hence write, in terms of quantiles:

$$e^1(\pi, \gamma) = 1 + \frac{1}{3}\pi, \qquad e^2(\pi, \gamma) = \frac{4}{3} + \frac{1}{3}\pi,$$

$$e^3(\pi, \gamma) = \frac{5}{3} + \frac{1}{3}\pi.$$

We may then compute that

$$v^i(\pi, \gamma_i) = \left(\frac{2+i}{3} + \frac{\pi}{3}\right)^2 \sqrt{\gamma_i}, \qquad i = 1, 2, 3.$$

The feasibility constraint computes to $7\gamma_1 + 9\gamma_2 + 11\gamma_3 = 18$. Indeed we may write the problem as:

(8.10)
$$\varphi^{E,3} = \sup_{\gamma_1, \gamma_2, \gamma_3} \int_0^1 \min_{i=1,2,3} \left(\frac{2+i}{3} + \frac{\pi}{3}\right)^2 \sqrt{\gamma_i} \, d\pi$$

s.t. $7\gamma_1 + 9\gamma_2 + 11\gamma_3 = 18$.

Examining the specification of $\varphi^{E,2}$ in (8.7ab) and of $\varphi^{E,3}$ in (8.10) allows us to deduce the formulation for $\varphi^{E,n}$, for any n:

$$\varphi^{E,n} = \sup_{\gamma} \int_0^1 \min_{i=1,\dots n} \left(\frac{n-1+i}{n} + \frac{\pi}{n} \right)^2 \sqrt{\gamma_i} d\pi$$

(8.11)

$$\text{s.t.} \quad \sum_{i=1}^n (2n-1+2i)\gamma_i = 2n^2, \quad \gamma \in \mathbf{R}_+^n.$$

Let us, before proceeding further, solve another problem. What does the Rawlsian mechanism [see (8.4)] converge to as n approaches infinity? This can be calculated by allowing the planner to choose a function $\varphi(e,\alpha) = \gamma(\alpha)e$, where $\gamma(\alpha)$ is an unrestricted function of α, so as to maximize minimum advantage over all individuals. The transfer rule $\varphi(e,\alpha)$ tailors the coefficient on effort exactly to fit each person. The effort response of α to the schedule $\varphi(e,\alpha) = \gamma(\alpha)e$ is, of course, still α. Thus, α's advantage will be $\alpha^2 \sqrt{\gamma(\alpha)}$. Hence the planner's problem is to choose the function $\gamma(\alpha)$ to

$$\sup_{\gamma} \inf_{\alpha} \alpha^2 \sqrt{\gamma(\alpha)}$$

(8.12)

$$\text{s.t.} \quad \int_1^2 \gamma(\alpha)\alpha d\alpha = 1.$$

I shall assume as well that $\gamma(\cdot)$ is restricted to be continuous.

We shall solve (8.12) as follows. Let us consider all functions $\gamma(\cdot)$ that render the individual $\alpha = 1$ the worst-off individual, that is,

$$\forall \alpha \in A \quad \alpha^2 \sqrt{\gamma(\alpha)} \geq \sqrt{\gamma(1)}$$

or $\gamma(\alpha) \geq \gamma(1)/\alpha^4$. Feasibility thus requires that $\int_1^2 (\gamma(1)/\alpha^4)\alpha d\alpha \leq 1$. This inequality can be integrated to deliver:

$$\gamma(1) \leq \frac{8}{3}.$$

Let us, now, choose $\hat{\gamma}(1) = 8/3$ and $\hat{\gamma}(\alpha) = 8/(3\alpha^4)$. $\hat{\gamma}$ is feasible, and, by its choice, is clearly the feasible function that renders individual 1 as well-off as possible among all allocation rules that render him the worst-off.

Note that, indeed, $\hat{\gamma}$ equalizes advantage for all $\alpha \in A$: $\alpha^2\sqrt{\gamma(\alpha)} = \sqrt{\frac{8}{3}}$ for all α. But it now follows that $\hat{\gamma}$ is the solution to (8.12). For suppose there were a function $\gamma(\alpha)$ that produced a value of the objective in (8.12) greater than $\sqrt{\frac{8}{3}}$. Then

$$\inf_{\alpha} \alpha^2 \sqrt{\gamma(\alpha)} > \sqrt{\frac{8}{3}},$$

which says $\gamma(\alpha) > 8/(3\alpha^4)$. This implies $\int_1^2 \gamma(\alpha)\alpha d\alpha > \int_1^2 (8/3\alpha^3)d\alpha = 1$, which contradicts feasibility.

Thus the limit of the Rawlsian transfer rules $\varphi^{R,n}$ as n goes to infinity is the transfer rule $\varphi(\alpha) = 8/(3\alpha^4)$.

We now return to the problem of computing what $\varphi^{E,n}$ converges to as $n \to \infty$. Recall that $\varphi^{E,n}$ is specified by a vector $\gamma^n \in \mathbf{R}_+^n$; we write $\gamma^n = (\gamma_1^n, \gamma_2^n, \ldots, \gamma_n^n)$. I will first show that as n becomes large, the value of the objective in (8.11) approaches a number greater than or equal to $\sqrt{\frac{8}{3}}$. For the n-partition, consider the vector $\bar{\gamma}^n$ defined by

(8.13) $$\bar{\gamma}_i^n = \frac{8}{3\left(1 + \frac{i}{n}\right)^4}, \qquad i = 1, \ldots, n.$$

$\bar{\gamma}^n$ may not be feasible, but in the limit it is. To see this, we compute the feasibility constraint of (8.11) at $\bar{\gamma}^n$:

$$\sum_{i=1}^n (2n - 1 + 2i)\frac{8}{3\left(1 + \frac{i}{n}\right)^4} = 2n^2 \iff$$

$$\sum_{i=1}^n \frac{2n - 1 + 2i}{n^2\left(1 + \frac{i}{n}\right)^4} = \frac{3}{4} \iff$$

(8.14) $$\sum_{i=1}^n \frac{2 - \frac{1}{n} + 2\frac{i}{n}}{n\left(1 + \frac{i}{n}\right)^4} = \frac{3}{4}.$$

As n gets large we may ignore the $\frac{1}{n}$ term in the numerator, and hence the last sum converges to

$$(8.15) \qquad \sum_{i=1}^{n} \frac{2\left(1+\frac{i}{n}\right)}{n\left(1+\frac{i}{n}\right)^4} = \sum_{i=1}^{n} \frac{\frac{2}{n}}{\left(1+\frac{i}{n}\right)^3} = 2\sum_{i=1}^{n} \frac{\frac{1}{n}}{\left(1+\frac{i}{n}\right)^3}.$$

But the last term in Equation (8.15) converges to the integral $2\int_0^1 (dx/(1+x)^3)$ which equals $\frac{3}{4}$. It follows that, in the limit, the vector $\bar{\gamma}^n$ is feasible. That is, for n large, there is a feasible vector γ^n for program (8.11) which yields an objective value arbitrarily close to the objective value engendered by $\bar{\gamma}^n$. This follows since the objective is a continuous function of γ^n.

Let us next compute what the objective of (8.11) converges to at the vectors $\bar{\gamma}^n$. Let us compute the term involved in the integrand of the objective of (8.11),

$$\left(\frac{n-1+i+\pi}{n}\right)^2 \sqrt{\bar{\gamma}_i^n},$$

which equals:

$$(8.16) \qquad \left(\frac{n-1+i+\pi}{n}\right)^2 \sqrt{\frac{8}{3\left(1+\frac{i}{n}\right)^4}} = \sqrt{\frac{8}{3}} \frac{\left(\frac{n-1+i+\pi}{n}\right)^2}{\left(1+\frac{i}{n}\right)^2}.$$

As $n \to \infty$, this term approaches $\sqrt{\frac{8}{3}}$, independently of π and i, since the numerator in (8.16) approaches $\left(1+\frac{i}{n}\right)^2$. It thus follows that the integral in (8.11) approaches $\sqrt{\frac{8}{3}}$.

We have therefore shown that:

$$(8.17) \qquad \limsup_{n\to\infty} \int_0^1 \min_{i=1,\dots,n} \left(\frac{n-1+i}{n} + \frac{\pi}{n}\right)^2 \sqrt{\bar{\gamma}_i^n} \, d\pi \geq \sqrt{\frac{8}{3}}.$$

The final task is to show equality holds in (8.17). It will then follow that $\bar{\gamma}^n$ becomes arbitrarily close to a solution of (8.11) as n becomes large.

Let $\{\gamma^n\}$ be any sequence of feasible solutions for (8.11). For each $\pi \in [0, 1]$, let

$$(8.18) \qquad i(\pi) = \arg \min_i \left(\frac{n - 1 + i + \pi}{n} \right)^2 \sqrt{\gamma_i^n}.$$

Then we may write the integral in (8.17) as

$$(8.19) \qquad \int_0^1 \left(\frac{n - 1 + i(\pi) + \pi}{n} \right)^2 \sqrt{\gamma_{i(\pi)}^n} \, d\pi;$$

and by the definition of $i(\pi)$, we have, for all i,

$$\pi \left(\frac{n - 1 + i(\pi) + \pi}{n} \right)^2 \sqrt{\gamma_{i(\pi)}^n} \le \left(\frac{n - 1 + i(\pi) + \pi}{n} \right)^2 \sqrt{\gamma_i^n}$$

$$\le \left(\frac{n + i}{n} \right)^2 \sqrt{\gamma_i^n}.$$

Hence, for any $i \le n$ the expression (8.19) is less than or equal to:

$$(8.20) \qquad \int_0^1 \left(\frac{n + i}{n} \right)^2 \sqrt{\gamma_i^n} \, d\pi = \left(\frac{n + i}{n} \right)^2 \sqrt{\gamma_i^n}.$$

Let $\frac{i}{n} \equiv \delta$; the expression on the right-hand side of (8.20) can be written $(1 + \delta)^2 \sqrt{\gamma_{\delta n}^n}$ where by the subscript "δn," I mean the closest integer to δn.
It follows that

$$(8.21) \qquad \begin{aligned} &\limsup_{n \to \infty} \int_0^1 \inf_\gamma \inf_i \left(\frac{n - 1 + i + \pi}{n} \right)^2 \sqrt{\gamma_i^n} \, d\pi \\ &\qquad \le \lim_{n \to \infty} \inf_{0 < \delta < 1} (1 + \delta)^2 \sqrt{\gamma_{\delta n}^n}. \end{aligned}$$

Now suppose

$$\lim_{n \to \infty} \inf_{0 < \delta < 1} (1 + \delta)^2 \sqrt{\gamma_{\delta n}^n} > \sqrt{\frac{8}{3}}.$$

It would then follow, for all δ, that

$$\lim_{n \to \infty} \gamma_{\delta n}^n > \frac{8}{3} \frac{1}{(1+\delta)^4}.$$

But this contradicts the feasibility constraint: for the earlier calculation leading to (8.15) shows that, if

$$\lim_{n \to \infty} \gamma_{\delta n}^n = \frac{8}{3} \frac{1}{(1+\delta)^4},$$

then $\{\gamma^n\}$ approaches a feasible solution which just exhausts the aggregate resource endowment.

This proves that, indeed, the inequality in (8.17) is an equation, and hence the solution of the program (8.11) gets arbitrarily close to $\bar{\gamma}^n$ as n gets large. Now, fixing $\alpha \in [1, 2]$ and taking a sequence of fractions $\left\{1 + \frac{i}{n}\right\}$ where $1 + \frac{i}{n} \to \alpha$, we see, from (8.13), that $\{\bar{\gamma}^n\}$ can be said to approach the function $\varphi(\alpha) = 8/(3\alpha^4)$. But $\varphi(\alpha)$ was shown to be the "Rawlsian" solution to the program (8.12). It therefore follows that, *as the partition of A becomes ever finer, $\varphi^{E,n}$ approaches the Rawlsian solution.* This result confirms the intuition that, as persons are held decreasingly responsible for their choices (that is, the number of types becomes infinite), the EOp mechanism approaches full equality of advantage.

Finally, we may compute the solution $\varphi^{E,1}$, when the partition into types is as coarse as possible—namely, when all individuals are of one type. In this case, the planner chooses a number γ to

$$\max_{\gamma} \quad \int_1^2 \alpha^2 \sqrt{\gamma} \, d\alpha$$

$$\text{s.t.} \quad \int_1^2 \alpha \gamma \, d\alpha = 1.$$

The solution is, trivially, $\gamma = \frac{2}{3}$: the planner announces the function $\varphi(e) = \frac{2}{3} e$.

To summarize the calculations, write $\tilde{u}(\alpha; \varphi)$ for the advantage of α under solution φ. Then we have:

$$\tilde{u}(\alpha; \varphi^{E,1}) = \alpha^2 \sqrt{\frac{2}{3}},$$

$$\tilde{u}(\alpha; \varphi^{E,2}) = \begin{cases} \alpha^2 \sqrt{1.109} & \text{for } 1 \le \alpha \le 1.5 \\ \alpha^2 \sqrt{0.351} & \text{for } 1.5 < \alpha \le 2 \end{cases}$$

$$\tilde{u}(\alpha; \varphi^{E,\infty}) = \sqrt{\frac{8}{3}}.$$

8.5.2 An Example in a Production Economy

In this example, we examine the issue of compensating individuals for low incomes, where income is a function of education received, and education chosen is a function both of a circumstantial variable beyond the individual's control (talent) and of a variable within the person's control (effort). We shall compare the action of the EOp, utilitarian, and Rawlsian mechanisms. Let *utility* be given by $u(x, e; a) = x - e^2/(2a)$, where x is income, e is years of education, and a is talent. In this case, we take advantage to be welfare as measured by utility. The relationship between education and income is given by $x(e) = \delta e$. In the population, "a" takes on positive values $a_1 < a_2 < \ldots < a_r$, with frequencies $p_1, \ldots, p_r$. People are viewed as not responsible for the value of "a."

We shall limit the set of feasible tax schemes $\mathcal{T}$ to linear income taxes, of the form $\tau(x) = d_0 + d_1 x$. Were an agent of type j an optimizer with utility function u, she would, facing the linear tax scheme (d_0, d_1), solve the problem

$$\max_e (1 - d_1)\delta e - \frac{e^2}{2a_j},$$

yielding $e = \delta a_j(1 - d_1)$. We shall assume, however, that, among those of type j, actual educational levels achieved are given by a random variable $e(d_1, a_j)$ which depends upon type and the tax scheme:

(8.22) $e(d_1, a_j)(y) = \delta a_j y(1 - d_1),$

where y is uniformly distributed on $[0, 1]$. In terms of our previous notation, $F_{d_1}^j$ is the uniform distribution on $[0, \delta a_j(1 - d_1)]$ for all (a_j, d_1). We may therefore write the education level, as a function of type (a_j) and quantile within type (π), as:

(8.23) $\hat{e}^j(d_1, \pi) = \delta a_j \pi (1 - d_1)$.

The interpretation of (8.22) may be that willpower is required to undertake the amount of education that, rationally, one should. Most people, because of weakness of will, only undertake a fraction of the education that they should. The EOp planner is an egalitarian who wishes to compensate persons for their differential native talent, that being beyond their control, but not for their weakness of will.

From (8.23) it follows that income levels, as a function of type and "willpower" are:

(8.24) $\hat{x}^j(d_1, \pi) = \delta^2 a_j \pi (1 - d_1)$.

We now define feasibility of a tax scheme (d_0, d_1) by the balanced budget condition:

$$d_1 \int_0^1 \sum p_i \hat{x}^i(d_1, \pi) d\pi + d_0 = 0$$

or

(8.25) $$d_0 = -d_1 \int_0^1 \sum_i p_i \hat{x}^i(d_1, \pi) d\pi.$$

Thus the set of feasible tax schemes $\mathcal{T}$ can be identified by the single parameter $d_1 \in [0, 1]$, where d_0 is given by (8.25). I shall, from now on, refer to the generic tax scheme as "d_1."

Substituting from (8.24) into (8.25), we have:

$$d_0 = -\sum_j p_j d_1 (1 - d_1) \delta^2 a_j \int_0^1 \pi d\pi$$

or,

(8.26) $$d_0 = d_1 (1 - d_1) \delta^2 \frac{\bar{a}}{2}$$

where

$$\bar{a} \equiv \sum p_j a_j.$$

We can then write the utility of a type j individual at the πth centile of his type with respect to education achieved as:

$$(8.27) \quad v^j(\pi, d_1) = \delta^2 a_j \pi(1 - d_1)^2 - d_0 - \frac{1}{2}\delta^2 a_j \pi^2(1 - d_1)^2,$$

where d_0 is given by (8.26).

Our task is to find d_1 to maximize $\int_0^1 \min_j v^j(\pi, d_1)d\pi$.

To find $\arg \min_j v^j(\pi, d_1)$, we examine the coefficient of a_j in (8.27),

$$\delta^2 \pi(1 - d_1)^2 - \frac{1}{2}\delta^2 \pi^2(1 - d_1)^2,$$

which has the same sign as $1 - \frac{1}{2}\pi$, and hence is positive for all $\pi \in [0, 1]$. It follows that for all π, $1 = \arg \min_j v^j(\pi, d_1)$, and so our maximization problem can be written:

$$\sup_{d_1} \left(\delta^2 a_1(1 - d_1)^2 \int_0^1 \left(\pi - \frac{1}{2}\pi^2 \right) d\pi - d_0 \right),$$

or, using (8.26) and integrating:

$$(8.28) \quad \sup_{d_1} \left(\frac{\delta^2 a_1(1 - d_1)^2}{3} + \frac{d_1(1 - d_1)\delta^2 \bar{a}}{2} \right).$$

We can factor out δ^2 from (8.28), and expand, and we have

$$(8.29) \quad \varphi^E(E) = \arg \sup_{d_1} [2a_1 - d_1(4a_1 - 3\bar{a}) + d_1^2(2a_1 - 3\bar{a})].$$

Since $a_1 = \min a_j$, we have $2a_1 - 3\bar{a} < 0$ and it follows that the function in brackets in (8.29) is concave in d_1. Hence setting its derivative with respect to d_1 equal to zero yields

$$\tilde{d}_1 = \frac{4a_1 - 3\bar{a}}{4a_1 - 6\bar{a}},$$

which is the required tax rate if $\tilde{d}_1 \in [0, 1]$. Noting the denominator of $\tilde{d}_1$ is negative, but the numerator can be either positive or negative or zero, we have

$$
(8.30) \quad \varphi^E(\mathcal{E}) = \begin{cases} 0 & \text{if } \frac{a_1}{\bar{a}} \geq \frac{3}{4} \\ \frac{1 - \frac{4}{3}\frac{a_1}{\bar{a}}}{2 - \frac{4}{3}\frac{a_1}{\bar{a}}} & \text{if } \frac{a_1}{\bar{a}} \leq \frac{3}{4}. \end{cases}
$$

In sum, the egalitarian mechanism φ^E does not redistribute at all if the variance among the $\{a_j\}$ is sufficiently small ($a_1/\bar{a} > 3/4$), but does tax, up to a maximum marginal tax rate of $d_1 = \frac{1}{2}$, as $a_1/\bar{a}$ approaches zero.

Next we calculate the utilitarian mechanism, φ^U, recalling this is equivalent to placing all individuals in a single type. We have

$$
\varphi^U(\mathcal{E}) = \arg\sup_{d_1} \sum_j \int_0^1 p_j(\delta^2 a_j \pi(1 - d_1)^2 - d_0
$$

$$
(8.31) \qquad\qquad - \frac{1}{2}\delta^2 a_j \pi^2(1 - d_1)^2)d\pi,
$$

which can be reduced to

$$
\varphi^U(\mathcal{E}) = \arg\sup_{d_1}[2(1 - d_1)^2 + 3d_1(1 - d_1)],
$$

which in turn implies $\varphi^U(\mathcal{E}) = 0$. There is no taxation under the utilitarian scheme.

Finally, we may compute the Rawlsian mechanism, φ^R, in which individuals are responsible neither for their type nor for their "effort":

$$
\varphi^R(\mathcal{E}) = \arg\sup_{d_1} \min_{j,\pi} \left(\delta^2 a_j \pi(1 - d_1)^2 - d_0 - \frac{1}{2}\delta^2 a_j \pi^2(1 - d_1)^2 \right)
$$

$$
= \arg\sup_{d_1} \min_{\pi} \left(\delta^2 a_1 \pi(1 - d_1)^2(1 - \frac{1}{2}\pi) + d_1(1 - d_1)\delta^2 \frac{\bar{a}}{2} \right)
$$

$$
= \arg\sup_{d_1} d_1(1 - d_1)\delta^2 \frac{\bar{a}}{2}
$$

$$
= \frac{1}{2}.
$$

In sum, we have

$$(8.32) \quad 0 = \varphi^U(\mathcal{E}) \le \varphi^E(\mathcal{E}) \le \varphi^R(\mathcal{E}) = \frac{1}{2}.$$

Since we can say, for linear tax schemes, that the degree of redistribution is measured by the size of d_1, it follows from (8.32) that φ^E redistributes no more than φ^R and no less than φ^U. Furthermore, (8.30) shows
that the inequalities in (8.32) are tight: there are nondegenerate environments $\mathcal{E}$ such that $\varphi^E = \varphi^U$, and there is a sequence of nondegenerate
environments $\mathcal{E}^k$ such that $\lim |\varphi^E(\mathcal{E}^k) - \varphi^R(\mathcal{E}^k)| = 0$. In words, φ^E may
prescribe any tax rate between what a Rawlsian and a utilitarian would rec-
ommend.

A comment on a difference between the example in §8.5.1 and in the
present section is in order. In §8.5.1, I assumed that the EOp mechanism
could indeed assign a different effort reward schedule to each type, while
in the example just completed, a single income tax function is used for
all types. In actual situations, something in between these two extremes
will usually be politically feasible. There are two advantages in constrain-
ing the EOp mechanism to use the same redistribution function for all
types: there will be, in this case, no reason for an individual to attempt
to dissemble about her type, and "backlash" will be minimized. (Backlash
occurs when members of one type resent the preferential treatment af-
forded to another type, with the political consequence of jeopardizing the
implementation of the EOp policy.) On the other hand, the advantage of
allowing differentiation of the policy according to types is, clearly, to increase the value of the EOp objective (fewer constraints). In the United
States, current tax policy is differentiated for some types who, almost everyone agrees, should receive preferential treatment (for example, people
with certain kinds of handicaps). Households with children also receive
differentiated tax treatment. In practice, it would be advisable, for both
incentive and political reasons, to constrain the EOp mechanism to using the same tax function (if redistribution of income is intended) for
many types. Thus use of the EOp mechanism will not, in general, require that individuals reveal their types. The (optimal) mechanism must
be computed, however, using data from a sample in which types are
known—specifically, from which labor-supply elasticities can be computed
by type.

8.6   Related Approaches to Equality of Opportunity

In this section I describe the approaches that Fleurbaey (1994, 1995) and Bossert (1995) have taken to the problem of equality of opportunity in their recent work.

Bossert (1995) supposes that a society, N, consists of n individuals, each of whom is characterized by a vector of traits $a_i = (a_i^R, a_i^S) \in \mathbf{R}^{r+s}$. a_i^R is the vector of "relevant" traits—the traits for which society will hold individuals responsible—and a_i^S is the vector of "irrelevant" traits—what I have called circumstances. Income (not utility) is assumed to be given by a function $f(a_i)$. Thus income is a function only of the individual's traits, and it is *not* affected by taxes. This, I believe, is the most restrictive assumption of Bossert's model. We write the various profiles of characteristics as $a = (a_1, \ldots, a_n)$, $a^R = (a_1^R, \ldots, a_n^R)$, and $a^S = (a_1^S, \ldots, a_n^S)$. Let the domain of possible traits be $\Omega \subset \mathbf{R}^{r+s}$.

A *redistribution mechanism* is a mapping $F : \Omega^n \to \mathbf{R}_{++}^N$ such that $\sum_{i=1}^n F_i(a) = \sum_{i=1}^n f(a_i)$ for all $a \in \Omega^n$. This is just the balanced budget condition: $F_i(a)$ is the income individual i receives if the profile of traits is a. The task is to find a mechanism F under which i's (post-tax) income is responsive to his relevant traits but not to his irrelevant traits.

Suppose that f is *additively separable in R and S*: that is, for all $a_i \in \Omega$, $f(a_i) = g(a_i^R) + h(a_i^S)$. This is clearly a strong restriction. In this case, there is an obvious redistribution mechanism, namely F^0, defined by

$$F_k^0(a) = g(a_k^R) + \frac{1}{n} \sum_{i=1}^n h(a_i^S), \qquad \text{for } k = 1, \ldots, n.$$

F^0 gives each individual the income generated by her relevant traits, and a lump sum equal to average income generated by society's irrelevant traits. F^0 implements equality of opportunity for *income* in the sense this chapter has proposed.

Bossert characterizes the mechanism F^0 with two axioms.

No Redistribution for Equal S (NR).

$$a_i^S = a_j^S \ \forall i, j \in N \quad \Rightarrow \quad F_i(a) = f(a_i), \qquad \text{for all } i \in N,$$

Group Solidarity in S (GS). $\forall a, \hat{a} \in \mathbf{R}^{n(r+s)}, \forall k \in N,$

$a_k^R = \hat{a}_n^R$ and

$$a_j = \hat{a}_j \; \forall_j \in N \backslash \{k\} \quad \Rightarrow \quad F_i(\hat{a}) - F_i(a) = F_j(\hat{a}) - F_j(a),$$

$$\forall i, j \in N.$$

NR states that if everyone's vector of irrelevant traits is identical, then there should be no redistribution. GS is an interprofile condition. Suppose under profiles a and $\hat{a}$, no individual's relevant traits differ, and, except for individual k, no individual's irrelevant traits differ either. Then the change of the income allocated to all individuals must be the same, that is, the gain or loss of income owing to a change in one person's irrelevant traits should be identical.

These are certainly appealing, if strong, axioms. Bossert proves:

Theorem 8.1. *A redistribution mechanism satisfies NR and GS iff f is additively separable in R and S and $F = F^0$.*

In particular, there is no redistribution mechanism satisfying NR and GS if f fails to be separable.

Bossert obtains a second characterization of F^0 with two more axioms.

Equal Distribution for Equal Relevant Traits (ER). $\forall a \in \Omega^n$:

$$a_i^R = a_j^R \; \forall i, j \in N \quad \Rightarrow \quad F_i(a) = F_j(a) \quad \forall i, j \in N.$$

Individual Monotonicity in Relevant Traits (IM). $\forall a, \hat{a} \in \Omega^n, \forall k \in N$:

$$a_k^S = \hat{a}_k^S \text{ and } a_j = \hat{a}_j \; \forall j \in N \backslash \{k\}$$
$$\Rightarrow \quad F_j(\hat{a}) = F_j(a) \quad \forall j \in N \backslash \{k\}.$$

ER is, informally speaking, the ethical dual of NR, and IM is the ethical dual of GS. It is therefore satisfying that Bossert establishes:

Theorem 8.2. *A redistribution mechanism satisfies ER and IM iff f is additively separable in R and S and $F = F^0$.*

Finally let us drop the restrictive assumption of additive separability in income. Let us further specify that the domain of traits Ω is itself a product space: $\Omega = \Omega_R \times \Omega_S$ where $\Omega_R \subset \mathbf{R}^r$ and $\Omega_S \subset \mathbf{R}^s$. Bossert proposes the following mechanism, F^*:

$$F_k^*(a) := \gamma \sum_{i=1}^n f(a_k^R, a_i^S), \quad \forall a \in \Omega^n, \quad \forall k \in N,$$

where γ is a real number chosen so that F^* satisfies the budget constraint, that is, $\gamma = \left(\sum_{i=1}^n f(a_i^R, a_i^S) \right) \left(\sum_{i=1}^n f(a_k^R, a_i^S) \right) / \sum_{j=1}^n \sum_{i=1}^n f(a_j^R, a_i^S)$. F^* allocates to individual k the average of the incomes he would have, were he to have been endowed alternatively, with the irrelevant (S) traits of *every* member of society, always retaining his own relevant (R) traits. F^* does not require f to be additively separable, and it is arguably an attractive implementation of equality of opportunity for income.

Bossert discovers an axiomatic characterization of F^*, relying on a new axiom:

Additive Responsiveness with Respect to Irrelevant Traits (AS). $\exists b : \Omega^n \to \mathbf{R}$ such that, $\forall a, \hat{a} \in \Omega^n, \forall k \in N$: if $a_k^R = \hat{a}_k^R$ and $a_j = \hat{a}_j \ \forall j \in N\backslash\{k\}$, then

$$\frac{F_j(\hat{a})}{b(\hat{a})} - \frac{F_j(a)}{b(a)} = f(a_j^R, \hat{a}_k^S) - f(a_j^R, a_k^S) \quad \forall j \in N.$$

The premise of AS states that we are comparing two profiles of traits, a and $\hat{a}$, in which the only difference consists in the irrelevant traits of an individual, k: thus k's vector of irrelevant traits has changed from a_k^S to $\hat{a}_k^S$. The axiom asserts that the income of *each* individual should change just as it would have were *her* vector of irrelevant traits to have changed from a_k^S to $\hat{a}_k^S$, with a scale adjustment to render such an income change feasible.

Bossert proves:

Theorem 8.3. *A redistribution mechanism F satisfies NR and AS iff F = F^*.*

Bossert's environment differs in two ways from that of the production-economy example of §8.5: society is interested in equalizing opportunity for income, rather than a more general advantage, and the production behavior of individuals is, as noted earlier, not responsive to the tax system chosen. The latter characteristic is, in my view, undesirably restrictive.

Fleurbaey (1994, 1995) studies the problem of equality of opportunity in a framework more traditional than Bossert's, in which individuals care about welfare, not income as such. Society consists of n individuals; individual i is characterized by a vector of nontransferable consumption talents/handicaps y_i and a preference order R_i on $\mathbf{R}_+ \times Y$, where Y is a space containing all possible values of y_i. Society has a fixed amount $\omega \in \mathbf{R}_{++}$ of a transferable good (money) to divide among the citizens. Let $y = (y_1, \ldots, y_n)$ and $R = (R_1, \ldots, R_n)$ be the profiles of "handicaps" and preferences. An economy is a quadruple $\mathcal{E} = \langle n, y, R, \omega \rangle$. A *solution* is a single-valued map φ on a domain of economies that assigns an allocation of ω to the individuals. Let $\varphi_i(\mathcal{E})$ be the amount of the transferable good assigned to i by φ; then we require $\sum \varphi_i(\mathcal{E}) = \omega$.

The implicit assumption is that individuals are responsible for their preferences but not for their handicaps. Fleurbaey introduces two axioms. Let $\mathcal{D}$ be the domain of economies such that preferences can be represented by utility functions $u_i(x, y)$, $x \in \mathbf{R}_+$, $y \in Y$, which are continuous and strictly increasing in x. The first axiom is:

Equal Resource for Equal Handicap (EREH).

$$\forall \mathcal{E} \in \mathcal{D}, \ [\forall i, j, \ y_i = y_j] \quad \Rightarrow \quad \varphi_i(\mathcal{E}) = \varphi_j(\mathcal{E}).$$

That is, if two individuals have the same handicaps, they should be assigned an equal amount of "money." This axiom is intended to capture the idea that individuals are responsible for their preferences.

The second axiom is:

Equal Welfare for Equal Preference (EWEP).

$$\forall \mathcal{E} \in \mathcal{D}, \ [\forall i, j, \ R_i = R_j] \quad \Rightarrow \quad (\varphi_i(\mathcal{E}), y_i) I_i \ (\varphi_j(\mathcal{E}), y_j)$$
$$\text{or } \varphi_i(\mathcal{E}) = 0 \ \text{ and } \ (0, y_i) R_i(\varphi_j(\mathcal{E}), y_j)$$
$$\text{or } \varphi_j(\mathcal{E}) = 0 \ \text{ and } \ (0, y_j) R_i(\varphi_i(\mathcal{E}), y_i).$$

EWEP says that, if two individuals i and j have the same preferences, then each of them should be indifferent between his "extended bundle" (x_i, y_i) and the extended bundle of the other (x_j, y_j), where $x_k = \varphi_k(\mathcal{E})$ for $k = i, j$. (The rest of the axiom tells us what should be done if it is impossible to find an allocation of money that engenders the stipulated indifference.) This axiom captures the idea that individuals are not responsible for their handicaps and require social compensation for them.

EREH and EWEP are strong axioms and it is not surprising, as Fleurbaey shows, that they are generally incompatible. Consider his example

(Fleurbaey 1995) with four individuals. Let $Y = \mathbf{R}_+$, let $\mathcal{E} = \langle 4; (1, 1, 3, 3);$ $(R, R', R, R'); 5 \rangle$ where R and R' are represented, respectively, by $u(x, y) = x + y$ and $u'(x, y) = x + 2y$. By EREH, $x_1 = x_2$ and $x_3 = x_4$. Assume $x_i > 0$ for all i. Then EWEP requires $u(x_1, y_1) = u(x_3, y_3)$, that is, $x_1 = x_3 + 2$, and $u'(x_1, y_1) = u'(x_3, y_3)$, that is, $x_1 = x_3 + 4$. These two equations are inconsistent. Similar reasoning shows there is no solution in the cases when some x_i is zero.

Because of this impossibility, Fleurbaey weakens these two axioms to:

EREH*.

$$\forall \mathcal{E} \in \mathcal{D}, [\forall i, j, y_i = y_j] \quad \Rightarrow \quad [\forall i, j, \varphi_i(\mathcal{E}) = \varphi_j(\mathcal{E})].$$

and

EWEP*.

$$\forall \mathcal{E} \in \mathcal{D}, [\forall i, j, R_i = R_j] \quad \Rightarrow \quad [\forall i, j, (\varphi_i(\mathcal{E}), y_i) I_i (\varphi_j(\mathcal{E}), y_j)]$$
$$\text{or } \varphi_i(\mathcal{E}) = 0 \text{ and } (0, y_i) R_i \ (\varphi_j(\mathcal{E}), y_j)$$
$$\text{or } \varphi_j(\mathcal{E}) = 0 \text{ and } (0, y_j) R_i \ (\varphi_i(\mathcal{E}), y_i).$$

EREH* requires that pairs of individuals receive the same money transfer only when *all* individuals share the same handicaps, and similarly EWEP* requires that pairs of individuals be indifferent between their extended bundles only when *all* individuals have the same preferences. There are, indeed, many solutions that satisfy EWEP* and EREH*. There is, however, no solution on $\mathcal{D}$ that satisfies EWEP*, EREH*, and *stability* (in the sense defined in §2.3): namely, that the solution is "consistent" with respect to the reallocation of the resource among subgroups of the original society (Fleurbaey 1995, Cor. 1).[6]

Indeed, Fleurbaey further weakens EREH* and EWEP* as follows. Let $\tilde{y} \in Y$ and $\tilde{R}$ be a fixed (vector of) handicap(s) and preference order on $\mathbf{R}_+ \times Y$.

---

6. Following is a formal definition of stability. Let $\mathcal{E} = \langle n, y, R, \omega \rangle$ be an economy and let $\mathcal{E}' = \langle m, y^G, R^G, \omega' \rangle$ be an economy where G is a subgroup of the set of individuals N, in the first economy, m is the cardinality of G, and y^G and R^G are the handicap and preference profiles of G. φ is *stable* iff whenever $\omega' = \sum_{i \in G} \varphi_i(\mathcal{E})$ then $\varphi_k(\mathcal{E}') = \varphi_k(\mathcal{E})$ for all $k \in G$.

Axiom $\tilde{y}-$ EREH*.

$$\forall \mathcal{E} \in \mathcal{D}, [\forall i, y_i = \tilde{y}] \;\Rightarrow\; [\forall i, j, \varphi_i(\mathcal{E}) = \varphi_j(\mathcal{E})].$$

Axiom $\tilde{R}-$ EWEP*.

$$\forall \mathcal{E} \in \mathcal{D}, [\forall i, R_i = \tilde{R}] \;\Rightarrow\; [\forall i, j, (\varphi_i(\mathcal{E}), y_i)\tilde{I}(\varphi_j(\mathcal{E}), y_j)]$$
$$\text{or } \varphi_i(\mathcal{E}) = 0 \text{ and } (0, y_i)\tilde{R}(\varphi_j(\mathcal{E}), y_j)$$
$$\text{or } \varphi_j(\mathcal{E}) = 0 \text{ and } (0, y_j)\tilde{R}(\varphi_i(\mathcal{E}), y_i).$$

$\tilde{y}$ is a *reference handicap* and $\tilde{R}$ is a *reference preference order*: thus axiom $\tilde{y}-$ EREH* states that when all individuals have the reference profile $\tilde{y}$, all should receive the same money transfer, and axiom $\tilde{R}-$ EWEP* states that when all individuals share the same preference order then each individual should be indifferent between her extended allocation and the extended allocation of all others.

Note that $\tilde{y} -$ EREH* and $\tilde{R} -$ EWEP* can trivially be simultaneously fulfilled: simply define a mechanism φ that splits the resource equally whenever $\mathcal{E}$ is such that for all i, $y_i = \tilde{y}$, and that assigns an "equal welfare" allocation whenever $\mathcal{E}$ is such that everyone's preferences are $\tilde{R}$. φ can be arbitrarily defined on all other environments. What Fleurbaey shows, however, is that if in addition φ must be stable, then these new axioms effectively characterize two solutions.

The $\tilde{R}$-*conditionally equal solution* is the allocation of the resource $(x_1, \ldots, x_n)$ such that $\forall i, j (x_i, y_i)\tilde{I}(x_j, y_j)$ or $x_i = 0$ and $(0, y_i)\tilde{R}(x_i, y_j)$ or $x_j = 0$ and $(0, y_j)\tilde{R}(x_i, y_i)$. This is just the leximin solution with respect to any utility function representing $\tilde{R}$. The $\tilde{y}$-*egalitarian equivalent solution* assigns that allocation $(x_1, \ldots, x_n)$ such that $\exists \tilde{x}, \forall i, (x_i, y_i)I(\tilde{x}, \tilde{y})$, or $x_i = 0$ and $(0, y_i)R_i(\tilde{x}, \tilde{y})$: that is, the extended consumption bundle of each individual is indifferent, for her, to a given reference extended bundle. We have:

Theorem 8.4 (Fleurbaey 1995, Prop. 9). $\tilde{R}$-*conditional equality is the only stable solution on $\mathcal{D}$ which satisfies EREH* and $\tilde{R} -$ EWEP*. The $\tilde{y}$-egalitarian-equivalent solution is the only stable solution (on a suitable domain) which satisfies $\tilde{y} -$ EREH* and EWEP*.*

In summary, Fleurbaey's program, in these articles, is to begin with a pair of axioms (EREH and EWEP) that, he proposes, capture the essential requisites of equality of opportunity as I have characterized it in this chapter, namely, that persons should not be compensated on account of what is within their control (which Fleurbaey, along with Dworkin, takes to be preferences), but should be compensated on account of their circumstances (beyond their control). These axioms are too strong to be compatible on any interesting domain of economies. Furthermore, he considers consistency of resource allocation with respect to subgroups to be desirable. He then progressively weakens the two initial axioms until they are, essentially, compatible with consistency; moreover, the weakening is "just right" in the sense that, finally, single solutions are characterized.

A general comment on impossibility theorems, which applies to those in this section in particular, appears in the final sentence in §8.7: it contrasts the approach of Bossert and Fleurbaey to the approach I have taken in §§8.3–8.5.

8.7   Conclusion

Amartya Sen's (1979) initial attack on welfarism was based on examples in which some individuals' welfares were offensive: a welfarist must treat the welfare a sadist derives from whipping another as equally worthy, in the social calculus, as welfare derived from having enough to eat (see Sen's example reproduced in §1.3). Ronald Dworkin's and Thomas Scanlon's attacks on welfarism are entirely different, being based on the view that welfarism does not hold individuals accountable for certain kinds of choices they should be held responsible for: in particular, choices following from tastes with which they identify. Richard Arneson and G. A. Cohen agree with Dworkin and Scanlon that any defensible egalitarian theory must allow differences in advantage (or welfare) which reflect the differential responsibility that individuals have or take, but disagree that a person should be held responsible for the choices she makes just because those choices follow from preferences with which she identifies: rather, the salient question is whether those choices devolved from preferences which were within or beyond a person's control. The issue of responsibility was absent in the writing of Kolm, germinal in the writings of Rawls and Sen, and became focal in the writings of Dworkin, Scanlon, Arneson, and Cohen. It must, of course, be added that libertarians and neo-Lockeans have all the while emphasized the element of responsbility in distributive justice, but they have, in my view, taken a shallow approach to it in not taking serious account of the social factors beyond an individual's control which influence his formation, and of which account should be taken in rectifying the laissez-faire distribution of advantage. For these latter thinkers, rights of self-ownership trump any redistributive imperative deduced from considerations of responsibility.

Although I believe this new articulation of responsibility in the theory of distributive justice, and of egalitarian theory in particular, is the signal achievement in the field of the last fifteen years, I have concentrated, in the last two chapters, on weaknesses and incompleteness in the arguments as they now stand. Principal among these is a satisfactory articulation of "advantage." Sen advocates "capability," some measure of the size of an individual's set of available functionings, as the correct measure of advantage; Arneson advocates opportunity for welfare, but, I have argued, does not succeed in proposing a test which will avoid the problem of the tamed housewife (that is, that truncated conceptions of welfare formed as a response to poor opportunities should not be taken at face value in the social calculus). Cohen admits the depth of the problem, but has not thus far committed himself to a way of resolving it. Some objective measure of a person's condition should, it seems, surely count in the measure of advantage salient for distributive justice, for a purely subjective measure does not appear to permit a solution to the tamed housewife problem. Along these lines, Sen's functionings appear to be the most promising proposal, although, as I mentioned in Chapter 5, I would prefer not to include among functionings such subjective characteristics as "happiness," as Sen does. There is a value, I think, to defining advantage as some aggregation of objectively measurable characteristics (such as Sen's more observable functionings) and subjective characteristics (such as happiness). Or, as Cohen has put it, there is a kind of "midfare," perhaps only conceivable as a vector, that characterizes a state between having resources and enjoying welfare. That midfare should surely count, as well as more subjective welfare, in the measure of advantage. (For a very different "objective" measure, see Van Parijs's proposal, described in this book's appendix on envy-freeness.)

The proposal for implementing equality of opportunity for advantage that I have articulated in §§8.3–8.5, it must be emphasized, does not solve the deep problems just described: it is a tool for arriving at the just distribution of resources once the problems of defining advantage and of distinguishing circumstance from volition have been solved. Perhaps this division of labor is the typical one between the philosopher and the economist in the search for a theory of distributive justice: the philosopher's task is to discover the correct conceptual elements of the theory, and the economist's is to produce a workable (in particular, feasible) social policy that makes acceptable compromises among those conceptual elements. Impossibility theorems are statements that no *un*compromising solution exists embodying all the conceptual necessities of a theory, but such theorems do not in general preclude the existence of acceptable compromises.

8.8 Appendix

In this appendix I study the EOp mechanism for an environment that is similar to the production economy of §8.5.2, but where advantage is taken to be income instead of utility. I include this example here because much actual redistributive policy in contemporary welfare states is designed to equalize income rather than welfare.

We shall limit the set of feasible tax schemes $\mathcal{T}$ to linear income taxes of the form $\tau(x) = d_0 + d_1 x$, as in §8.5.2. The data of the problem consist in the following: for any tax scheme, denoted $d = (d_0, d_1)$, there is a frequency distribution of education levels achieved among each type. Let $e^i(\pi, d)$ be the education achieved at the πth centile of the distribution of education in type i at tax scheme d. Since taxes are to be purely redistributive, a tax scheme d is admissible if and only if

$$(A8.1) \qquad \sum_{i=1}^{r} p_i \int_0^1 (d_1 \delta e^i(\pi, d) + d_0) d\pi = 0.$$

This just says that the average tax is zero, so the government's budget balances. From (A8.1), we may write

$$(A8.2) \qquad d_0 = -d_1 \delta \int_0^1 \sum p_i e^i(\pi, d) d\pi,$$

and henceforth, admissible tax schemes may be parameterized by the single variable d_1. Indeed, note that the integral in (A8.2) is just average education achieved in the population at the tax scheme d_1; let us write $\bar{e}(d_1) \equiv \int_0^1 \sum p_i e^i(\pi, d_1) d\pi$.

Advantage, in this case, is just (after-tax) income; thus we may write the advantage function as

(A8.3) $v^i(\pi, d) = (1 - d_1)\delta e^i(\pi, d_1) - d_0.$

Substituting from (A8.3) into (8.3), we have

$$\varphi^E = \arg\sup_{d_1} \left[(1 - d_1)\delta \int_0^1 \min e^i(\pi, d_1)d\pi + d_1\delta\bar{e}(d_1) \right],$$

or

(A8.4) $\varphi^E = \arg\sup_{d_1} \left[(1 - d_1)E(d_1) + d_1\bar{e}(d_1) \right],$

where $E(d_1) := \int \min_i e_i(\pi, d_1)d\pi$.

Let us next compute the Rawlsian and utilitarian solutions. By substituting from (A8.3) into (8.5), we see the utilitarian solution is

(A8.5) $\varphi^U = \arg\sup_{d_1} \bar{e}(d_1);$

and substitution of (A8.3) into (8.4) yields:

(A8.6) $\varphi^R = \arg\sup_{d_1} \left[(1 - d_1)R(d_1) + d_1\bar{e}(d_1) \right],$

where $R(d_1) := \min_i e^i(0, d_1)$.

Let us now further specialize the example so that we may compute numerical solutions for the three mechanisms. Suppose that individuals are choosing their education levels by maximizing utility functions of the form $u(x, e, a) = x - (1/2a)e^2$; the different distributions of education by type are engendered by different distributions of the parameter "a" by type.[7] Thus, an individual is not responsible for the distribution of a for his type, but is responsible for where she sits in that distribution. An individual with this utility function, facing a tax scheme (d_1, d_0), chooses e to

$$\max(1 - d_1)\delta e - \frac{1}{2a}e^2;$$

---

7. Here I depart from the environment of §8.5.2, for the sake of variety.

or $e = (1 - d_1)\delta a$. Thus we may write $e^i(\pi, d) = (1 - d_1)\delta a^i(\pi)$, where $a^i(\pi)$ is the value of "a" at the πth quantile of the a-distribution characteristic of type i. Substituting this expression into (A8.4) yields:

(A8.7) $\varphi^E = \arg\sup\limits_{d_1} \left[(1 - d_1)^2 A + d_1(1 - d_1)\bar{a} \right],$

where $A = \int_0^1 \min_i a^i(\pi) d\pi$ and $\bar{a} = \int_0^1 \sum p^i a^i(\pi) d\pi$. We can expand the bracketed term in (A8.7) to $A + d_1(\bar{a} - 2A) + d_1^2(A - \bar{a})$. Since $A \leq \bar{a}$, this last expression is a concave function of d_1. Consequently, we can compute that, if d_1 is restricted to lie in the interval $[0, 1]$, then

(A8.8) $\varphi^E = \max\left(0, \dfrac{1 - 2\alpha^E}{2(1 - \alpha^E)} \right),$

where $\alpha^E := A/\bar{a}$. Note the maximum marginal tax rate is achieved when $A = 0$ (and $\varphi^E = \frac{1}{2}$); if $\bar{a} \leq 2A$, however, then there is no redistribution ($\varphi^E = 0$). The size of $\bar{a} - 2A$ depends on how much the parameter "a" varies across types.

Similarly, we may compute the utilitarian tax scheme using the above expression for $e^i(\pi, d)$: we get

(A8.9) $\varphi^U = \arg\sup\limits_{d_1} [\bar{a} - d_1\bar{a}] = 0.$

There is no redistribution under the utilitarian scheme. Finally, the Rawlsian tax scheme is

$$\varphi^R = \arg\sup\limits_{d_1} \min\limits_{i,\pi} \left[(1 - d_1)^2 \delta^2 a^i(\pi) - d_0 \right]$$

$$= \arg\sup\limits_{d_1} \min\limits_i \left[(1 - d_1)^2 a^i(0) + d_1(1 - d_1)\bar{a} \right]$$

$$= \arg\sup\limits_{d_1} \min\limits_i \left[a^i(0) + d_1\left(\bar{a} - 2a^i(0) \right) + d^2\left(a^i(0) - \bar{a} \right) \right].$$

Again, the bracketed term is a concave function of d_1, since $a^i(0) \leq \bar{a}$, and we compute

(A8.10) $\varphi^R = \max\left(0, \dfrac{1 - 2\alpha^R}{2(1 - \alpha^R)} \right),$

where $\alpha^R := (\min_i a^i(0))/\bar{a}$. Noting that $a_0 \leq A \leq \bar{a}$, we may conclude, from (A8.8), (A8.9), and (A8.10), that $\alpha^R \leq \alpha^E$ and

(A8.11) $\varphi^U \leq \varphi^E \leq \varphi^R$;

that is, for the case of quasi-linear utility, the equal-opportunity mechanism always redistributes at least as much as the utilitarian mechanism and no more than the Rawlsian mechanism.

Furthermore, inequality (A8.11) is tight: we can produce environments where $\varphi^E = \varphi^U$ and environments where $\varphi^E = \varphi^R$. The former occurs when $\bar{a} < 2A$, and the latter occurs when $a_0 = A$. "$a_0 = A$" occurs when one type consists of individuals, all of whom have the same low value of a, namely a_0, and there are no other individuals in society who have a lower a-value. Although this may be a singular environment, we can clearly approach it as closely as we wish and still maintain a nonatomic distribution of a-values in the "least motivated" type.

If we return to the more general (non-quasi-linear) formulation at the beginning of this example, is the inequality (A8.11) still true? The following example shows it is not, in general. Let there be two types, with

$$e_1(\pi, d) = \alpha d_1 + \beta \qquad \text{for all } \pi,$$

$$e_2(\pi, d) = \max(0, \beta - \varepsilon d_1^2) \quad \text{for all } \pi,$$

where $p_1 = .8$, $\alpha = .01$, $\beta = .5$, $\varepsilon = .1$. Note that, for all d_1 and π, $e^2(\pi, d) < e^1(\pi, d)$ (except at $d_1 = 0$, where the two education levels are equal). It follows that, in this case, $\varphi^E = \arg\sup_{d_1}((1 - d_1)\hat{e}^2(d_1) + d_1\bar{e}(d_1))$ where $\hat{e}^2(d_1) := e^2(\pi, d)$. The functions $\bar{e}(d_1)$ [for φ^U, see (A8.5)] and $(1 - d_1)\hat{e}^2(d_1) + d_1\bar{e}(d_1)$ [for φ^E, see (A8.6)] can be plotted with *Mathematica*; we then see that $\varphi^U \cong .2$, while $\varphi^E = 0$. Now clearly we can introduce small perturbations so that, in each type, there are slight variations in education attained, so that e^1 and e^2 depend on π as well, and this result will not be altered. Thus in general, the equal-opportunity mechanism does not redistribute more than the utilitarian mechanism.

The above counterexample to inequality (A8.11) is perhaps an artifact of the restriction of tax schemes to be linear in income and independent of type. Suppose tax schemes τ may be, more generally, continuous functions of income and education, and different across types. Research question: What restrictions on $e^i(\pi, \tau)$ are sufficient to preserve something like inequality (A8.11)? A conjecture might be that, when the admissible set $\mathcal{T}$ of tax schemes is large, and if $e^i(\pi, \tau)$ are "rationalizable" as the optimal efforts generated by "reasonable" classes of utility functions, then the "amount of redistribution" from the "fortunate" to the "unfortunate" types accomplished by the equal-opportunity mechanism lies in between that accomplished by utilitarianism and Rawlsianism. With more general tax schemes, however, we cannot so easily measure that amount by the marginal taxation of income, as we can in the case of linear income taxes.

We may easily extend the analysis of the last example to allow tax schemes to be linear in income *and* education $[\tau(x, e) = d_0 + d_1 x + d_2 e]$, always retaining the assumption of quasi-linear utility. A tax scheme $\tau = d_0 + d_1 x + d_2 e$ induces an optimal choice of education $e = a(\delta(1 - d_1) - d_2)$ with the quasi-linear utility function of the last example. Now consider the linear income tax scheme $\tau' = d_0 + d_1' x$ where $d_1' = d_1 + d_2/\delta$. This also induces an education choice of $e = a(\delta(1 - d_1) - d_2)$. Furthermore, the taxes collected from each individual are the same under τ' and τ. Without loss of generality, then, linear income tax schemes include general linear tax schemes, with the possible relaxation of the restriction that $d_1 \in [0, 1]$. Keeping education (and hence income) non-negative, however, requires $d_1 \leq 1$.

We may, however, wish to allow $d_1 < 0$. This changes the above analysis as follows: when $\alpha^E > \frac{1}{2}$, then the equal-opportunity mechanism will involve a *marginal* income transfer (not tax) and a lump sum *tax*. [Check, from (A8.8), that φ^E becomes negative in this case when the non-negativity restriction on d_1 is removed.] The utilitarian planner now maximizes $1 - d_1$ [see (A8.9)] with no non-negativity restriction: there is no solution. Let us, however, see what happens for d_1 large in absolute value and negative. The income of an agent whose preference characteristic is "a" is non-negative if and only if

$$(1 - d_1)^2 \delta^2 a + \delta^2 \bar{a} d_1 (1 - d_1) \geq 0$$

or, since $1 - d_1 > 0$ for d_1 "large" and negative, if and only if:

$$\frac{a}{\bar{a}} \geq \frac{|d_1|}{1 - d_1}.$$

As $|d_1| \to \infty$, it follows that the only individuals who maintain non-negative incomes are those whose a-characteristic is at least average. Thus if we allow incomes to be arbitrarily negative, then (approximate) utilitarianism implements a transfer from the "untalented" to the "talented," a not uncommon utilitarian characteristic. Finally the same remarks apply to the Rawlsian mechanism as applied to the equal-opportunity mechanism.

Appendix: Envy-Free Allocations

Let $\omega \in \mathbf{R}_+^n$ be a commodity vector of n goods, let $\rho = (R^1, \ldots, R^H)$ be a preference profile of H persons on the commodity space, and let $x = (x^1, \ldots, x^H)$ be a feasible allocation of ω among these individuals. x is said to be *equitable* if and only if no individual "envies" another, that is, if and only if, for all $i, j = 1, \ldots, H$, $x^i R^i x^j$. x is said to be *fair* if and only if it is equitable and Pareto efficient. The definition of equity is due to Foley (1967), and fairness was apparently first introduced by Schmeidler and Yaari in an unpublished paper (see Daniel 1975, p. 96). According to Kolm (1972, p. 18), this notion of equity was suggested by the Dutch physicist Ehrenfest to Jan Tinbergen in the early 1950s. Varian (1974) brought the concept into the full view of the economics profession.

The notion of fairness (so defined) has attracted a good deal of attention among economists, as a criterion of justice, because it provides a way of narrowing the set of Pareto optimal allocations—sometimes, as we shall see, to a unique allocation—without introducing comparability of welfare: fairness is a strictly ordinal concept. As I discussed in §1.1, many economists believe that interpersonal comparisons of well-being are impossible, an inference that they draw (mistakenly) from the fact that interpersonal comparability is not necessary for general equilibrium theory.[1] It is, I believe, for this reason that fairness has achieved its prominence in the economics literature.

---

1. Note that the *conclusion* that interpersonal comparisons are impossible may be true, even though the stated *inference* is false.

In this appendix I briefly report on two aspects of the fairness concept: first, its association with equal division Walrasian equilibria, and second, its relationship to the issue of personalized, and hence internal, resources (like endorphins). I attempt no thorough review of the literature, as several useful introductions to the subject are available: see, for instance, Thomson and Varian (1985) and Moulin (1995, chap. 4). The most comprehensive study of the topic is Thomson (1994).

Recall that an equal division Walrasian equilibrium (EDWE) allocation is a Walrasian allocation associated with initial equal, private ownership of the economy's endowments. (Some of these endowments could be firms or indivisible goods, in which cases every individual must be an equal shareholder.) Note that an EDWE is fair: it is equitable because any individual could have purchased the consumption of any other with her own income, as all incomes are the same, and it is efficient since it is Walrasian. When preferences are quasi-concave, goods are divisible, and technologies are convex, EDWE allocations exist, and so fair allocations exist: usually, there are many more fair allocations (than the EDWE).

What is of more interest is the converse: under certain conditions, in an exchange economy with a continuum of agents, the only fair allocations are the EDWE. Varian (1976) first proved this result, under the condition that preferences are representable by a *differentiable* utility function $u(x, t)$, where x is the commodity vector and t is an index of the agents (say, in the interval $[0, 1]$). (For a quick proof, see Thomson and Varian [1985].) The assumption that tastes vary continuously (even differentiably) across individuals is, unfortunately, a strong one, and Varian shows that without it, the result is false. Nevertheless, under this assumption, we have that fairness characterizes a generally "small" set of allocations, and indeed, ones that have an independent appeal, in the sense that the initial equal incomes of individuals correspond to an obvious notion of justice.

Zhou (1992) dispenses with the assumption of continuity of preferences across individuals in the continuum, strengthens the notion of fairness to "strict fairness," and proves that the only strictly fair allocations are EDWE. An allocation in a finite economy is *strictly fair* if and only if, for all coalitions S of individuals, and for all $h \notin S$, h does not prefer the average bundle of S, $(1/|S|) \sum_{i \in S} x^i$, to x^h.

The second issue, of the relationship between personalized goods and fairness, is best introduced with the consideration of production economies. One of the early "problems" with the concept of fairness was the putative general nonexistence of fair allocations in production economies.

Pazner and Schmeidler (1974) provided an example of a production economy in which no fair allocation existed. A subtle but important change, however, was, perhaps inadvertently, introduced in the definition of fairness in these examples. The Pazner-Schmeidler example involved two individuals, with preferences over goods and leisure, who are differentially talented in the production of goods. An allocation was said to be fair if it is Pareto efficient and no individual would prefer to consume the goods-leisure bundle of another.

But this is, formally and importantly, not the same concept as the original definition. For in a production economy with one produced good, call it corn, and two consumer-workers Adam and Betsy, there are not two goods (corn and leisure), but three goods: corn, Adam's leisure, and Betsy's leisure. The economy's endowment consists of amounts of these three goods, and each consumer has preferences defined on $\mathbf{R}^3_+$; each individual's consumption set consists, however, of a coordinate plane in commodity space, because neither individual can consume the other's leisure time. Now the EDWE allocations in this production economy *do constitute* fair allocations in the original sense, where we allocate a 50% share of the firm that produces the goods to each individual: the original argument applies (if Adam preferred Betsy's bundle of goods he could have purchased it). Note that these allocations are associated with a private ownership economy in which Adam initially owns one-half of "his" leisure and one-half of Betsy's, and the same is true of Betsy. (Indeed, these fair allocations constitute what Dworkin called "slavery of the talented," as the individual with the higher wage at Walrasian equilibrium has to toil to purchase her expensive leisure.)

When Pazner and Schmeidler said there were, in general, no fair allocations in production economies, and when Varian (1976) agreed, they were substituting for the original definition of "equitable" a new definition in which an allocation of goods and leisures is deemed equitable if and only if no individual envies another's goods bundle and her *level* of leisure. Thus the elements of a certain set of personalized goods, {Adam's leisure, Betsy's leisure}, are implicitly declared "equivalent" in the sense that, when asking if he prefers Betsy's consumption bundle to his own, Adam can substitute the good "Adam's leisure" for the good "Besty's leisure."

But if we admit the attractiveness of this new concept, it can be applied as well to exchange economies. Consider an exchange economy with two individuals, Aziza and Bogdan, with three goods: corn, gin, and scotch. Aziza likes only corn and gin and Bogdan likes only corn and scotch. Suppose

Aziza's preferences are represented by the utility function $C^\alpha G^{1-\alpha}$, and Bogdan's by $C^\beta S^{1-\beta}$, and suppose the aggregate endowment is $(\overline{C}, \overline{S}, \overline{G}) = (1, 2, 1)$. Consider the set of allocations which divide the corn in any way between Aziza and Bogdan, give all the scotch to Bodgan, and give all the gin to Aziza. It is trivial to observe that each of these is a fair allocation (in the original sense of the term). Now suppose, instead, that we "identify" scotch with gin: each is alcohol, but Aziza and Bogdan have personalized tastes for different kinds of alcohol, as Adam and Betsy had personalized tastes for different kinds of leisure. We will say that Aziza does not *level-envy* Bogdan if she would not prefer his bundle of corn and alcohol to hers, where she substitutes her gin for his scotch. Let C be the amount of corn going to Aziza. The condition for Bogdan not level-envying Aziza at a Pareto-efficient allocation is:

$$(1 - C)^\beta 2^{1-\beta} \geq C^\beta,$$

and the condition for Aziza not level-envying Bogdan at a Pareto-efficient allocation is:

$$C^\alpha \geq (1 - C)^\alpha 2^{1-\alpha}.$$

These conditions imply that

$$\left(\frac{1 - C}{2C}\right)^\alpha \leq \frac{1}{2} \leq \left(\frac{1 - C}{2C}\right)^\beta,$$

an impossibility if $\alpha > \beta$. Thus, in general, level-envy-free allocations do not exist in *exchange* economies, either.

Daniel (1975) provided a general definition of "level-envy-freeness"; he named the concept "personally equitable," with the corresponding notion of personally fair allocations. (Thus an allocation is *personally equitable* if and only if no individual level-envies another, where the individual substitutes his personal consumption goods for the analogous personal consumption goods of the other.) Daniel defines an allocation as *balanced* if and only if, for all individuals h, the number of persons who personally envy h is equal to the number of persons whom h personally envies. An allocation is *just* if and only if it is Pareto efficient and balanced. Daniel's main result is that, under an arguably reasonable set of assumptions, just allocations always exist. Indeed, we can observe that "just" allocations do exist in the Aziza-Bogdan example. For the condition that each of Aziza and Bogdan level-envy the other (which is an instance of a balanced allocation) is:

$$\left(\frac{1-C}{2C}\right)^{\beta} < \frac{1}{2} < \left(\frac{1-C}{2C}\right)^{\alpha},$$

which is true for many allocations when $\alpha > \beta$. But when $\alpha \leq \beta$, then envy-free allocations exist, as we have observed, which are also balanced, and so balanced allocations exist for any positive pair (α, β).

The original concept of equitable allocation can declare far too many allocations just in the case where preferences differ drastically. Consider Aziza and Bogdan's world, in the case $\alpha > \beta$, where all efficient allocations are fair. Neither, that is, has a claim at the bar of justice under its fairness interpretation, regardless of the distribution of corn, as long as Aziza gets all the gin and Bogdan gets all the scotch. (Dworkin would allow the two each to insure himself against a low lot of corn, even if being gin- or scotch-loving was not an insurable harm.) To consider a formally equivalent example, with perhaps more bite, consider an economy with poor Muslims, who only like corn and beef, and rich Hindus, who only like corn and pork. Much more pork than beef will be produced (assuming effective-demand-driven production), and the final allocation, where Hindus consume a lot of pork and corn, and Muslims a little beef and corn, will be envy-free.

Daniel's move to personally fair allocations is, in my view, a good one, for it allows us, as it were, to reduce the degree of individual responsibility for idiosyncratic preferences (if we wish to). To permit Aziza to envy Bogdan's alcohol consumption, rather than his scotch consumption, effectively in-sures her against having been born with an idiosyncratic taste for gin. How, in general, we decide which goods should be declared "equivalent" for the purposes of the level-envy test has not been addressed; I would suggest an appeal to Sen's functionings here. Adam's leisure and Betsy's leisure are "equivalent" because they each bring about a certain functioning, namely, relaxation; Aziza's gin and Bogdan's scotch similarly engender the same functioning, perhaps also a kind of relaxation. (One should also at this point recall Kelvin Lancaster's [1971] preferences over characteristics, for which perhaps idiosyncratic commodities enter as household-production inputs.) What I aim to point out now is that, in pursuing this tack, of iden-tifying equivalent pairs of goods, we are led to making interpersonal com-parisons of a kind, to saying that different goods may do the same thing for different people. Thus, to make the no-envy test more attractive (in my view) as a measure of distributive justice, we are led to introduce a certain degree of interpersonal commensurability which dedicated ordinalists, to whom the "fairness" approach appeals, would deny. For who am I to say that gin does for Aziza what scotch does for Bogdan? If I can say that, does whatever allows me to assert it also perhaps allow me to make full interpersonal comparisons of their degrees of well-being? I leave this question as an exercise in political philosophy for the reader.

There are precious few references to fair allocations (of course, always in the technical sense) among political philosphers. Dworkin (1981b) originally motivates his clamshell auction, as a preamble to his proposal for resource egalitarianism, with the observation that the allocation thus arrived at, which has the EDWE property, is envy-free. But that observation appears to be gratuitous for his theory; indeed, in Chapter 8 I attempted to summarize his theory without mentioning fairness at all. What seems much more salient for Dworkin's resource egalitarianism than its envy-free property is that the EDWE allocation corresponds to an obvious kind of "resource equality," equality of initial property rights.

Finally, Van Parijs (1995) proposes a modification of fairness as a principle of distributive justice. He defines an allocation $x = (x^1, \ldots, x^H)$ of goods among H individuals with preference profile $\rho = (R^1, \ldots, R^H)$ to exhibit *undominated diversity* if and only if there is no pair $\{i, j\}$ such that for all h, $x^i P^h x^j$. This is a much stronger requirement than fairness (that is, all fair allocations exhibit undominated diversity but not conversely), and in general undominatedly diverse allocations do not exist. The proposal, of course, is purely ordinal. Yet despite its inherently agnostic position on interpersonal comparability, it achieves a certain objectivity in the sense that the *distribution* of preferences is an objective feature of a society. I think giving every individual a veto in the vote on the question whether i is better off than j at the allocation x, as Van Parijs does, is too radical, but I think that a modification of his proposal in which an allocation would be declared just (or undominatedly diverse) if and only if for all ordered pairs $\{i, j\}$, the members h of some coalition S of significant size report that $x^i R^h x^j$, has an appeal. In particular, in a large economy, this modified principle would be objective (in the sense of depending only on the distribution of preferences, a social, not individual characteristic), non-subjective (in not depending at all on any individual's preferences), yet still ordinal. It substitutes a consensus of personal views for the interpersonal commensurability of well-being.

References

Arneson, R. 1989. "Equality of opportunity for welfare." *Philosophical Studies* 56, 77–93.

———— 1990a. "Liberalism, distributive subjectivism, and equal opportunity for welfare." *Philosophy & Public Affairs* 19, 159–194.

———— 1990b. "Primary goods reconsidered." *NOÛS* 24, 429–454.

———— 1991. "Lockean self-ownership: Towards a demolition." *Political Studies* 39, 36–54.

Arrow, K. J. 1951. *Social choice and individual values.* New York: Wiley.

———— 1963. *Social choice and individual values.* 2d ed. New York: Wiley.

Arrow, K., and G. Debreu. 1954. "Existence of an equilibrium for a competitive economy." *Econometrica* 22, 265–290.

Barry, B. 1989. *Theories of Justice.* Vol. 1. Berkeley: University of California Press.

Bergson, A. 1938. "A reformulation of certain aspects of welfare economics." *Quarterly Journal of Economics* 52, 310–334.

Billera, L., and R. Bixby. 1973. "A characterization of Pareto surfaces." *Proceedings of the American Mathematical Society* 41, 261–267.

Binmore, K. 1987. "Nash bargaining theory III." In Binmore and Dasgupta (1987).

———— 1993. "Bargaining and morality." In Gauthier and Sugden (1993).

Binmore, K., and P. Dasgupta, eds. 1987. *The Economics of Bargaining.* Oxford: Basil Blackwell.

Binmore, K., A. Rubinstein, and A. Wolinsky. 1986. "The Nash bargaining solution in economic modelling." *Rand Journal of Economics* 17, 176–188.

Black, R. D. Collison. 1987. "Utility," pp. 776–778. In J. Eatwell, M. Milgate, and P. Newman, eds., *The New Palgrave: A Dictionary of Economics.* Vol. 4. London: Macmillan.

Blackorby, C., W. Bossert, and D. Donaldson. 1993. "Intertemporal population ethics: A welfarist approach." University of British Columbia.

Blackorby, C., and D. Donaldson. 1982. "Ratio-scale and translation-scale full interpersonal comparability without domain restrictions: Admissible social-evaluation functions." *International Economic Review* 23, 249–268.

―――― 1984. "Social criteria for evaluating population change." *Journal of Public Economics* 25, 13–33.

Blackorby, C., D. Donaldson, and J. Weymark. 1980. "On John Harsanyi's defences of utilitarianism." Discussion Paper 80-4, Department of Economics, University of British Columbia.

―――― 1984. "Social choice with interpersonal utility comparisons: A diagrammatic introduction." *International Economic Review* 25, 327–356.

Border, K. 1981. "Notes on von Neumann–Morgenstern social welfare functions." California Institute of Technology.

―――― 1983. "Social welfare functions for economic environments with and without the Pareto principle." *Journal of Economic Theory* 29, 205–216.

―――― 1985. "More on Harsanyi's utilitarian cardinal welfare function." *Social Choice and Welfare* 1, 279–281.

Bordes, G., and M. Le Breton. 1989. "Arrovian theorems with private alternatives domains and selfish individuals." *Journal of Economic Theory* 47, 257–282.

―――― 1990. "Arrovian theorems for economic domains: The case when there are simultaneously private and public goods." *Social Choice and Welfare* 7, 1–18.

Bossert, W. 1995. "Redistribution mechanisms based on individual characteristics." *Mathematical Social Sciences* 29, 1–17.

Broome, J. 1991. *Weighing Goods.* Oxford: Basil Blackwell.

―――― 1993. "A cause of preference is not an object of preference." *Social Choice and Welfare* 10, 57–68.

Butts, R., and J. Hintikka, eds. 1977. *Foundational Problems in the Social Sciences.* Dordrecht: D. Reidel.

Campbell, D. 1992. *Equity, Efficiency, and Social Choice.* New York: Oxford University Press.

Chew, S. H., L. G. Epstein, and U. Segal. 1991. "Mixture symmetry and quadratic utility." *Econometrica* 59, 139–163.

Cohen, G. A. 1986. "Self-ownership, world-ownership and equality." In F. Lucash, ed., *Justice and Equality Here and Now.* Ithaca: Cornell University Press.

―――― 1989. "On the currency of egalitarian justice." *Ethics* 99, 906–944.

―――― 1992. "Incentives, inequality, and community." In G. B. Peterson, ed., *The Tanner Lectures on Human Values.* Vol. 13. Salt Lake City: University of Utah Press.

―――― 1993. "Equality of what? On welfare, goods, and capabilities." In Nussbaum and Sen (1993).

―――― 1995a. "The Pareto argument for inequality." In Cohen (1995b).

―――― 1995b. *Self-Ownership, Freedom, and Equality.* Cambridge: Cambridge University Press.

Coulhon, T., and P. Mongin. 1989. "Social choice theory in the case of von Neumann–Morgenstern utilities." *Social Choice and Welfare* 6, 175–187.

Daniel, T. E. 1975. "A revised concept of distributional equity." *Journal of Economic Theory* 11, 94–109.

d'Aspremont, C., and L. Gevers. 1977. "Equity and the informational basis of collective choice." *Review of Economic Studies* 44, 199–209.

Debreu, G. 1954. "Representation of a preference ordering by a numerical function." In R. Thrall, C. Coombs, and R. Davis, eds., *Decision Processes*. New York: Wiley.

——— 1964. "Continuity properties of Paretian utility." *International Economic Review* 4, 235–246.

Deschamps, R., and L. Gevers. 1978. "Separability, risk-bearing, and social welfare judgments." *European Economic Review* 10, 77–94.

Diamond, P. 1967. "Cardinal welfare, individualistic ethics, and interpersonal comparisons of utility: Comment." *Journal of Political Economy* 75, 765–766.

Dixit, A. 1978. "Lecture notes on social choice theory."

Domotor, Z. 1979. "Ordered sum and tensor product of utility structures." *Theory and Decision* 11, 375–399.

Donaldson, D., and J. Weymark. 1988. "Social choice in economic environments." *Journal of Economic Theory* 46, 291–308.

Donaldson, D., and J. E. Roemer. 1987. "Social choice in economic environments with dimensional variation." *Social Choice and Welfare* 4, 253–276.

Dworkin, R. 1981a. "What is equality? Part 1: Equality of welfare." *Philosophy & Public Affairs* 10, 185–246.

——— 1981b. "What is equality? Part 2: Equality of resources." *Philosophy & Public Affairs* 10, 283–345.

Elster, J. 1979. *Ulysses and the Sirens*. Cambridge: Cambridge University Press.

——— 1992. *Local Justice: How Institutions Allocate Scarce Goods and Necessary Burdens*. New York: Russell Sage Foundation.

Elster, J., and J. E. Roemer, eds. 1991. *Interpersonal Comparisons of Well-Being*. New York: Cambridge University Press.

Epstein, L., and U. Segal. 1992. "Quadratic social welfare functions." *Journal of Political Economy* 100, 691–712.

Fishburn, P. C. 1984. "On Harsanyi's utilitarian cardinal welfare theorem." *Theory and Decision* 17, 21–28.

Fleurbaey, M. 1994. "On fair compensation." *Theory and Decision* 36, 277–307.

——— 1995. "Three solutions to the compensation problem." *Journal of Economic Theory* 65, 505–521.

Foley, D. 1967. "Resource allocation and the public sector." *Yale Economic Essays* 7, 45–98.

Gaertner, W., and M. Klemisch-Ahlert. 1992. *Social Choice and Bargaining Perspectives in Distributive Justice*. New York: Springer-Verlag.

Gauthier, D. 1986. *Morals by Agreement*. Oxford: Oxford University Press.

—— 1993. "Uniting separate persons." In Gauthier and Sugden (1993).

Gauthier, D., and R. Sugden. 1993. *Rationality, Justice, and the Social Contract.* Ann Arbor: University of Michigan Press.

Georgescu-Roegen, N. 1987. "Ophelimity," pp. 716–718. In J. Eatwell, M. Milgate, and P. Newman, eds., *The New Palgrave: A Dictionary of Economics.* Vol. 3. London: Macmillan.

Gevers, L. 1979. "On interpersonal comparability and social welfare orderings." *Econometrica* 47, 75–90.

—— 1986. "Walrasian social choice: Some simple axiomatic approaches." In W. Heller, et al., eds., *Social Choice and Public Decision Making: Essays in Honor of K. J. Arrow.* Vol. 1. New York: Cambridge University Press.

Gibbard, A. 1976. "Natural property rights." *NOÛS* 10, 77–86.

—— 1991. "Constructing justice." *Philosophy & Public Affairs* 20, 264–279.

Grunebaum, J. O. 1987. *Private Ownership.* London: Routledge & Kegan Paul.

Hammond, P. 1976. "Equity, Arrow's conditions, and Rawls' difference principle." *Econometrica* 44, 793–804.

—— 1979. "Equity in two person situations: Some consequences." *Econometrica* 47, 1127–1136.

—— 1992. "Harsanyi's utilitarian theorem: A simpler proof and some ethical considerations." In Selten (1992).

Harsanyi, J. 1953. "Cardinal utility in welfare economics and in the theory of risk-taking." *Journal of Political Economy* 61, 434–435.

—— 1955. "Cardinal welfare, individualistic ethics, and interpersonal comparisons of utility." *Journal of Political Economy* 63, 309–321.

—— 1975. "Nonlinear social welfare functions: Do welfare economists have a special exemption from Bayesian rationality?" *Theory and Decision* 6, 311–332.

—— 1977a. *Rational Behavior and Bargaining Equilibrium in Games and Social Situations.* Cambridge: Cambridge University Press.

—— 1977b. "Nonlinear social welfare functions: A rejoinder to Professor Sen." In Butts and Hintikka (1977).

Hausman, D. M., and M. S. McPherson. 1995. *Economic Analysis and Moral Philosophy.* Cambridge: Cambridge University Press.

Hildenbrand, W., and A. Kirman. 1988. *Equilibrium Analysis.* New York: Elsevier Science Publishers.

Howe, R. 1987. "Sections and extensions of concave functions." *Journal of Mathematical Economics* 16, 53–64.

Howe, R., and J. E. Roemer. 1981. "Rawlsian justice as the core of a game." *American Economic Review* 71, 880–895.

Hurwicz, L., D. Schmeidler, and H. Sonnenschein, eds. 1985. *Social Goals and Social Organziation: Essays in Memory of Elisha Pazner.* New York: Cambridge University Press.

Kalai, E. 1977. "Proportional solutions to bargaining situations: Interpersonal utility comparisons." *Econometrica* 45, 1623–1630.

——— 1985. "Solutions to the bargaining problem." In Hurwicz, Schmeidler, and Sonnenschein (1985).

Kalai, E., and M. Smorodinsky. 1975. "Other solutions to Nash's bargaining problem." *Econometrica* 43, 513–518.

Kolm, S. C. 1972. *Justice et équité*. Paris: Centre National de la Recherche Scientifique.

——— 1995. *Modern Theories of Justice*. Cambridge, Mass.: MIT Press.

Kymlicka, W. 1990. *Contemporary Political Philosophy*. Oxford: Oxford University Press.

Lancaster, K. 1971. *Consumer Demand: A New Approach*. New York: Columbia University Press.

Le Breton, M., and J. Weymark. 1994. "An introduction to Arrovian social welfare functions on economic and political domains." In N. Schofield, ed., *Social Choice and Political Economy*. Dordrecht: Kluwer Academic Publishers.

Loomes, G., and R. Sugden. 1982. "Regret theory: An alternative theory of rational choice under uncertainty." *Economic Journal* 92, 805–824.

MacKay, A. 1980. *Arrow's Theorem: The Paradox of Social Choice*. New Haven: Yale University Press.

Makowski, L., and J. Ostroy. 1987. "Vickrey-Clarke-Groves mechanisms and perfect competition." *Journal of Economic Theory* 42, 244–261.

——— 1992. "Vickrey-Clarke-Groves mechanisms in continuum economies." *Journal of Mathematical Economics* 21, 1–35.

Mas-Colell, A. 1980. "Remarks on the game theoretic analysis of a simple distribution of surplus problem." *International Journal of Game Theory* 9, 125–140.

——— 1989. "An equivalence theorem for the bargaining set." *Journal of Mathematical Economics* 18, 129–139.

Maskin, E. 1977. "Nash equilibrium and welfare optimality." Department of Economics, MIT.

——— 1978. "A theorem on utilitarianism." *Review of Economic Studies* 45, 93–96.

——— 1979. "Decision-making under ignorance with implications for social choice." *Theory and Decision* 11, 319–337.

——— 1985. "The theory of implementation in Nash equilibrium: A survey." In Hurwicz, Schmeidler, and Sonnenschein (1985).

May, K. 1954. "Intransitivity, utility, and the aggregation of preference patterns." *Econometrica* 22, 1–13.

Milnor, J. 1954. "Games against nature." In R. Thrall, C. Coombs, and R. Davis, eds., *Decision Processes*. New York: John Wiley.

Moulin, H. 1987. "A core selection for pricing a single output monopoly." *Rand Journal of Economics* 18, 397–407.

——— 1988. *Axioms of Cooperative Decision Making*. New York: Cambridge University Press.

——— 1990. "Joint ownership of a convex technology: Comparison of three solutions." *Review of Economic Studies* 57, 439–452.

———— 1995. *Cooperative Microeconomics*. Princeton: Princeton University Press.

Moulin, H., and J. E. Roemer. 1989. "Public ownership of the external world and private ownership of self." *Journal of Political Economy* 97, 347–367.

Myerson, R. 1981. "Utilitarianism, egalitarianism, and the timing effect in social choice problems." *Econometrica* 49, 883–897.

Nash, J. 1950. "The bargaining problem." *Econometrica* 18, 155–162.

———— 1953. "Two-person cooperative games." *Econometrica* 21, 128–140.

Nehring, K. 1995. "A theory of rational decision with incomplete information." Department of Economics Working Paper 95-13. University of California, Davis.

Nozick, R. 1974. *Anarchy, State, and Utopia*. New York: Basic Books.

Nussbaum, M., and A. Sen. 1993. *The Quality of Life*. Oxford: Clarendon Press.

Ostrom, E. 1990. *Governing the Commons*. New York: Cambridge University Press.

Ostroy, J. 1980. "The no-surplus condition as a characterization of perfectly competitive equilibrium." *Journal of Economic Theory* 22, 183–207.

Pareto, V. 1896. *Cours d'économie politique professé à l'université de Lausanne*. Vol. 1. Lausanne: F. Rouge.

Parfit, D. 1984. *Reasons and Persons*. Oxford: Oxford University Press.

Pazner, E., and D. Schmeidler. 1974. "A difficulty in the concept of fairness." *Review of Economic Studies* 41, 441–443.

Peters, H. J. M. 1992. *Axiomatic Bargaining Game Theory*. Dordrecht: Kluwer Academic Publishers.

Rawls, J. 1971. *A Theory of Justice*. Cambridge, Mass.: Harvard University Press.

———— 1975. "Fairness to goodness." *Philosophical Review* 84, 536–555.

———— 1980. "Kantian constructivism in moral theory." *Journal of Philosophy* 77, 515–572.

———— 1982. "Social unity and primary goods." In A. Sen and B. Williams, eds., *Utilitarianism and Beyond*. Cambridge: Cambridge University Press.

———— 1985. "Justice as fairness: Political not metaphysical." *Philosophy & Public Affairs* 14, 223–251.

Roberts, K. 1980a. "Possibility theorems with interpersonally comparable welfare levels." *Review of Economic Studies* 47, 409–420.

———— 1980b. "Interpersonal comparability and social choice theory." *Review of Economic Studies* 47, 421–439.

Roemer, J. E. 1985. "Equality of talent." *Economics and Philosophy* 1, 151–181. Reprinted in Roemer (1994).

———— 1986a. "Equality of resources implies equality of welfare." *Quarterly Journal of Economics* 101, 751–784.

———— 1986b. "The mismarriage of bargaining theory and distributive justice." *Ethics* 97, 88–110.

———— 1987a. "A public ownership resolution of the tragedy of the commons." Department of Economics Working Paper No. 295, University of California, Davis.

———— 1987b. "Egalitarianism, responsibility, and information." *Economics and Philosophy* 3, 215–244. Reprinted in Roemer (1994).

———— 1988. "Axiomatic bargaining theory on economic environments." *Journal of Economic Theory* 45, 1–31.

———— 1989. "A public ownership resolution of the tragedy of the commons." *Social Philosophy and Policy* 6, 74–92.

———— 1990. "Welfarism and axiomatic bargaining theory." *Recherches Economiques de Louvain* 56, 287–301.

———— 1993a. "Distributing health: The allocation of resources by an international agency." In Nussbaum and Sen (1993).

———— 1993b. "A pragmatic theory of responsibility for the egalitarian planner." *Philosophy & Public Affairs* 22, 146–166.

———— 1994. *Egalitarian Perspectives: Essays in Philosophical Economics.* New York: Cambridge University Press.

Roemer, J. E., and J. Silvestre. 1989. "Public ownership: Three proposals for resource allocation." Department of Economics Working Paper No. 307, University of California, Davis.

———— 1993. "The proportional solution for economies with both private and public ownership." *Journal of Economic Theory* 59, 426–444.

Roth, A. 1979. *Axiomatic Models of Bargaining.* Berlin: Springer-Verlag.

Rubinstein, A. 1982. "Perfect equilibrium in a bargaining model." *Econometrica* 50, 97–110.

Rubinstein, A., Z. Safra, and W. Thomson. 1992. "On the interpretation of the Nash bargaining solution." *Econometrica* 60, 1171–1186.

Scanlon, T. 1975. "Preference and urgency." *Journal of Philosophy* 72, 665–669.

———— 1986. "Equality of resources and equality of welfare: A forced marriage?" *Ethics* 97, 111–118.

———— 1988. "The significance of choice." In S. McMurrin, ed., *The Tanner Lectures on Human Values.* Vol. 8. Salt Lake City: University of Utah Press.

Selten, R., ed. 1992. *Rational Interaction: Essays in Honor of John C. Harsanyi.* Berlin: Springer-Verlag.

Sen, A. 1976. "Welfare inequalities and Rawlsian axiomatics." *Theory and Decision* 7, 243–262.

———— 1977. "Non-linear social welfare functions: A reply to Professor Harsanyi." In Butts and Hintikka (1977).

———— 1979. "Utilitarianism and welfarism." *Journal of Philosophy* 76, 463–489.

———— 1980. "Equality of what?" In S. McMurrin, ed., *The Tanner Lectures on Human Values.* Vol. 1. Salt Lake City: University of Utah Press.

———— 1985. *Commodities and Capabilities.* Amsterdam: North-Holland.

———— 1986. "Social choice theory," pp. 1073–1181. In K. Arrow and M. Intriligator, eds., *Handbook of Mathematical Economics.* Vol. 3. Amsterdam: North-Holland.

———— 1987. *The Standard of Living.* Cambridge: Cambridge University Press.

———— 1992. *Inequality Reexamined.* Cambridge, Mass.: Harvard University Press.

———— 1993. "Capability and well-being." In Nussbaum and Sen (1993).

Sikora, R. 1978. "Is it wrong to prevent the existence of future generations?" In R. Sikora and B. Barry, eds., *Obligations to Future Generations.* Philadelphia: Temple University Press.

Steiner, H. 1994. *An Essay on Rights.* Oxford: Blackwell.

Strasnick, S. 1976a. "Social choice theory and the derivation of Rawls' difference principle." *Journal of Philosophy* 73, 85–99.

———— 1976b. "The problem of social choice: Arrow to Rawls." *Philosophy & Public Affairs* 5, 241–273.

Thomson, W. 1991. "Bargaining theory: An axiomatic approach." Department of Economics, University of Rochester.

———— 1994. "Fair allocations." Department of Economics, University of Rochester.

Thomson, W., and T. Lensberg. 1989. *Axiomatic Theory of Bargaining with a Variable Number of Agents.* New York: Cambridge University Press.

Thomson, W., and H. Varian. 1985. "Symmetry theories of justice." In Hurwicz, Schmeidler, and Sonnenschein (1985).

Van Parijs, P. 1995. *Real Freedom for All: What if Anything Can Justify Capitalism?* Oxford: Clarendon Press.

Varian, H. 1974. "Equity, efficiency, and envy." *Journal of Economic Theory* 9, 63–91.

———— 1976. "Two problems in the theory of fairness." *Journal of Public Economics* 5, 249–260.

von Neumann, J., and O. Morgenstern. 1944. *Theory of Games and Economic Behavior.* Princeton: Princeton University Press.

Waldron, J. 1988. *The Right to Private Property.* Oxford: Clarendon Press.

Walzer, M. 1983. *Spheres of Justice: A Defense of Pluralism and Equality.* New York: Basic Books.

Weymark, J. 1991. "A reconsideration of the Harsanyi-Sen debate on utilitarianism." In Elster and Roemer (1991).

———— 1993. "Harsanyi's social aggregation theorem and the weak Pareto principle." *Social Choice and Welfare* 10, 209–221.

Yaari, M., and M. Bar-Hillel. 1984. "On dividing justly." *Social Choice and Welfare* 1, 1–24.

Young, H. P. 1994. *Equity.* Princeton: Princeton University Press.

Zeuthen, F. 1930. *Problems of Monopoly and Economic Welfare.* London: Routledge & Kegan Paul.

Zhou, L. 1992. "Strictly fair allocations in large exchange economies." *Journal of Economic Theory* 57, 158–175.

———— 1994. "Harsanyi's utilitarian theorems: Concise proofs and infinite societies." Yale University.

Index